INTRODUCTIONS
TO
TRADITIONAL
ASTROLOGY:

Abū Ma'shar & al-Qabīsī

TRANSLATED AND EDITED BY
BENJAMIN N. DYKES, PHD

The Cazimi Press
Minneapolis, Minnesota
2010

Published and printed in the United States of America
by the Cazimi Press
621 5ᵗʰ Avenue SE #25, Minneapolis, MN 55414

© 2010 by Benjamin N. Dykes, Ph.D.

ISBN-13: 978-1-934586-15-0

ACKNOWLEDGMENTS

I would like to thank the following friends and colleagues, in alphabetical order: Chris Brennan, Frank Clifford, Martin Gansten, Demetra George, Philip Graves, Richard Schacht, and Robert Schmidt.

TABLE OF CONTENTS

BOOK ABBREVIATIONS

TABLE OF FIGURES

Note: All figures by Benjamin Dykes (not in original Latin or Arabic texts)

INTRODUCTION

§1: Purposes of this book

Introductions to Traditional Astrology (*ITA*) is an introduction and resource text for students of traditional astrology. It is not exactly a course, but would be invaluable for those taking a course as well as studying alone, whether as new or continuing students. It covers material spanning all areas of the traditional period: Hellenistic, medieval Arabic and Latin, Renaissance and early modern astrology.

At its core are two short works by famous astrologers of the 9th and 10th Centuries: Abū Ma'shar's *Abbreviation of the Introduction* and al-Qabīsī's *Introduction to the Science of Astrology*. In many sections, I have also added material from Abū Ma'shar's *Great Introduction to the Science of the Stars* and from other sources.[1] These texts also provide a unifying historical and conceptual center for the traditional period generally, as an elaboration of Hellenistic practice, and as the foundation of later European astrology. *ITA* thus covers fundamental astrological concepts and methods from about 100 BC to 1700 AD, with its center in 9th Century Baghdad.

ITA is also the technical introduction and entry-point to my *Essential Medieval Astrology* (*EMA*) series:[2] a cycle of translations in all branches of traditional astrology (again, focusing on Persian and Arabic writers). Recently I completed the natal installments of the cycle as *Persian Nativities* I-III, and I will soon release the horary installments. But no matter which branch interests you, all techniques in traditional astrology come down to the primary principles, concepts, and methods presented in this book. The other introduction to the *EMA* series will be an "invitation" to traditional astrology, directed at curious modern students. It will offer a more philosophical look at key approaches and ideas in traditional astrology, including matters of fate and freedom, prediction techniques and time, how we look at signs, and so on. It will also include helpful reading lists, astrologer biographies, and more.

---

[1] Although I have translated the *Gr. Intr.* excerpts from Latin, I have reviewed the Arabic versions of them for clarity and corrections. It is clear to me now that we very much need a complete translation of *Gr. Intr.* directly from the Arabic.
[2] See Appendix G.

If we think of these two introductions in terms of quadruplicities, *ITA* is the "fixed" book, a concentration of instructions and information for use in all branches of astrology. The invitational book will have a "movable/cardinal" and "mutable/common" function: it will offer some challenges to modern astrology, stimulate a deeper experience of traditional astrology and thought generally, provoke more sophisticated conversations about issues astrologers care about, and expose people to a variety of alternative outlooks and practical methods.

§2: The primary authors and texts

In this section, let me describe the lives and works of several of the authors represented in *ITA*; in the next section I will describe the overall organization and special features of the book.

Abū Ma'shar. Abū Ma'shar Ja'far bin Muhammad bin 'Umar al-Balkhī was one of the most significant astrologers of the medieval period. He was born on August 10, 787 AD, in medieval Khurāsān, today near Balkh, Afghanistan.[3] According to ibn al-Nadīm, he died on March 8th or 9th, 886 AD. He lived in Baghdad and first took up astrology at age 47, allegedly in response to a challenge from the Arab astrologer and scientist, al-Kindī. According to a famous story, Abū Ma'shar had had a scoffing attitude towards astrology and those who practiced it, until al-Kindī challenged him to learn something about it first. He was soon converted to astrology and became a prolific and highly influential author in several branches of astrology, particularly in mundane techniques.

One major work was the *Great Introduction to the Science of the Stars* (*Gr. Intr.*), translated into Latin by both John of Spain (in 1133) and Hermann of Carinthia (in 1140).[4] Its eight books begin with some philosophical and scientific justifications for astrology, which later formed the backbone of Bonatti's *BOA* Tr. 1. Subsequent books cover all areas of basic concepts, from attributions of the signs and planets and houses, to dignities, planetary configurations, special degrees in the zodiac, some predictive material, and Lots.[5] Again, this material was mined by Bonatti and others for centuries. In

---

[3] See *PN3*, pp. 1 and 134.
[4] The oldest existing copy of *Gr. Intr.* in Arabic is from 939 AD: Istanbul, Carullah 1508, published in facsimile by Sezgin in 1985 (see *Abbr.* p. 7).
[5] In 2011-12 I plan on releasing a translation of John's Latin version.

ITA, I have liberally inserted sections from this book (using Lemay's critical edition of John's translation).

After writing *Gr. Intr.*, Abū Ma'shar turned extracts from it into a shorter textbook called the *Abbreviation of the Introduction* (*Abbr.*). This book was translated in the 12th Century by Adelard of Bath, who paired it with material on astrological talismans and pseudo-Ptolemy's famous *Centiloquium*. According to Burnett *et al.*, *Abbr.* was never popular in either the Arabic East or Latin West, "perhaps because of competition from several other popular short introductions."[6] But it might also have remained on the margins because it was included with magical material rather than with the standard astrological compendia. As of 1994, when Burnett *et al.* published the critical edition of the Arabic and Latin, only two Arabic manuscripts of it were known. In forming their edition, Burnett's group compared their Arabic *Abbr.* against the oldest copy of *Gr. Intr.*, but also found that Adelard's Latin was helpful—even in establishing the correct reading of competing or unclear Arabic passages. Since Adelard's Latin also contains more material than the Arabic *Abbr.*, it may reflect a fuller version of *Abbr.* now lost.[7] My new translation of Adelard forms one of the two key texts of *ITA*, supplemented by sections from John's Latin version of *Gr. Intr.*

Al-Qabīsī. The second core text is al-Qabīsī's *Introduction to the Science of Astrology*. Abū al-Saqr 'Abd al-'Azīz bin 'Uthmān bin 'Alī al-Qabīsī (d. 967) was a mathematician and astronomer active in the friendship circle of Sayf al-Dawla (the Emir of Aleppo from 945-67 AD), who also composed some astrological works. According to the historian al-Nadīm, al-Qabīsī was the student of the astrologer al-'Imrānī, who wrote a famous work on elections.[8] In a treatise on the testing of astronomers and astrologers, al-Qabīsī outlined a fivefold division of astrology (which he called the "Craft of Judgments"): this is simply the four traditional branches (mundane, nativities, questions, elections), with annual natal techniques[9] as a separate category. He believed that astrology should be kept from dilettantes, and in his book on testing he

---

[6] *Abbr.* p. *vii.*

[7] For example, *Abbr.* III.54-62, IV.34-36, and VII.8-73; also information on tastes and lands in *Abbr.* I.

[8] I plan to translate al-'Imrānī's book from the Latin version for the electional portion of the *EMA* cycle.

[9] See VII.2 below for al-Qabīsī's brief account of these, and Appendix F for others' versions in the three volumes of my *Persian Nativities*.

divided astrologers into four categories: from the fully competent astrologer who understands the mathematics involved and the reasoning behind inter-pretations, to those who can only perform mechanical tasks (like using astrolabes and such).

Al-Qabīsī's *Introduction* was translated by John of Spain, and became one of the most popular introductions to astrology for many centuries. Important portions of it are clearly drawn from Abū Ma'shar's *Abbr.* or the *Gr. Intr.*, but there is plenty more material in it, including brief reviews of several natal and mundane predictive techniques: these reviews may help students who have not already been acquainted with the lengthier treatments in *Persian Nativities.* Burnett *et al.* produced a critical edition of the Arabic and Latin in 2004, and *ITA* contains my own translation of the Latin, with corrections and adjust-ments based on the Arabic edition.

Adelard of Bath. The more popular translations of astrological works from the 12th Century were by John of Spain, whose literal and simple Latin style makes them very easy to read. In my Introduction to *PN1*, I describe how John's terminology supplanted those of competitors such as Hugo of Santalla and Hermann of Carinthia: thus we speak today of planetary "exalta-tions" (John), not "kingdoms" or "supremacies" (Hugo). The same thing may be said about Adelard of Bath (ca. 1080-1152 AD), whose translation of *Abbr.* calls the planetary falls or descensions "slaveries" (*servitus*), and the sign of detriment an "estrangement" or "alienation" (*alienatio*). Although Ade-lard's translations of astronomical and mathematical material were initially influential, ultimately both his terminology and works were neglected.

Adelard was from Bath,[10] born just after the Norman Conquest and a few years before the First Crusade. His father was likely Fastred (a Germanic name), a tenant of the Bishop of Wells (and his successor, John of Tours), both continental bishops. Adelard seems to have been an educated country gentleman rather than an academic, suggested in part by his familiarity with now-lost English methods of hawking (preserved in his *Treatise on Birds*). He is known to have studied at Tours, and had an early interest in astronomical and mathematical sciences. Some of his works are constructed as dialogues with a (fictional?) nephew, who is supposed to represent less sophisticated northern European learning, while Adelard's own persona is up to date on the new and exotic Arabic and eastern contributions to learning—of which

---

[10] In what follows I draw on several of the articles in Burnett 1987.

Adelard himself would be an early translator. But in order to write such works, he also had to know traditional Latin learning.

Around 1112, Adelard began his encounter with eastern learning in southern Italy (particularly Salerno), where he was exposed to and discussed various scientific questions with unnamed Greek scholars. After Italy he traveled to France, and probably before 1116 he wrote a work called *On the Same and the Different*. Although the title is a clear reference to Plato's *Timaeus* (which was enjoying scholarly popularity at the time), the book is really a description of the seven liberal arts modeled on earlier Latin literature. Probably around this same time, he wrote *On the Rules of the Abacus*, possibly also in France.

In the early 1120s, Adelard returned to England and participated in the intellectual circle of the Bishop of Hereford and Prior of Malvern. Here he translated three astrological works, which apparently tended to be included together: (1) *Abbr.*, (2) an incomplete version of pseudo-Ptolemy's *Centiloquium*, and (3) *Thābit's Book of Talismans, following Ptolemy and Hermes*. This latter work includes a description of magical images, prayers and incenses, the material bases for talismans and rings, and so on. Adelard's translation of *Abbr.* remained virtually unknown for reasons suggested above, but with the work on talismans he may also have helped jump-start the medieval magical tradition of carved gems and astro-magical images, some of which were "even on episcopal croziers."[11] Burnett suggests[12] that Adelard's translation shows he was not fully confident with Arabic at the time, but in my own view Adelard's choice of Latin words was sometimes more perceptive than that of fully fluent Arabists such as John of Spain.

Around 1126, Adelard translated the astronomical tables of al-Khwārizmī, and between 1125-50 he went on to translate Euclid's *Elements* from an Arabic source.[13] Near the end of his life he wrote *On the Work of the Astrolabe* (ca. 1150), and, if North is right, Adelard was a tutor of sorts to the future Henry II, and is responsible for casting most of the ten astrological charts on royal matters described in his article, covering years from the 1130s to about 1150.[14] If true, it would show that northern European and English royalty

---

[11] Margaret Gibson, "Adelard of Bath," in Burnett 1987 p. 16.

[12] Burnett 1987, p. 135.

[13] There are three versions of the *Elements* attributed to Adelard, of which "Adelard II" is considered the most secure.

[14] North, "Some Norman Horoscopes," in Burnett 1987, p. 160.

were solidly committed to Arabic-era astrology just a few decades into the First Crusade.

Other works pretty solidly attributed to Adelard include *Natural Questions* and *On Music* (in which Adelard notes that teenage boys of his day just want to sit around and listen to music: some things never change).

§3: Structure of ITA

In order to take the best advantage of *ITA*, readers must understand how I have structured it. Since *Abbr.* is composed largely of excerpts from *Gr. Intr.*, and al-Qabīsī's book is often based on *Abbr.*, it makes sense to put parallel discussions in these three works into the same sections of *ITA*. One could reconstruct *Abbr.* and al-Qabīsī entirely by putting these sections in numerical order, but for my purposes I have followed the organization of *Abbr.* for Books I-VII, and put al-Qabīsī's material on predictive and interpretive methods at the end as Book VIII. Each section heading is my own, followed by the relevant sections of the core works, almost always in the following order: *Abbr.*, *Gr. Intr.*, al-Qabīsī, other astrologers—occasionally with my own comments following. Below is an example of the structure, with further descriptions of each type of excerpt:

§XX.1: Dykes's section numbering and heading

[*Abbr.* XX.1] Leading excerpts from Abū Ma'shar's *Abbr.*, almost completely in numerical order based on Burnett *et al.*'s critical edition of Adelard's Latin. In almost every instance, I adhere to Adelard's Latin without corrections from the Arabic unless necessary: this offers an alternative perspective on some technical terms and style (which is sometimes informative in Book III).[15]

[*Gr. Intr.* XX.1.1] Corresponding excerpts from *Gr. Intr.*, citing the book, section and line numbers from Lemay's edition of John of Spain's Latin. I have also corrected and amended every instance in

---

[15] However, in Book V (on planetary natures), I have not corrected Adelard's list of planetary attributes except where absolutely necessary: there is enough overlap between the lists that readers should not feel they are missing anything.

which John's meaning departs from the Arabic, though for the most part I do not make John's vocabulary conform to my new standards.

[al-Qabīsī XX.1] Parallel excerpts in al-Qabīsī (citing Burnett *et al.*'s critical edition), with strict adherence to my standardized Arabic technical vocabulary here and in my commentary. These excerpts do not appear in numerical order, since al-Qabīsī arranged his own book differently.

[*Other sources* XX] Relevant quotes or passages from other authors, usually giving advice on their use in reading charts.[16]

Comment by Dykes. Occasionally (and throughout Book III) I offer commentary on concepts and their uses.

In sum, each section ideally has the closely-related perspectives of Abū Ma'shar and al-Qabīsī (with updated standardized vocabulary), delineation advice and comments from other traditional astrologers, and (especially in Book III) commentary by me.

§4: Planetary relationships: Book III

In my own view, Book III is the heart of the *ITA*. It establishes special technical vocabulary for planetary relationships which is sometimes surprising and informative. In *ITA*, I have now adopted a standardized vocabulary almost exclusively based on the Arabic, which in some cases differs from what we have inherited from the 17th Century English astrologers (or even John of Spain's Latin), including from some of my own previous translations. As an example, in III.14 I explain why I no longer use the word "prohibition" for a planet blocking another from completing a connection by degree. Instead, I use the more concrete and accurate "barring" or "blocking."

It is useful to compare *Abbr.*, *Gr. Intr.*, and al-Qabīsī on their organization here. My impression is that *Abbr.* takes a bit more care in its organization. For instance, in *Gr. Intr.* Abū Ma'shar did not list domain (III.2) in the list of

---

[16] For excerpts from ibn Ezra's *Beginning of Wisdom* (*BW*), I have had to reconstruct some of the Latin sentences using Epstein, due to the extremely terse style of the Latin.

planetary configurations, and al-Qabīsī casually inserts it later; but *Abbr.* puts it at the top of the list, allowing it to be grouped with advancement and retreat (III.3-4), yielding intriguing ideas I explore in my commentary. Moreover, al-Qabīsī's definitions are sometimes briefer, more abstract, or organized in a way that does not reveal their distinctness. For example, al-Qabīsī's definition of assembly (III.5) is rather bare, and is treated alongside aspects instead of being set apart and emphasized, as Abū Ma'shar treats it. Al-Qabīsī also treats separation (III.8) as practically a throwaway sentence in his paragraph on connection (III.7)—when in fact the Arabic terminology and concept of separation deserves its own examination. Thus it seems that even by al-Qabīsī's time, planetary relationships were being considered more mechanical and abstract via dry jargon, instead of richly and concretely.

I also include many diagrams and lengthy commentary on the meanings of the Arabic and Latin words, as well as comparing the planetary relationships with one another. One might indeed ask whether this is necessary, since on the surface the texts are simply defining astronomical scenarios. And from a modern perspective, this attention to conceptual and linguistic detail might seem tedious and picky. But these complaints arise from two sources: (1) the abstraction and increasingly stale nature of our jargon over the centuries, so that it is hard to reflect on exactly what inspired particular terms; and (2) a modern emphasis on psychological and spiritual interpretations.

I address the nature of our jargon (and the importance of recapturing its richness) in my comments in Book III. But let me address the issue of tedium and pickiness directly, because many people confuse accuracy and detail with loosely-defined notions of fate, and believe that an abundance of precise concepts implies some objectionable notion of fate or determinism. First of all, the metaphysical status of fate is totally different from the exactness of a science. Even if our lives are *in fact* determined down to the smallest detail, our *knowledge* of that determinism through a given *science or discipline* might be either imprecise or only general. For example, it may be that astrology can ultimately only describe types, instead of every singular detail of the world: if so, then even a completely precise astrology can only be precise about types instead of every particular feature of a fully deterministic world.

But here we are talking about the value of conceptual precision in a science.[17] Much modern astrology is characterized by a lack of detail or rigor in

---

[17] Please note that I am *not* talking about modern statistical attempts to prove that astrology "works," but rather the qualitative precision of interpretation.

its concepts, in part because it has made psychology a centerpiece of attention. Much psychology (not to mention spirituality) is difficult to pin down and define, so any astrology which defines itself in their terms invites a corresponding looseness of expression. But for our medieval astrologers, astrology was a science, closely related to astronomy and mathematics, and even expressed something of God's mind: so even if something like a nativity describes many potential outcomes or general types, they at least wanted to define the range of those outcomes well, through precise terminology. If astrology is really supposed to give us insight into our past, present, and future, from mental attitudes to concrete events in life, we should not complain about that. We might argue that a given definition is right or wrong, and even agree that a given meaning in a chart is only general and does not extend down to the smallest detail of our lives; but we owe it to these astrologers and astrology itself to *take the definitions themselves seriously.* So for instance, when Abū Ma'shar comments that a certain planetary scenario will involve a matter escaping one's grasp, and that some other thing will confront or come into one's path (III.23.2), we are obliged to note that he is not just speaking casually, but using technical Arabic terms already defined: escape (III.22) and obstruction (III.21). This can add qualitative detail to chart readings, but also expresses the fact that Abū Ma'shar sees his role as expounding a well-defined discipline with interrelated technical concepts.

What is more, the fact that these configurations can be grouped according to themes (see Appendix B), embodies a kind of philosophical commentary on what astrology does. For if the concepts deriving from different planetary scenarios are related in certain ways, then planetary conditions are not merely static and unrelated states or properties, but they are all part of a grander process of planetary flowing, relating, connecting, separating, loneliness, rescue, generating and constructing or falling apart and destructing, and so on: and so *we who are born, ask questions, or perform elections, are born or asking or making choices within a process of worldly and spiritual generation and corruption.* The nativity should show the general arc of many areas of life: whether they are on an ascending or descending arc, following a theme of successful completion, or corruption, or cooperation, or isolation, and so on—and likewise for horary and electional charts. We need a clear and rich vocabulary to describe these processes, and Book III contains the medieval attempts to do so. I think a proper understanding of these processes could lead to new and deeper ways of reading charts and understanding the meanings of our lives.

§5: Planetary conditions: Book IV

In IV.1-IV.4.1, our authors define four categories of planetary condition in terms of two contrasting pairs: (1) good fortune and bad fortune, and (2) power and impotence (or more usually, strength and weakness). At first the titles and meanings of these categories might seem like a superficial grouping into good/bad, and strong/weak: terms which are often overused and left unexamined in traditional literature. But the Arabic terms help clarify what each category is trying to capture, and hopefully we will be able to make their recognition and use more widespread.

The Arabic term for "good fortune" (*saʿādah*) means "happiness, bliss, prosperity, good fortune." It is the same Arabic word used for the Lot of Fortune. "Bad fortune" (*nuḥūsa*) means "bad luck, misfortune," and is related to the verb "be calamitous, ominous, unlucky, disastrous." Clearly, these conditions should pertain not only to the conventionally good and bad qualities displayed by planets in them, but they should have to do more specifically with outcomes. If we compare our astrologers on these individual conditions, that does seem to be the case. But I emphasize "conventional" goods, since much astrology focuses on conventional notions of benefit and harm: wealth, for instance, or poverty, health or sickness, fame or obscurity. A more spiritual or philosophical approach might frame enlightenment and happiness in other terms, even though the planets will still often indicate such conventional goods and evils.

The Arabic term for "strength" (*quwwah*) means "power, strength, capacity," with an emphasis on *being able* to do something. Its opposite, "impotence" (*duʿf*), means "weakness, feebleness," and is related to the verb to "become weak, frail, impotent, flabby, to slacken, abate." This is significant: it is not so much that a planet is *actually* doing something—that would be more a question of advancement and retreat[18]—but that it is in a *position* to do something either in a taut and forceful, or slack and frail, way. In the Arabic lexica, power is related to being strong, upright, standing, and supported;[19] but impotence conjures the image of a frail and flabby man: thus these categories have to do with the difference between a planet's activity

---

[18] That is, angularity. See III.2-3.
[19] There is a connection here between angles (which connote firmness and fixity, see I.12 below) and planetary "strength."

being like a toned and practice athlete, being sharp and timely, versus being lazy, lax, slovenly, and clumsy.

Thus in traditional astrology, we have several ways of determining what a planet does and how it does it: for instance, being slack at providing good outcomes, powerful at providing bad outcomes. And in each case, the planet might be more (angular, succeedent) or less (cadent) engaged in what it is doing: a powerful planet indicating good outcomes, but cadent in the 6th, might be unengaged and unhelpful as a whole, unless perhaps it is for indicating positive 6th-house matters.

§6: Whole-sign versus quadrant-based houses

People familiar with traditional astrology will be aware of "whole sign" and "quadrant" houses. Still, it is worth reviewing the difference between them here, since whole-sign houses are becoming more popular—making it even more important for traditional astrologers to decide what house system to use. Moreover, I discuss some new information and interpretive possibilities below.

Quadrant-based houses are the familiar house systems such as Porphyry, Alchabitius Semi-Arc, Placidus, and Regiomontanus. They are created by dividing the celestial quadrants between the horizon and meridian, as mentioned by al-Qabīsī in I.12 below. The zodiacal degree falling on each of the divisions is called a "cusp" (Lat. *cuspis*, "point"), and marks the beginning of a new house. Because the zodiacal distance between the Ascendant and Midheaven changes depending on latitude and other factors, quadrant-based house systems sometimes yield "intercepted signs" (signs without a cusp on them) and signs with multiple and intermediate cusps (for example, both the second and third house cusps might fall onto the second sign).

A variation on quadrant-based houses is the equal house system, in which houses are measured by equal 30° increments from the rising degree of the Ascendant itself; again, the degree beginning each division is a cusp marking a new house.[20] This method seems to have been used by Ptolemy in his treatment of longevity (*Tet.* III.11). Many traditional astrologers also adapted

---

[20] Since the degree marking the tenth house must match the corresponding degree in the rising sign, it follows that in equal houses, the Midheaven does not mark the beginning of the tenth house.

a recommendation by Ptolemy, that planets within 5° prior to a house cusp will be considered to have topical significance for that house, even though they are not actually in it. In equal houses, there are no intercepted signs or multiple, intermediate cusps on signs, though each house still overlaps two signs.

Whole-sign houses result from treating each sign itself as being identical to a house, so that all of the rising sign is the first house, all of the second sign counts as the second house, and so on. Like equal houses, the degree of the Midheaven does not automatically begin the tenth house, since it moves around between the ninth and eleventh signs. In whole-sign houses, there are no intermediate cusps and no intercepted signs.

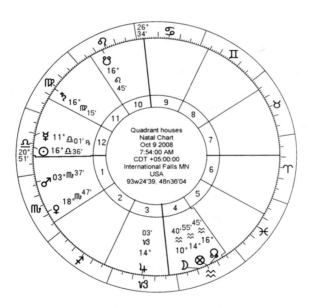

Figure 1: Quadrant-based houses (Alchabitius Semi-Arc)

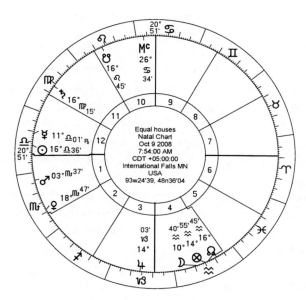

Figure 2: Equal houses

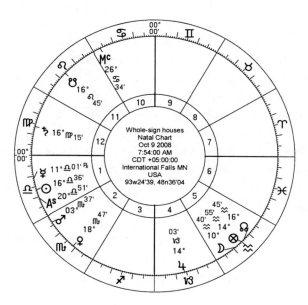

Figure 3: Whole-sign houses

In all of the figures above, the degree of the Ascendant is at 20° 51' Libra, and the Midheaven is at 26° 34' Cancer. In the quadrant-based figure, the Sun has first house significations because he is within 5° of the cusp—though many people would agree that he also has twelfth house significations because he is actually in the twelfth (though the first house significations would counted as more important). Mercury is in the rising sign, but he is a twelfth-house planet because he is in the twelfth quadrant-based region and not within 5° of the cusp. Mars is in the second sign but in the first topical house. Jupiter is in the fourth sign, but in the third quadrant region and so in the third house.

The equal house figure is very similar, but the degree of the Midheaven at 26° 34' Cancer is not identical to the tenth-house cusp: rather, the tenth-house cusp is the degree corresponding to the Ascendant, at 20° 51' Cancer. If there had been a planet within 5° prior to 20° 51' Cancer, it would be considered a tenth-house planet.

In the whole-sign figure, all of Libra is the first house, and so both Mercury and the Sun are first-house planets (though the Sun would be more significant because he is closer to the horizon). Mars and Venus are each in the second house. Jupiter is in the fourth house because he is in the fourth sign. All of Cancer is the tenth house, but the degree of the Midheaven in it has special significance for tenth-house matters, just as in the other systems.

Already in the Perso-Arabic period, there were disagreements not only about which quadrant-based houses to use (when an astrologer used them, that is), but whether one should favor them over whole-sign houses. Māshā'allāh mentions some of this controversy in I.12 below. If we compare Abū Ma'shar and al-Qabīsī, we see that al-Qabīsī occasionally emphasizes or strongly suggests using quadrant systems for delineating house topics, even if the corresponding text in Abū Ma'shar does not. But one thing is certain: as time went on, quadrant-based houses eventually triumphed. One element in their triumph was the new ability of Arabic-language scholars to perform the calculations to create them—which corresponded exactly with the 9th Century explosion in new systems.[21] But an ability to do something requires a motivation, even if the ability and its success ultimately overwhelm and disguise the original motivation. In my Introduction to *Works of Sahl &*

---

[21] See for example Edward S. Kennedy, "The Astrological Houses as Defined by Medieval Islamic Astronomers," in Edward S. Kennedy, *Astronomy and Astrology in the Medieval Islamic World* (Aldershot, Hampshire and Brookfield, Vermont: Ashgate Publishing, 1998).

Māshā'allāh I tried to reconstruct some of the reasoning that might have contributed a well-meaning astrologer's motivation for such a switch.[22] But I think we must recognize a combination of professional preferences, mathematical abilities, and translation errors at work, too. I return to this below.

There was even linguistic ambiguity over what sort of house system a particular author meant. For example, in the quadrant-based and equal systems, if a planet "aspects the Ascendant," it means it aspects the degree on or just around the cusp itself. But in traditional texts employing whole signs, it means the planet aspects the rising sign itself, regardless of where the rising degree actually falls. For the exact degree, the traditionalists often specified "the degree of" the Ascendant.

Likewise, there was great ambiguity over certain important concepts and words which I must describe at some length here: (1) being "angular" or "pivotal" or in a "stake"; (2) being "busy" or "advantageous" or "advancing"; (3) being "strong" or "powerful"; and (4) house topics. For it seems that at least some astrologers used both quadrant/equal houses and whole-sign houses simultaneously, but perhaps for different purposes; and there is more than one way to understand how to distribute these four concepts across the house systems. Let me briefly describe the problems and how some astrologers seemed to create their own solutions.

(1) Already in antiquity, the word which we translate as "angle" or "pivot" (Gr. *kentron*, Ar. *watad*) was used to describe three distinct things: (a) a whole-sign angular house (such as the tenth sign), (b) one of the axial degrees, and (c) a region of power which followed those axial degrees. Obviously, this makes it difficult to know exactly what a particular author means. For instance, in the whole-sign figure above, Libra is an angle or pivot because it is (a) the Ascendant (by whole sign), and nothing in the second sign (Scorpio) would be considered angular. But 20° 51' Libra is also an angle or pivot because it is (b) the axial degree itself. Finally, (c) an indeterminate region following 20° 51' is also angular and considered a region of power, and any planet in that region—even if it is in the second sign—could be considered angular. It is easy to know how large this degree-based region is if we use quadrant and equal houses: the angle is precisely the region of the house itself. Thus in the quadrant-based figure, the angle extends from 20° 51' Libra to 24° 44' Scorpio.

---

[22] *WSM* pp. *ff.*

(2) As explained in my comment to III.4 below, the houses are distinguished into those which are "busy" or "advantageous" or "advancing," and those which are "not busy" or "unadvantageous" or "retreating"—and there were two ways of making this distinction. One way is sign-based, because the busy places include the rising sign itself and six others which aspect it. This approach was advocated by Timaeus and adopted by astrologers like Sahl bin Bishr (via Dorotheus). The other way is explicitly stated as though it pertains only to signs, but it could and was interpreted according to quadrant and equal houses as well: in this second way, all four angles and all four succeedents are busy or advantageous or advancing, and all the rest (i.e., the cadents) are unbusy or unadvantageous or retreating. This approach was advocated by Nechepso and adopted by Abū Ma'shar and al-Qabīsī; and while I think Abū Ma'shar might have used whole signs, al-Qabīsī definitely uses quadrant houses. Planetary actions will be interpreted differently depending upon one's use of these houses. For example, in the figures above Mercury is busy (etc.) by being in the Ascendant by whole signs, but unbusy (etc.) by being in the twelfth by quadrant or equal divisions.

I have already mentioned that (3) houses were also granted a certain amount of strength based on their relationship to the angles, where angles are the strongest, the succeedents strong to middling, and the cadents weak. There is evidence (see below) that some astrologers viewed the quadrant divisions as referring to regions of power, while still using the signs for (4) topical meaning. So for example, a planet might be in the rising sign and therefore indicate first-house matters; but if it were far away from the degree of the Ascendant itself (like Mercury in the figures above), it might be considered weak in that signification. Likewise, a planet in the tenth sign would indicate profession and actions, but if it were far away from the Midheaven (which still retains an analogical meaning for profession and actions), it might not be particularly stimulated or quantitatively strong. However, in quadrant-based and equal house systems, the signs are not used for topical matters at all, so the region of power becomes identical to the region indicating the topic. In that case, every planet indicating friends (the eleventh house) would be strongish, and every planet indicating religion (usually, ninth house) would be "weak." But does it make sense that religious indicators are by definition weak?

Evidence that some astrologers used signs for topics but quadrant divisions for power, comes from Dorotheus[23] and a parallel text in Antiochus and Porphyry.[24] The text from the Arabic Dorotheus is also evidence for how some astrologers may have been encouraged to adopt quadrant-based houses straightforwardly for both power and topics. Recall that in both of the ways of determining the busy (or advantageous or advancing) houses, the rising sign is considered busy. But the seven-place, whole-sign approach advocated by Porphyry and Dorotheus[25] does not consider the second sign to be busy. In their discussion of this seven-place approach, Antiochus and Porphyry state that *sometimes*, if a late degree is rising in the Ascendant, then degrees in the spatial region following it, *even if in the second sign*, will be "co-busy" or "jointly busy" with the Ascendant. Dorotheus considers the regions of greatest power (or perhaps, busyness or advantageousness) to extend up to 15° from the axes.[26]

Let us return to our figures above and see how this would actually work in a chart. In all three figures, the degree of the Ascendant is at 20° 51' Libra. Now look at Mars, at 3° 37' Scorpio. If we followed the eight-place, whole-sign version of busyness advocated by Nechepso, then Mars is definitely busy, because all succeedent signs are busy. In fact, according to quadrant and equal houses, Mars is in the first house and therefore busy as well. But if we follow the seven-place, whole-sign approach of Timaeus and Dorotheus, then Mars is not obviously busy because he is in the second sign. However, the degree of the Ascendant is rather late, and he is with in 15° of it: therefore he falls under the special exception described above, and is considered "co-busy" or "jointly busy" even though he is in the second sign.

In other words, the Timaeus-Dorotheus theory allows normally unbusy planets to be *jointly* busy, provided that they fall into a certain region of *power*. It *does not* make a planet in an unbusy sign change its *life topic*: in this case, Mars is *not made into a first-house planet*, he is simply a jointly-busy, *second-house* planet. He is more relevant to the generality of life because he is (jointly) busy, but he is still a second-house planet indicating finances in particular. In

---

[23] *Carmen* I.5 and I.7.7-8.
[24] See Schmidt 2009, p. 279. In my discussion of Dorotheus in *WSM*, I did not yet know about the Antiochus-Porphyry material.
[25] This approach is also advocated by Rhetorius and Sahl. See my comment to III.4 below.
[26] *Carmen* I.7.7-8, I.26.3-8, III.1.23.

quadrant and equal systems, *this distinction is ignored*, because in them the regions of power and house topics wholly coincide.

If this were simply how things stood, we could say that whole signs are to be used for topics, but that regions of power could be measured from the Ascendant (and probably from the Midheaven and the other axial degrees), either using quadrant houses, or Dorotheus's 15° for the regions. And we might look at Ptolemy's use of equal houses[27] as a kind of unfortunate misstatement, in the sense that he uses the equal house regions of power but misleadingly calls them by their normal house names. But the Arabic edition of Dorotheus which has come down to us[28] is worded in a manner somewhat differently than the Antiochus and Porphyry passages, and I believe this Arabic passage erroneously inspired a wider use of quadrant-based houses for topics themselves.

After describing the seven-place version of busy places, which he also calls "good" and "strong,"[29] Dorotheus turns to rules for distinguishing natives with a good and healthy upbringing from those without one. He wants us to examine planets in *all* of the signs of the seven-place approach (I.7.3), then considers whether planets in the signs are of the proper sect (I.7.4-5), and then whether they are benefic (I.7.6). Clearly, Dorotheus is employing very generic considerations of busyness and sect and planetary quality, but *here* to assess the overall chart support for the native's life as a whole. So, if there are planets in the busy or advantageous places, of the correct sect, and benefic, then things look good for the native as a whole. Then Dorotheus adds the second-sign exception found in Antiochus and Porphyry: if a planet is in the second sign within 15° of the Ascendant, it has "power *as if it were in* the Ascendant" (I.7.7). As it stands, this is simply a restatement of the second-sign exception from Antiochus and Porphyry, though again in the context of the native's life. So far, so good: after all, the very general assessment of the chart for upbringing (in terms of angularity and power) was a staple of traditional astrologers. But then the Arabic goes further: if a planet were in the second sign and further away than 15°, it has no power "in the Ascendant" and indicates those who will have "no upbringing" (I.7.8). This is actually a significantly different statement. In the first place, Antiochus and

---

[27] *Tet.* III.11.

[28] The edition of 'Umar al-Tabari (itself not a complete translation of the Pahlavi and/or Greek). Māshā'allāh also had translated his own version, but it only survives in a few fragments.

[29] *Carmen* I.5.

Porphyry (and the true Dorotheus) did not say that planets in the second sign would actually have power "in the Ascendant," but rather that they would be "jointly busy," a kind of upgrade from a normally unbusy condition. But the Arabic Dorotheus links a region of power to a specific topic: life. Moreover, the Arabic says that if the planet were further away than 15°, it indicates "no upbringing"—but what the text should (and probably did) read is that such a planet cannot be considered "jointly busy" for the *overall* assessment of the chart. Thus again, what should have been a general observation about chart support seems to be made more specific to the rising sign and the topic of life.

Finally, another of the 15° rules in Dorotheus links this second-sign exception to life—without mentioning the second sign or busyness. In *Carmen* III.1.23, the Arabic Dorotheus assesses the primary releaser for longevity,[30] and says that if there is a benefic in the Ascendant, between the rising degree and 15°, it should be "mixed with" the releaser. I am not sure how one "mixes" another planet with the releaser, but we see again the ambiguity between what was originally a region of power, the Ascendant, and a topic of life or longevity.

These are the types of considerations which I believe led ancient and medieval astrologers to begin identifying regions of power more and more with house topics, so that by the High Middle Ages of Latin Europe, a "house" meant almost exclusively a region of power measured from an axial degree, which was identical to a topic of life. Although there had been controversy over different systems before, this is very different from a whole-sign topical system overlaid with busy or advantageous signs and regions of power.

If we allow signs to signify topics, but the quadrant divisions to indicate something like "power," then this problem is largely solved: all planets in the rising sign will indicate first house matters, and will be central to life because of it; but they might be weak in power even if they are central to life. Consider arthritis: some arthritis might always be on one's mind (in the rising sign), but might never be debilitating or really problematic (cadent in power); but other arthritis might be on one's mind (in the rising sign) but very painful and distracting (angular in power). Other planets and signs could work in roughly the same way: signs for topics, quadrant divisions for intensity.

I would like to propose the following as a possible solution to these issues, employing all of the schemes we have discussed so far: (1) adopt whole

---

[30] See "releaser" and related terms in the Glossary.

signs for topics; (2) apply Nechepso's eight-place scheme to signs in order to identify pivotal and busy *topics* relevant to conventional well-being;[31] (3) apply Nechepso's eight-place scheme to quadrant-based dynamical divisions, to assess planets' overall activeness and engagement in the chart (which I associate with advancement and retreat in III.3-4); (4) apply Timaeus's seven-place scheme to identify topics more directly advantageous to the native's sense of well-being.[32]

§7: Orbs

Since the medieval period, English-language astrologers have been used to speaking about "orbs" (Lat. *orbis*): spans of degrees within which two planets are said to be effectively connected. There are several versions in the literature: orbs based on type of aspect (modern), a 3° range (Hellenistic), a 6° range (al-Qabīsī), and unequal orbs based on the planets involved (Abū Ma'shar).[33] All of these are described in *ITA*. But readers should also be aware that the Arabic word does not really mean "orb." Rather, the Arabic authors speak of the size or power of a planet's "body, mass, bulk, volume" (*jirm*). For the unequal planetary orbs, it does seem strange that these degrees of power should be related to a planet's "body" or "volume," since we might expect them to derive from planet's brightness: but fainter planets like Saturn and Jupiter have larger ranges than a brighter and nearer planet such as Venus. The ranges of equal degrees (such as 3° or 6°) are undoubtedly based on other unknown considerations. Still, if we start from the notion of body or bulk or volume, we might begin to understand why orbs work as they do, and which version is preferable.

---

[31] This is already used by traditional astrologers in assessing conventional happiness and prosperity, when judging the triplicity Lords of the sect light. See "Prosperity" references in Appendix F.

[32] The distinction between busy/advantageous/advancing planets relative to the chart as a whole versus for the native, is suggested by Schmidt (2009, p. 289). But Schmidt does not distinguish Nechepso's scheme for whole signs and for quadrant-based divisions as I do here. I also do not agree with his analysis of other aspects of the passages and concepts.

[33] Not to say that the 6° and planet-based orbs began with al-Qabīsī and Abū Ma'shar, but they report them thusly in II.6 below. There are other degree-based regions too, such as being in the same bound or within 15° of the same sign (see II.6 and III.5).

§8: Lots: Book VI

Book VI is relatively straightforward. I only capitalize the names of the Lots of Fortune and Spirit (and the variant titles for Spirit), because their names are relatively stable: it does not make sense to me to insist on capitalized letters for the varied names of other Lots, when we should be understanding their meaning and formulas instead. Also, there is some controversy in traditional literature over whether or not to reverse certain Lots, and Abū Ma'shar himself wades into these controversies (with an occasional comment or observation by me). My own view is that all or most of the Lots are intended to be reversed.

BOOK I: SIGNS AND HOUSES

§I.1: Introductory comments

[*Abbr.* I.2-4] Anyone inquiring into the higher knowledge of philosophy with faithful study, scrutinizes the admirable effects of heavenly [things] in the sensible[1] world—indeed, inasmuch as the likenesses of superior forms [are] appearing above this lower world with a certain natural motion,[2] and portending the preconception[3] of future matters— he can hardly obtain it without an awareness of the degrees of the circles and signs, [and] moreover what planet [is] the Lord of a sign, and which parts they occupy in them; even their nature (and no less that of the signs); it is even fitting to know beforehand which ones of them are northern, but [also] which are southern. However, the specifics of these were stated more expansively in the *Greater Introduction*, but now in a more abridged way, closer to [how] things should be introduced.

[al-Qabīsī I.2-3] The Introduction of al-Qabīsī to the judgments of the stars, interpreted by John of Spain.

With an extended life being requested for Sayf al-Dawla, and the lastingness of his honor, and the protection of his goods, and the extension of his rule, let us begin what we want to describe. Since I have seen an assembly of certain ancients (from among the authorities of the mastery of the judgments of the stars) write books which they call introductions to this mastery, but, of those things which are *appropriate* to an introduction they have not scrutinized diligently all the things which are *necessary* in that mastery, and certain ones publish what is necessary in a sprawling way, and since I have determined that what is necessary in it has been lost; also that I have observed certain people

---

[1] Reading *sensibili* for *sensili*.
[2] This statements suggests the existence of eternal Forms (in Plato's sense), which are represented by the planets circling the sublunar ("lower") world.
[3] Normally we would take this to mean a preconception or anticipatory notion in the mind of the astrologer, and this seems to be the case in the Arabic text. But to my mind, Adelard's statement really suggests a preconception in the mind of God, who has rationally ordered the universe: thus the stars would foretell something which will happen according to the rational ordering of God and His mind.

not having begun on the path of teaching in the order in which they have published it, I have taken up the writing of this book: and I have made it an introduction, and I have gathered in it whatever is necessary for this mastery from the statements of the ancients, in the manner of an introduction.

[*Abbr.* I.1] And so, in the first place,[4] we will speak about the nature of the signs, [and their] proper qualities [and] effects; but secondly about the proper qualities of the stars according to themselves and their quantities, and what affections they have from the Sun; but thirdly about the twenty-five[5] bearings of the planets; fourthly, we must speak about the good fortune and power of the stars, but also [their] misfortune and impotence, even the unsoundness of the Moon, and an acquaintance with their twelfth-part; fifthly, about the nature of the planets and what they signify over the lower world, and which one is in charge over what day or hour; sixthly, about the names of the Lots; seventhly, about an acquaintance with the *firdārīyyāt*[6] and the bounds of the stars according to the philosophers of the Egyptians,[7] and also the differences of [their] degrees.

[al-Qabīsī I.4] And I have not introduced the necessary reasonings for the defense of what we have published, since they are in Ptolemy's book which is called the *Tetrabiblos*,[8] and in my own book which I wrote in confirmation of the mastery of the judgments of the stars[9] (and in destroying the letter by 'Ali bin 'Isa on its annihilation),[10] of the reasoning which could be sufficient for this. And I have divided [the book] into five sections:

The first section, on the essential and accidental being of the circle of signs.

---

[4] Each of the following seven headings corresponds to a Book below.
[5] From "domain" to "reception," III.2-25 below. I would group largesse and recompense together (III.24), and treat generosity and benefits (III.26) as the twenty-fifth.
[6] VII.2-8. Note that these periods include the Persian *firdārīyyāt* proper and the usual planetary years (greater, middle, lesser).
[7] Lat. *Medorum*, i.e., of Medes.
[8] See *Tet.* I.1-3. For other sources, see *Gr. Intr.* I-III, and BOA (or *Bonatti on Basic Astrology*) Tr. 1.
[9] A book by al-Qabīsī containing test questions for aspiring astrologers.
[10] A book by al-Qabīsī defending astrology from a critic.

The second section, on the natures of the seven planets and what is proper to them and what they signify.

The third section, on those things which happen to the seven planets in themselves, and what happens to them from each other.

The fourth section, on the explanation of the [technical] terms of the astrologers.[11]

The fifth section, on all of the Lots.[12]

§I.2: List of signs and planets and Nodes

[*Abbr.* I.5] Therefore, the circle is divided into 360°, not to mention into twelve signs: but the first of the signs is Aries, the second Taurus, the third Gemini, the fourth Cancer, the fifth Leo, the sixth Virgo, the seventh Libra, the eighth Scorpio, the ninth Sagittarius, the tenth Capricorn, the eleventh Aquarius, the twelfth Pisces.

[al-Qabīsī I.5-6] The first section, on the essential or accidental being of the circle of signs. The belt of the circle of signs is divided into twelve equal parts according to the division of the circle of signs, and these twelve parts are called "signs," and they refer to the images which are under that same zodiacal circle, which are: Aries, Taurus, Gemini, Cancer, Leo, Virgo, Libra, Scorpio, Sagittarius, Capricorn, Aquarius, Pisces.

---

[11] Most of this material is in Book VIII below.
[12] Omitting: "and the explanation of them in the degrees."

♈   Aries
♉   Taurus
♊   Gemini
♋   Cancer
♌   Leo
♍   Virgo
♎   Libra
♏   Scorpio
♐   Sagittarius
♑   Capricorn
♒   Aquarius
♓   Pisces

Figure 4: Symbols of the signs

[*Abbr.* I.6] But each one of these is divided into 30°; but the degrees into 60'. According to the same [method] a minute can be divided into seconds, and the seconds into thirds, and the thirds into fourths, in an unending way.[13]

[al-Qabīsī I.7] And each one of these signs is divided into thirty equal parts, which are called "degrees," and a degree is divided into 60', and a minute into 60", and a second into sixty "thirds," and [others] follow likewise: namely the "fourths" and "fifths," going on up to infinity.

[*Abbr.* I.7] But the seven planets are these: the first [is] Saturn, the second Jupiter, the third Mars, the fourth the Sun, the fifth Venus, the sixth Mercury, the seventh the Moon. [8] But each one of these holds onto its own dignities[14] in the signs, and also its apogee[15] and Dragon.[16]

---

[13] These further divisions into smaller parts are used by astrologers such as Abū Ma'shar for mundane calculations over great periods of time, such as in *BRD*.

[14] Ar. *ḥaẓẓ*, which means something's good fortune or allotment, which it has to itself apart from others.

[15] Lat./Ar. *awj*, here and throughout.

[16] That is, its Node. The Moon's Nodes are the most well-known, but all planets have them. See *BOA* pp. 201-02 (also in *Bonatti on Basic Astrology*).

♄	Saturn
♃	Jupiter
♂	Mars
☉	Sun
♀	Venus
☿	Mercury
☽	Moon
- -	- - - - - - - - - - - - -
☊	Head of the Dragon (North Node)
☋	Tail of the Dragon (South Node)

Figure 5: Symbols of the planets and Nodes

[al-Qabīsī I.12] But of all the wandering planets which are borne in these signs (not that they are *in* them, but they are borne under them in their forward movement), the one higher and nearer to the circle of the signs, and slower in course, is Saturn, then Jupiter, then Mars, then the Sun, then Venus, then Mercury, then the Moon—who is closer to the earth and quicker in course than all [the others]. Certain significations are even signified by the Head of the Dragon and the Tail in addition to the planets, just as we will make clear in what follows.

[al-Qabīsī I.13] Also, the planets have powers in these signs, certain ones by nature, certain ones by accident. The ones which are by nature are these: domicile, exaltation, bound, triplicity and face. But of those which are by accident, they are those which we will deal with in an appropriate place.

§I.3: Significations of the signs

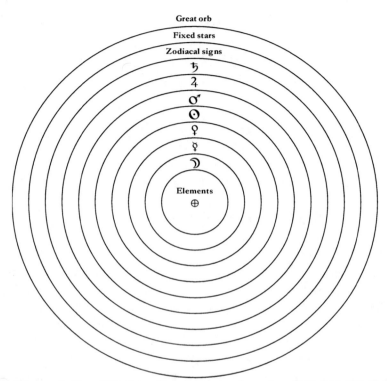

Figure 6: Simplified medieval cosmos based on Māshā'allāh[17]

♈

[*Abbr.* I.9-14] And so, Aries is a domicile of Mars, but the kingdom of the Sun in its nineteenth degree; but the slavery of Saturn in the twenty-first. Its faces[18] [are] three, each one holding onto 10°; but its first face is that of Mars, the second that of the Sun, the third that of Venus. Its nature [is] hot and dry, fiery, choleric, the taste bitter, the sex masculine, rejoicing by day, convertible,[19] [pertaining to] new sprouts, increasing the day beyond an

---

[17] *On the Knowledge of the Motion of the Orb,* §§15-17.
[18] See a complete table of the Chaldean faces or decans in I.5 below.
[19] I.e., movable.

equality of hours, its arising less than 30°, and it is indirect.[20] But the shape [is] imperfect, [it is] liable to anger, two-colored, two-formed, libidinous, of few children (sometimes none),[21] royal, four-footed, hoofed, of imperfect voice. Its part in a man [is] the head and face. But in lands, Babylonia, Persia, Palestine and Azerbaijan.[22]

[*Gr. Intr.* VI.9.1210-14] Of regions, Aries has Babylonia and Persia and Palestine and Azerbaijan. And of regions, sandy places and places for the grazing of sheep, and furnaces, and places in which one works by fire, and the hiding places of robbers; also, houses covered in wood.

[al-Qabīsī I.25] And every one of the signs has a proper signification in these things which it signifies: of the creation of men, crops, and regions and so on. Of the body of a man, Aries has the head and face; and of regions Babylon and Persia, and Azerbaijan and Palestine.

	Domicile	Exaltation	Detriment	Fall
♈	♂	☉ (esp. 19°)	♀	♄ (esp. 21°)
♉	♀	☽ (esp. 3°)	♂	
♊	☿		♃	
♋	☽	♃ (esp. 15°)	♄	♂ (esp. 28°)
♌	☉		♄	
♍	☿	☿ (esp. 15°)	♃	♀ (esp. 27°)
♎	♀	♄ (esp. 21°)	♂	☉ (esp. 19°)
♏	♂		♀	☽ (esp. 3°)
♐	♃		☿	
♑	♄	♂ (esp. 28°)	☽	♃ (esp. 15°)
♒	♄		☉	
♓	♃	♀ (esp. 27°)	☿	☿ (esp. 15°)

Figure 7: Table of major dignities and corruptions/debilities[23]

---

[20] That is, "crooked."

[21] The Ar. says it sometimes indicates twins.

[22] Many of these place names are in the Middle East or Asia, reflecting the political interests of the time; I will address them in the mundane installment of the *EMA* series, tentatively titled *Astrology of the World*.

[23] In traditional texts there is widespread inconsistency between cardinal and ordinal numbers. For example, the exaltation of the Sun is variously given as "nineteen" degrees

	Body part
♈	Head, face
♉	Neck, throat
♊	Shoulders, arms, hands
♋	Upper chest, breast
♌	Middle trunk, heart
♍	Belly, intestines
♎	Upper pubes, hips
♏	Genitals and anus
♐	Thighs
♑	Knees
♒	Shins
♓	Feet

Figure 8: Simplified table of sign-limb correspondences[24]

[*Abbr.* I.15-20] Taurus is a domicile of Venus, the kingdom of the Moon in its third degree, but the slavery of none in it. Its three faces: the first one that of Mercury, the second that of the Moon, the third that of Saturn. Its nature [is] cold and dry, earthy, melancholic, its taste acidic,[25] the sex feminine, nocturnal, firm, [pertaining to] sprouts, increasing the days, an imperfect shape, a diminished limb, libidinous, of few children (sometimes none), of imperfect voice, four-footed, hoofed. However, every plant and whatever is rooted in the earth belongs to it. But in a man, the neck and throat. In lands, however, al-Suwād, [Māhīn], Hamadhān, and the cities [of the Kurds].

[*Gr. Intr.* VI.9.1215-19] Of regions, Taurus has al-Suwād, Māhīn,[26] Hamadhān, and [the cities of] the Kurds who live in the mountains. And of provinces, lands of little water in which one sows [seed], and all

---

(19°), and the "nineteenth" degree (18°). My sense is that the authors probably meant "at the end of the nineteenth degree, namely at 19°."

[24] See also I.4 for the use of these correspondences for pain and illness.

[25] Or, "vinegary" (*acetosus*).

[26] Reading with Burnett for the Ar. *māhīr*.

fertile tilling [places], and every place close to mountains, also gardens and the forest and trees and waters and places of elephants and cows.

[al-Qabīsī I.26] Taurus has trees which are planted, and of the body of a man the neck and Adam's apple; and of regions al-Suwād, Māhān, Hamadhān, and [the land of] the Kurds.

II

[*Abbr.* I.21-26] Gemini: a domicile of Mercury; however, the kingdom of the Head of the Dragon in its third degree, but the slavery of the Tail in the same one.[27] Its faces [are] three, of which the first [is] that of Jupiter, the second that of Mars, the third that of the Sun. Its nature: hot and moist, airy, sanguine, its taste sweet, the sex masculine, diurnal, two-formed, a spring [sign] but its furthest part is of the solstice; many-faced,[28] of all flying things, the majority of it over tall trees, a human shape, eloquent, lacking children, powerful in voice,[29] shapely, generous, benevolent. But in men, having the chest and arms.[30] In lands, Jurjān, Armenia, Azerbaijan, [Jīlān, Burjān, Mū-qān,] Egypt, and Barqa.

[*Gr. Intr.* VI.9.1220-24] Of regions, Gemini has Jurjān and Armenia and Azerbaijan and Jīlān and Burjān[31] and Mūqān, also Egypt and the regions of Barqa, and it has partnership in Isfahān and Kirmān. And of places, mountainous ones, and whatever is cultivated in the earth, and [rubble][32] and hills, also places of hunters and of those playing backgammon, and those who have fun and sing.

[al-Qabīsī I.27] The sign of Gemini is generous, of a good mind; of the body of a man it has the shoulder and arms and hands; and of re-

---

[27] The attribution of exaltations to the Nodes is Persian and/or Indian, but I have never seen it used practically.
[28] Reading with the Arabic for "many-formed." I take this to be a psychological statement, i.e., inconsistent or shifting or two-faced.
[29] Reading with the Ar. for "sparse in words."
[30] Ar.: shoulders, upper arms, hands.
[31] Lemay reads: Buzjān.
[32] Translation tentative.

gions Jurjān and [Greater] Armenia and Azerbaijan and [Mūqān and] Jīlān and Egypt and Barqa.

[*Abbr.* I.27-32] Cancer is the domicile of the Moon, but the kingdom of Jupiter in its fifteenth degree, the slavery of Mars [in the] twenty-eighth. Its three faces: the first one that of Venus, the second that of Mercury, the third that of the Moon. Its nature: cold and moist, watery, phlegmatic, its taste salty, the sex feminine, nocturnal, turning[33] from spring to summer, its beginning decreasing the days, of many children, without voice. Its part [is] over creeping things and what swims, and trees middling [in height], and running waters and rain-waters. But in a man, having the breasts and the heart, the stomach, the sides and the spleen and lungs. In lands, Lesser Armenia, Eastern Khurāsān, [China and Marw al-Rūd], but it is a partner in the land of Balkh [and Azerbaijan].[34]

[*Gr. Intr.* VI.9.1225-29] Of regions, Cancer has Lesser Armenia and Marw al-Mūqān and Numidia (which is part of Africa), and the eastern region of Khurāsān, and Sind, and Marw al-Rūd. And it has partnership in Balkh and Azerbaijan. And of places, bushes and thickets[35] and coasts and riverbanks, and bluffs, also the places of trees.

[al-Qabīsī I.28] Of trees, Cancer has those which are moderate[36] in height; and of the body of a man the chest, heart, stomach, ribs, spleen and lungs; and of regions, Lesser Armenia and the eastern region of Khurāsān, and China, and it has a partnership in Balkh and Azerbaijan.

---

[33] I.e., movable.
[34] The Latin has, "and Helewez and some [parts of] Africa."
[35] Or perhaps, "jungle."
[36] Reading with the Ar. for *aequales*.

♌

[*Abbr.* I.33-38] Leo is the domicile of the Sun, [and there is] no kingdom
or slavery in it. Its first face [is] that of Saturn, the second that of Jupiter, the
third that of Mars. Its nature: hot and dry, fiery, choleric, its taste bitter, masculine, diurnal, firm, according to the summer, four-footed, having the teeth
and claws in wolves; a partner in tall trees; imperfect [in shape], liable to anger, libidinous, lacking children, of imperfect voice, making things up,[37] false,
malevolent, troubled, sad. In a man, having the upper part of the stomach
and the heart and the sinews[38] and the sides and ribs.[39] In lands, those of the
Turk up to the end of the inhabited world [in] Sogdiana and Nishapur.[40]

[*Gr. Intr.* VI.9.1230-34] Of regions, Leo has those of the Turk up to
the end of the inhabited [world] which follows it, and Sogdiana and
Nishapur.[41] And [delightful things][42] and adornments. And of places,
deserts[43] and rivers [which are] hard to cross, and earth that is gravel-
like and every place of abundance, and the mansions of the rich
(namely palaces), and mountains and hills, also higher places and
strong fortresses.

[al-Qabīsī I.29] Leo has tall trees; clever and cunning, and of much
anguish and sorrow; and of the body of a man the stomach, heart,
flanks and back; and of regions, that of the Turk up to the end of the
inhabitable region.

♍

[*Abbr.* I.39-44] Virgo is a domicile of Mercury; his kingdom [is] even in its
fifteenth degree; but the slavery of Venus in the twenty-seventh [degree] of

---

[37] *Artifex* ("craftsman, actor"), but following the sense of the Arabic.
[38] Or perhaps, the nerves (*nervi*).
[39] Including the back part of the rib cage.
[40] Following the Ar. Instead of Sogdiana, the Latin follows *Gr. Intr.* by including royal
places, sandy deserts and fortresses.
[41] Following *Abbr.*
[42] Translation uncertain.
[43] The Arabic is uncertain: possibly also valleys or caverns or grottoes.

it. Its first face [is] that of the Sun, the second that of Venus, the third that of Mercury. Its nature: cold and dry, earthy, melancholic, the taste acidic, feminine, nocturnal, double, weak, its end-part is of the equinox, three-formed (each one of them a flying one), a little dark, with a human figure, sterile, of great voice, shapely, generous, benevolent. In a man, the buttocks and the intestines [and the diaphragm].[44] But in lands: Jarāmaqa, Syria, the Euphrates, al-Jazīra, and Persia following Kirmān.[45]

> [*Gr. Intr.* VI.9.1235-39] Of regions, Virgo has Jarāmaqa and Syria, and the Euphrates, and al-Jazīra;[46] and, of the regions of Persia, those following Kirmān. And of places, every land in which one sows [seed], and places where women stay, also those of jokers and those singing and walking around.[47]

> [al-Qabīsī I.30] Virgo has whatever is sown from seeds, and it is generous, of a good mind; and of the body of a man it has the belly, the innards, the diaphragm and [small] intestines; and of regions, Jarāmaqa and Syria and the Euphrates, and al-Jazīra, and Persia.

♎

[*Abbr.* I.45-50] The sign of Libra is a domicile of Venus, but the kingdom of Saturn in its twenty-first degree, the slavery of the Sun in its nineteenth. Its first face [is] that of the Moon, the second that of Saturn, the third that of Jupiter. Its nature: hot and moist, airy, sanguine, of the male sex, diurnal, convertible, autumnal, decreasing the day, its arising over 30°, indirect, two-colored, two-formed, a little dim. Its part [is] in tall trees, with a human shape, middling in pleasures and longing, of few children (sometimes twins),[48] of a lively voice, shapely, benevolent to all. In a man, having the

---

[44] Adding with the Ar.
[45] Following the Ar. The Latin has: "the cities, Africa and Shem and Arabia and all grain-lands, places of female musicians and musicians."
[46] John believes this refers to Spain, but it is also a familiar name for the Arabian peninsula and regions in modern Iraq (both of which are more likely).
[47] *Spatiantium.*
[48] Reading with the Ar. for *nullorum* ("none").

[backbone],[49] lower parts of the belly and the pubic area. In lands, the Roman [Empire][50] up to Africa, and Upper Egypt[51] up to Ethiopia, and [the boundaries of Barqa] and Kirmān, Sijistān, Kabul, [Tukhāristān, Balkh, and Hirāt].[52]

[*Gr. Intr.* VI.9.1240-47] Of regions, Libra has the region of the Romans and whatever is in their boundaries up to Africa, and those which are in its circuit; and the upper parts of Egypt up to the boundaries of Ethiopia, and Barqa, also Kirmān and Sijistān, and Kabul and Tabaristān and Balkh and Hirāt. And of places, every place in which one sows in the peaks of mountains, and every land in which there are palm trees, and places of hunting with hawks, and every observation post and road, also every lofty and elevated place,[53] or sandy level plains.

[al-Qabīsī I.31] Libra has tall trees, and is generous, of a good mind; of the body of a man, having the backbone,[54] the lower parts of the belly, the navel, and the private parts, the hips,[55] intestines[56] and buttocks; and of regions the land of the Romans[57] and what follows its boundaries up to Africa; having Egypt up to the boundary of Ethiopia and Barqa; it even has Kirmān and Sijistān and Kabul and Tabaristān, Balkh and Hirāt.

♏

[*Abbr.* I.51-56] The sign of Scorpio is a domicile of Mars, but the slavery of the Moon in its third degree. Its first face [is] that of Mars, the second that of the Sun, the third that of Venus. Its nature: cold and moist, watery,

---

[49] Adding with the Ar.
[50] I.e., the Byzantine Empire.
[51] Following the Ar. (Lat. *Shahid Mediae*).
[52] Following the Ar. The Latin follows *Gr. Intr.*: "and places for hunting and fowling and the peaks of mountains."
[53] The Arabic also has connotations of shining and and splendid places.
[54] The Lat. reads "loins."
[55] Particularly the waist.
[56] *Ilia.*
[57] That is, the Byzantines.

phlegmatic, feminine, nocturnal, firm, autumnal, [dark],[58] its part [is] in wolves and in every swimming thing, and in rivers and in orchards; of many children, liable to anger, a liar, occupied in evil, good-looking, generous, mute. In a man, having the private parts and the sperm. In lands, the Hijāz, the countrysides[59] of the Arabs up to the Yemen, Tangier, [Qūmis and Rayy and part of Sogdiana].[60]

[*Gr. Intr.* VI.9.1248-53] Of regions, Scorpio has the lands of the Hijāz, and the countrysides of the Arabs up to the Yemen, and Tangier and Qūmis [and] Rayy and partnership in Sogdiana. And of places it has the places of vineyards and mulberries and the rest of similar things of that which is in a garden, and every stinking and horrid place, also prisons and places of grief and sorrow, and destroyed houses and the hollows of scorpions.

[al-Qabīsī I.32] Scorpio has trees moderate in height; generous, of a good mind;[61] and of the body of a man it has the private parts, the testicles, bladder, anus and thighs; and of regions the land of the Hijāz, and the countrysides of the Arabs and its boundaries up to the Yemen, and Tangier and Qūmis and Rayy, and it has partnership in Sind.

[*Abbr.* I.57-62] The sign of Sagittarius is a domicile of Jupiter, but the kingdom of the Tail of the Dragon in its third degree [and] the slavery of the Head of [the Dragon] in the same one.[62] Its first face [is] that of Mercury, the second that of the Moon, the third that of Saturn. Its nature: hot and dry, fiery, choleric, its taste bitter,[63] masculine, diurnal, two-colored, autumnal, its end point that of the winter solstice, imperfect, arising indirectly, of a twin

---

[58] Adding with the Ar.

[59] Or, the deserts.

[60] Following the Ar. The Latin follows *Gr. Intr.*, putting Persia after Tangier and adding "all stinking places and prisons and the habitations of scorpions."

[61] I do not know how al-Qabīsī gets this description of Scorpio's mind: perhaps the original read "*not*" of a good mind, *etc.*

[62] The attribution of exaltations to the Nodes is Persian and/or Indian, but I have never seen it used practically.

[63] Reading *amarus* with the rest of the fiery signs, for "acidic" (*acidus*).

figure, divided into two halves (the first half that of a human figure, royal, ruling; the second half four-footed, of an undivided hoof); its part [is] in wolves, [insects of the earth],[64] of few children, of a small voice, dutiful, profitable.[65] In a man, the legs.[66] In lands, [Baghdad and al-Jibāl, Isfahān, places of the Herpads[67] and fire-worshippers].[68]

[*Gr. Intr.* VI.9.1254-58] Of regions, Sagittarius has mountains and Rayy and Isfahān. And of places, it has gardens and every place which is irrigated for a season, and it signifies the places of the Herpads and fire-worshippers, and the places of the rest of the sects, and smooth desert, also places of animals and bulls and calves.

[al-Qabīsī I.33] Sagittarius: ingenious and clever; of the body of a man it has the thighs; and of regions,[69] Baghdad, al-Jibāl, Isfahān, places of the Herpads and fire-worshippers, and Ethiopia.

♑

[*Abbr.* I.63-69] The sign of Capricorn is a domicile of Saturn, but the kingdom of Mars in its twenty-eighth degree, but the slavery of Jupiter in the fifteenth. However, its first face [is] that of Jupiter, the second that of Mars, the third that of the Sun. Its nature: cold and dry, earthy, melancholic, an acidic[70] taste, feminine, nocturnal, convertible, wintry, its beginning increasing the day, of a round shape, incomplete [in figure];[71] of two wills and natures (for the first part [is] earthy and dry, sometimes powerful over beasts and sterile [men], the second part watery, flowing,[72] of many children, foul;[73]

---

[64] Adding with the Ar.

[65] The Ar. reads, "master of stratagem, cunning."

[66] Particularly the thighs.

[67] Reading with Burnett (Ar. *herābdhah*).

[68] The Latin has only "mountains and places having fires."

[69] John switched some of the places between Sagittarius and Capricorn; reading with the Ar.

[70] Or, "vinegary" (*acetosus*).

[71] Reading with the Ar. for "jealous," but jealousy could make sense for a Saturnian sign.

[72] *Fluxilis*, as water flows. But it also has bad moral connotations, and part of Capricorn is indeed known as "lecherous."

[73] The Ar. has the last part of Capricorn also indicating birds.

having grassy land and what is like grass;[74] of a good life, a mediocre voice, tending to anger, cautious,[75] panicky, sad, libidinous, [dark].[76] In a man, the knees. In lands, Ethiopia and the banks of the Indus,[77] [Makrān, Sind, Oman and Bahrain] and Hind up to the Hijāz.[78]

[*Gr. Intr.* VI.9.1259-68] Of regions, Capricorn has Ethiopia and Makrān and Sind, and the river of Makrān, and the shore of the sea which follows those regions, and Oman, and the two seas[79] up to Hind its boundaries up to Sind, and the Ahwaz, and the boundaries of the land of the Romans. And of places it has palaces and portals and gates and gardens, and every irrigated place, also rivers and the flowing down of waters and rivers, and irrigation canals, and ancient cisterns[80] and every riverbank above which there are trees, and a shore at which there are plantings, and places of dogs and foxes, also wild beasts and predatory animals, and the lodging-places or staying-places of foreigners and resident slaves,[81] and places in which fires are lit.

[al-Qabīsī I.34] Capricorn: of a good life, a tendency to anger, cautious and clever, of much sorrow;[82] of the body of a man, having the knees; and of regions Ethiopia and Mahrūbān, Sind and Oman up to the two seas and up to Hind.

[*Abbr.* I.70-75] The sign of Aquarius is a domicile of Saturn, the estrangement[83] of the Sun. Its first face is that of Venus, the second that of

---

[74] The Ar. adds "insects of the earth."
[75] The Ar. adds, "master of stratagem."
[76] Adding with the Ar.
[77] Lat. *Elden.*
[78] Following more the Ar. (which has "up to Sind and Hind."). The Latin follows *Gr. Intr.* by adding "flowering regions and meadows, places of dogs and wild asses, wolves and the places of the Arabs."
[79] Lit., "Bahrain."
[80] John reads, "fishponds" (Lat. *piscinas*).
[81] Or, "residents and slaves."
[82] Reading with the Ar.: John switched some of the places between Sagittarius and Capricorn.
[83] That is detriment.

Mercury, the third that of the Moon. Its nature: hot and moist, airy, sanguine, its taste sweet, masculine, diurnal, firm, wintry; its part [is] in tall trees, flowing waters, of a human shape, few children (occasionally none), of a small voice. In a man, the shins up to the feet. In lands, [al-Suwād], Kūfa,[84] [the rear of the Hijāz, the land of the Copts in] Egypt, [and western Sind].[85]

[*Gr. Intr.* VI.9.1269-77] Of regions, Aquarius has al-Suwād toward the mountains, and Kūfa and its parts, and the rear of the Hijāz, and the land of the Copts of Egypt, and the western region of the land of Sind, and it has partnership in the land of Persia. And of places, it has places of waters and flowing rivers and seas and canals and whatever is in them, and everything which is dug by hoes, not to mention every place which is irrigated by water, also places in which there are aquatic birds and the rest of birds, and every place in which there is a vineyard or in which wine is sold or whores provide lodging,[86] and every mountainous and uncivilized land.

[al-Qabīsī I.35] Aquarius: of the body of a man it has the legs and the lower ankles; and of regions al-Sawād, and Kūfa and its parts, and the land of the Hijāz and part of the land of Egypt,[87] and the western region of the land of Sind.

♓

[*Abbr.* I.76-82] Pisces is a domicile of Jupiter, the kingdom of Venus in its twenty-seventh degree, the slavery of Mercury in the fifteenth degree of it. The first one of its faces [is] that of Saturn, the second that of Jupiter, the third that of Mars. Its nature: cold and moist, watery, phlegmatic, its taste salty, feminine, nocturnal, two-bodied, wintry, its end-point equinoctial. Its first part is marshy, the other [part is set] over trees of mediocre height. To it belong wolves and all [animals] of waters, and ponds.[88] Indifferent to

---

[84] And the region around it. The Latin adds "up to Africa and Media [Egypt]."

[85] Following the Ar. The Latin is closer to *Gr. Intr.*, adding "forested areas" and "watery and meadow" regions.

[86] Or, "scrub," in the sense of a massage parlor or bathhouse.

[87] Namely, that of the Copts (Ar.).

[88] Ar.: "stagnant waters."

women,[89] of many children, imperfect, mute, [cautious, master of stratagem, rash, assuming many colors].[90] In a man, the feet. In lands, Tabaristān, [what is north of Jurjān],[91] part of the Roman[92] [Empire], the land from the Byzantine Empire to Syria,[93] al-Jazīra, [Egypt], Alexandria and the sea of Yemen.[94] And these indeed are the natures and proper qualities of the signs.

[*Gr. Intr.* VI.9.1278-85] Of regions, Pisces has Tabaristān and the northern parts of the land of Jurjān, and it has partnership in the land of the Romans up to the land of Syria, and al-Jazīra and Egypt and Alexandria, and whatever is in the circuit of Egypt and the Red Sea (namely the sea of the Yemen), and the eastern region of the land of the Hind. And of places, it has whatever comes up to the sea and its shores, also lakes and thickets and shores of the sea, and fish, also places of angels[95] and hermits,[96] and places of beating [the breast] and sorrow.

[al-Qabīsī I.36] Pisces: cautious and clever, commingled,[97] of much color; of the body of a man, having the feet; and of regions Tabaristān and the northern region of the land of Jurjān, and a partnership in Roman[98] [lands] up to Syria, and it has al-Jazīra and Egypt and Alexandria and the sea of Yemen.

---

[89] Ar.: "moderate in libido."
[90] Adding with the Ar.
[91] The Latin has: "parts of France."
[92] That is, Byzantine.
[93] Lat. *Soliman.*
[94] The Latin follows *Gr. Intr.* by adding "coasts and places of prayer and the places of angels."
[95] Lemay does not mark this as a mistake, but the Arabic reads "of a queen." If so, it might be related to the fact that Venus is exalted in Pisces.
[96] Or, "worshippers." This could relate to Pisces as being the ninth house of the *Thema Mundi* (see III.6.2 below); also, Jupiter and Venus are rulers of Pisces, and both are religious planets.
[97] Ar.: "promiscuous," probably because it is both watery and common.
[98] That is, Byzantine.

§I.4: The signs in pain and illnesses: al-Qabīsī

[al-Qabīsī I.37-48] And since certain planets signify pain, and they have a limb proper to them in each sign, let us therefore treat of the pains of the planets in the signs. And let us begin with Aries: in Aries, Saturn has the chest, Jupiter the belly, Mars the head, the Sun the thighs, Venus the feet, Mercury the legs, the Moon the knees.

In Taurus: Saturn the belly, Jupiter the chest,[99] Mars the neck, the Sun the knees, Venus the head, Mercury the feet, the Moon the legs.

In Gemini: Saturn the belly, Jupiter the private parts and what follows them, Mars the chest, the Sun the legs and ankles, Venus the neck, Mercury the head, the Moon the thighs.

In Cancer: Saturn the manly parts and what follows them, Jupiter the thighs, Mars the chest, the Sun the feet, Venus the arms and shoulders, Mercury the eyes, the Moon the head.

In Leo: Saturn the private parts and what follows them, Jupiter the thighs and knees, Mars the belly, the Sun the head, Venus the heart, Mercury the shoulders and throat, the Moon the neck.

In Virgo: Saturn the feet,[100] Jupiter the knees and what follows them, Mars the belly, the Sun the neck, Venus the belly, Mercury the heart, the Moon the shoulders.

In Libra: Saturn the knees and what follows them, Jupiter the eyes and what follows them, Mars the private parts and what follows them, the Sun the shoulders, Venus the [belly and][101] head, Mercury the belly, the Moon the heart.

In Scorpio: Saturn the ankles and what follows them, Jupiter the feet, Mars the head, arms and thighs, the Sun the heart, Venus the private parts and what follows them, Mercury the back, the Moon the belly.

In Sagittarius: Saturn the feet, Jupiter the legs and head, Mars the feet and hands, the Sun the belly, Venus the thighs and arms, Mercury the private parts and the heart, the Moon the back.

In Capricorn: Saturn the head and feet, Jupiter the knees and eyes, Mars the legs and shoulders, the Sun the back, Venus the thighs and

---

[99] Lat. "back."
[100] The Ar. reads "thighs," but feet seem to fit better to me.
[101] Reading with the Ar.

heart, Mercury the private parts and what follows them, the Moon the thighs and what follows the private parts.

In Aquarius: Saturn the head and neck, Jupiter the shoulders, chest and feet, Mars the ankles and heart, the Sun the private parts and what follows them, Venus the knees and what follows them, Mercury the thighs and heart, the Moon the private parts.

In Pisces: Saturn the shoulders, arms and neck, Jupiter the heart and head, Mars the ankles and the belly, the Sun the thighs and what follows them, Venus the neck and back, Mercury the legs and private parts, the Moon the thighs.

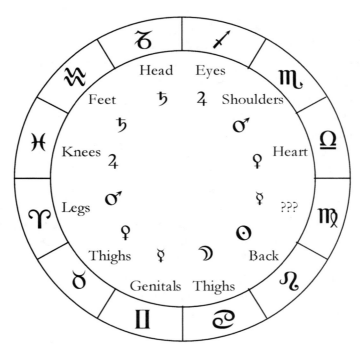

**Figure 9: Pain/illness distribution of planets
based on Capricorn**

§I.5: The faces: al-Qabīsī

[al-Qabīsī I.20] On the face. But the faces of the signs are these: each sign is divided into three equal parts; each part consists of 10° and they are called "faces," the beginning of which is from the first degree of the sign of Aries.[102]

♈	♂ 0°-9°59'	☉ 10°-19°59'	♀ 20°-29°59'
♉	☿ 0°-9°59'	☽ 10°-19°59'	♄ 20°-29°59'
♊	♃ 0°-9°59'	♂ 10°-19°59'	☉ 20°-29°59'
♋	♀ 0°-9°59'	☿ 10°-19°59'	☽ 20°-29°59'
♌	♄ 0°-9°59'	♃ 10°-19°59'	♂ 20°-29°59'
♍	☉ 0°-9°59'	♀ 10°-19°59'	☿ 20°-29°59'
♎	☽ 0°-9°59'	♄ 10°-19°59'	♃ 20°-29°59'
♏	♂ 0°-9°59'	☉ 10°-19°59'	♀ 20°-29°59'
♐	☿ 0°-9°59'	☽ 10°-19°59'	♄ 20°-29°59'
♑	♃ 0°-9°59'	♂ 10°-19°59'	☉ 20°-29°59'
♒	♀ 0°-9°59'	☿ 10°-19°59'	☽ 20°-29°59'
♓	♄ 0°-9°59'	♃ 10°-19°59'	♂ 20°-29°59'

Figure 10: Chaldean faces (decans)

[al-Qabīsī I.21] If therefore you had degrees in some sign and you wanted to know of which of the planets they are, take the signs from the beginning of Aries up to the whole sign which is before the sign about which you wanted to know the face, and triple them, and add [three] on top of how much there was, and [subtract by sevens], and count what remained from Saturn, through the succession of planets: and where the numbering would be ended will be the [planet ruling] the first face of that sign; whence, were the degrees up to the tenth degree of that sign, [the face will be ruled by] that planet with which the number was ended; and from 10 up to 20, that of the one which succeeds it. Therefore, it will be of the face of that planet in whose 10° of the sign it was.[103]

---

[102] Omitting the rest of al-Qabīsī's description, as the values and rulerships match the following table. I have put in the actual degrees of the faces, whereas al-Qabīsī's table simply puts "10°" in each cell.

[103] I have adapted this paragraph from the Latin, trying to shorten it and making the counting start with Saturn (which is how the Arabic reads).

Example: 16° Virgo (second face of Virgo)	
Number of signs up to ♍ (♈, ♉, Ⅱ, ♋, ♌):	5
Multiplied by 3:	15
Add 3:	18
Subtract multiples of 7. Remainder:	4
Count down from ♄ (♄, ♃, ♂, ☉):	☉
(Therefore, 1ˢᵗ face of ♍ ruled by ☉)	
Second face of Virgo ruled by:	♀

Figure 11: Example of deriving a face Lord

§I.6: Exaltation, detriment, fall

[*Abbr.* I.83-84] However, in the above-stated signs are also the estrangements[104] and slaveries[105] of the stars. And estrangement is the opposite of a domicile, but slavery [the opposite] of a kingdom,[106] in the same degree.

[al-Qabīsī I.14a] The domiciles are these: Aries and Scorpio, domiciles of Mars; Taurus and Libra, domiciles of Venus; Gemini and Virgo, domiciles of Mercury; Cancer, the domicile of the Moon; Leo, the domicile of the Sun; Sagittarius and Pisces, domiciles of Jupiter; Capricorn and Aquarius, domiciles of Saturn.

But the seventh sign from the domicile of each planet is said to be to be the detriment of that same planet.

[al-Qabīsī I.15] These are the exaltations of the planets:[107] The Sun is exalted in Aries (this is in its nineteenth degree), the Moon in the third degree of Taurus, Saturn in the twenty-first degree of Libra, Jupiter in the fifteenth degree of Cancer, Mars in the twenty-eighth degree of Capricorn, Venus in the twenty-seventh degree of Pisces, Mercury

---

[104] Detriment (Ar. *wabāl*: "unhealthiness, evil results, harm").

[105] Fall. Ar. *hubūṭ*, "downfall."

[106] Ar. *sharaf*, "honor, distinction, nobility."

[107] In my diagram below I have followed the more common practice of treating the signs themselves as the exaltations, instead of using the specific degrees.

in the fifteenth degree of Virgo, the Head of the Dragon in the third degree of Gemini and the Tail in the third degree of Sagittarius.[108]

However, in the seventh sign from the exaltation of each planet will be its descension in a like degree. For example, just as the Sun is exalted in the nineteenth degree of Aries, so does he fall in the nineteenth degree of Libra; and thus with the rest. However, Ptolemy[109] made all of Aries be the exaltation of the Sun, and all of Taurus the exaltation of the Moon, and likewise the rest.

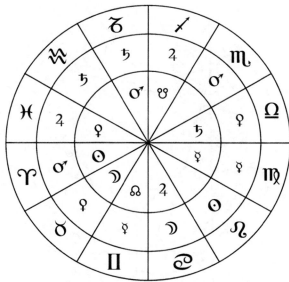

Figure 12: Planetary domiciles (outer) and exaltations (inner)

---

[108] The exaltations of the Nodes derive from Persian and/or Indian lore; they do not appear in earlier Greek astrology.
[109] *Tet.* I.20.

§I.7: The triplicities

[*Abbr.* I.85] One must even know that the threefold signs are of the same nature:

[al-Qabīsī I.16a] But we distinguish the triplicities thus: for every three signs which seem to agree in one nature make a triplicity, and they are called by the same name.

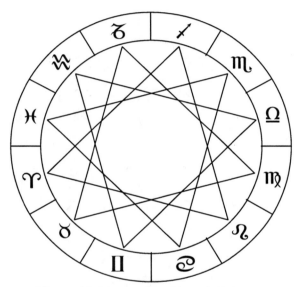

Figure 13: Signs related by triplicity

	Primary	Secondary	Partnering
Fire	☉	♃	♄
Air	♄	☿	♃
Water	♀	♂	☽
Earth	♀	☽	♂

Figure 14: Dorothean triplicity Lords

[*Abbr.* I.86] Aries, Leo, [and] Sagittarius [are] triangular, fiery, eastern, collecting and filling up; the diurnal judge of these is the Sun and [then] Jupiter, but the nocturnal one Jupiter and [then] the Sun; sharing with them by day and night [is] Saturn.

[al-Qabīsī I.16b] Therefore, Aries, Leo and Sagittarius make the first triplicity, because each one of these signs is masculine, diurnal, fiery (namely hot and dry), choleric, bitter in taste. And this triplicity is also eastern, the Lords of which are: in the day the Sun, and in the night Jupiter, and their partner in the day and night is Saturn.

[*Abbr.* I.87] Then Taurus, Virgo, [and] Capricorn [are] generous of provisions[110] and power, triangular, earthy, southern; their diurnal judge [is] Venus and [then] the Moon; but the nocturnal one [is] the Moon and [then] Venus; sharing with them by day and night [is] Mars (but Mercury has a share in Virgo).

[al-Qabīsī I.16c] The second triplicity is that of Taurus and Virgo and Capricorn, because these signs are feminine, nocturnal, earthy (namely cold and dry), melancholic, acidic in taste, southern. Also, the Lord of this triplicity are: in the day Venus, in the night the Moon, the partner of whom in the day and night is Mars.

[*Abbr.* I.88] Then Gemini, Libra, [and] Aquarius [are] giving and emptying, triangular, airy, western; the diurnal judge of these [is] Saturn and [then] Mercury, but the nocturnal one Mercury and [then] Saturn; sharing with them by day and night [is] Jupiter.

[al-Qabīsī I.16d] The third triplicity is that of Gemini, Libra and Aquarius, because these signs are masculine, diurnal, airy (namely hot [and] moist), sanguine, western, sweet in taste, the Lords of whose triplicity are: in the day Saturn and in the night Mercury; also, their partner in the day and night is Jupiter.

[*Abbr.* I.89] Finally, Cancer, Scorpio [and] Pisces [are] overflowing[111] and filling up, triangular, watery, northern; their diurnal judge [is] Venus and

---

110 *Census.*
111 Reading with the Ar. for "taking."

[then] Mars, but the nocturnal one Mars and [then] Venus; sharing with them by day and night [is] the Moon.

[al-Qabīsī I.16e] But Cancer, Scorpio and Pisces make the fourth triplicity, because these signs are feminine, nocturnal, northern, watery, phlegmatic, cold [and] moist, salty in taste, the Lords of whose triplicity are in the day Venus and in the night Mars, the partner of whom in the day and the night is the Moon.

§I.8: Analogies of the dignities: al-Qabīsī and others

[al-Qabīsī I.23] Certain people even gave such a comparison concerning this matter, saying that if a planet were in its own domicile it is like a man at home and in his own rule; and if it were in its own exaltation it is like a man in his own kingdom and glory; and if it were in its own bound it is like a man among his parents and relatives; and while it was in its own triplicity it will be like a man in his own honor and among his allies and underofficials. And if it were in its own face, it will be like a man in his own mastery.[112] These are the general, essential powers of the planets in the signs.

[BW VIII.78] If a planet were in its house, it is just like a man in his own home.

[BW VIII.79] But in its own honor,[113] it is just like someone in the loftiness of his station.

[BW VIII.57] A planet as the Lord of the Ascendant: if it were in its own triplicity and the Lords of the signs of the triplicity look at it, many [relatives] will be present as helpers.
[BW VIII.81] But in [its own] triplicity, [it is] just like one among his own relatives.[114]

---

[112] That is, in his own profession or job.
[113] Exaltation.
[114] Reading just as Epstein, but *propinquos* can also mean "neighbors" or people "nearby."

[*BW* VIII.80] A planet in its own bound [is] just like a man in his own seat.

[*BOA* II.2.14] And the philosophers found by long experience, that at such a time that a planet is in those degrees which are assigned to him as his bound in every sign, that it more strongly imprints in inferior things, than when it is in the other degrees of that same sign. And therefore they are called "bounds" because just as bounds are fixed by fields, they impose an end [limit], and they divide field from field; so those degrees assigned to a planet as its bound, impose an end on its virtue, and they divide the virtue of one planet from the virtue of the next.

[*BW* VIII.82] In [its] face: as one in [beautiful] ornaments and vestments.

[*Judgment* 26] If the malefic planets were in a peregrine sign, and if they were not in their own domiciles (nor in the exaltation, nor in triplicity), they increase evil and their impediment is made greater; and if they were in signs in which they have testimony, they are restrained from evil, and altogether there will not be an impediment.

[*Judgment* 41] If a planet were on a foreign journey,[115] that is, if it were not in one of its own dignities (as is the exaltation, face, and so on), its mind and nature becomes cunning.[116] And if it were not[117] in its own domicile or exaltation and it were direct, and in a good place from the Ascendant, or in the Midheaven or in the eleventh, it will be good.

[*BW* VIII.23] If a bad one were peregrine, its malice will increase.

[*BW* VIII.87] A planet in a place in which it wholly lacks dominion is like someone outside of his own homeland.

[*Judgments* 50] And know that the Lord of the Ascendant (or the Moon), if it were in the opposition of its own domicile (that is, in the seventh of its own domicile), the master of the question[118] will dread the purpose concerning which he asked: for it will be severe for him.

---

[115] *In peregrinatione.*

[116] *Callidus.*

[117] This seems to indicate a mitigating condition.

[118] That is, the querent.

[*BW* VIII.86] But if it is in the detriment of its domicile, it is like one who is antagonistic toward himself.

[*Judgments* 9] If a planet were in its own descension, it signifies sorrow and prison and distress.

[OR Ch. 10] [A planet in its own fall] will hate [its situation] on account of [its] hatred which it has towards its own place.

[*BW* VIII.31] If a planet were in its disgrace, it denotes pain and difficulty.

[*BW* VIII.88] A planet in the house of the opposite of its height,[119] is like one doing down from his dignity.

---

[119] *Augis*, reading with Epstein instead of "apogee."

§I.9: Classifications of the signs: Abū Ma'shar

§I.9.1: Straight/crooked signs

[*Abbr.* I.90-91] Of the signs, six arise directly, but the others indirectly. Indirectly [are] from the first [degree] of Capricorn to the last one of Gemini; but directly [are] from the first [degree] of Cancer to the last one of Sagittarius.[120]

[al-Qabīsī I.8b] And six of them are said to be ascending directly: that is from the beginning of Cancer to the end of Sagittarius; and six are said to be ascending crookedly: that is, from the beginning of Capricorn to the end of Gemini.

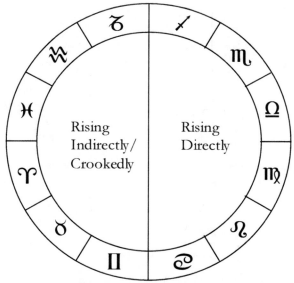

Figure 15: Signs ascending directly/indirectly

---

[120] Those ascending directly have greater ascensional times; those ascending crookedly have lesser ones.

§I.9.2: *Commanding/obeying signs, signs of equal daylight*[121]

[*Abbr.* I.92] In a certain way, those which arise indirectly obey[122] those which rise directly, [namely] [because] their days are equal to their days, giving themselves to them for prosperous actions:[123] for example, Gemini and Cancer, Taurus and Leo, Aries and Virgo, Pisces and Libra, Aquarius and Scorpio, Sagittarius and Capricorn.

[al-Qabīsī I.8c] And those ascending crookedly obey those ascending directly: that is, two signs which were of one longitude from the beginning of Cancer obey each other: as Gemini [obeys] Cancer, Taurus Leo, Aries Virgo, and Pisces Libra, Aquarius Scorpio and Capricorn Sagittarius.

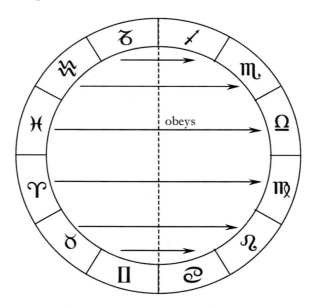

**Figure 16: Commanding/obeying signs (*Abbr.*), antiscion signs,
agreeing in strength/power and equal daylight**

---

[121] Ptolemy *Tet.* I.16 likewise calls these signs equal in daylight, but instead of commanding and obeying, these are his "seeing and hearing" signs. But he does not specify which is which.
[122] Reading with the Arabic for "love" (*amant*).
[123] Ar.: they signify agreement and friendship.

§I.9.3: Agreeing in strength or power

[*Abbr.* I.93] And so, these whose days are equal are friendly to each other, and they consent in good effects and agree in power.

[*Gr. Intr.* VI.4.1068-71] Also, the signs obeying each other are named in another way, that is, the "very powerful signs" and those "agreeing in strength," namely those for which the hours of the day of one of them are like the hours of the day of the other. And we will describe this in what follows, if God wills.

[*Gr. Intr.* VI.5.1098-1117] Secondly are the signs agreeing in strength. And the Persians call all [sets of] two signs from among them "very powerful." Also, they are said to obey each other. And they are the signs in which, if the Sun were in one of them, the hours of its day come to be equal just as the hours of the day of the other sign, as: Cancer and Gemini, Taurus and Leo, Aries and Virgo, Pisces and Libra, Aquarius and Scorpio, also Capricorn and Sagittarius. For the hours of the day of one of these signs are equal to the hours of the day of the other sign.

And[124] let us begin in one of these from the end of a sign, and in the second one from the beginning, as: the hours of the day of the thirtieth degree of Gemini, which are like the hours of the day of the first degree of Cancer; and the hours of the day of the twenty-ninth degree of Gemini are like the hours of the day of the second degree of the sign of Cancer. And the hours of the tenth degree of Gemini are like the hours of the twentieth degree of the sign of Cancer. And the hours of the day of the last degree of Taurus [are] like the hours of the day of the first degree of Leo. And [it will be] according to this up to where the hours of the day of the thirtieth degree of Virgo [are] like the hours of the first degree of Aries, and the hours of the end of Libra are like the hours of the beginning of Pisces. And the hours of the beginning of Scorpio [are] like the hours of the end of Aquarius, and the hours of the beginning of Sagittarius [are] like the hours of the end of Capricorn.

[al-Qabīsī I.54] And two degrees which were of one longitude from the beginning of the movable signs are said to be co-powerful and

---

[124] This matching of individual degrees also describes the antiscia or "shadow" degrees.

partners in virtue: like the twentieth degree of Capricorn or Cancer with the tenth of Sagittarius and Gemini; and the twentieth degree of Aries and Libra with the tenth degree of Pisces and Virgo; and thus with the rest.

§I.9.4: Commanding/obeying in concord and esteem[125]

[*Abbr.* I.94-95] Moreover, those which arise indirectly are even said to follow those which do so directly, [going] in another direction: for Gemini obeys[126] Leo, Taurus Cancer, Capricorn Virgo, Pisces Scorpio, and Capricorn Scorpio, and Aquarius Sagittarius. But Aries and Libra, [and] Capricorn and Cancer, do indeed have obedience[127] between themselves but not to a good effect: for they are opposites.

[*Gr. Intr.* VI.4.1057-67] Therefore, the signs of crooked ascension obey the signs of direct ascension, and they signify concord and esteem. And they signify more than this if they aspected each other from an aspect of friendship: as for example the sign of Gemini, which obeys Leo; and Leo Gemini; and Taurus Cancer, and Cancer Taurus; also Capricorn Virgo, and Virgo Capricorn; and Scorpio Pisces and Pisces Scorpio; also Sagittarius Aquarius and Aquarius Sagittarius; even Capricorn Scorpio and Scorpio Capricorn. However, Aries [obeys] Libra and Capricorn Cancer, but they are contrary in esteem. Because even though one of them obeys its companion, still they aspect each other from the opposition.

---

[125] This section may be based on something like the anonymous scholion to Paul Ch. 8 on his seeing and hearing signs (see diagram below). Note too that these trines and sextiles cross the crooked/direct divide, and involve signs of the same gender. But I do not see why not all signs are included.
[126] Reading with the Arabic for "love" (*amant*).
[127] Reading with the Arabic for "love" (*amant*).

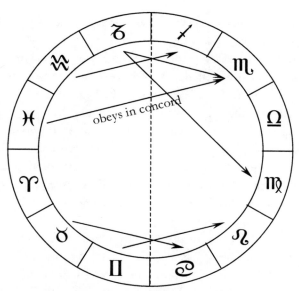

Figure 17: Commanding/obeying signs in concord and esteem

§I.9.5: Agreeing in the circle and ascensions[128]

[*Abbr.* I.96] Moreover, all those whose degrees [of ascension are] equal, are friendly to each other: Aries and Pisces, Taurus and Aquarius, Capricorn and Gemini, and the rest like these.

[*Gr. Intr.* VI.5.1079-97] One, that there would be two signs agreeing and partnering in the zone: this is that the longitude of each of them would be equally on the side of the circle of the equinox, and the ascensions of one of them are like those of the other, as for example Aries with Pisces, and Taurus with Aquarius, and Gemini with Capricorn, also Cancer with Sagittarius, and Leo with Scorpio, and Virgo with Libra. These signs agree with each other by ascensions.

For in one of these signs it begins through the concord of their ascensions with the other, from the beginning of the sign, but in the

---

[128] For a table of ascensional times calculated according to degrees of latitude, see www.bendykes.com. Ptolemy *Tet.* I.15 likewise lists these signs (as does Paul Ch. 12), but they also function as Ptolemy's commanding and obeying signs: the signs of northern declination (Aries through Virgo) are commanding, and those of southern declination (Libra through Pisces) are obeying.

other it begins from the end of the sign. Because the ascensions of the first degree of Aries agree with the ascensions of the last degree of Pisces. And the ascensions of the tenth degree of Aries agree with the ascensions of the twentieth degree of Pisces. And the ascensions of the end of Pisces are like the ascensions of the beginning of Pisces. Also, the ascensions of the beginning of Taurus are like the ascensions of the end of Aquarius, and the ascensions of the end of Taurus are like the ascensions of the beginning of Aquarius. And according to this example, the ascensions of the twentieth degree of Virgo come to be like the ascensions of the tenth degree of Libra, and the ascensions of the last degree of Virgo like the ascensions of the first degree of Libra.

[al-Qabīsī I.9] And two signs which were of one longitude from the beginning of Aries are said to be "agreeing in the journey,"[129] as Aries and Pisces, Taurus and Aquarius, Gemini and Capricorn, Cancer and Sagittarius, Leo and Scorpio, Virgo and Libra.

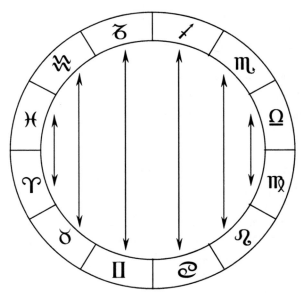

**Figure 18: Signs agreeing in ascensions
(and Ptolemy's commanding/obeying)**

---

129 Or, "the path" (Ar.).

§I.9.6: Agreeing in the journey

[*Abbr.* I.97] Moreover, any two which are the domiciles of one [planet]: Capricorn and Aquarius belong to Saturn, Sagittarius and Pisces belong to Jupiter, and those like these.

[*Gr. Intr.* VI.5.1118-25] But thirdly are the signs agreeing in the journey. This is that two signs would belong to one planet: as Aries and Scorpio, which are domiciles of Mars; and like Taurus and Libra, which are domiciles of Venus; and Gemini and Virgo, which are domiciles of Mercury; also Sagittarius and Pisces, which are domiciles of Jupiter; and Capricorn and Aquarius, the domiciles of Saturn. For each of these signs is in the journey of its Lord. But Cancer and Leo are the domiciles of the luminaries, [and are] in one journey, because each of them is the [sole] domicile of its Lord.

[al-Qabīsī I.14b] And if two signs were the domiciles of one planet, they are said to be "agreeing in the belt."

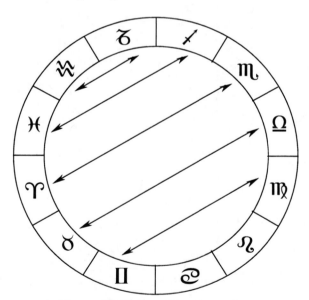

Figure 19: Signs with same ruler:
Agreeing in the "journey" (*Abbr.*) or "belt" (al-Qabīsī)

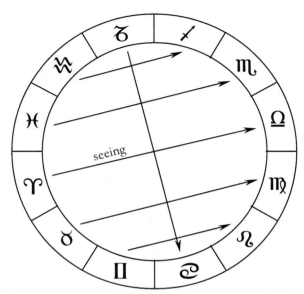

Figure 20: Seeing/hearing signs from Paul Ch. 8[130]

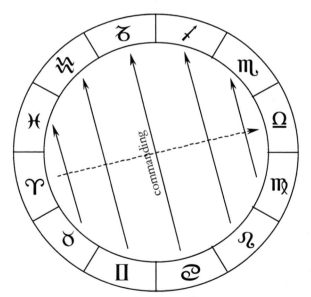

Figure 21: Commanding/obeying signs from Paul Ch. 9[131]

---

[130] Paul does not explicitly say how Capricorn and Cancer are related, but it is easy to see that all of the other crooked signs see the direct signs: thus it makes sense that Capricorn would see Cancer. My own sense is that these are the signs to be used for the synastry techniques in *BA* III.12.1-3 and III.12.7-8.

§I.10: Classifications of the signs: al-Qabīsī

§I.10.1: Northern/southern

[al-Qabīsī I.8a] And six of these signs are northern: that is, from the beginning of Aries up to the end of Virgo; and six southern: that is, from the beginning of Libra up to the end of Pisces.

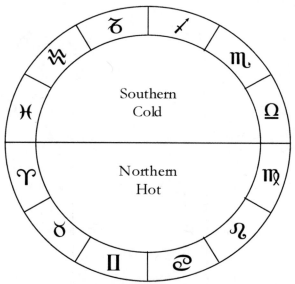

Figure 22: Hot/cold, northern/southern signs

§I.10.2: Solar/lunar halves of the zodiac

[al-Qabīsī I.10a] And the half of the circle which is from the beginning of Leo up to the end of Capricorn is called the "greatest half," and it is the Sun's half: because the Sun has sovereignty in this whole half just like the planets do in their own bounds. And the other half,

---

131 Paul does not explicitly say how Aries and Libra are related, but the other signs of northern declination command the signs of southern declination: so it is reasonable to suppose that Aries commands Libra.

which is from the beginning of Aquarius up to the end of Cancer, is called the "least half": because the Moon likewise has sovereignty in this whole half, just like the Sun does in the greatest one.

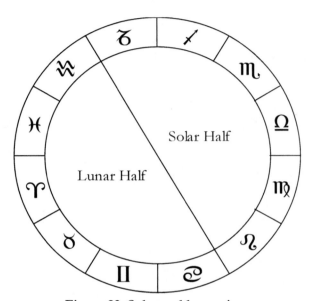

Figure 23: Solar and lunar signs

§I.10.3: Hot/cold halves of the zodiac

[al-Qabīsī I.10b] And that half which is from the beginning of Aries to the end of Virgo is called the "hot half," and the other which is from the beginning of Libra to the end of Pisces is called the "cold half."[132]

---

[132] This is because daylight and heat grow when the Sun is in the hot half (spring through summer), and diminish when he is in the cold half (autumn through winter).

§I.10.4: *Quarters of the zodiac*[133]

[al-Qabīsī I.11] And that fourth of the circle which is from the beginning of Aries up to the end of Gemini is called the hot, moist, spring-like, child-like, sanguine quarter. And the one which is from the beginning of Cancer up to the end of Virgo is said to be the hot, dry, summery, youthful, choleric quarter. And the one which is from the beginning of Libra up to the end of Sagittarius is said to be the cold, dry, autumnal, melancholic quarter, and it signifies the decline of middle age. And the one which is from the beginning of Capricorn up to the end of Pisces is said to be the cold, moist, defective, senile, wintry, phlegmatic quarter.

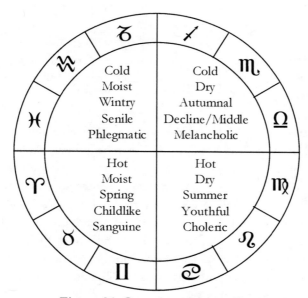

Figure 24: Quarters of the zodiac

---

[133] See a similar grouping for the quarters in I.11 below.

§I.10.5: Quadruplicities

[al-Qabīsī I.17] Also, four of these signs are said to be movable: that is, Aries, Cancer, Libra and Capricorn; and four fixed: that is, Taurus, Leo, Scorpio and Aquarius; but the remaining four are common: that is, Gemini, Virgo, Sagittarius and Pisces.

[BW VIII.47] If a planet were in a fixed sign, it denotes everything fixed [and] stable. And if it were in a movable one, it will be transformed. And if it were in a common one, it signifies a stable thing partly [completed], and partly changeable.

[Judgments 46] If planets were in fixed signs, they signify fixity—that is, firmness and the stability of matters concerning which the question comes to be. And if they were in common signs, they signify the loosenings of matters and repetitions, and other things will be attached to that matter (or some such other thing). And if they were in movable signs, they signify the speed of the conversions or changes of matters into good or evil.

[On Elect. §§12a-17 passim] Know that the movable signs signify the mobility of matters, quickly [so], and there is nothing lasting in them, nor is their time prolonged. But it is good to sow seed in them, to buy, sell, and to be betrothed to a woman (all of these are successful under them);[134]...And everything which you might begin in them (whose stability you want), will not be stable; but every unstable work (and hastenings) which you wanted to do, begin under them...And the faster [of] the movable ones are Aries and Cancer, for they have more crookedness and more mobility. Indeed Libra and Capricorn are the stronger and more temperate.

Next, the fixed ones are appropriate to every work whose stability and prolongation is sought, and what its author wants to be durable. And it is good and useful to build in them, and to celebrate a wedding—after the engagement was in the movable ones.[135] And if a woman were divorced by her husband in them, she will not return to

---

[134] This parenthetical comment belongs to the translator or a later editor.
[135] I.e., a quick engagement (movable) but a long celebration (fixed).

him. Indeed in judgments and inceptions in them, there will not be confidence[136] afterwards, unless the testimonies of the benefics would be multiplied in them[137]...But Scorpio is lighter than all the fixed [signs], and Leo more fixed; Aquarius is slower and worse, indeed Taurus is more level [or even].

The[138] common signs are useful in partnerships and brotherhood, and whatever might be worked in them often will be repeated. Indeed to buy and to celebrate a wedding in them will not be useful nor advantageous, and there will be trickery and deception in them ...all of the good and evil which comes to a man in them is doubled upon him; and if someone dies in them, then after him another person near him[139] will die in that place. And alteration,[140] and the washing of the head and the beard, and the purification of gold and silver are appropriate in them, and sending boys [to learn their] letters.

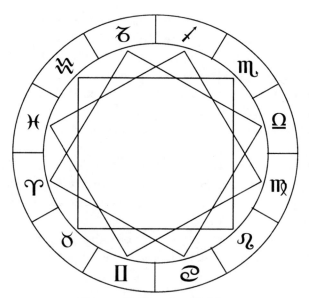

Figure 25: Quadruplicities

---

[136] *Fiducia.*
[137] For this last point Crofts reads, "There is no satisfaction after making a judgement or starting an enterprise, unless the testimonies of the benefics are manifold."
[138] See *Carmen* V.4.1.
[139] *In proximo*; following Crofts, signifying a neighbor or someone related, hence the evil is doubled in relation to the *first* dead person.
[140] According to Crofts, this is resettling one's home from one place to another.

§I.10.6: Further classifications of the signs: al-Qabīsī

[al-Qabīsī I.24] And the figures of the signs follow these: because in the signs are certain signs which are said to be rational: that is, Virgo, Gemini, Libra, Aquarius and the first half of Sagittarius, because these images in the circle are shaped in the images of men. These are also said to be those having beautiful voices. These also thrive if they were in the east.

And certain ones are said to be those having wings: that is, Gemini, Virgo and Pisces.

Certain ones four-footed: that is, Leo and Sagittarius.

And certain ones of them are domesticated: that is, Aries, Taurus and Capricorn; and these thrive if they were in the north.

And of the signs certain ones are defective: that is, Aries, Taurus, Cancer, Scorpio and Capricorn.

And certain ones of them and are said to be having many offspring: that is, Cancer, Scorpio and Pisces; and these thrive if they were in the west.

And certain ones are sterile: that is, Gemini, Leo and Virgo.

And certain ones are having few children: that is, Aries, Taurus, Libra, Sagittarius, Capricorn and Aquarius.

And certain ones are said to be very wanton: that is, Aries, Taurus, Leo and Capricorn.

And of the signs certain ones are said to be having half a voice: namely those which are formed in the images of bleating, lowing, and roaring animals, like Aries, Taurus, Leo, Capricorn, and the last part of Sagittarius.

And certain ones are lacking in voice, namely those which are formed in the images of animals lacking in voice: like Cancer, Scorpio, and Pisces.

§I.10.7: *Joys of the planets by sign: al-Qabīsī*

[al-Qabīsī I.14c] However, the signs in which the planets, when they enter [them], are said to rejoice in them, according to Dorotheus,[141] are these: Saturn is said to rejoice when he enters Aquarius, and Jupiter in Sagittarius, Mars in Scorpio, Venus in Taurus, and Mercury in Virgo.[142]

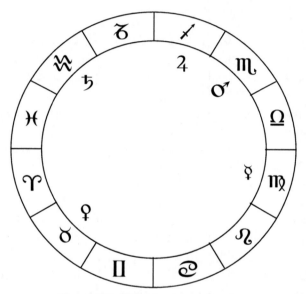

Figure 26: Planetary joys by sign

<hr />

[141] *Carmen* I.1.9.

[142] Except for Mercury, note that the planets rejoice in the domiciles of their sect: the nocturnal planets in their feminine/nocturnal domiciles, the diurnal ones in masculine/diurnal ones. Mercury probably rejoices in Virgo because he is also exalted there. Sahl's *Introduction* has the Sun in Leo and the Moon in Cancer as well.

§I.11: Quarters of the circle

[*Abbr.* I.98-102] However, at any hour the circle is divided into four parts. The first one [is] from the rising up to the Midheaven: and it is called eastern, masculine, advancing.[143] But another from the Midheaven up to the west: and it is called female, southern, retreating. The third from the west up to the middle of the lower hemisphere: western, masculine, advancing. The fourth from the lowest middle up to the east: northern, female, retreating.

[al-Qabīsī I.56a] However, the quarter which is from the Ascendant to the Midheaven (which is the twelfth, eleventh, tenth houses) is said to be the eastern, masculine, arriving quarter: it signifies the beginning of life, and is called childlike, sanguine, spring-like.

And the next part, which is from the Midheaven up to the degree of the western sign which is above the circle of the western hemisphere (which is the ninth, eighth, seventh houses), is southern, feminine, retreating: it signifies middle age and is called the completion of youth, summery, choleric.

Also, the third part, which is from the west up to the degree of the fourth house, which is upon the circle of midday [but] below the earth (which is the sixth, fifth, fourth houses) is western, masculine, arriving: it signifies the end of life and is called autumnal, melancholic, and is of middle age.

But the fourth part, which is from the fourth house up to the Ascendant (which is the third, second, and ascending houses) is northern, feminine, retreating: it signifies what happens to a man after his death, or his arrangement with respect to his leftover assets or what will be said about him (that is, whether he would be praised or blamed); and this part is called senile, phlegmatic, defective, wintry.

---

[143] The terms for advancing/arriving and retreating in this section are the same as for advancing and retreating planets in III.3-III.4 below.

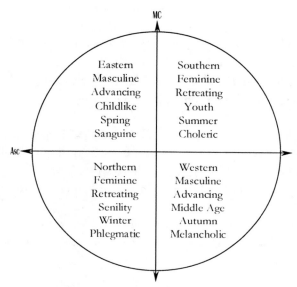

Figure 27: Quarters of the circle

[*Abbr.* I.103-04] Moreover, were any part of the circle above the earth, it is usually called "right," but the lower [part] "left." According to certain people the two upper parts are even called masculine and right and advancing, but the two lower ones female and left and retreating.

[al-Qabīsī I.56c] And whatever of the circle were above the earth is called "to the right," and what is below the earth is called "to the left."

[*Abbr.* I.105] Moreover, from the lowest middle up through the east to the upper middle, it is called "ascending"; but from the upper middle through the west to the lowest middle [it is] "descending."

[al-Qabīsī I.56b] And those two parts which are from the Mid-heaven up to the Ascendant, and from the Ascendant up to the fourth house, this half is called the "ascending half." And the remaining parts are called the "descending half."

§I.12: Angularity of the houses[144]

[*Abbr.* I.106-07] Likewise, the four above-stated parts are divided over the twelve signs, and they call each one of them a domicile. They call the first domicile of each above-stated quarter "firm,"[145] but [also] the one following "firm,"[146] [and] the third one "removed from a firm one."

[al-Qabīsī I.56d] And the Ascendant and fourth, seventh and tenth are called "stakes";[147] and the second house and the fifth, eighth, and eleventh are called "succeeding to the angles"; but the third and the sixth, the ninth and twelfth are said to be "cadent"[148] from the angles.[149]

[al-Qabīsī I.56e-f] If therefore a planet were in an angle or in its succeedent, it is said to be advance; and if it were in the cadents from the angles, it is said to fail.[150]

---

[144] See also III.3-III.4 below.

[145] Ar. *watad*, "stake." See the passage from al-Qabīsī immediately below.

[146] It is considered advancing and strong, but it is a succeedent to a stake (*watad*).

[147] These were called "pivots" by the Greeks and some Latin translators, but are usually called "angles" (lit. "corners") due to the popularity of John of Spain's translation. The Latin manuscripts of al-Qabīsī contain a comment by John or a later scribe: "...which we call 'angles' because it sounds more beautiful."

[148] Lit., "falling."

[149] The diagram below is somewhat idealized, since both Greek and Arabic writers called the signs and the regions measured from the axial degrees by the same name (Gr. *kentron*, Ar. *watad*), without always clarifying which they meant in a given situation. See my Introduction §6 and the quote from Māshā'allāh below.

[150] Following the Latin. In the Arabic and in III.3-4 below, these are distinguished as "advancing" and "retreating"; but ancient people associated moving forward and making progress with being successful and making money, and moving backwards and failing with poverty just as we do today. See my comments on advancing and retreating in III.3-4.

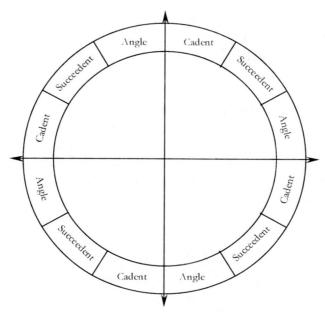

Figure 28: Angularity of houses

[*Abbr.* I.108] They distinguish each one of these by its own proper name.[151] But these domiciles are those signifying all lower things. Therefore one must speak about the significations of the twelve domiciles.

[al-Qabīsī I.55] But because, with God aiding, we have already made the essential being of the circle of the signs known, now let us mention even [its] accidental [being]. For, the circle is figured at every hour in such a figure that is divided into four parts, which the circle of the horizon and the circle of the meridian divide; and each part of these is divided into three unequal parts according to the ascensions of the ascending sign, and in this way the circle is divided into twelve parts, which are named "houses." Also there are named the "cusps,"[152] the work of which is laid out in the *Zij*.

Therefore, the beginning of the division is the Ascendant, the beginning of which is on[153] the circle of the eastern horizon; then follows

---

[151] That is, according to what they signify below.
[152] Lit. "pinpoints" (Lat. *cuspides*) or "centers" (Ar. *marākiz*).
[153] Reading with the Ar. for "above."

the second house and the third, and the rest of the houses up to the twelfth.[154]

[al-Qabīsī I.57a] And each of these houses signifies something about the being of men.

[BA I.4] Nevertheless also, in terms of assigning the arisings [of degrees], much disagreement can be observed [among] the astrologers: of which a certain portion [of the astrologers] attribute the 5° [above] its arising as being associated with the arising degree...On the other hand, others, with the degree of the east being found in 29 [degrees] of any sign, want to ascribe that entire sign to the east.[155]

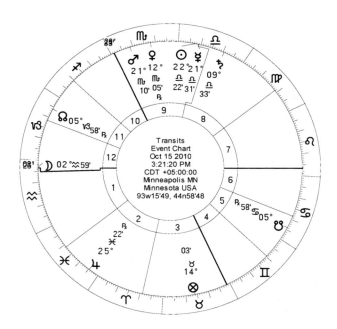

Figure 29: A chart with quadrant-based houses and cusps

---

[154] Al-Qabīsī obviously favors a quadrant-house division of houses, though he did not explicitly call for that when speaking about angularity in the passage above.
[155] This quote is meant to illustrate that even in the 8th Century AD, there was some dispute over whether houses should be measured from cusps (and even a few degrees before the cusp), or in terms of whole signs.

§I.13: Significations of the houses

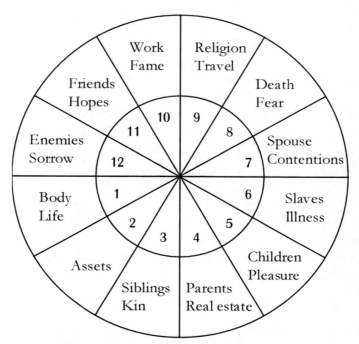

Figure 30: Basic meanings of the houses

[*Abbr.* I.109] And so, the domicile occupying the rising [place] is called the horoscope; the effect of this [is] over the body and life of a man itself, and all of his undertakings.

[al-Qabīsī I.57b] For the first house, whose beginning arises in the circle of the eastern horizon, is called "the Ascendant": this signifies [the soul],[156] bodies and life and the beginnings of works—namely of interrogations and orating and speech and rumors, and whatever the one asking is thinking about in his own mind; and it signifies the beginning of life.[157] And al-Andarzaghar said: in a nativity the first Lord of the triplicity of the Ascendant signifies life and the nature of the native or of the one asking, and his delights and pleasures, and what he esteems or what he hates, and what good or evil finds him at the be-

---

[156] Adding with the Ar.
[157] See below for a figure showing the angular triads grouped according to age.

ginning of his life. And the second Lord of the triplicity signifies life and the body and virtue and the middle of life. And the third Lord of the triplicity signifies what its companions signified, and it signifies the end of the matter[158] at death.

[*Abbr.* I.110] The second domicile [is] over possessions and dealings.[159]

[al-Qabīsī I.58] The second house is the house of assets and the means of livelihood and underofficials.[160] And it signifies the end of the years of life (that is, the end of youth). And al-Andarzaghar said about the Lords of the triplicity of the house of assets, namely about the first, second and third: see which one of them is stronger in being and place: you will make this one deservedly the authority over assets and the significator of their acquisition. Which if it were in the Midheaven, he will find this from the king; and if it were in the house of faith, it will be better. Likewise, the first Lord of the triplicity gives assets at the beginning of life, the second one in the middle, and the third at its end.

[*Abbr.* I.111] The third, over full siblings and blood-kin, and the relatives of the wife,[161] and [it is] also over [religion, jurisprudence, rumors, messengers],[162] and movement in place.

[al-Qabīsī I.59] The third house: of brothers and sisters, also kinsmen and those [who are] esteemed, faith and religion, commands and legates, changes[163] and short journeys; and it signifies the condition of life before death. Al-Andarzaghar said: the first Lord of the triplicity of the house of brothers signifies older brothers, and the second one the middle ones, but the third one the younger ones; and their worthiness will be according to their places.

---

[158] Reading with the Ar. for "life."
[159] Tentatively following Burnett for *usus*; but *usus* refers specifically to activities surrounding livelihood and supporting oneself. The Ar. reads "income" (*ma'āsh*).
[160] Or, "helpers" (Ar.): that is, human support (as opposed to financial support).
[161] That is, in-laws (broader sets of kin through marriage).
[162] Reading with the Ar. for "reading and knowledge."
[163] Especially in the sense of moving one's place of residence.

[*Abbr.* I.112] The fourth, over parents (namely, the father and mother) and their predecessors, and what part of the land he is going to occupy, treasures and all hidden things.

[al-Qabīsī I.60] The fourth house: of fathers and real estate and the end of matters and treasures and all concealed and hidden things; and of the being of the life of men, it signifies the end. Al-Andarzaghar said the first Lord of the triplicity of the house of fathers signifies fathers, the second cities and lands, but the third the ends of matters and prisons.

[*Abbr.* I.113] The fifth, over his desires[164] and children.[165]

[al-Qabīsī I.61] The fifth house: of children and delights, [eating and drinking],[166] legates and donations; and it signifies what is going to be after death (namely in terms of praise or blame). Al-Andarzaghar said: the first Lord of the triplicity of the house of children signifies children and life, the second delight, but the third signifies legates.

[*Abbr.* I.114] The sixth, over illness and slaves and his beasts.

[al-Qabīsī I.62] The sixth house: of infirmities and slaves; it signifies the end of life and whatever is going to be before old age. Al-Andarzaghar said: the first Lord of the triplicity of the house of infirmities signifies infirmities and recovery from infirmities, the second one signifies domestics and slaves, the third signifies what will find him in terms of those, and their usefulness and works. And [the house] is a significator of beasts[167] and flock-animals and all four-footed things, and their strength, also their multitude or scarcity, [and] by the custom of their being in his hand or their going out from it;[168] also prison and detention.[169]

---

[164] *Libidinem.*

[165] The Ar. reads "children, messengers, and guidance," but pleasure is in fact one meaning of the fifth.

[166] Adding with the Ar.

[167] The Ar. adds, "riding," which is normally not associated with the sixth.

[168] The Ar. seems to refer only to the native keeping *animals* or their running away; but the Latin is phrased to as to include the keeping or manumission of slaves.

[169] Reading *detentionis* for *retentionis.*

[*Abbr.* I.115] The seventh, that of wives and nuptials, [controversies, oppositions.][170]

[al-Qabīsī I.63] The seventh house: of women and nuptials, contentions too and partnerships and opponents;[171] and it signifies the middle of the end of life towards old age. Al-Andarzaghar said: the first Lord of the triplicity of the house of women signifies women, the second one contentions, the third uniting [with others].[172]

[*Abbr.* I.116] The eighth, that of fear and death [and inheritance].[173]

[al-Qabīsī I.64] The eighth house: of death; it signifies fear and death and inheritance, [and the assets of women, and thefts, and the conditions of opponents, and poisons];[174] and it signifies the end of the years of life after old age. Al-Andarzaghar said: the first Lord of the triplicity of the house of death signifies death, and the second one ancient things, and the third inheritance.

[*Abbr.* I.117] The ninth, that of travel and pilgrimage, laws and divine contemplation, philosophy and the arts, writings and [rumors and][175] visions.

[al-Qabīsī I.65] The ninth house: of pilgrimages and travels,[176] faith and religion, wisdom,[177] philosophy and books, also letters and legates, reports and dreams; and it signifies the beginning of [the second] half of life. Al-Andarzaghar said: the first Lord of the triplicity of the house of pilgrimage signifies pilgrimage and everything which happens on it, the second one signifies faith and religion and the good state of these

---

170 Adding with the Ar.
171 Reading with the Ar. for "opposites."
172 That is, partnerships and agreements.
173 Adding with the Ar.
174 Adding with the Ar. "Poisons" (*sumūm*) can also mean "hot wind" (*simūm*), which does not make much sense here.
175 Adding with the Ar.
176 Or more directly, "absence" (Ar.), as found in medieval horary questions about absent people.
177 The Ar. reads, "sciences," which traditionally referred to organized bodies of knowledge of many types, not just the natural sciences.

things and their manner,[178] and the third one is the significator of wisdom and dreams, also stars and omens and their truth and lying in this.

[*Abbr.* I.118] The tenth, that of the kingdom and dealings,[179] fortune, reputation,[180] silence,[181] duties[182] and labors [and mothers].[183]

[al-Qabīsī I.66] The tenth is the royal house, and [is] of works and loftiness, also of a kingdom and memory[184] and voice,[185] and masteries and mothers;[186] and it signifies the middle of the years of life. Al-Andarzaghar said: the first Lord of the triplicity of the royal house signifies work and exaltation, and the highest station; the second one signifies [one's] voice and courage in the same; the third signifies its stability and durability.

[*Abbr.* I.119] The eleventh, that of hope, fortune, riches, fame,[187] companions.

[al-Qabīsī I.67] The eleventh house: of trust and fortune and praise, also friends and underofficials, [recompense, clothing, scents, dignity, affection, and joy];[188] and it signifies the end of the middle of the years of life, and after the middle of life. Al-Andarzaghar said: the first Lord of the triplicity of the house of trust signifies trust, and the second one friends, the third signifies their usefulness.

[*Abbr.* I.120] The twelfth, that of suffering, enemies, prisons, [envy and slander], pains, wants, [and riding animals].[189]

---

[178] The Ar. refers to one's *eminence* in religious matters.
[179] See footnote above.
[180] Reading *famae* (and with the Ar.) for *formae*.
[181] Possibly a reference to Saturn in an archetypal relation to the tenth.
[182] Also, offices and responsibilities (*officiorum*).
[183] Adding with the Ar.
[184] That is, of whether or not one is remembered by others (i.e., one's lasting reputation).
[185] That is, the influence of one's voice and commands.
[186] The Ar. adds, "and whatever job the native does." This is potentially important as showing daily activity instead of one's higher vocation.
[187] In the sense of good praise from others, and not merely reputation in general.
[188] Adding these items from the Ar.
[189] Adding bracketed material based on the Ar. Note that envy and slander are meant to cover a variety of malicious and crafty thoughts and deeds.

[al-Qabīsī I.68] The twelfth is the house of enemies and labor and sorrow, envy and whispering, clever tricks and devices, and beasts [for riding].[190] And it signifies[191] what will happen to mothers in their conception, in terms of good or bad. Al-Andarzaghar said: the first Lord of the triplicity of the house of enemies signifies enemies, the second one labors,[192] but the third signifies beasts [for riding] and flock-animals.

This is what the twelve houses signify.

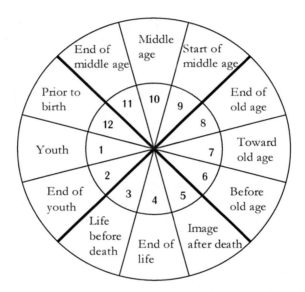

Figure 31: Angular triads and ages of life (al-Qabīsī)

---

[190] Adding with the Ar.
[191] Following the Ar., omitting "the end of life and."
[192] Or, "suffering" (Ar.).

§I.14: House meanings according to angularity: al-Qabīsī

[al-Qabīsī I.71] And in the signification of the houses, it is said that the angles signify strength and advancement,[193] but the cadents weakness and retreat[194] (except that the ninth and third signify public things[195] and the twelfth and sixth signify hiddenness and being covered and the low quality of things. But the angles and the Lords of the angles signify the greatness of honor and value and fortune, and being stimulated and being far from falling; and the presence of falling is the contrary of fortune: that is, disgrace and misfortune.

[al-Qabīsī I.72] But concerning the succeedents of the angles, the one which succeeds the tenth (that is, the eleventh) signifies strength and middling fortune from friends [and] from that direction in which there was trust. And the one which follows the fourth (that is, the fifth) signifies middling fortune through donations and reverence, and it is a cause of children with reverence, happiness and joy. However, the one which succeeds the Ascendant (which is the second) likewise [signifies] middling fortune by reason of assets and underofficials. But the one which succeeds the seventh (which is the eighth) signifies middling fortune from inheritance and from hidden things.

§I.15: The Lords of angles in the angles: al-Qabīsī

[al-Qabīsī I.73-I.76] These are also the significations of the Lords of the angles when they are present in the angles. The presence of the Lord of the Ascendant in the Ascendant signifies his fortune and acquisition through himself and through his family.[196] And through [its] presence in the tenth it signifies [it] through the king and through higher masteries. And if it were in the seventh, through meetings and contentions[197] and wives. Also, by its presence in the fourth it signifies

---

[193] Reading with the Ar. for "perfection."
[194] Reading with the Ar. for "detriment."
[195] Lat. "appearance" (*apparitionem*); Ar. "fame, reputation" (*shuhrah*).
[196] The Ar. does not mention the family, but this is consistent with the fact that the Lord of the Ascendant will be in its own "house" or "household"—particularly in a whole-sign system, when it would be in its own domicile.
[197] Reading more with the Ar. for "sowers" (*satores*).

fortune through real estate and through the causes of fathers and through the drawing out of waters, and through populating [lands] and [the building of cities and][198] from ancient and deep-rooted things.

Also, the Lord of the tenth, through its presence in that same tenth, signifies fortune through a great kingdom and higher masteries. And through its presence in the seventh, fortune through a kingdom, and victory in contentions and from the purposes of wives. And through its presence in the fourth, through a kingdom and the causes of [land-based] taxes and the cultivation of lands and the building of cities, through the diverting of rivers and the guarding of cities and from ancient things. And by its presence in the Ascendant, through a kingdom and cleverness and through petitioning[199] the king [and] from the matters of the common masses.

But the presence of the Lord of the seventh in the seventh signifies fortune through business deals and meetings, also through[200] women and contentions.[201] And through its presence in the fourth, through the meetings of women and business matters, through the causes of fathers and real estate and the cultivation of land. And by its presence in the Ascendant, through meetings and business matters, through the causes of medicine and astronomy and through spiritual[202] works and cleverness and the rest suchlike. And through its presence in the tenth, fortune through meetings and business deals and through wives and through the causes of the king.

But the presence of the Lord of the fourth in the fourth signifies fortune from the cultivation of land and [its] produce, through the causes of fathers and ancient things. And through its presence in the Ascendant it signifies fortune from the cultivation of the earth and [its] produce, through skill and the depth of counsel. And through its presence in the tenth, it signifies success from the cultivation of the earth and [its] produce, through the causes of the king and masteries. And its presence in the seventh signifies fortune from the cultivation of the

---

[198] Adding with the Ar.
[199] Reading *petitionem* and with the Ar. for *propinquitatem.*
[200] Omitting *nutritiones.*
[201] Reading more with the Ar. for "sowers" (*satores*).
[202] Or, "mental" (Ar. *nafsāniyyah*).

earth and [its] produce, through the causes of wives and contentions[203] and through business deals.

The Lords of the angles signify these things through their presence in the angles. You will do likewise concerning the presence of the Lords of the rest of the houses, but we have only introduced the Lords of the angles because they are an example for the rest.

§I.16: Planetary joys by house

[*Abbr.* I.121] However, Mercury rejoices in the horoscopic domicile, but the Moon in the third, Venus in the fifth, Mars in the sixth, the Sun in the ninth, Jupiter in the eleventh, Saturn in the twelfth.[204]

[al-Qabīsī I.70] And each one of the planets has a certain power (namely from among the accidental powers) in one of these houses, which is said to be a "joy." Because Mercury rejoices in the Ascendant, and the Moon in the third, also Venus in the fifth and Mars in the sixth, the Sun in the ninth and Jupiter in the eleventh, but Saturn in the twelfth.

---

[203] Reading more with the Ar. for "sowers" (*satores*).
[204] As Robert Schmidt has pointed out, note that the diurnal planets rejoice above the earth, the nocturnal ones below it, and Mercury (who can partake of either sect) in a domicile which is partly above, partly below.

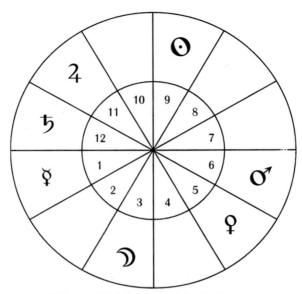

Figure 32: Planetary joys by house

§I.17: The colors of the places: al-Qabīsī

[al-Qabīsī I.69] The twelve houses even signify colors, and they are these: for the ascending house and the seventh are white, the second and twelfth green, the third and eleventh orange,[205] the fourth and tenth red, the fifth and ninth honey-colored, but the sixth and eighth are black.

---

[205] The Ar. reads "yellow": probably something like a light saffron is meant.

§I.18: The victor (*mubtazz*) of a topic: al-Qabīsī

[al-Qabīsī I.22] And since (with God assisting) we have already treated of the powers[206] of the planets in the signs (which are the domicile, exaltation, triplicity, bound and face), now therefore let us treat of their virtues in them. For the Lord of a domicile has five strengths, and the Lord of the exaltation four, and the Lord of the triplicity three, and the Lord of the bound two, and the Lord of the face one. And certain people put the bound before the triplicity.[207]

[al-Qabīsī I.77] And if you wished to know the planetary dominator of a matter, you will look to see which one of the planets is of more authority in the house of the matter, and [look] at the planet which signifies the nature of that matter (just as we will state in the nature of the planets in its [own proper] place), [and the Lot of the topic],[208] in terms of the strengths which we said before; and the one which was stronger than all the others in the place of the matter, that one will be its dominator.[209]

For example, if there were a question about assets, and you wanted to know which one is its dominator, and the second house (which signifies assets) was the fifth degree of the sign of Aries: since it is a domicile of Mars, Mars has five strengths in this place; it is also the exaltation of the Sun, and [so the Sun] has four strengths in it; it is even the triplicity of the Sun,[210] and he has three [more] strengths in it (therefore the Sun has seven strengths); and it is the bound of Jupiter, and he has two strengths there; it is even the face of Mars, and he has one strength there. Therefore, Mars has six strengths there, and the Sun seven. Therefore the Sun takes the position of first place there, and he himself dominates here in the house of assets. Likewise, you will look in the place of the Lot of Assets and the Lot of Fortune, and you will make Jupiter (who is naturally a significator of assets) the part-

---

[206] Ar. *ḥuẓūz* (sing. *ḥaẓẓ*), "shares, portions."
[207] See footnote in VII.4.
[208] Adding with the Ar. See below.
[209] To be clear: the victor for the house is a primary significator, but we must combine its information with *other* general significators and Lots. See the end of the instructions below.
[210] In a diurnal chart. Note that only the primary triplicity Lord receives points.

ner of these, and you will mix the significations of the Lots and the testimonies of the planets; you will do this for all the houses and you will
know their dominator.[211]

---

[211] This is ambiguous. Al-Qabīsī could mean one of three things: (a) we should find the
victor for each of these other places; (b) we should combine the dignities of the second
house and the Lots together and find a compound victor for all positions taken together;
or (c) find the victor for the second house alone, but we are to look at the relevant Lots
and natural significators individually without making them part of a victor calculation. I
think (c) is the more likely and is closer to the more ancient practice, even if we allow the
use of victors. I would like to point out that this victor procedure is not very informative:
if we follow al-Qabīsī and use Dorothean triplicity rulers and Egyptian bounds, and only
assign points to the primary triplicity Lord, then the victor will always be either the domicile or exalted Lord of the place—with only two exceptions: Mars will win in a few
degrees of Pisces, and Venus in a few degrees of Cancer. Since one should be looking at
exalted Lords when delineating houses anyway, the whole effort seems unrewarding.

BOOK II: PLANETS IN THEMSELVES AND SOLAR PHASES

§II.0: Introduction and celestial circles

[al-Qabīsī III.1] The third section, on those things which happen to the planets in themselves and from each other.[1]

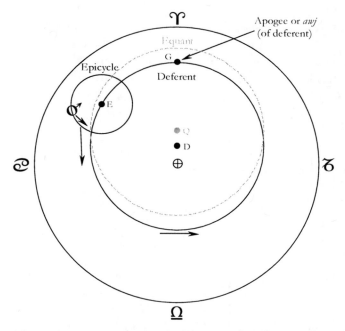

Figure 33: Deferent, epicycle, equant, and apogee (*awj*)

---

[1] In the diagram below, the symbol for the earth (⊕) is the center of the universe and the zodiac. Mars (representing planets generally) travels counterclockwise on his epicycle with center *E*. The whole epicycle travels counterclockwise on his deferent circle, with center *D*. Note that the deferent is "eccentric," that is, its center *D* does not coincide with the earth. Point *G* is the apogee (Ar. *awj*) of the deferent, its furthest position from the center of the earth. The equant circle (with center *Q*) is a special circle used to measure a planet's mean motion: according to al-Biruni, planets do not move equal distances in equal times on the deferent, but at different rates; we use the equant circle to determine mean motions and positions.

§II.1: Ascending/descending in the apogee

[*Abbr.* II.1-5] But the individual planets have diverse proper qualities in themselves. For each one is raised high in the circle of the apogee,[2] and when it is raised high it seems both less bright and smaller to us, and it moves forward less when fewer than 90° are contained between it and the Head of its apogee[3] from the front or back part. If however there were 90° on either side, the light and size and motion will be balanced. But if it went beyond this place, the light and size and motion will be increased.

[al-Qabīsī III.2a] The signification of the planets in themselves is that [if] a planet would be ascending in the circle of its apogee, [it is] less in light and magnitude and course: that is, if there were less than 90° between it and its apogee, in front or behind. If however there were [exactly] 90° between it and the apogee, it will be equal in light and magnitude and course. But if it were outside of these places, it will be descending in the circle of the apogee, and it will appear greater in light and magnitude, and quicker in course.

[*BW* VIII.83] When a planet is in its own apogee, it is just like someone who is on his own horse.

	2010 AD
♄	22° ♑
♃	2° ♎
♂	23° 30 ♌
☉	9° 30' ♋
♀	9° 30' ♋
☿	9° ♏

Figure 34: Approximate apogees of the planets (2010), based on al-Bīrūnī

---

[2] Reading with the Ar. for "signs" (*signorum*). The apogees (Ar. *awj*) of the planets change slightly over the years, moving forward in the order of signs by about 1° in every 66 years (according to al-Biruni, §195).
[3] Reading with the Ar. for "being raised high" (*sublimationis*).

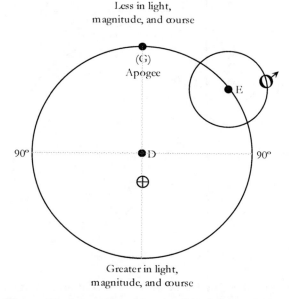

Figure 35: Ascending/descending in the apogee

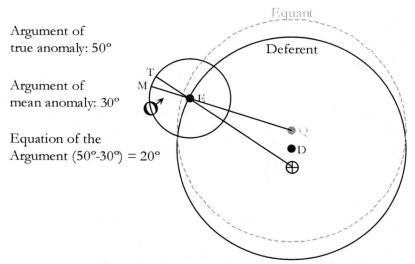

Figure 36: Arguments of anomalies and equation of the argument[4]

---

[4] In this diagram, we measure the distance of a planet (here, Mars) from the apogee of its epicycle. But the apogee can be determined from our perspective at the center of the earth

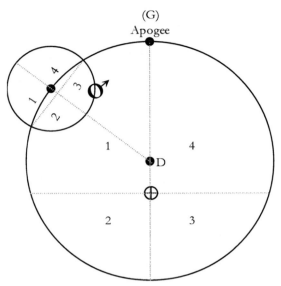

Figure 37: Quadrants of the deferent and epicycle[5]

§II.2: Increasing/decreasing in number

[*Abbr.* II.6] However, there are certain hours in which the number increases, but certain ones in which it decreases; even others in which it neither increases nor decreases. For if the argument[6] were less than 180°, it increases. But if more, it decreases. But if [exactly] 180°, neither one nor the other.

[al-Qabīsī III.2b] And if its calculated portion[7] were less than 180°, it will be increasing the number; and if it were more, it will be decreasing the number; and if its calculated portion were of [exactly] 180° or 360°, it will be neither increasing nor decreasing the number.

(to *T*) or from the center of the equant (to *M*). Mars's distance from *T* is the argument of the "true" anomaly, and from *M* is the "mean" anomaly. In this diagram I have posited that Mars is 50° from *T* and 30° from *M*. The difference between them is the "equation of the argument," in this case 20°. Obviously all of these values will change as Mars continues moving on the epicycle.
[5] For the Moon, al-Biruni says the quadrants of the epicycle are numbered differently, starting clockwise from the upper right quadrant.
[6] Ar. "anomaly."
[7] I.e, its "mean anomaly" (Ar.).

§II.3: Increasing/decreasing in computation[8]

[*Abbr.* II.7] It is even fitting to know that sometimes [there is a time] when the computation is increased, and when it is made less, and when it is neither increased nor made less. Indeed it is increased whenever the equation is added to the mean.[9] But it is made less while it is being subtracted from it. And when it is neither added to nor made less, it is found in the circle of the obliquity, in the path of the Sun.

[al-Qabīsī III.2c] And if the calculated equation[10] is added on top of the average course, it is said to be increasing the number; and if the equation is subtracted, it is said to be subtracting the number.

§II.4: Increasing/decreasing in speed

[*Abbr.* II.8] But there is also this: that if the superior planets went beyond their average motion, their motion is said to be increased. But when they subtract from the average, the motion [is] diminished. But if they neither add nor subtract, then the motion is called balanced.

[al-Qabīsī III.2d] And if some one of the three higher planets goes more than its own average course, it is said to be increasing the course; and if it goes less, it is said to be subtracting; and if it goes [its middle course] exactly, it is said to be even in course.

[*Abbr.* II.9] But the motion of Venus and Mercury are named because of the motion of the Sun: for if they went beyond the average motion of the Sun, their motion [is] increased. But if they moved forward less than the average, [it is] diminished. But should they neither add nor subtract, it is said to have an average course.

---

[8] See the figure of quadrants above. According to Wright's correction to al-Biruni §203, a planet will be increasing in calculation if it is in epicycle quadrants 1 and 2, and decreasing 3 and 4. In the figure above, Mars is decreasing because he is in the 3rd epicycle quadrant.
[9] This is to find the true longitude of a planet.
[10] Or, "equated equation" (Ar.).

[al-Qabīsī III.2e] And if some one of the inferior planets goes more than the course of the Sun, it will be increasing the course; and when it goes less, it will be subtracting the course; and when it goes [the Sun's course] exactly, its course will be even. However, the condition of the luminaries in [their] course is just like the condition of the higher planets.

[*Judgments* 13] If a planet were slow (that is if it walks slowly), it puts aside[11] its own number[12] or its own promise. That is, it makes a delay in number or its own promise, both in the good and the bad. It does likewise if it were in the domiciles of Saturn or Jupiter. And in the domiciles of the light planets, it hastens.

[*BW* VIII.94] Slow in course, like an exhausted person, without power in the course of his journey.

[*BW* VIII.95] A quick planet: like a young man running.

♄	00° 02' 01"
♃	00° 04' 59"
♂	00° 31' 27"
☉	00° 59' 08"
♀	00° 59' 08"
☿	00° 59' 08"
☽	13° 10' 36"

Figure 38: Average daily motions of the planets

---

[11] *Postponit*, the origin of our "postpone."
[12] This seems to refer to timing techniques—such planets will manifest more slowly and take more time.

§II.5: Planetary nodes, northern and southern latitudes

[*Abbr.* II.10] But there is also this, that they are called northern and southern with respect to the path of the Sun. For from [their] own Head of the Dragon up the Tail, they are called northern; but from the Tail up to the Head, southern.[13]

[al-Qabīsī III.3] Also, a planet becomes northern when it crosses its own [northern] Node.[14] If therefore a planet crossed the aforesaid cutting [of the ecliptic], and there were less than 90° between the planet and the cutting itself, the planet will be ascending northern. And if it were from 90° up to 180°, it will be descending northern. And if it passed by this number, going towards 270°, it will be descending southern. And if it crossed this number, going to 360°, it will be ascending southern.

This is the condition of the planets in themselves.

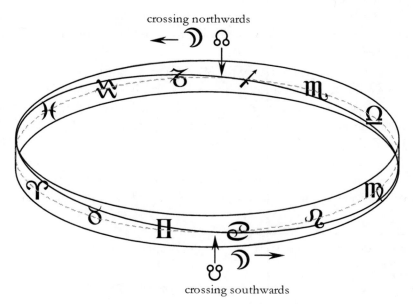

Figure 39: Nodes and latitude of Moon

---

[13] See IV.2-IV.3 and IV.5 for these position as indicating power or impotence.
[14] *Jawzahirr*, from the Pahlavi for "dragon."

§II.6: Planetary orbs[15]

[*Abbr.* II.11-12] But one should not pass over the fact that the individual stars have determinate degrees of their power, in front and behind. And so the Sun has 15° of his power in front of himself and the same amount behind himself. The Moon, 12° in front and the same amount behind. Saturn and Jupiter, 9° in front and the same amount behind. But Mars, 8° in front and the same amount behind. Finally, Venus and Mercury: 7° in front and the same amount behind.

[*Gr. Intr.* VII.4.354-89] And the orbs of the seven planets have an amount of strength in their places, which we have already described in the preceding section.[16] Therefore, if one planet is being joined to another, if there were the quantity of one-half (or less) of the orb of each of them between them—that is, in front or behind—the signification of their conjunction with each other will manifest, [divided between them].[17] But if one of them were in the degrees of the strength of the other's orb, but the other were not commingled with the degrees of the orb of that planet which is conjoining to it, their signification will be weaker.

For example: if Saturn and the Moon were in one sign, and the longitude which was between them were less than 12° in front or behind, Saturn will be in the strength of the Moon's orb, but the Moon will not be in the strength of Saturn's orb until there are less than 9° between them (by a trifling amount).[18]

But if each of them were in the strength of its companion's orb, the signification of their conjunction will be strengthened. And if in addition it were in one bound, they will be stronger in signification.[19] And

---

[15] It is worth noting that the Arabic does not call these "orbs," but refers to the "body" or "mass" of a planet (*jirm*). Our own notion of a planetary "orb" for aspects may therefore conceal the rationale for these values.

[16] I.e., in a paragraph matching the one in *Abbr.* immediately above (*Gr. Intr.* VII.3.333-39).

[17] Translation somewhat uncertain.

[18] Saturn's orb will not begin to touch the Moon until she is 9° away from him.

[19] This seems to reflect a version of Hellenistic "neighboring" (Gr. *homoroēsis*) according to Rhetorius; Antiochus and Porphyry want this only to apply to planets aspecting each other by sign while they happen to be in bounds ruled by the same planet. See Schmidt 2009, pp. 187-91.

by how much more one of them approached the other, the signification of those things which they signified will be increased by that much
more. And if they met by their own bodies, they will be effected to the
limit of their signification over good and evil. And when one of them is
separated from the other, their signification is weakened. And by how
much more they were elongated, they will be weakened that much
more in signification, up to where one of them goes out from the sign
in which the other was. If however there were the quantity of half the
orb of each of them between them, and one was going toward the
other, their signification will be stronger than if that same quantity of
degrees were between them while one of them is being separated from
the other.

And if the planets were each in two different signs, and one of them
were in the strength of the other's orb by the number of aforesaid degrees, they are not said to be "conjoined,"[20] on account of the
difference of their signs—but each of them is said to be in the strength
of the other's orb, and the commingling of their orbs will have signification over some small matter [compared with] what they signify when
they are conjoined.[21]

♄	9°
♃	9°
♂	8°
☉	15°
♀	7°
☿	7°
☽	12°

Figure 40: Size of planetary bodies/orbs, in front and behind

---

[20] That is, "assembled" in the same sign. See III.5.
[21] See also III.5 on assembly in one sign, III.6 on aspects from different signs, and III.7
on connections by degree.

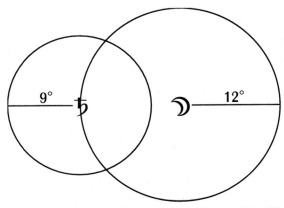

Figure 41: Saturn in the body/orb of the Moon: Abū Ma'shar

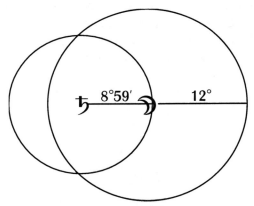

Figure 42: The Moon in the body/orb of Saturn: Abū Ma'shar

§II.7: Relations to the Sun

[*Abbr.* II.13] It must also be stated what properties they receive from the Sun; however, in the *Greater Introduction* [this was treated] more expansively, but here however [we will state only] what is necessary.

[al-Qabīsī III.4] But concerning their condition with respect to each other, let us deal with what happens to the five planets in relation to the luminaries.

§II.8: Right and left of the Sun

[*Abbr.* II.14] Therefore, each of the superior planets (Saturn, I say, or Jupiter, or even Mars), if they departed from a meeting [with the Sun], it will be called "right" with respect to [the Sun] until the Sun reaches the opposite degree. But if the Sun crossed the opposite [degree], the planet will be called "left" of him.

[*Gr. Intr.* VII.2.143-46] And so Saturn and Jupiter and Mars, from the time at which they have departed from the Sun up to where they are opposed to him to the minute, are "right" of him. And from the time of their opposition up to where they are joined to him, they are "left" of him.

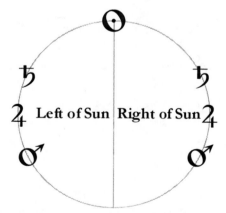

Figure 43: Right and left of Sun (superiors): Abū Ma'shar

[*Abbr.* II.15] However, Venus and Mercury, departing from the Sun toward the east, until they return to him, are said to be "right." But retreating from him until when they return to the aforesaid first place, they are called "left."[22]

[*Gr. Intr.* VII.2.146-51] However, Venus and Mercury, from the time at which they are departed from the Sun and they were retrograde on the eastern side, until they go direct and hasten and are attached to the Sun and are joined to him, they are "right" of him. And from where they are departed and were direct towards the west until they stand still in the west so that they go retrograde and the Sun touches them and they are joined to him, they are "left" of him.

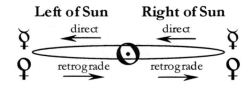

Figure 44: Right and left of Sun (inferiors), Abū Ma'shar

[*Abbr.* II.16] Also the Moon, departing[23] until she comes to the opposite, will be called "left." But if she crossed the opposite, "right."

[*Gr. Intr.* VII.2.151-54] On the other hand, the Moon, from where she is departed from the Sun until she is opposed to him, is "left" of him. And when she crosses his opposition until she is conjoined to him again, she is "right" of him.

---

[22] Reading "right" and "left" with the Ar., as the Latin had it backwards.
[23] That is, increasing in light in her first two phases.

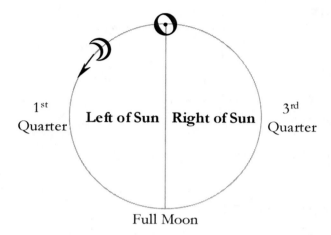

Figure 45: Right and left of Sun (Moon), Abū Ma'shar

§II.9: The rays and combustion—al-Qabīsī

[al-Qabīsī III.7] And every planet, from where it is covered by the rays of the Sun until it appears from under the rays, is called "burned up." And while it is beginning to enter the rays, it is said to have "undertaken to be burned." And while it is being concealed under the rays and it were within them, it is called "oppressed." And if it were with the Sun in one degree, and there were 16' or less between them, and likewise its latitude 16', it is called "united."[24] And when it has crossed that same union, seeking an exit, until it appears, it is called "escaped."

[al-Qabīsī III.10b] And when a planet has gone out from under the rays, and it was connected to no planet, it is said that it is in "its own light."

[*Judgments* 29 (second part)] Because if a planet were under the rays, combust, or in the opposition of the Sun, it will be weak, since in this place there is no usefulness nor anything of the good for benefic planets, nor anything of evil for the malefic ones: because the benefics signify a modicum of the good if they were under the rays, and likewise if the malefics were under the rays their impediment will be less.

---

[24] Or, "in the heart" (Ar.): see below.

[*Judgments* 39] If planets were under the rays, they will be weak in all matters: that is, if there were less than 12° between them and the Sun (unless a planet is in the degree of the Sun, because then it will be strong).

[*BW* VIII.89] But one under the rays of the Sun is just like one being in prison.[25]

[*BW* VIII.90] Burned up: like one condemned to death.

[*BW* VIII.98] A planet in the heart of the Sun: like one sitting with the king in the same seat.

[*BOA* III.2.7] And a planet is said to have "escaped" by similarity with a sick person whom fever has let go, nor however has he yet gotten better so that he could be said to be freed; nor is he fully freed. However, he is out of danger while he gets better, after which he is said to be freed. And so it is with a planet when it enters combustion: it is like one who begins to grow ill…And [after it is separated from the Sun by a few degrees]…until it goes out from under the rays, it is like a sick person whose sickness ceases and is visibly diminishing; and [when] it is wholly freed from combustion, [it is] like a sick person completely freed from sickness, but [who] has not yet resumed his previous powers, however is safe from the illness.

---

25 *Existens in loco carcerum.*

§II.10: Synodic cycle, easternness and westernness

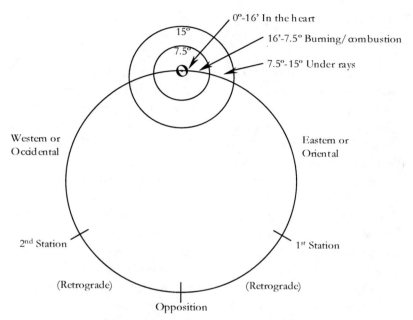

Figure 46: Generic synodic cycle with Sun (superiors)

§II.10.1: The superior planets

[*Abbr.* II.17-21] Moreover, Saturn and Jupiter and the Mars take up eight properties from the Sun. The first, when they meet the Sun in the same place, [within 16' before or after him].[26] The second, when the Sun recedes from Saturn by 15°, from Jupiter by the same amount, from Mars by 18°. The third, when there are 90° between the Sun and any of those three.[27] The fourth, when, appearing in the first station, [any of them] begins to go retro-

---

[26] Adding with the Ar.: that is, in the "heart," *kaṣmīmī* or *ṣamīm*, often spelled "cazimi." This also applies to the inferior planets, Mercury and Venus and the Moon.

[27] If we compare Abū Ma'shar with al-Qabīsī, we see that Abū Ma'shar wants easternness to end at 90°: this is because—on average—that is approximately where the Midheaven would be if the Sun were on the horizon: thus the planet would be both eastern relative to the Sun himself, and in the eastern quadrant of the heavens relative to us. Abū Ma'shar might also be picking up on statements by Ptolemy in *Tet.* IV.5, where Ptolemy defines easternness in terms of quarters measured from the Sun (for purposes of spousal age or when the native marries).

grade. The fifth, if the Sun were in its opposite. The sixth, if they were beginning to move forward at the second station. The seventh, if they were
distant from the Sun by 90°. The eighth, if they were removed from the Sun
by 15° or fewer, and they are already being hidden by him.

[al-Qabīsī III.8a] And from where the higher [planets] appear from
under the rays and they begin to arise in the morning before the Sun
(that is, when they are closer to the circle of the eastern horizon), until
they go to the opposition, are called "eastern" and "right." And from
where they cross the opposition until they are again conjoined to the
Sun, they are called "western," "left."

[al-Qabīsī III.9] But the three higher ones, from where they go out
from under the rays of the Sun, they are called "eastern," and they are
said to be "increased in strength" up to 30° from the Sun. And after
this up to 30° more, they are called "eastern, strong." And when they
transit the Sun by 60°, the planets are called "eastern, going toward
weakness" until they go to retrogradation: then they are called "eastern,
retrograde" until they are in opposition [to the Sun]. After this, they
will be "western, retrograde," namely when they transit the opposition,
until they reach direct motion. Then, from direct motion up to 60° after direct motion, until their distance from the Sun is 30°, they are said
to be "western, strong." Then, from a distance of 60° after direct motion they are called "western, going toward weakness."[28] Then they
become "western, weak," until they enter under the rays of the Sun.

---

[28] In the figure below, I have represented the planets' second station as though it occurs
120° from the Sun, so that this period of strength ends at 60° from the Sun.

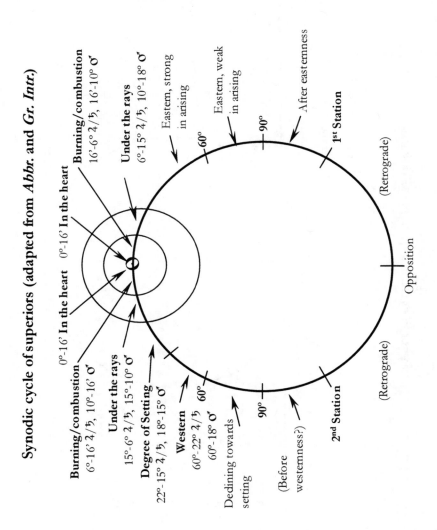

Figure 47: Synodic cycle of superiors: Abū Ma'shar

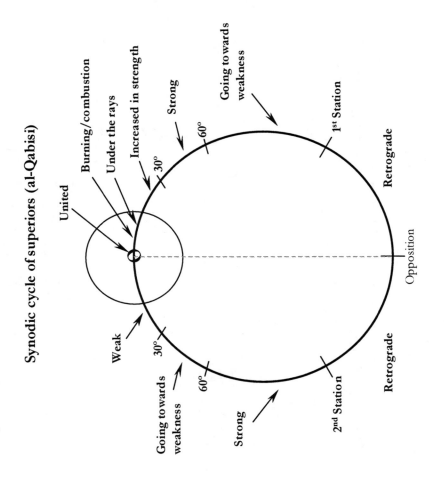

Figure 48: Synodic cycle of superiors: al-Qabīsī

§II.10.2: *The inferior planets*

[*Abbr.* II.22-26] However, Venus and Mercury have eight properties from the Sun, and the first is when they meet the Sun. The second, if they receded from the Sun toward arising [while retrograde], by 7°. The third, if in the first station they are already [stationary and beginning to go direct.][29] The fourth, when—in 7° from the Sun—they approach him from the opposite direction.[30] The fifth, when they meet the Sun again. The sixth, when they were likewise distant from[31] the Sun by 7°, and then they appear at the first [part] of the night. The seventh, when they make a retrograde[32] course in the first[33] station. The eighth, if when approaching [by retrogradation] they were removed from the Sun by 7°.

[al-Qabīsī III.8b] But Venus and Mercury, from where one of them is separated from the degree of the Sun in the middle of its retrogradation, and it appears, until it is being burned up by the Sun in its direct motion, are called "eastern." And from where they are separated in their direct motion from the degree of the Sun, until they are burned up again, they are called "western." And if they were in their arising,[34] they are called "right" and are said to be masculine; and in their setting,[35] they are called "left" and are said to be feminine.

[al-Qabīsī III.10a] Also, from where the inferiors are separated from the Sun and are retrograde, they are called "eastern, weak," and they do not stop being thus until they come to their direct motion. Then they become "eastern, strong" until their distance from the Sun is just like the distance of the Sun from them at the hour of retrogradation. Then, they become "eastern, weak" until they are put under the rays, and then they are "united." Then, they become "burned up, going out toward appearance," up to where they are seen. And from where they are separated from the Sun in direct motion up to the hour of their retrogradation, until they are retrograde with the Sun, they will be "weak."

---

[29] Reading with the Ar., the Latin has this condition backwards.
[30] I.e., now in direct motion, and opposite where they were in their epicycle earlier.
[31] Omitting "the opposite of."
[32] Reading for "direct."
[33] Reading for "second."
[34] Or, "easternness" (Ar.).
[35] Or, "westernness" (Ar.).

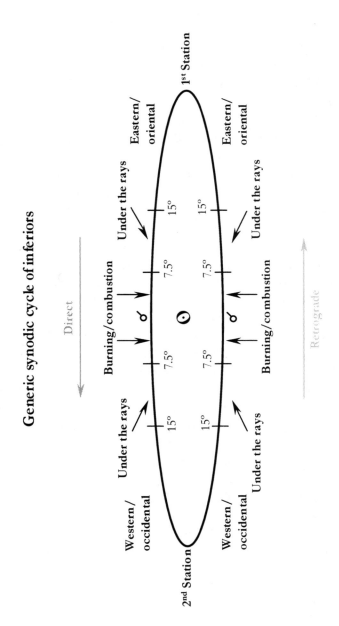

Figure 49: Generic synodic cycle of inferiors

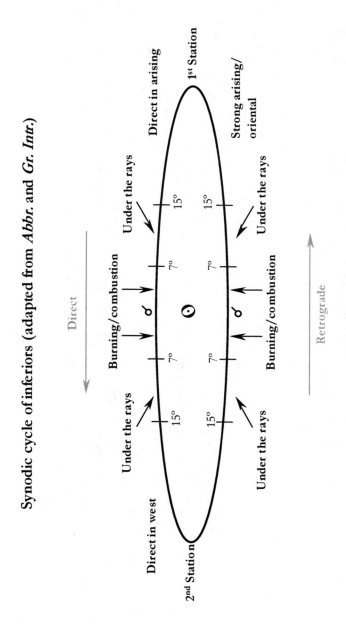

Figure 50: Synodic cycle of inferiors (Abū Ma'shar)

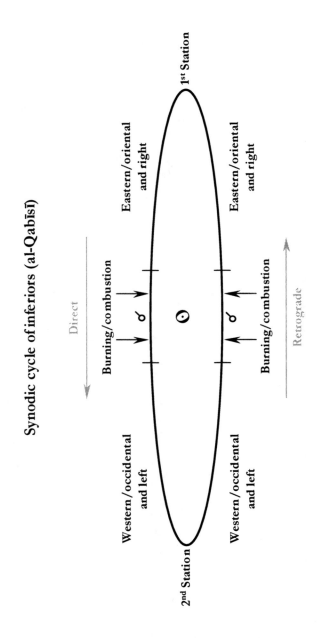

Figure 51: Synodic cycle of inferiors (al-Qabīsī)

§II.10.3: Analogies of easternness and westernness

[*BW* VIII.96] Eastern: like one fulfilling his desire.

[*BOA* V.54] [When a planet is coming out of the rays and is direct,][36] it is said to be stronger than it could be in every matter, like someone is who has left a battle, all of his enemies having been completely overcome, and he is resting, and rejoices in his victory; nor does he fear anyone else who will rise up against him, or who will resist him in anything; for he is then cheerful, of good spirit, of a good disposition, blessed in every way.

[*BOA* V.56] [When a planet has arisen out of the rays, and is direct,][37] it will be strong and well-fitted to perfect what it indicates, just like a man who was sick, and now is wholly freed, and has resumed all his powers; and just like a building which had already fallen, and now is restored, and newly raised, and improved in all of its parts; thus it is with all of the aforesaid planets so disposed.

[*BOA* III.2.5] [When superiors come out from under the rays, eastern up to 30°, they are like] a sick man who, after a crisis, is increased in his strength and full health, until he resumes his former vigor, and returns to the state in which he had been before he began to fall ill, and stays more carefree.

[*BOA* III.2.5] [When superiors come out from under the rays, eastern from 30° to 60°, they are like one] "who has escaped an illness does not fear it, and has already resumed all his powers, or rather after the complete freeing and resumption of his powers he is sometimes made more fleshy and stronger than usual, if however his complexion is well disposed to be able to take them on."

[*BW* VIII.97] Western: like a lazy man.

---

[36] I.e., an eastern superior or western inferior.
[37] I.e., an eastern superior or western inferior.

[BOA V.56] [When a planet is direct and moving toward the rays, it][38] is like an impediment by which a man is impeded who is already beginning to get sick, so that the illness has already prevailed so much that the sick person is thought to have fallen: he practically cannot help himself without the aid of another; and like a building which has already started to go to ruin, nor is there anyone who would protect it so it does not fall down. And by how much more the planet is far from the Sun, it impedes by that much less.

[BOA III.2.8] And it is a certain impediment for [western superior planets approaching the rays], not a middling one, because they begin to fear coming again to combustion: just like a man who, when someone is following him, begins to get tired in his flight, and sees the one who is following him catching up to him, and sees that he is faster than himself, and is approaching him: for he fears that he cannot escape his grasp.

---

[38] I.e., an eastern inferior or western superior.

§II.10.4: Analogies of stations and retrogradation

[*Judgments* 48] If a planet were to stand toward retrogradation (that is, if it were in its first station), it signifies the dissolution of a purpose, and disobedience; and if it were to stand toward direction (that is, if it were in its second station), it signifies forward direction after the slowness or duress of the matter. And every planet which is a significator and wished to go direct (that is, if it were in its second station) signifies the renewal of the actions of matters, and their action and strength or forward movement. And if it were in the first station, wishing to go retrograde, it signifies their destruction and slowness and dissolution.

[*BW* VIII.33] A planet in the first station [about to go retrograde] is like a man ignorant of what he should do, whose bad end is [already] present. And if it were in the second station [about to go direct], it is like one hoping for some matter, nor will his hope be disappointed.

[*BW* VIII.91] Standing toward retrogradation is like a nervous person on account of fearing bad things in the future.

[*Judgments* 10] A retrograde planet signifies disobedience, and contradiction, and turning back and taking back, and diversity or discord.

[*BW* VIII.32] A retrograde planet signifies antagonism[39] and the dissipation of everything considered.

[*BW* VIII.92] Retrograde: like one returning, and pulling back.[40]

[*BW* VIII.93] Stationary in the second station: like one hoping for good.

---

[39] Reading with Epstein for *revelationem*.
[40] Epstein's reads: "rebellious and defiant."

§II.10.5: *The Moon*

[*Abbr.* II.27-31] The Moon also [has] eight properties from the Sun: the first, when she is conjoined to him. The second, if she receded from him by 12°. The third, if she were distant from him by 90°, and appears [in her] half-[phase]. The fourth, if she would be distant from the opposite of the Sun by 12°. The fifth, when she would be opposed to him. The sixth, if she would add 12° on top of the opposite. The seventh, whenever she pursues him [while] removed by 90°, and she appears [in her] half-[phase]. The eighth, if moreover she would be distant from the Sun by 12°.[41]

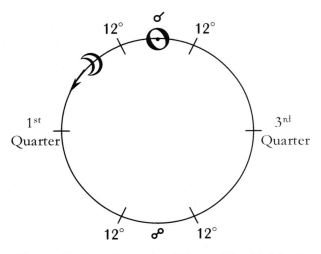

Figure 52: Synodic cycle of Moon (Abū Ma'shar)

---

[41] The Moon is corrupted or experiences misfortune in several of these places: see IV.5 below.

§II.11: Facing: al-Qabīsī

[al-Qabīsī III.5] And from this, let us state what Ptolemy said about "facing":[42] this is if there were, between a planet and the Sun, when the planet was western (that is, when it is following the Sun),[43] exactly as much as there is between the domicile of that planet and the domicile of the Sun, in terms of signs—or, if there were between the planet and the Moon (when it is eastern of the Moon),[44] exactly as much as there is between the domicile of the planet and the domicile of the Moon in terms of signs. Because a planet, when it follows up upon the Sun, and it was namely Saturn in the sixth sign from the Sun, and Jupiter in the fifth, Mars in the fourth, Venus in the third, Mercury in the second—then it is said to be in the "facing" of the Sun. Likewise, if this number of signs were counted for any planet, between any planet and the Moon [when she is] following up upon [that planet], it is said to be in the "facing" of the Moon.

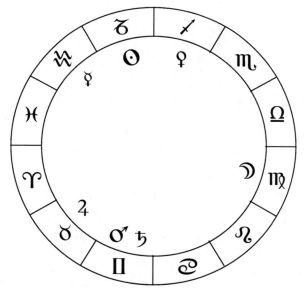

**Figure 53: Mercury, Jupiter, Saturn in facing of Sun;
Mars in facing of Moon**

---

[42] *Tet.* I.23.
[43] In primary motion, i.e., rising after the Sun, up to 180°.
[44] That is, rising before the Moon by primary motion, up to 180°.

§II.12: Solar phases and elemental qualities: al-Qabīsī

[al-Qabīsī II.41a] And certain people said that the Moon, from the conjunction to the first half of her light, will have moisture as her nature; and from the middle of her light up to fullness her nature will be heat; and from the fullness up to the second half of her light her nature will be dryness; and from the second half of her light up to the conjunction, her nature will be coldness.

[al-Qabīsī II.42] But the rest of the planets,[45] from their arising[46] up to their first station, will be in the nature of moisture;[47] and from their first station up to the opposition of the Sun their nature will be heat;[48] and from this place up to their second station their nature will be dryness;[49] and from their second station up to their first hiddenness their nature is cold.[50]

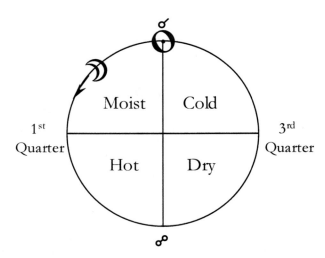

Figure 54: Lunar phases and elemental qualities: al-Qabīsī

---

[45] This probably applies only to the superiors.
[46] Or, "easternness" (Ar.).
[47] John adds: "and they signify childhood."
[48] John adds: "and they signify youth."
[49] John adds: "and they signify completed age."
[50] John adds: "in senility."

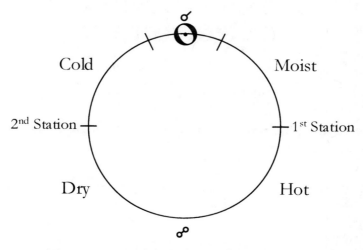

Figure 55: (Superior) planets' cycles and elemental qualities: al-Qabīsī

[al-Qabīsī III.10c] This is the condition of the planets with the luminaries.

BOOK III: PLANETARY CONFIGURATIONS

§III.1: List of configurations

[*Abbr.* III.1-2] But next we must speak about the bearings[1] of the planets. There are however twenty-five, the names of which are these:

- domain,
- advancement,
- retreat,
- assembly,
- regard,
- connection,
- disregard,
- emptiness,
- wildness,
- transfer,
- collection,
- reflection,
- barring,
- pushing nature,
- pushing power,
- pushing two natures,
- pushing management,
- returning,
- revoking,
- obstruction,
- escape,
- cutting of light,
- largesse,
- recompense,
- reception.[2]

---

[1] *Habitudinibus*, in the sense of how one carries oneself or behaves.
[2] This list omits generosity and benefits (III.26), friendship and enmity (III.27), and body-guarding (III.28), the last two of which are from al-Qabīsī. In terms of the list of twenty-

§III.2: Domain

Arabic: Domain (*ḥayyiz*)
Hermann: Alternation (*vicissitudo*)
Adelard: Suitability (*competentia*)
Cf. Greek "sect" (*hairesis*)

[*Abbr.* III.3] "Suitability" is if a masculine[3] planet were above the earth by day (but below the earth by night) and in a masculine sign, but a feminine planet below the earth by day ([but] above the earth by night)—with Mars alone being excepted, [since] he, though he is male, is still [nocturnal].[4]

[*Gr. Intr.* VII.1.133-38] For if a planet were according to this condition, it will be in its "domain," and it will have a strong nature, signifying temperance[5] and fitness.[6] Which if it took certain things away from these which we have said, it will be taken away from the nature of the tempering. And if it were different from all of this, it will be in the contrariety of its domain, and this will signify corruption[7] and the contrariety of the tempering.[8]

[al-Qabīsī I.78] Also, of the accidental powers of the planets is the *ḥalb*:[9] this is if a diurnal planet were above the earth in the day, and below the earth in the night; and a nocturnal planet above the earth in the night and below the earth in the day. And if in addition a masculine planet were in a masculine sign and a feminine planet in a feminine

---

five, I myself would group largesse and recompense together, and make generosity and benefits the twenty-fifth, even though *Gr. Intr.* treats the latter as offshoots of reception.

[3] As with many medieval astrologers on this topic, Abū Ma'shar has conflated being masculine with being diurnal. See comment below, and source texts in *Anth.* III.5 and Paul Ch. 6.

[4] Reading for the Latin "womanly."

[5] *Temperamentum.* This word indicates restraint, balance, and a good mixture of qualities.

[6] *Aptationem.* Note the overlap in meaning with Adelard's "suitability."

[7] Or, "detriment" (Lat. *detrimentum*). This suggests that the planet's activities will involve imbalance and excess, so that what it produces is unstable and lacks unity.

[8] See also V.11 below.

[9] Currently I do not know the source or meaning of this word.

sign, it is said to be in its "domain." And its strength will be like a man in a place of his success, acquisition, and fortune.[10]

[*BW* VIII.75] The testimony of a significator from the category of domain denotes every good thing prepared for is [going to be] there.

[*BW* VIII.84] In [its] domain, [it is like someone doing something] proportionate to himself.

[*BW* VIII.85] A planet in the opposite of domain is just like one who is [involved in something] inappropriate to himself.

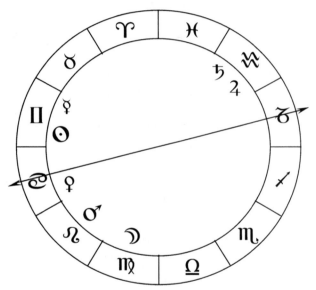

Figure 56: Planets in their domains in a diurnal chart

---

[10] Neither *Gr. Intr.* nor al-Qabīsī include this item in the list of planetary configurations, but rather with the varied accidental powers of the planets. To me this indicates that Abū Ma'shar re-thought his organization for *Abbr.*

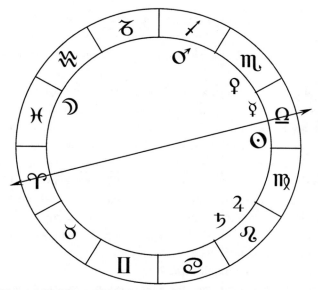

Figure 57: Planets in their domains in a nocturnal chart

Comment by Dykes. Domain is an intensification of another sect-related condition in which planets are said to "rejoice":[11] *ḥalb*, which al-Qabīsī describes as being like domain except that the planets do not need to be in signs of the same gender as themselves. In the diurnal figure above, all planets are in their domains: the diurnal planets are above the horizon with the Sun, and the nocturnal planets are below the horizon (*ḥalb*); furthermore, each planet is in a sign of its own gender (*ḥayyiz*). Likewise in the nocturnal figure, the nocturnal planets are above the horizon away from the Sun, while the diurnal ones are below it with him (*ḥalb*); furthermore, each planet is in a sign of its own gender (*ḥayyiz*).

The Arabic *ḥayyiz* is a translation of the Greek *hairesis*,[12] which is now often translated simply as "sect," but the Arabic and Greek share other, important core meanings. *Hairesis* suggests the taking or seizing of something, as well as *taking/choosing sides* (it is the root of our English "heretic"). Likewise, *ḥayyiz* has as its verb root *ḥāza*, which means both to gain possession of something, to take sides, be inclined toward one thing over another, and to favor one side over another. But *ḥāza* also has a sense of competition, namely *victory* in achieving this, and keeping others away from something

---

[11] Schmidt 2009, p. 88.
[12] See Schmidt 2009, p. 88.

over which one has gained control. All of these ideas help us understand the traditional notion of sect,[13] in which planets are first of all divided into different sects or domains, and take turns having a kind of dominance over a chart.

The Arabic not only suggests that the planets take sides generally speaking, but that in a chart of a given sect, they have inclinations to occupy the side of the horizon which bears an analogy to their own quality: diurnal planets want to be on the same side of the chart as the Sun, while the nocturnal planets want to be on the opposite side, each planet also wanting to be in a sign whose gender is conformable with it. *Gr. Intr.* captures this well by speaking of the planets being well-tempered and fit when they are in such a condition. In fact, Ptolemy's rationale for the sects of the planets is based precisely upon the idea that each planet belongs to the sect that reinforces moderate qualities and tempers extreme qualities.[14]

The Latin translators amplify these ideas in different ways.[15] Hermann's "alternation" (*vicissitudo*) captures the alternation between night and day, emphasizing that the planets *take turns* fulfilling a *role* (Lat. *vicis*) in the governance of the chart. However, alternation focuses on who has control, not *what* is being controlled or what control *means* to the one who has it.

I find Adelard's "suitability" (*competentia*) more intriguing, and it certainly reflects the Latin *BW* excerpts. First of all, it does suggest correspondence and proportion, which might simply indicate an appropriate match between a planet of a given sect and the place it is in. But secondly, it also connotes being *competent*, in the sense that one's task is proportionate to one's ability. In other words, Adelard captures the Arabic's notion of intentionality and purpose: that the planets are trying to achieve or do something. Third, the Latin connotes belonging and "falling to" someone, as though a task belongs to one and has fallen to one.

Finally, I note that when Hugo of Santalla translated Māshā'allāh's *BA*, he regularly translated these sect notions with Latin words which mean "at rest" and "restless" or "worried,"[16] and related Arabic words suggest that a helpful sect placement brings happiness and luck.

---

[13] See V.11 below.

[14] *Tet.* I.7.

[15] John of Spain tends simply to use the transliteration *haiz*, and so does not contribute to the discussion.

[16] See my Introduction to *BA*, pp. *xxv-xxix*.

From these texts and considerations we can conclude that domain involves the following two principal concepts: (1) balance in a planet's activities, and (2) fitness and proportionality to the task, both in terms of a planet's fitness to the chart and its role in it, and in terms of its being in places fitting or proportionate to *itself*. To these we can add more descriptive terms of a planet's operation: Adelard's competence and Hugo's "at rest" (and their opposites: incompetence, disproportionality, restlessness and nervousness, possibly being erratic or hasty). These terms can help us understand how to interpret planets signifying events and people in charts.

So, in general I suggest that:

- The sect of the chart shows *to whom* responsibility for the chart primarily falls, by sect status.
- Planets in their domain—particularly those of the sect of the chart—possess the *competence* to act, and in a more calm, reasonable, balanced, and confident manner.
- Planets not in their domain will connote unease and disquiet, less competence or fitness to act constructively.

It is as though the planet's relationship to domain identifies the right planet for the job of managing the chart: some default choices are naturally suited to step in to take charge, or rather it is their natural "place" to do so (sect), but not all are *well* suited or competent (domain), and even then not all will be very *inclined* to take chart, or have the lasting power to do so (advancing and retreating, see III.3-4).

§III.3: Advancement

Arabic: Advancement (*'iqbāl*)
John: "Advancement, profit" (*profectus*)
Adelard: "Approach" (*accessus*)
Cf. Greek "pivots" (*kentra*)
Cf. Greek "succeedents" (*epanaphora*)
Cf. Greek "busy, advantageous" (*chrēmatistikos*)

[*Abbr.* III.4] Advancement is if a planet were in a firm sign[17] (which is the first [sign] of a quarter), or in that which is the second from it.[18]

[al-Qabīsī I.56e] If therefore a planet were in an angle or in its succeedent, it is said to be advancing...[19]

[*BW* VIII.63] If the testimony of a significator were from the category of uprightness [or what follows it], it signifies a good end in all matters.
[*BW* VIII.101] A planet in an angle is like a man in his [own] place.
[*BW* VIII.102] In a succeedent, like one hoping.

§III.4: Retreat

Arabic: Retreat, flight (*'idbār*)
John: Making worse (*deterioratio*)
Adelard: Withdrawal, retreat (*recessus*)
Cf. Greek "decline, cadent" (*apoklima*)
Cf. Greek "unadvantageous" (*achrēmatistikos*)

[*Abbr.* III.5] Retreat is if a planet were in the third domicile,[20] which is called "remote."[21]

---

[17] That is, an angular sign.
[18] That is, a succeedent. The Ar. does not specify these as signs, but simply as the "stakes" and "what comes after them."
[19] I have repeated this passage from I.12 above. The Latin reads "successful" or "advancing" (*proficere*).

[al-Qabīsī I.56f] ...and if it were in the cadents from the angles, it is said to retreat.[22]

[*BW* VIII.64] If the testimony of a significator were from the category of being slantwise, it signifies the matter will be abandoned.

[*BW* VIII.103] In a cadent, like one changing over, [away] from his place.

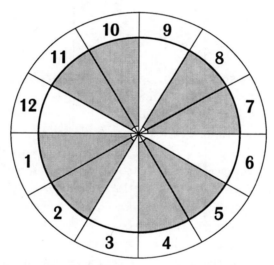

**Figure 58: Eight advantageous places: Nechepso,
Abū Ma'shar, al-Qabīsī**

---

[20] That is, the third house counted from an angle. The Ar. says "houses," which ambiguates between whole signs and quadrant houses.

[21] That is, "cadent."

[22] I have repeated this passage from I.12 above. The Latin reads, "fail" (*deficere*).

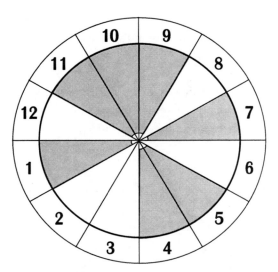

Figure 59: Seven advantageous places (gray):
Timaeus, Dorotheus, Sahl

Comment by Dykes. Advancement and retreat are meant to be understood together, and they derive from Hellenistic astrological concepts of being busy or advantageous (advancement), and unbusy or unadvantageous (retreat). The eight-place scheme of Abū Ma'shar and al-Qabīsī goes back to Nechepso, one of the two earliest and legendary elaborators of Hellenistic astrology.[23] In fact there was another version of the Hellenistic "busy" or "advantageous" places, a seven-place arrangement according to Timaeus and possibly Hermes.[24] But let us first look at the Arabic and Latin.

On its face, the Arabic word for advancement means approaching something, drawing near something, but also to *show concern or interest* in something, with the notion of good fortune and *prosperity* accompanying this interest; its verb root *qabila* not only means to confront, but to *assent to* something and be *willingly occupied* with it. John's *profectus* does indeed suggest profit and motion toward something, but Adelard seems to capture the Arabic better: *accessus* does mean approaching and drawing near, but also to occupy oneself

---

[23] Firmicus Maternus reports (III.1.1, e.g.) that a semi-legendary pharaoh (Nechepso) and priest (Petosiris) elaborated and preserved astrological doctrines originated by figures such as Asclepius, Hermes, and Hanubio. A textbook attributed to the latter survived for many centuries, with excerpts found in authors as late as Hephaistio of Thebes (c. 415 AD).
[24] See Schmidt 2009, pp. 279.

with something and to assent to it. What this suggests is that advancing planets will show *active assent, engagement,* and *success* in whatever they signify—
whether that is helpful or harmful.

On the other hand, the Arabic "retreat" and its verb root *dabara* mean to
turn one's back, to dodge or escape, to face the other way, and for time or an
opportunity to elapse or pass by. It also can mean to trail behind someone.
Adelard's *recessus* captures these notions well but does not have quite the
richness of the Arabic. Taken with advancement, retreat suggests that such
planets are more likely to show opportunities missed, ignored, or responsibilities dropped.

Now, this eight-place version of advancement (with four retreating places)
is identical to that attributed to Nechepso and endorsed by Serapio,[25] and
both Abū Ma'shar and al-Qabīsī also reference it in I.12 above. But it seems
not to have been the most widespread prior to the 9th Century, because there
is another, seven-place version attributed to Timaeus[26] and possibly Hermes,
which was also reported in the influential works of Antiochus, Porphyry,
Rhetorius,[27] Dorotheus,[28] and later Sahl: the seven busy or advantageous
places are the four pivotal or angular places (Ascendant, tenth, seventh,
fourth), the fifth and eleventh, and the ninth. The remaining places are not
busy, or unadvantageous. This was the version which Sahl and Māshā'allāh
would have gotten from Dorotheus, especially since they clearly rely on the
related "15° rules" in *Carmen*—which helped inspire the use of quadrant-
based house systems.[29] Sahl explicitly uses the seven-place arrangement of
Timaeus and Dorotheus in his *Introduct.* §4,[30] where he says that these seven
places are more "praiseworthy" and "stronger" and have more "profit" than
the rest.

The diagrams above illustrate both the Nechepso and Timaeus versions.
Both agree on the angular signs and the eleventh and fifth as being busy or

---

[25] Schmidt, *ibid.*

[26] Timaeus was an early astrologer of the Hellenistic period, with natal material on parents
preserved by Valens (*Anth.* II.32; cf. *BA* III.4.1), and other material on fugitives and
thefts. I will have more to say about the latter in my forthcoming translation of *The Book of
the Nine Judges*.

[27] Rhetorius Chs. 27-28.

[28] *Carmen* I.5 and I.7.3-9.

[29] See §4 of my Introduction above, and the related discussion in my Introduction to
WSM.

[30] I do not currently have the Arabic of Sahl's text, but I have no doubt it uses the words
for advancement and retreat.

advantageous; they also agree that the third, sixth, and twelfth places or signs are unbusy or unadvantageous. But they disagree on the ninth, eighth, and second. What accounts for the differences? The technical difference is that Nechepso's places are strictly related to the angles, and from this it is obvious why Abū Ma'shar and al-Qabīsī (or their Arabic sources) used "advancement" for these places: the angular or pivotal places are considered the most powerful, and the succeedent places advance toward them by primary motion. By such a criterion, the eighth and second places must be considered advancing (or advantageous), but not the ninth. On the other hand, Timaeus makes all of his advantageous places either be the ascending sign itself, or signs aspecting it: by that criterion, the eighth and second cannot be advantageous, but the ninth can be. (No one seems to want to make the third place busy or advantageous.)

Schmidt suggests an interpretive difference which seems promising:[31] (1) by being related to the angles alone, the Nechepso version adopted by Abū Ma'shar and al-Qabīsī identifies planets busy or advantageous or advancing *in the life as a whole*, regardless of the specific relation they have toward the native as an individual. This is consistent with the pairing of advancement and retreat with domain (see below), because domain describes a planet's role in the chart as a whole. But (2) by being configured to the ascending sign, the Timaeus-Dorotheus version adopted by Sahl identifies planets which are more directly busy and advancing relative to the native and his *interests as an individual*.

From all of these considerations, we can conclude that the type of advancement and retreat used by Abū Ma'shar and al-Qabīsī is based on the following three notions: (1) a planet's interest, engagement, and active *assent* in its activity, (2) its overall staying power in life (in that angular places especially are "pivotal" and "firm"), and (3) its overall usefulness and advantage primarily in performing its own activities and according to its own place and rulerships—though not necessarily for its conventional advantage to the native, since sect conditions like domain may make it less fit or balanced. The planet is engaged and committed (advancing) or less reliable and present (retreating), apart from it being a good fit or being balanced in its responsibilities (domain).[32]

---

[31] *Ibid.*, p. 289.
[32] The texts here are ambiguous as to whether angles by whole sign or quadrant-based divisions are meant. See §4 of my Introduction above.

I would also point out that these first three terms (domain, advance, retreat) are all conditions based on primary motion: as in a sports match when opposing teams take turns with the ball, planets take turns with their responsibilities and who has control of the play in accordance as the heavens turn: they advance and retreat, gain and lose ground and control, are more aggressive and engaged or distracted, retiring, and not obviously involved.[33] After this, the rest of our concepts will mainly concern secondary motion or motion through the zodiac, and what the planets actually do with and to each other.

In conclusion, I argue that these first three configurations form a group indicating the level of opportunity, responsibility, competence, and willingness on the part of the planets (or the people they represent) to act. Just as people may be given responsibility for something (sect), this may not mean they are fully competent (domain); nor does it indicate whether or not they actively and obviously assent to or get involved in the matters they signify (advancement, retreat). I suggest that a planet belonging to the sect of the chart has been given responsibility for promoting the native's life; being in its domain (or not) will show the extent to which it is balanced and competent; its condition of advancement or retreat will show how directly and completely and willingly it is involved in producing matters.

---

[33] It is important to remember that one difference between angular (or pivotal) and cadent places is their public nature (see *PN3* II.9). Angular and succeedent places are more public and show more obvious influences and involvement; cadent places are less public and show things which are more behind the scenes. Thus, while the twelfth is cadent or retreating, it does not mean that the native will not have active enemies at all because of the weakness of the place: it means rather that they will be not as well noticed, working behind the scenes, and so on. Remember that the twelfth is in aversion to the Ascendant, and so signifies things that are more private or go unnoticed.

§III.5: Assembly

Arabic: Association, comparison (*muqārana*)
John, Hermann: Conjunction, uniting (*coniunctio*)
Adelard: Assembly (*concilium*)
Cf. Greek: Assembly (*sunodos*)
Cf. Greek: Co-presence (*sumparousia*)

[*Abbr.* III.6-9] "Assembly" is if planets met in one sign, especially if there were less than 15° between them: by how much less, [it is] that much better. But whichever of them were stronger in that place,[34] its effect will be greater. Which if one or more of them occupied certain degrees of the other's power,[35] and they blended together, then they will be particularly effective in their effects. If however they were in different signs, [then] even if one is not very removed from the other, still they will not be said to be assembled.[36]

[*Gr. Intr.* VII.5.742-61] But the conjunction of the planets to each other is that a light one is joined to a slower one. And they come to be in eight ways: namely the conjunction which comes to be in one sign, and the seven conjunctions by aspect.

Therefore, the conjunction in one sign is that two planets would be going in direct motion in one sign, and the one of them lighter in course is in less degrees than the slower one. Then, so long as the one lighter in course remained less [in degrees] than the slow one, it will be going toward the conjunction of it, through the unity of the sign. And once it was with it in one degree and minute, it perfects its own conjunction with it.

And the beginning of the power of the conjunction in one sign[37] (and the complexion of the nature of the conjoined ones) is if there were 15° between them. And by how much more one of them drew near the other, the conjunction will be stronger by that much more until they are joined. This will be if they were in one sign.

---

[34] Ar.: "in itself."
[35] This refers to being in their orbs: see above, II.6.
[36] That would be a connecting aspect: see the next section. See also II.6 on out-of-sign orbs.
[37] In other words, assembly is already in effect if they are in the same sign; but it will not have the special power of mixing the planets until they are at least 15° away.

If however they were in different signs and there were few degrees between them, that conjunction is not noted as being the same as a conjunction which comes to be in one sign, but they will be com- plected through their nature by a weak complexion.[38]

And if one planet were conjoined to many planets by a number of different degrees, and it were lighter than them, it is joined first to the one closer to it.

[al-Qabīsī I.18b] And if two planets were in one sign, they are said to be "associated."

[BW VIII.104] United planets [are] like two people who are in a fel- lowship.

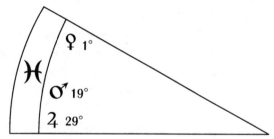

Figure 60: Planets assembled in same sign and within 15°

Comment by Dykes. This and the next few definitions form a very important second group in traditional astrology: the aspect and testimony group. Here we begin to see a very close association between the Hellenistic Greek and the Perso-Arabic concepts, which seems to weaken in later Latin and Renais- sance astrology. With "assembly," we begin to distinguish both same-sign versus different-sign relationships, and those *within* the same sign. In Helle- nistic texts, there are three ways for planets in the same sign to be associated: (1) simply by being in the same sign, (2) by being within 15° of each other, and (3) by being within 3° of each other. Early Arabic astrologers recognize all three ways,[39] even if they usually substitute orbs or being in the same bound for (3). But later Latin and Renaissance astrology tends not to consis-

---

[38] See a similar statement in II.6 above.
[39] Note that Māshā'allāh recognizes a 3° range in *BA* II.10.

tently distinguish or recognize (1) and (2), and definitely tends towards planetary orbs for (3). In the figure above, all three planets are assembled in the same sign, but only Mars and Jupiter are assembled within 15°.

The straightforward dictionary meaning of the Arabic *muqārana* is frankly rather odd on its own: what does it mean to say that two planets in the same sign have a "comparison"? The term only becomes clearer if we look at its verb root *qarana*, which not only means (1) to connect or unite, but (2) to associate and *draw a parallel* between two things, and also connotes (3) companionship and peer relations.

Likewise, although the Latin *coniunctio* does mean to connect or unite or conjoin, its verb root *coniungo* means to juxtapose two things or to use or perform two actions at the same time, and also connotes bonds of friendship and familiarity. It also carries the interesting meaning of establishing communication between people.

Adelard's *concilium* or "assembly" has the closest match to the Greek "assembly" (which also refers to fellow-travelers), and suggests a group of people working and deliberating together on a common project.

My own sense is that the best Latin words for capturing these ideas would have been *associatio* (association) or even *sodalitas* (companionship, fellowship). But what all of these words do capture is a sense of *joint action* or *similarity of purpose* between planets, but in a looser way than the close, 3° or orb-based range. And this is perhaps where the Arabic notion of "comparison" comes in, since comparison suggests the search for similarity between two apparently different things, on the basis of some third standard. In this case, the sign occupied by two (or more) planets acts as their common basis and means of comparison, and provides a context for loose joint action. One might imagine employees in the same company but who work in different departments: they do not have a close personal connection even though they agree in trying to promote the general agenda of the company as a whole. Just so, perhaps planets which are assembled each contribute jointly to what they signify by house, but without the kind of close and consistent partnership and directness (or perhaps even awareness) which one might expect from a close bodily conjunction.

§III.6: Aspect or regard

Arabic: Regard (*naẓar*)
John: Aspect (*aspectus*)
Hermann, Adelard: Regard (*respectus*)
Cf. Greek: Testimony, bearing witness (*marturia, epimartureō*)
Cf. Greek: Right, left (*dexios, euōnumos*)

§III.6.1: Aspects and right/left defined

[*Abbr.* III.10-12] But there are seven regards (and the eighth [is] when they meet in one [sign]): two hexagonal ones (one in front, the other behind), two trigonal ones (one in front, the other behind), two tetragonal ones (one in front, the other behind), finally [there is] one opposite. Therefore, the hexagonal regard generates half-friendship, the tetragonal one dislike, but the trigonal one the highest friendship, the opposite malevolence. But the third sign and the fourth and the fifth are regarded "on the left," but the ninth and tenth and eleventh "on the right."[40]

[*Gr. Intr.* VII.5.722-41] In fact the aspect of a planet comes to be to the noted signs which are seven signs: namely the third from it, the fourth, fifth, and seventh, the ninth and tenth and eleventh. And it looks at all of the degrees of the whole sign, and everything which is in them (of the planets and the Lots, and so on).

And its aspect to any degree of these signs will be stronger to the degree which was closer in affinity to the degree of its sign by number: like to 60 and 90 and 120 and 180 by equal degrees. But if it were farther from these degrees in the aspect, its aspect will be weaker. But its aspect to the eleventh sign and the third from it is the sextile aspect, and to the tenth and fourth from it is the square, and to the ninth and fifth sign from it is the trine. But to the seventh from it is the opposite.

---

[40] I have adjusted the Latin slightly to clarify the direction of aspects: if a planet were in Aries, then its left or sinister aspects would be cast to the third, fourth, and fifth signs (Gemini, Cancer, Leo); its right or sinister aspects would be cast to the eleventh, tenth, and ninth signs (Sagittarius, Capricorn, Aquarius). This paragraph not only defines dexter and sinister aspects, but underscores that out-of-sign aspects are not used.

However, it looks at the ninth and tenth and eleventh sign from the right;[41] but it looks at the third, fourth, and fifth from the left.[42] Therefore, in these areas are the aspects of the seven planets to the signs, and to every thing in them, and they look at each other.

But the signs which do not aspect are four: that is, the second from it, the sixth and the eighth and the twelfth.[43] And the number of the degrees of these four signs comes to be 120°, following the quantity of the trine aspect.[44]

[al-Qabīsī I.18a] On regarding. The signs are even said to look at each other: this is [that] every sign looks at the third one in front of it and the third one after it (which is the eleventh), and this aspect is called the sextile, and it is an aspect of esteem.[45] And it looks at the fourth one in front of it and the fourth one after it (which is the tenth), and this aspect is called the tetragonal raying, one of discord and medium enmity. It also looks at the fifth sign in front of it and at the fifth one after it (which is the ninth), and this aspect is called the trigonal raying, and it is an aspect of concord.[46] It even looks at the seventh by opposition, and it is an aspect of enmity. And if planets were in these signs aspecting each other thusly, they are said to look at each other: this is a regard.[47]

[al-Qabīsī I.18c] When a planet is in some sign, its rays will be in those signs which look at that sign, in a like degree and minute.

[*BW* VIII.105] Those which look at each other by a sextile aspect, [are] like two people seeking[48] friendship together.

[*BW* VIII.106] But by a trine aspect, like two men who are equal in nature.

[*BW* VIII.107] But by a square, like two who are seeking rulership each for himself.

---

[41] These are often called "dexter" aspects (Lat. *dexter*, "right").

[42] These are often called "sinister" aspects (Lat. *sinister*, "left").

[43] These places are "in aversion" to whatever sign we are considering.

[44] This is the first of several "120° concepts" we will encounter.

[45] Or, "friendship" (Ar.).

[46] Or, "compatibility" (Ar.).

[47] Note that al-Qabīsī defines aspects solely in terms of whole-sign configurations, and not by exact degrees or orbs.

[48] Reading *petentes* for *potentes*.

[*BW* VIII.108] If they are in the opposite aspect, just like two people battling each other strongly.

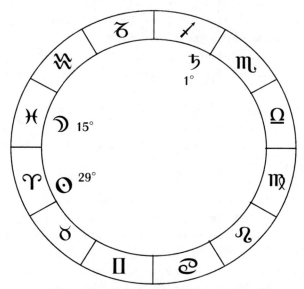

Figure 61: Saturn regarding the Moon and Sun[49]

---

[49] In this figure, the Moon and Sun each regard Saturn toward the right; Saturn regards the Moon and Sun toward the left; the Sun and Moon do not regard each other.

§III.6.2: The Thema Mundi and aspects

[*Mathesis* III.1.1-2] And so, those who followed Asclepius and Ha-nubio (to whom the most powerful divine power of Mercury committed the secrets of this science) wanted this to be the birth chart of the world[50]...And so, they want the fates of men to be arranged ac-cording to this birth chart and according to these conditions of the stars, and according to how they bear witness to this birth chart,[51] and according to these reasonings, just as is contained in that book of As-clepius which is called *Myriogenesis*, so that nothing at all in the individual birth charts of men would seem to be alien to this birth chart of the world.

[*BOA* II.2.13] And it is said that the sextile aspect is a good aspect, and it is an aspect of medium (but not complete) friendship and con-cord. And it is said to be an aspect of medium friendship, because it is drawn from Venus and from the luminaries, since the domiciles of Ve-nus aspect the domiciles of the luminaries from a sextile aspect, as was said above...And the square aspect is said to be moderately bad, and it is an aspect of medium enmity and discord, but not of the complete [sort]. And it is said to be an aspect of medium enmity, because it is drawn from Mars and from the luminaries, since the domiciles of Mars regard the domiciles of the luminaries from a square aspect, as was said above...But the trine aspect is said to be a good aspect, and it is an as-pect of perfect friendship, and of perfect agreement, and complete goodness. And it is said to be an aspect of perfect friendship and agreement because it is drawn from Jupiter and from the luminaries, since the domiciles of Jupiter aspect the domiciles of the luminaries from a trine aspect...But the aspect of the opposition is said to be an evil aspect, and it is an aspect of extreme enmity, and extreme malice, and extreme disagreement. And such an aspect is said to be of extreme enmity, because it is drawn from Saturn and from the luminaries, since

---

[50] See the figure below. The planets in black represent the position of the planets in this birth chart of the world (*Thema Mundi*). Firmicus states that the planets were each at 15° of their respective signs, which is not important for our purposes here.

[51] Or, "according to the testimonies they bear towards this birth chart" (*testimonia quae huic geniturae perhibent*).

the domiciles of Saturn aspect the domiciles of the luminaries from the opposition.

Figure 62: The Thema Mundi and aspects

Comment by Dykes. The Arabic *naẓar*, like its root verb *naẓara*, indicates on the one hand "looking at," "contemplating." But it also has a more specific legal and intellectual meaning of deciding between things, drawing comparisons between them, and even to try a legal case. There is also a sense that two planets in signs which are configured to each other have a kind of equality and correspondence, just as the Arabic word for assembly above had to do with "comparison."

The Latin *aspectus* and *respectus* likewise mean to notice, look at, turn one's mind toward something, or to show concern for. Unlike assembly in the same sign (which shows a loose similarity of purpose), aspects or regards suggest active concern and attention. But one might well ask how merely looking at something could imply an important or focused relationship: after all, mere looking seems rather passive. My sense is that aspecting or regarding[52] is like when campaigning politicians say they will find solutions after

---

[52] I have not tried to decide absolutely between these two terms, both of which are well-attested to in the Latin literature. On the one hand, "regard" is a true English verb which

"looking at" everything. Aspecting or regarding by whole sign (the closer the degree, the better) is like planets paying attention to each other and forming a relationship, though it does not imply a common purpose (assembly) or a firm partnership (connection).

These definitions of aspecting or regarding fit well the ancient definitions of "witnessing" or "testifying,"[53] which specifically point out that such witnessing may be by whole sign alone or by exact degree. In fact, the Arabic definitions include all three of the Greek notions which define an aspect: the whole-sign vs. exact degree distinctions, what each type of configuration (square, opposition, et cetera) means, and the right-left distinction.

Recently, Robert Schmidt has argued that witnessing or testifying proper requires that aspecting planets actually complete their connection by exact degree before they leave their own respective signs.[54] Surely, both the Greek and Arabic traditions would emphasize applying aspects which complete, especially in a horary context; but I do not agree with Schmidt's interpretation. Unfortunately I cannot address all of the details and nuances involved in my reasoning here, but my current view is this: the Greek texts speak of witnessing or testifying first as a very general notion (covering both by signs alone and by degree), and then get more precise by addressing particulars such as same-sign (assembly) versus different-sign (aspect) relationships, and the difference between distant, close applying, and separating relationships (see below). Although the order is a little bit changed in the Arabic authors, the same basic approach appears here: first, Abū Ma'shar and al-Qabīsī deal with same-sign relationships (assembly); then they deal with different-sign configurations generally (aspect), and the right-left distinction; in the next section they will address the close applying connections between planets by degrees (assembly, connection). So, planets witness or testify to each other simply by being in signs which aspect, even if there is not an applying connection by degree; but how we interpret their relationship will ultimately depend on whether a planet is applying (and how close it is), or separating and what happens afterwards.[55]

---

bears the connotations better (to look at, to form opinions about); but, while "aspect" is not really a verb, it has been in use as a verb and a noun by astrologers for centuries, and I am reluctant to insist on changing it.

[53] Schmidt 2009, pp. 127-29 and 139.

[54] Schmidt 2009, pp. 130-31.

[55] Some Arabic-language works also speak of a planet's rulership over a sign as being a form of "testimony" in it, but that is a different context.

§III.7: Connection

Arabic: Connection (*'ittiṣāl*)
John: Connection/conjunction (*coniunctio*)
Hermann #1 and Adelard: Application/attachment (*applicatio*)
Hermann #2: Attachment (*ligatio*)
Cf. Greek: Joining (*sunaphē*)
Cf. Greek: Attachment, adherence (*kollēsis*)

§III.7.1: Connection by longitude

[*Abbr.* III.13] One application is in longitude, another in latitude.

[*Abbr.* III.14] However, one application of longitude [is] in the same sign, the other in a different one. But of the one which is in different ones, one [is] without a regard,[56] the other with a regard (whether hexagonal or tetragonal or trigonal). However, whichever one it was, if it reaches the one which it pursues closely, it is already the end of the application.

[*Gr. Intr.* VII.5.795-05] But the conjunction of an aspect by longitude is if there were planets in signs which look at each other (namely from a sextile aspect or a trine, or from the square aspect or the opposition). And if it were so, and the one quicker in course went toward the conjunction of the slower one, until the quick one in its own sign is in a like degree and minute to that of the slower planet, in the sign in which it is. And if they were alike, its conjunction is perfected.

But the beginning of the power of the conjunction of an aspect is if there were 12° between both planets. And by how much more one of them drew near to its companion by aspect, it will be stronger for it.[57]

[al-Qabīsī III.11a] But the condition of the planets toward each other is this. There is connection: this is if there were two planets in two signs looking at each other, and the lighter one in its own sign were in less degrees than was the more weighty one in its own sign,

---

[56] I believe Abū Ma'shar is speaking about relationships not based upon aspects but rather on having the same ascensions and so on: see I.9 above and III.25 below.
[57] See additional material on orbs and aspects in II.6.

and there were 6° or less between them:[58] then the lighter one would be going toward the connection of the weightier one. And if their degrees were equal, its connection is perfected. And if it crossed over it, it will be separated from it. This connection is called the connection in longitude.

[*BA* II.10] Moreover, it is said [to be] a [corporal] application whenever a light one which is said to be applying, stood apart from the heavier one to which it applies, by 3° and just short of that, or at least it would be regarding the same [star] from the trigon or tetragon or hexagon or opposition by [that] whole number of degrees.

[*BW* VIII.3] The conjunction or aspect of the Moon with a planet signifies everything which is going to be, and everything about which the querent hopes. And if this planet were fortunate, [it will be] good; but if a bad one, bad.

[*BW* VIII.99] Aspecting: like a man seeking what he wants.

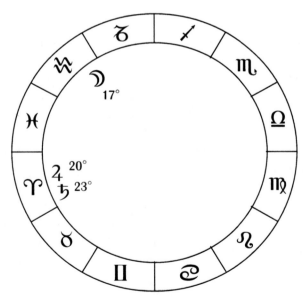

Figure 63: Moon connecting to Jupiter, Jupiter connecting to Saturn

---

[58] According to Schmidt (2009 p. 162), this 6-degree interval comes originally from Olympiodorus.

§III.7.2: Connection by latitude

[*Abbr.* III.15-19] But one [kind of] application according to latitude comes to be in the same sign, the other in a different one. [In the same sign, they must be in the same degree of longitude and ecliptical latitude.][59] But of the one which comes to be in a different one, [the opposition is] when one ascends in the north [and] the other descends in the north; another when one ascends in the south, the other descends in the same region; another[60] when one ascends in the north, the other descends in the south, or the other way around. But this application comes to be when the one which is more remote from the path of the Sun applies its own motion to the nearer one.[61] And so when it reaches it, the application is already ended.

[al-Qabīsī III.11.b] But the connection in latitude is that two planets would be joined by longitude, and, if their connecting were by assembly, their latitude would be equal (that is, in one direction).[62] And if the connecting were from the opposition, their latitudes would be equal: so that the latitude of one is ascending in the north, and that of the other descending in the north.[63]

But if it were something other than [such a] connection,[64] it will be[65] if one is ascending northern, and the other descending southern.

Comment by Dykes. All of these Arabic and Latin words share a basic meaning: to bring two distinct things into a close relationship, connecting or attaching them together. This is even true for the English version, "application," which suggests bringing oneself to bear upon something. Moreover, these terms also imply a closer relationship than mere aspecting or assembling: ʾ*ittiṣāl* and *coniunctio* in particular mean a transmission and communication of information, and *coniunctio* also implies putting several

---

[59] Adding based on the Ar.
[60] I.e., the other aspects.
[61] The Ar. and other manuscripts have the planet with less latitude moving toward the one with greater latitude.
[62] That is, on the same side of the ecliptic.
[63] John adds: "or that of one ascending in the south and that of the other descending in the south," just as *Abbr.* says.
[64] Burnett takes this to be a conjunction in latitude by some other type of aspect.
[65] Following the Ar. and omitting "an applying conjunction of longitude and not latitude."

things into one continuous structure. Thus, an (applying) connection creates a more focused association and mixture and pursuit between two planets than does assembly or aspecting.

It is unfortunate that the Arabic, unlike the Greek, does not distinguish connections within the same sign (*kollēsis*) from those in different signs (*sunaphē*). This means that in any text it might be unclear whether an author means one or the other—or indeed, if he cares whether it is one or the other.

The difference in degree range deserves a bit of comment. Note that Māshā'allāh's *BA* accurately reports the Greek 3° range, but by the time of Abū Ma'shar this becomes 12°, with al-Qabīsī apparently concluding that with a 12° interval, each planet gets a standardized orb of 6°. Of course in the later tradition, these connections by body or aspect become particular to the orbs of each individual planet. Other texts say that connections within the same bound are particularly important.[66]

---

[66] See for instance III.8 and II.6.

§III.8: Disregard or separation

Arabic: Averting, diverting, disregarding (*inṣirāf*)
John, Hermann: Splitting up or separation (*separatio*)
Adelard: Neglect or disregard (*neglectio*)
Cf. Greek: Falling/flowing off (*aporroia*)
Cf. Greek: Crossing over (*parallagê*)

[*Abbr.* III.20] Disregard is when, an application of longitude or latitude being ended, the quicker crossed over[67] the slower, and it disregarded it.

[*Gr. Intr.* VII.5.762-80] And when the light one goes across the slower one by one minute or less, it is already separated from it. If however a planet were separated from another by the conjunction which comes to be in one sign, and it were not joined to another, one of them will be in the nature of its companion so long as they were in the sign in which they are joined. And the complexion of their nature will be stronger if they were in one bound and not yet elongated by a quantity of one-half of the body[68] of the one which was less in degrees. And if one of them went out from the bound in which they were conjoined, this will be weaker for their complexion. And if in addition their elongation were more than the quantity of half the orb of each of the planets, this will be weaker for the complexion of their nature. But if another planet encountered it while it is being separated from [the slower one], before it goes out from the bound in which they had been assembled, or before it is elongated from the first planet by the quantity of half the orb of the one lesser in degrees, the light planet will be in the nature of both planets, namely of the one to which it is being joined, and the one from which it is being separated. And once it was separated from the second planet by orb, its condition with it will be like its condition with the first planet which was separated from it.

---

[67] *Transierit.* This Latin verb does also carry connotations of deserting someone.
[68] I.e., "orb."

[*BA* II.16] Therefore, whenever any stars regarded each other by a lesser number of degrees,[69] they judge the regarding to be effective. If they and the aspect cross beyond, there will be a shaking.[70]

[*BW* VIII.4] The separation of the Moon from a planet signifies what is past; and if she would be separated from the conjunction or aspect of a fortune, good was present; but if of a bad one, evil.

[*BW* VIII.100] A separating planet is like one regretting a matter.[71]

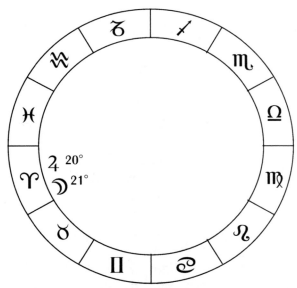

Figure 64: The Moon disregarding/separating from Jupiter

Comment by Dykes. This term begins the third group of definitions, which define a basic lack of connection. On its face, "disregard" or "separation" or "splitting up" stands simply in contrast to "regard" and "attachment" above. But actually, these terms and texts suggest deeper meanings and explicitly introduce an interesting Greek term not otherwise defined by Abū Ma'shar or al-Qabīsī. First, let us look at these terms and their implications.

---

[69] Probably the 3° range.
[70] *Quassatio.* In other words, separating aspects are in some sense "shaky."
[71] Epstein reads, "changing his mind," which is also appropriate.

The Arabic *inṣirāf* has as its verb root *ṣarafa*, which means to turn away from, especially to turn one's gaze away from something: note the aspect language of looking and paying attention. It also means to disregard, abandon or relinquish, to dismiss, and to act independently.[72] Finally, it means to cause water to be diverted from its course.

Adelard uses the unusual term *neglectio*, which on its surface simply means "neglect," but its verb root *neglego* has the more specific meaning of ignoring, disregarding, doing nothing about some matter, and particularly to fail to show proper observance of or reverence for some duty. If we put these notions together with the Arabic, we see that a separating planet abandons and ignores the other planet, acts independently and pays attention to something else. This immediately suggests more concrete chart interpretations than simply that two planets now lack a connection. For example, if two planets signify the partners in a relationship, then a separating aspect between them shows an active *neglect* or *disregard*, or one partner *not paying attention* anymore. For disregard or separation is not simply a lack of connection, but an *active denial* of a connection which was *already assumed to exist*.

We must also address John's word *separatio* ("separation"), because compared with "disregard" it does not seem to go well with the rich meanings of previous configurations: assembling, forming a relationship, communicating, and so on. Actually, *separatio*—along with Hugo's reference to "crossing beyond" in the excerpt from *BA*—directly addresses another Greek definition not included here. After defining witnessing or testimony and then right and left aspects, Greek writers such as Antiochus and Porphyry and Rhetorius defined *parallagē*, which means "crossing over."[73] In dealing with this definition, Robert Schmidt recently concluded that "crossing over" pertains specifically to the aspect of opposition.[74] For when one planet crosses the opposition of another, it will switch from being on the right side of it to the left, or *vice versa*. However, there is a much simpler explanation to which I alluded earlier. That is, these early definitions simply describe in a general way what happens in any aspect whatsoever. First, they begin with entirely general descriptions of aspects by whole sign and degree. Then, they define right and left aspects with respect to the position a planet is in. But thirdly, they define "crossing over," which is what happens when (1) a planet passes

---

[72] Note the connection to the concept of a planet being "in its own light" (II.9).

[73] The Arabic-language versions seem to derive from Rhetorius because his definition omits mention of the "isosceles line" common to both Antiochus and Porphyry.

[74] Schmidt 2009, p. 147.

from one side to the other of the degree of an exact figure such as a square, but also (2) when the *rays* of two planets cross over each other after having been united in an exact aspect.

The diagram below explains what I mean. Let the Moon be in early Capricorn, applying to a square defined by Jupiter's position in Aries. (Let's suppose Jupiter is stationary so as to keep things simple.) She is in a whole-sign aspect which will soon be connected by degree, and the square will be defined as being on her left, a left square. But from Jupiter's perspective, she is on the right of *his* square aspect. Once the square is completed, she will cross over from being on the right side of his square to being on the left. However, this crossing over also involves another perspective. For her rays are like lines of sight: until the aspect is perfected, she will be looking to the right of him, and he will be looking at her left. When the aspect is exact, their lines of sight will coincide. Immediately afterwards, their lines of sight will *cross over* and be *diverted* away in the opposite direction: the Moon's square ray will now turn away to Jupiter's left, and his will divert to her right.

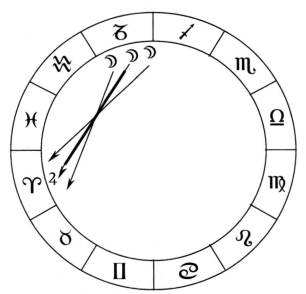

**Figure 65: The Moon crossing over and diverting or
separating from Jupiter**

Clearly then, this notion of crossing over appears in any aspect whatever, and not simply in the opposition. But it also shows that John's use of *separatio* was not amiss, because it is precisely at the moment of crossing over that the planets' lines of sight *split apart*. In other words, some translators emphasize the diversion of sight and attention into different directions, while others emphasize the splitting of the coinciding lines themselves.

From this we can conclude that the Arabs and Latins did address the Hellenistic notion of "crossing over," even if they did not define it separately. Moreover, this simpler way of understanding aspects combines aspects, right and left, applications, crossing over, and separation in a way which pertains to all aspects and not only to the opposition.

§III.9: Emptiness of course

Arabic: Emptiness of the course (*khalā' al-sayir*)
John: Empty/void in course (*vacuus cursu*)
Hermann, Adelard: Solitude (*solitudo*)
Cf. Greek: Emptiness of the course (*kenodromia*)

[*Abbr.* III.21] Solitude is if, a little after disregard, some star attaches to it in none of the above-stated ways, but neither does it attach to any [star] while it is in that sign.

[*Gr. Intr.* VII.5.965-67] The emptying of the course is if a planet would be separated from the conjunction of another planet by [bodily] conjunction or by aspect, and it would not be joined to another so long as it were in that same sign.

[al-Qabīsī III.12] And if one planet is being disregarded by another, and it is being connected to none of the planets so long as it is in that same sign, [its] course is said to be "empty."

[*Judgments* 6] If the Moon were void in course…it signifies futility and annulment, and turning back from that same purpose, and the impediment of that same purpose.

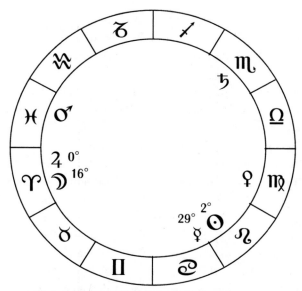

Figure 66: Medieval emptiness of course

Comment by Dykes. This and the next definition may be difficult to distinguish at first; they also depart from the Greek definitions in Antiochus, Porphyry, and Rhetorius Ch. 112. Here, emptiness of course is an intensification of disregard or separation, in which the separating planet does not *complete* a connection by body or ray so long as it is in its current sign. But the definition does not rule out whole-sign aspects as wildness does below. In the figure above, the Moon is void in course or is undergoing an emptiness of course while she is in Aries: she has separated from both the Sun and Jupiter, and cannot complete a square with Mercury while she is in Aries, since he will leave Cancer before she can reach him.

The Arabic *khalā* has several interesting meanings which are reflected in Hermann's and Adelard's *solitudo* (but not in John's "void" or *vacuus*): to be forsaken, deserted, abandoned; to be empty and isolated. These meanings specifically refer to a condition in which a *past* condition is no more, and in which there is little hope of anything further happening: thus we have an immediate interpretation for a planet (especially the Moon) in such a condition. The fact that emptiness in course only holds good for the current sign, is a function of the idea that aspects and connections require an appropriate sign relationship: each new sign provides new opportunities for planets to make a real connection. Thus a planet which will soon make a connection in the next sign, has new but *different* opportunities forthcoming—just as people do when leaving something behind and striking off in new directions.

The Hellenistic definition of emptiness was stricter (and referred only to the Moon): the Moon was not allowed to complete a connection within *the next 30°*, regardless of sign boundaries. That would indeed be rarer than the emptiness of course defined here. In fact, the Hellenistic definition is one of several which either restrict planets to, or forbid them from being in, a total of 120° of the zodiac. In the diagram below, the Moon is at 15° Aries, and in order to have an empty course she cannot complete a connection by body or ray within the next 30°. This can only happen if all other planets fall somewhere in a total of 120° of the zodiac, which are equivalent to *the four signs in aversion to the rising sign*.[75] In other words, all other planets must be in the longitudinal equivalent to the Moon's twelfth, eighth, sixth, and the second—in equal houses from the Moon's position, if you like. Below I have indicated the spaces forbidden to the other planets in gray, indicating the degrees where the forbidden areas begin and end. Of course if she were in some other degree, the corresponding forbidden areas would begin from that.

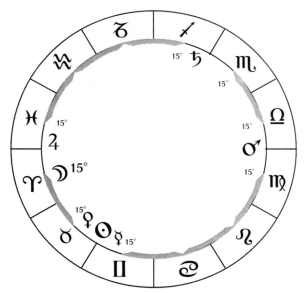

Figure 67: More restrictive Hellenistic emptiness of course

---

[75] That is, the twelfth, second, sixth, and eighth: these signs are not configured in a classical aspect to the rising sign.

§III.10: Wildness

Arabic: Wildness (*waḥashī*)
John: Wildness (*feralitas*)
Hermann: Estrangement (*alienatio*)
Adelard: Annullment (*abolitio*)
Cf. Greek: Emptiness of the course (*kenodromia*)

[*Abbr.* III.22] Annullment is when a planet has already been fully disregarded, and solitude undergone:[76] this is however particularly appropriate to the Moon.

[*Gr. Intr.* VII.5.968-76] But "wildness" is if a planet is in a sign and another one does not look at it at all. And if it were so, it is called "wild." And this happens more to the Moon.

[al-Qabīsī III.13] And if a planet were in some sign, and another planet did not look at this sign so long as it were in it, it is said that it is "wild."

---

[76] The Arabic reads, "it is a planet which no planet regards at all." Adelard clearly links wildness to the previous conditions as though part of a process.

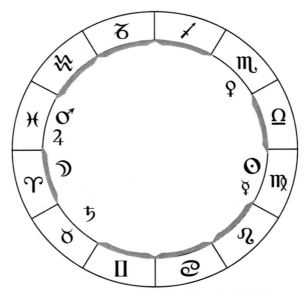

Figure 68: Example of a medieval wild Moon

Comment by Dykes. The medieval notion of wildness (sometimes called a "feral" planet) involves more stark isolation than either the Hellenistic or medieval emptiness of course, and is also more common. For not only can a wild planet not complete any connection while in its current sign (like emptiness of course), other planets cannot even aspect the wild planet's sign. (But the definition might allow the planet from which it is separated to be in the same sign.) In the figure above, the Moon has most recently separated from a bodily connection with Jupiter in Pisces (even though the definition might allow him to be in Aries in an earlier degree). However, because other planets must be in aversion to her current sign, she is totally alone.[77] Thus medieval wildness is both more lonely than Hellenistic emptiness and more common: since sign boundaries are respected (rather than the next 30°) and the separated planet seems to be allowed in the same sign, a planet separating from a bodily connection might only be wild for the remaining few degrees of its current sign: for example, if Jupiter were around the middle of Aries and the Moon were wild in only the last few degrees. But in the figure above I have constructed the example so that the Moon is wholly wild, in order to illus-

---

[77] The gray areas indicate where other planets are forbidden to be.

trate how close wildness is to the Hellenistic definition, including with its 120° aversion range of permitted degrees. In fact, this figure is identical to a "maximal" form of enclosure by sign (IV.4.2 below).

The Latin and Arabic descriptions of a wild Moon, and the meanings of the terms used, are striking and evocative. In the first place, Adelard brings his earlier theme of neglect to bear and heightens its intensity with one of cutting all ties: the Latin *abolitio* or "annulment" means the destruction and cancellation of connections and ties. On the other hand, this separation and cancellation or even abandonment also has a silver lining: the Latin *abolitio* also has the legal meaning of dropping a charge or even providing amnesty for a past act. If we return to the image of two partners separating, the destructive theme is negative in that it shows neglect, ignoring, and abandonment; but on the other hand, this abandonment also indicates the ability to begin anew with a cancelled past. Such an option is not fully available with a planet which has only had an empty course (III.9) or merely been separated (III.8), since such planets are still allowed to have other planets aspect their sign: a wild planet is not allowed even to have whole-sign relationships to other planets—but it would then enter the next sign with a clean slate.

The rest of the terms bring other ideas to bear. Following John of Spain, this condition is often called being "feral," (*feralitas*), which of course means "undomesticated, wild," as with a feral cat or dog. The idea here is that such a planet or person lacks civilizing connections with other people. The 17th Century astrologer Morin said that such a planet "will act simply in accordance with its own nature...[and] indicates something unusual—good or ill—depending on the nature of the planet; for example, Saturn feral in the first indicates a hermit or monk."[78] In other words, a wild planet may indeed act on its own, but like someone living in the wilderness this isolation might lead to unusual results untempered by normal social and mental associations. If aspects (even by whole sign) are understood in terms of light and knowledge and connections, wildness suggests people and activities whose natures are not known, hidden, and potentially disturbed or disturbing.

The dangers lurking in medieval wildness are more evident in the Arabic "wildness" (*waḥashī*) and Hermann's "estrangement"(*alienatio*). The Arabic

---

[78] Morin 1974, pp. 91-92. Morin may not have required the other planets to be fully in aversion to Saturn for him to be wild, but his comment is in the spirit of medieval wildness.

verb *waḥasha* does indeed mean to be deserted, lonely, forlorn, and to be alienated or estranged; also to become wild or brutal in the sense of lacking moderating moral and social restraints (one might also think of being "stir-crazy"). It also (like *feralitas*)[79] means to be anxious or gloomy, indicating the outlook of a planet which is not only empty in its course but in aversion to other relationship opportunities with other planets. Hermann's "estrange-ment" not only bears this notion of being estranged, alienated, and hostile, but even of being numb, insensible, or in shock, and finally of being mentally deranged: it is interesting to note that early psychiatrists were known as "alienists," as though their patients had become deranged by being estranged from their own normal minds.

And so, with wildness we complete a beginning-to-end series of concepts which began with a basic relationship of light and knowledge ("regard" or "aspect"), common purpose and close connections ("assembly," "connec-tion"), to a diverging of perspective, neglect, and loneliness, a darkness before the dawn of new opportunities and relationships. In the next two concepts, we will go beyond the immediate connection of two planets to those mediated by a third planet.

---

[79] The lexicon seems to say that the meaning of gloominess and that of wildness come from different Latin roots, but both of them can be gleaned from *feralitas* itself, and both of these meanings are also in the Arabic.

§III.11: Transfer

Arabic: Transfer (*naql*)
John, Hermann, Adelard: Transfer (*translatio*)

[*Abbr.* III.23-24] Transfer is in two ways: one, if a star elongating itself[80] from [another] star and pursuing[81] another closely, transfers the nature of the first one to the other one; the other one, if a star applies itself to a star, with another one applying to it: and it transfers the nature of the first into it.

[*Gr. Intr.* VII.5.977-82] Also, "transfer" comes to be in two ways. Namely one, if a light planet would be separated from a weighty one, and would be joined to another, and would transfer the nature of the one from which it is being separated, to the one to which it is being joined. Secondly, that a light planet would be joined to a planet slower than itself, and the slow one would be joined to another planet, and the slow planet would transfer the nature of the light planet to the one to whom it is being joined.

[al-Qabīsī III.14] And if a light planet is being diverted from a weightier planet, and were connected to another, it transfers the nature of the first to the second. A planet even transfers the nature in another way: this is that a light planet would be connected to a planet more weighty than itself, and the weightier one again to one more weighty than itself: then the middle one transfers the nature of the light one to the weightier one.

[*BW* VIII.56] If a planet transferred the light from the Lord of the Ascendant to the Lord of what is asked about, [the matter] will be perfected through the work of a mediator.

---

[80] Ar. "separating."
[81] Ar. "applying to."

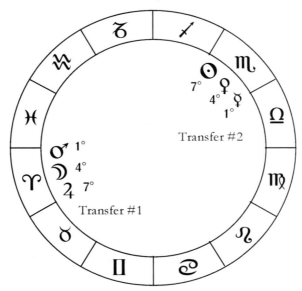

Figure 69: Transfer

Comment by Dykes. Our Latin and Arabic sources agree on the basic concept of a "transfer," with its dual sense of transmission: that of information and reports (Arabic) or responsibility, credit, and blame (Latin). The Arabic sense of transferring information fits well with the general theme of looking and light being analogous to testifying and knowledge, whereas the Latin sense of transferring responsibility helps us gain a concrete sense of what this means astrologically: the middle or transferring planet bears responsibility for bringing the other two planets together, and (depending upon the issue at hand) that responsibility for the matter finally rests with the planet to which everything is transferred. Bonatti says that the transferring planet can indicate what type of person makes this connection by its house position or rulership,[82] but such comments seem more appropriate to a transfer between planets which regard each other from different signs, or even the second form of reflecting the light (III.13), which is a transfer between two planets in aversion to each other.

Bonatti (and Lilly, following him) argues that a transfer—or at least a truly effective one—requires the transferring planet to be in one of the dignities of the planet from whom it is separated, on the theory that "a planet does not

---

[82] *BOA* Tr. 6 Part 1, Ch. 1 (p. 359).

give something in a place in which it promises nothing," or that the transferring planet cannot transfer something unless it is granted it by the first planet.[83] And one might wonder whether a dignity relation must be involved, since the definitions say middle planet transfers the *nature* of the first one to the last: in III.15 we will see "pushing nature" or classical reception, where a planet applies to one of its dispositors; and in III.25, Abū Ma'shar expands classical reception to include cases where the dispositor is the one applying. If Abū Ma'shar meant that classical reception or pushing nature (or pushing power, III.16) were involved, we would want to see him use the word "pushing." But he does not. On the left in the figure above, the Moon separates from Mars from his own domicile, and applies to the body of Jupiter from his triplicity. On the right, Mercury applies to Venus and she applies in turn to the Sun: this example does not fulfill any of the requirements laid out by Bonatti/Lilly or classical reception.

---

[83] *BOA* Tr. 3 Part 2, Ch. 11 (p. 215); *CA* pp. 125-26.

§III.12: Collection

Arabic: Collection (*jamᶜ*)
John, Hermann: Collection (*collectio*)
Adelard: Conjunction, connection (*coniunctio*)

[*Abbr.* III.25] "Collection"[84] is if two or three (or however many) [planets] are applying themselves to some star situated in its own place:[85] whence it collects their [light and receives their] natures.

[*Gr. Intr.* VII.5.983-84] Also, "collection" is if two or more are being joined to one planet, and it collects their lights and receives their natures.

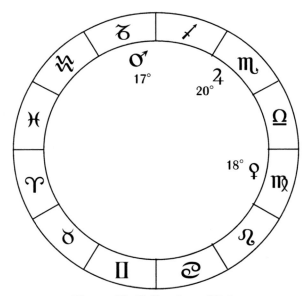

Figure 70: Collection of light

---

[84] I will follow the Arabic instead of Adelard's "conjunction, conjoining," because of its association with an applying conjunction.
[85] This does not mean its own dignity, but simply that it is in a given place and the others are moving toward it.

Comment by Dykes. Collection of light is the third of the primary ways in which planets are properly connected. Although the definitions do not obviously require that the planets be in particular dignities, the statements that the collecting planet "receives their natures" does recall pushing nature (III.15), and this is clearly the spirit in which Bonatti and Lilly read it. Lilly says that both of the applying planets must receive the collecting planet,[86] and Bonatti says they must "commit their virtue" to it,[87] which sounds like pushing power but may indeed simply be a case of reception or pushing nature as well. I have constructed my example so as to follow Bonatti and Lilly. Venus, the Lady of the 7th, is in a separating trine with Mars, the Lord of the Ascendant. But they are both connecting within 3° to Jupiter by a sextile, and Jupiter is received by both: by Mars from Mars's domicile and triplicity, and by Venus from her triplicity.

Collection of light also reminds us that whether planets are being properly connected or prevented from doing so, depends on context. Note that Venus is in a later degree than Mars: if the planets we wanted to connect were Mars and Jupiter, then we might well believe that Venus would prevent this connection in the manner of barring (III.14). (Although barring explicitly requires at least two planets to be in the same sign, we might wonder whether that is strictly required or only a function of the example chosen.) But in our scenario, Mars and Venus are not competing to reach Jupiter first (barring), nor are we trying to get Venus to connect Mars and Jupiter (transfer of light). Instead, we are trying to connect Mars and Venus: thus Jupiter collects their light.

---

[86] *CA* p. 126.
[87] *BOA* Tr. 6 Part 1, Ch. 2 (p. 360).

§III.13: Reflection

Arabic: Reflecting the light (*radd al-nūr*)
John: Rendering (*redditus*)
Adelard: Shifting, cross-changing (*transmutatio*)

§III.13.1: Reflection of light #1

[*Abbr.* III.26] Moreover, shifting is in two ways: one, if neither [of] two stars pertaining to our topic[88] applies to [nor regards][89] the other, [instead] applying themselves to [or regarding][90] others—whence the intention of the topic is turned in a different direction.[91]

[*Gr. Intr.* VII.5.985-90] However, the "rendering of light" comes to be in two ways. One, if one planet or two were significators, [and] one of them would not be joined to its companion, nor would they be looking at each other,[92] but they are looking at some planet or are being joined to it, and that planet at whom they are looking (or to whom they are being joined) will be looking at one of the places of the circle, and it will render their light to that place which it is aspecting.

[al-Qabīsī III.15a] If however one of two planets is not being connected to the other, but each is being connected to [yet] another, then, if that third planet looked at some one of the places of the circle, it reflects their light to that place: and this is called the "reflecting of light."

---

[88] *Thema*, here and below. This is clearly the "quaesited" in horary.
[89] Adding with the Ar.
[90] Adding with the Ar.
[91] *Pervertitur*, which I would normally translated as "turned awry," i.e., somehow twisted or spoiled. See below.
[92] By definition this means they must be either separated within the same sign, or in aversion to each other.

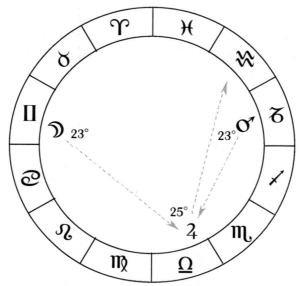

Figure 71: Reflecting the light #1

§III.13.2: Reflection of light #2

[*Abbr.* III.27] The other [kind of shifting]: if no regard[93] is had between the Lord of the horoscope and that of the topic, but the Lord of the sign of the topic applies to another star which likewise applies to the Lord of the horoscope,[94] and offers[95] the light[96] of the Lord of the topic to the Lord of the horoscope.

[*Gr. Intr.* VII.5.990-93] Secondly, that the Lord of the Ascendant and the Lord of the matter are not looking at each other, or they are separated. Which if some planet transferred light between them, it reflects the light of one of them to the other.

---

[93] Reading with the Ar. and *Gr. Intr.*; the Latin has them not being connected.
[94] The Latin is more specific about who is doing what: the Ar. is similar to the *Gr. Intr.* below, speaking only of a third planet moving between them.
[95] *Praebet.* That is, "reflects."
[96] Reading with the Ar. for "nature."

[al-Qabīsī III.15b] Again, if one of two planets is not being con-nected[97] to the other, but another [third] planet transfers the light between each, it reflects the light of one to the other: and this is like-wise called a "reflecting of light."

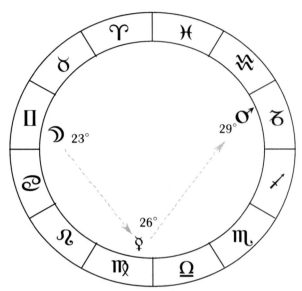

Figure 72: Reflecting the light #2

Comment by Dykes. In order to understand the reflecting of light, we must first refer to a simpler version described by Māshā'allāh in his *On Reception.*[98] In this work, Māshā'allāh gives instructions on how to choose the significator for the querent in a horary chart. Normally this role goes by default to the Lord of the Ascendant, but Māshā'allāh places some restrictions on this rule. If the Lord of the Ascendant cannot aspect the rising sign, then we must find some planet to which it applies, such that this *second* planet aspects the rising sign: if so, then the Lord of the Ascendant's light will be reflected to the As-cendant, and it can act as the primary significator.[99] So Māshā'allāh seems to

---

[97] This should probably read "is not regarding the other," i.e., being in aversion from it, following *Abbr.* and *Gr. Intr.*

[98] See my *Works of Sahl & Māshā'allāh*, pp. 444-46.

[99] John of Spain's translation of Māshā'allāh uses the same word there as he does here for reflection, but at the time I translated it as "render." This will be corrected in future edi-tions.

have viewed reflection as a way to overcome aversion: if a planet and sign cannot see each other, the light can be reflected from one to the other via an intermediary.

Both types of reflection in Abū Ma'shar and al-Qabīsī offer variants on this simple form, and in fact both types of reflection are really transfer and collection of light from aversion. The second type is a transfer of light from a position of aversion: if one planet is in aversion to a second one, its light can reach it by being reflected through a third. The text makes no suggestion as to whether any dignities must be involved, which was an open question above (III.11-12), but we must imagine that the result will be more certain if the applications involve proper dignity relations (pushing nature or pushing power, below). Moreover, we can see why this is not called a straightforward "transfer": just as we use a mirror to see something otherwise invisible to us by means of reflected light, so the first planet indirectly sees the other planet in aversion by means of the middle, reflecting planet.

In fact, reflection of both types offers insight into what takes place in connection, transfer, and collection. In those cases, the planets connecting or being linked by a transfer or collection *must* see each other, and it is as though the transferring or collecting planet recognizes there is a relationship between them: because *there is* a relationship, namely one of aspect or regard; it is just that they are in degrees which do not allow their aspect or regard to become a full-fledged connection. Still, the transferring or collecting planet sees that there is an objective form of communication and relationship between them, even if it is only by sign. But in reflection, the reflecting planet cannot recognize any relationship between the other two planets—it has no reason to, because they are in aversion to each other, not seeing or communicating. Thus, in the second type of reflection, the fact that the light of the first planet is reflected to the other has a touch of uncertainty to it, a bit of luck or perhaps with some indirection in the result: the reflecting planet takes the light from the first planet, and—what? It must simply go on its way, and just happens to apply next to the other planet, without having any idea that that is important.

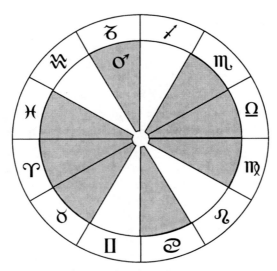

Figure 73: Potential perfection proper (gray) and reflection (white)

This idea of linking planets without a connection or knowledge also helps to explain the first type of reflection, which is not much more than collection from aversion: two planets we want to be linked are in aversion, but each applies to a third planet which collects their light. However, there is a twist: instead of simply retaining the light and perfecting the matter, the reflecting (collecting) planet sends the light elsewhere. Again, since there is no objective relationship between the two planets by sign, why should the reflecting (collecting) planet assume it is supposed to do anything special with their light? So, it simply sends its own light on as usual. But we may suppose that this reflecting onto somewhere else could be good or bad. Looking back at Māshā'allāh's version, perhaps this reflection to the Ascendant or some other important place will be valuable and helpful; if not, maybe it will make things turn out badly. But in either case, we see again the lack of relationship and awareness affecting the situation. It's as though the collecting planet takes things into its own hands, and we must cross our fingers that it's going to do the right thing with it.

With reflection, we reach the end of our "perfection" series, definitions of a perfecting relationship: the first three demand an aspect by sign (connect, transfer, and connection), which provides a kind of awareness and intentionality, a meeting of minds which enables a relationship. Reflection can be seen either as a more uncertain option covering aversion, or simply as a variation on transfer and connection,[100] in any event offering a second-best alternative but with no guarantees. As the figure above shows, these two groups together define all whole-sign places of the chart in terms of its possible perfections: Mars can potentially connect, have a transfer or collection with, any planet in a gray place; it can potentially have a reflection with any planet in a white place.

---

[100] By definition there could not be a connection from aversion.

§III.14: Barring or blocking

Arabic: Barring, blocking, prohibition (*man ͨ*)
Latin authors: Prevention, prohibition (*prohibitio*)
Cf. Greek: Intervention (*mesembolēsis*)

§III.14.1: Barring #1

[*Abbr.* III.28] Barring is likewise in two ways: one [is from assembly],[101] whenever two planets fit for application are barred by a third one coming in between.

[*Gr. Intr.* VII.5.994-1002] Also, prohibition comes to be in two ways. One, from the conjunction. This is if there are three planets in one sign, in different degrees, and the weightier one is in more degrees. Then, the middle one prohibits the one who was less in degrees from the conjunction of the weighty one, until it crosses over it. Like if Saturn were in Aries in the twentieth degree, and Mercury were in the same [sign] in the fifteenth degree, and Venus in the same [sign] in the tenth degree. Therefore, Mercury prohibits Venus lest she be joined to Saturn, until [Mercury] crosses over [Saturn]. After this, there will be a conjunction of Venus with Saturn.

[al-Qabīsī III.16a] Barring follows. And it comes to be in two ways, namely one from association. This is if there were three planets in one sign but in different degrees, and the weightier one were in more degrees: then the one which is the middle one bars the prior one (namely the one which is in fewer degrees) so that it would not be connected to the weightier one, until [the middle one] passes over it.

[*BW* VIII.52] If a planet were barring between [two planets], it signifies a separation between the one seeking and the matter sought.
[*BW* VIII.65] If the testimony of the significator will be from the category of barring, it signifies the destruction of the matter after [there was] hope.

---

[101] Adding based on the Ar.

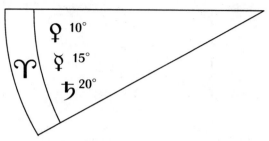

Figure 74: Barring #1 (by assembly)

§III.14.2: Barring #2

[*Abbr.* III.29] The other [kind of prohibition is] whenever, with two planets meeting in the same sign, and with one of them fit to be applied to another, the application of [a regarding one] is barred through the one conjoined in that place—unless the one which is outside the sign is distant by fewer degrees (for thus [the one in the sign] does not bar).

[*Gr. Intr.* VII.5.1003-1010] The second prohibition is from an aspect. This is that two planets would be in one sign, and the lighter one is joined to a weighty one, and another planet would be joined to that weighty one by an aspect. Therefore, the one which was with it in one sign prohibits the aspecting one, and it destroys its conjunction if their degrees were equal. But if the degrees of the aspecting one were closer to the conjunction than the degrees of the one which is being joined to it [by body], there will be a conjunction of the aspecting one, because it is joined to it before the conjunction of the other one.

[al-Qabīsī III.16b] In the second way: that two planets would be in one sign, and the lighter one is being connected to the weightier one, [and] the other [third one] is also being connected to the same weightier one by aspect. The one which is with [the weightier one] in one sign bars the aspecting one from the connection of the weightier one—if however the degree of the one which is being assembled, and the one which is aspecting, were equal. But if the one which is aspecting were closer to the degree of the weightier one, there will be a connection of the aspecting one.

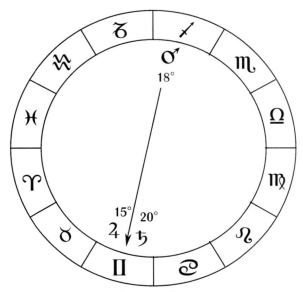

Figure 75: Barring #2 (by aspect)

Comment by Dykes. This term is sometimes called "prohibition" in English texts, but I have chosen the term "barring" because it is not only an accurate alternative, but is more concrete and descriptive of the astrological scenario. The Arabic *manʿ* comes from the verb *manaʿa*, which (like the Latin *prohibeo*) has the concrete sense of physically blocking or barring someone from doing something; only in the more abstract legal and moral senses do the Arabic and Latin have to do with "prohibition": as we all know, signs which say "X is strictly prohibited" does not physically stop people from breaking the rules. Here, a planet or its ray physically bars an applying planet from completing a desired connection.

Barring is the most direct counterpoint to all of the types of connecting and perfection we have seen thus far: the barring planet simply prevents the rays from going where they would otherwise. In the next group of definitions, we will circle back and look at what planet actually do when they connect with each other, so for now barring stands alone as a form of preventing a connection. Later on we will see other forms of failed perfection which involve planets in other signs as well as retrogradation.

The only other comment to make here is that barring is the same as the Hellenistic "intervention,"[102] and like intervention it can be both helpful or harmful. If it prevents the connection we want, then it is unhelpful. But in IV.4.2 below, we will see that barring is helpful in breaking a situation of enclosure or besieging. In the figure below, the Moon is enclosed or besieged by both malefics; but Venus casts her ray between the Moon and Mars, constructing a barrier and form of aid that liberates the Moon from the besieging.

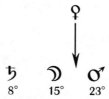

Figure 76: Barring as breaking an enclosure/besieging

---

[102] Schmidt 2009, pp. 200-01.

§III.15: Pushing nature

Arabic: Pushing nature (*dafʿ al-ṭabiyyʿah*)
John: Pushing of nature (*pulsatio naturae*)
Hermann, Adelard: Gift of nature (*donum naturae*)

[*Abbr.* III.30] A gift of nature is if some one of the planets occupying the domicile of another applies itself to it; whence its own nature is gifted, from its own host. It comes to be not dissimilarly even in the place of [a planet's] kingdom and face and the rest of the dignities.

[*Gr. Intr.* VII.5.1011-1014] Moreover, the pushing of nature is that a planet would be joined to the Lord of the sign in which it is (or to the Lord of its exaltation, or to the Lord of its bound, or to the Lord of its triplicity, or to the Lord of its face): and it will push the nature of that same planet to it.

[al-Qabīsī III.17] And if a planet is being connected to the Lord of the sign in which it is, or to the Lord of its exaltation or the Lord of the rest of the dignities in which it was, it is said to push the nature of that planet to it.

[*BW* VIII.61] If the testimony of the significator were from the category of pushing nature, it portends great joy in the matter.

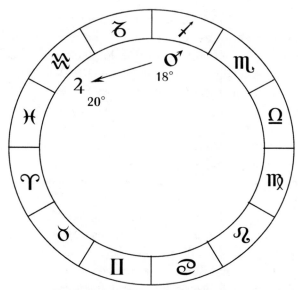

Figure 77: Mars pushing his nature to Jupiter

Comment by Dykes. The categories of "pushing" are among the odder in medieval astrology, and unfortunately references to them virtually died out in the Latin tradition after the first wave of 12ᵗʰ Century translations.[103] Let me describe the terminology and then discuss what I currently believe they mean.

The Arabic *dafʿ* ("pushing") comes from the verb *dafaʿa*, which does mean to push or shove something away from oneself; but it also means to hand something over, as well as to gush or stream forth (as a spout of water). Since the applying planet is always considered the pusher, the pushing planet sends a stream of something to another planet which is then responsible for it. Latin authors like John used *pulsare* (which normally means to "hit" or "beat," but can also mean to impel or give a push to something) or *committere*, emphasizing the "handing over." It is likely that the Persian or Arabic origi-nators of this terminology were thinking of light and water metaphors which we have already seen in terms such as disregard/separation, reflection, re-gard, and so on.

---

[103] Exceptions would the be occasional comment about "committing disposition" (i.e., pushing management) in authors such as Bonatti and Lilly, but neither author seems to have a fixed sense of what these types of pushing mean.

But there are four things which are pushed: nature, power, two natures (actually a combination of nature and power), and management. The Arabic *ṭabiyyʿah* ("nature") has an important career in philosophy, since it refers to something's fundamental nature, disposition, or character, which plays a central role in Aristotelian and other metaphysics and physics. Its root verb *ṭabaʿah* means to make an impression on something, or to have the propensity for doing something, or even to take on something's character—all of which recalls the famous image of something being impressed into soft wax, which retains the form of what was pressed.

Here, the applying or pushing planet presses or hands over its propensities and characters to the other planet, which receives the pushing and takes them on. In the figure above, Mars is in the domicile of Jupiter, and he is applying and pushing his nature onto Jupiter. Since Mars is in a dignity of the one receiving the pushing, this is a case of what I later call "classical" reception (III.25). For medieval and later astrologers, if a planet applies to the Lord of its domicile or exaltation (or preferably two of the lesser dignities), then it is "received" by that Lord. The Lord not only receives the pushing of the influence or nature, but also receives the pushing planet as a host does a guest.

In the future we may develop a richer sense of how this pushing works, and how it differs from other types. But we might ask: what does the dignity add here? My sense is that the receiving planet (here, Jupiter) denotes a level of *acceptance* and *adoption* of the pushing planet (Mars) into its home. So, the receiving planet is more willing to take on the qualities of whatever Mars means in this particular chart. In Abū Ma'shar's *Gr. Intr.*, it often seems to have to do with taking on the elemental qualities (hot, cold, wet, dry) of the pushing planet. But we will have to do more textual research and work with charts to see what else the Persians meant by pushing power. For more on classical reception, see III.25 below.

§III.16: Pushing power

Arabic: Pushing power (*daf˓ al-quwwah*)
John: Pushing strength (*pulsatio fortitudinis*)
Hermann: Gift of virtue (*donum virtutis*)
Adelard: Gift of power (*donum potentiae*)

[*Abbr.* III.31] A gift of power is whenever some one of the stars occupy-ing[104] either its own domicile or other dignities, [applies to] another one [and] exhibits its own power to [it].

[*Gr. Intr.* VII.5.1015-18] Also, the pushing of strength is that a planet would be in its own proper domicile or in its own exaltation (or in its own bound or in its own triplicity or face), and it would be joined to another planet, and it would push its own strength to it.

[al-Qabīsī III.18] And if it were in some one of its own dignities, and it were connected to another planet, it will give its own strength to it.

[*BW* VIII.48] If a planet were receiving power in a bad place, it de-notes evil.
[*BW* VIII.51] If the Lord of the Ascendant gave power to the Lord of the house of the matter sought, what is sought will be gotten according to his wishes; but if it were the contrary, [the attainment of] the matter will be without labor.
[*BW* VIII.59] If the significator belonged to the category of pushing strength, it signifies the matter is perfected according to his wish.

---

[104] Adelard reads *occupanti* instead of *occupans*, as if the *other* planet were in the domicile. I have changed this word and rearranged the clauses to fit the Ar. better.

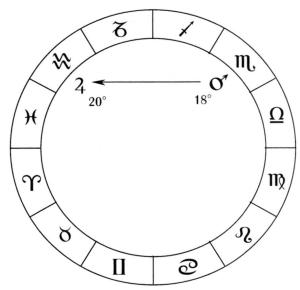

Figure 78: Mars pushing his power to Jupiter

Comment by Dykes. The Arabic *quwwah* refers to strength, vigor, and potency, while its root verb *qawiyya* means to be strong, to have influence over something, and to cope with or be able to manage something: the emphasis here is on strength as a *capacity*, not so much on wielding it. Adelard's *potentia* matches these ideas well, referring to the condition of being influential, powerful, and being able to control or exercise control.

In pushing power, the dignity relation is reversed from pushing nature. Instead of the applying or pushing planet being in another's dignities and applying to that very Lord, the applying planet is in one of its *own* dignities: thus it is in a position of power, control, and capability. It is able to push more than just its nature, and so it impresses this power upon the planet receiving the impulse. In the figure above, Mars is in his own domicile of Scorpio, so when connecting with Jupiter, he pushes and communicates his power to Jupiter.

To my mind, pushing power must mean that the planet receiving the impulse is able to take advantage of the control and competence it gains from the pusher: it must be able to cope with and manage whatever is signified, in a more authoritative and capable way. Just as pushing nature suggested that the intrinsic qualities and significations of the pusher would be impressed upon the receiver, so pushing power suggests that the receiver will get the benefit of the pushers essential (and possibly accidental) strengths.

§III.17: Pushing two natures

Arabic: Pushing two natures (*dafᶜ al-ṭabiyyᶜatīn*)
John: Pushing of two natures (*pulsatio utrarumque naturarum*)
Hermann: Gift of a twin nature (*donum geminae naturae*)
Adelard: Gift of two natures (*donum duarum naturarum*)

§III.17.1: Pushing two natures #1

[*Abbr.* III.32] A gift of two natures comes to be in two ways: one, if some one of the planets situated in a place of dignity applies itself to another having dignity in that same place.

[*Gr. Intr.* VII.5.1019-22] Likewise, the pushing of both natures comes to be in two ways. One, that a planet would be in a sign in which it has some dignity, and it would be joined to another which even has a dignity there. Like Venus, if she was being joined to Jupiter from out of Pisces.

[al-Qabīsī III.19a] And if it were in some one of its own dignities, and it were connected to a planet which [itself] even has a portion of the dignity in that same place, it even pushes both natures to it.

[*BW* VIII.62] The testimony of a significator from the category of the pushing of two natures, signifies the joy of the one seeking, and of him about whom it is asked.

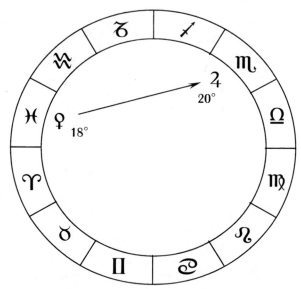

Figure 79: Pushing two natures type #1

§III.17.2: Pushing two natures #2

[*Abbr.* III.33] The other [gift of two natures]: whenever a star applies itself to a star, each of which [is of the same sect and appears in a place of that sect].[105]

[*Gr. Intr.* VII.5.1022-24] Secondly, that a planet would be joined to a planet which was of its own domain:[106] like if a diurnal planet was being joined to a diurnal planet, or a nocturnal one to a nocturnal one.

---

[105] Reading more with the Arabic for "appears in its luckiness [*felicitate*]," evidently a synonym for a sect-related condition. The Arabic explains that it is two diurnal planets connecting to each other, and in a diurnal place (and likewise for nocturnal planets in a nocturnal place). I take the "place" to be a sign, but it could be domain proper (III.2 above).

[106] That is, of its own sect.

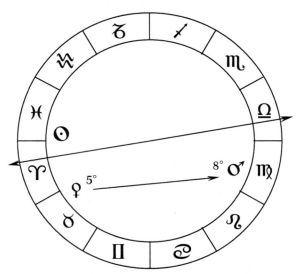

Figure 80: Pushing two natures type #2

Comment by Dykes. Pushing "two natures" is something of a misnomer. In the first figure, Venus in Pisces is connecting to Jupiter in Scorpio: really, she is pushing her own nature and pushing her own power at the same time. Likewise, in the second figure there is no pushing of nature at all: rather, Venus in her *ḥayyiz* is connecting to a fellow nocturnal planet, Mars in *ḥalb* and in a nocturnal sign. (Al-Qabīsī might have omitted the second type precisely because it does not push nature.) The point seems to be that the planets involved enjoy a similar status: they are the domicile and exalted Lords of the same sign, or they are sect-mates and each in a favorable sect condition.

§III.18: Pushing management

Arabic: Pushing management (*daf al-tadbīr*)
John: Pushing of arrangement (*pulsatio dispositionis*)
Hermann, Adelard: Gift of counsel (*donum consilii*)

[*Abbr.* III.34] A gift of counsel is when, with the planets applying in some place, one of them gives counsel to the other. Indeed if they were in trigonal or hexagonal [places], or together,[107] [it is] good; but in tetragonal or opposite ones, the contrary.

[*Gr. Intr.* VII.5.1025-32] However, the pushing of arrangement is if a planet would be joined to a planet, in whatever way the conjunction was, and it would push its own arrangement to it. Which if it were from the sextile or trine aspect and there were reception between them, the pushing itself will be with concord. But if it were from a conjunction and there were a complexion between them, it will even be from concord. And if it were to the contrary of what we have said, the pushing of arrangement will be without concord.

[*Introduct.* §5.13] An example of [pushing arrangement and nature] is: if the Moon or one of the planets was in Aries, and was being joined to Mars (or she was in Gemini and was being joined to Mercury). And the Moon, if she were in Taurus or in Cancer, pushes each (namely strength and arrangement); and if she were not in these two signs, she still pushes arrangement.

[*BW* VIII.60] If a significator were of the category of pushing authority, it denotes the matter will be revealed to another.

---

107 The Ar. reads, "or with reception."

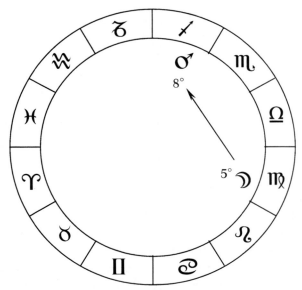

Figure 81: The Moon pushing management to Mars

Comment by Dykes. The final member of the "pushing" family is pushing management. The Arabic *tadbīr*, derived from *dabara*, has two primary groups of meaning: the first is more conceptual, dealing with planning, organizing, arranging, and designing; the second is more practical: managing, steering, regulating, conduct the business of something (especially household management). Of our Latin authors, John focuses on the practical side, where *dispositio* or arrangement (sometimes translated as "disposition") refers to how things are administered, ordered, arranged, allotted. Hermann's and Adelard's *consilium* emphasizes the conceptual side: deliberation, advice, planning.

The definitions above, particularly with the help of Sahl's example, make it clear that pushing management does not require any dignity relationship. In other words, pushing management takes place in *every* connection, though its import might be overshadowed by the special effects of pushing nature of power; and when there are no dignities involved, it is the *only* thing which happens. This will take place when the pusher is peregrine (not in any of its own dignities) and is not in any dignity of the one receiving the pushing. In the figure above, the Moon is peregrine in Virgo, connecting to Mars, and she is not in any of his dignities: thus she only pushes management. The fact that pushing management is wholly generic could be the reason that al-Qabīsī omitted it from his list.

Well, what does pushing management mean? If we compare it with the other forms of pushing, it seems that pushing nature impresses the natural features of the pushing planet; pushing power impresses its capability and authority; pushing management impresses the *rulership duties* of the pusher. So for instance, in the above example the Moon is the Lady of the fourth. If she were pushing nature, she would impress Lunar things upon Mars's behavior; if she were pushing power, he would benefit from her strength and authority; and in any case, by pushing management she impresses at least some of her rulership duties over home, land and parents upon him, so that he becomes partly responsible for those matters. This is a more precise way of expressing how planets combine than what we often read, namely that one should "mix" all of the significations together. Moreover, it helps us understand a bit more how to use other planets as time lords and in transits: for example, if a planet is acting as the profected Lord of the Year, we might track not only its transits but those of the planets to which he is pushing management, both in the nativity and at the solar revolution: for those planets are receiving his management and will share the responsibility of steering the period—for better or worse, depending upon their condition and the type of aspect involved.

§III.19: Returning

Arabic: Returning (*radd*)
Latin authors: Returning, restoring (*redditus, reditio*)

[*Abbr.* III.35-36] Returning is when, with one star being placed under the Sun, another one applies itself to it. But since [the first one] is burdened by the Sun, it returns to the other what it is unable to keep. But secondly, if some one of the planets applies itself to another, retrograde one[108]—but, burdened by the necessity of retrogradation, it returns what it had acquired[109] from it.

[*Abbr.* III.37-40] However, [in] this returning [is] sometimes usefulness, sometimes unusefulness. Usefulness, however, is threefold. The first, when [the burdened one] receives the one pushing.[110] The second, when the one receiving is running forward [and each] were in a firm sign[111] or in the one following from it.[112] The third, [if the burdened one is cadent but the pusher is in a firm or succeedent sign].[113] Because if it had kept [what was given] when it was burdened, the intention of the present topic would have been burdened; but if [what was pushed] is received [back] by the other [while in a firm or succulent sign], it consoles.[114]

[*Abbr.* III.41-42] But unusefulness [is] twofold. The first, when a free [but cadent] star applies itself to a burdened [but firm or succeedent] star, but the burdened one returns the application to it (whence the intention of the present topic is frustrated).[115] The second one [is] whenever, with each being burdened, the returning falls into severity (whence the present topic is deprived of both a beginning and an end).[116]

---

[108] Reading *retrogrado* for *retrogradus* to be more in line with the Ar.
[109] Or, "drawn on" (*traxerat*).
[110] Reading with the Ar. for *redditionem*. That is, if it is a case of pushing nature.
[111] An angular sign.
[112] A succeedent.
[113] Adding based on the Ar., overlooked by Adelard.
[114] Adding based on the Ar., in order to make the meaning clearer.
[115] I have reconstructed the sentence based on the Ar. and *Gr. Intr.* Adelard seems not to have understood which planet was doing what, and reads: "The first, when a burdened star applies itself to a free star, but the free one returns the application to it (whence the intention of the present topic is frustrated)."
[116] The applying planet represents the beginning of the matter or its current state, and the receiving planet its future state or endpoint.

[*Gr. Intr.* VII.5.1033-1058] But "returning" comes to be in two ways. One, that a planet would be joined to a planet under the rays, and it would not be able to retain what it received from it, and thus it will return it. Secondly, that a planet would be joined to a retrograde planet, and it returns to it what it received from it on account of its retrogradation.

Then perhaps the returning will be with fitness, or perhaps it will be with detriment.[117] But returning with fitness comes to be in three ways: one that the planet to which it is pushed is receiving the pusher. Secondly, that the pusher is direct in course, and the one to whom it is pushed is burned up or retrograde, and both are in an angle or in the follower to an angle. Third, that the planet [receiving the pushing] would be burned up or retrograde [or] cadent from the angles, and the pushing planet in an angle or in a follower to an angle. But if they were so, and the cadent or burned or retrograde one received the arrangement, it destroys the matter. If however the receiver returned to the pusher and the pushing one were in an optimal place, it will make the matter fit after destruction.

Also, its returning with destruction comes to be in two ways. One, that the pushing one would be cadent, and the retrograde or burned one to which it is being pushed is in an angle or in one following an angle. And since it returned to the pusher what it received from it (on account of its retrogradation or burning), and it was not advanced by it,[118] the matter will be destroyed after it was moving forward. Secondly, that the pushing one and the receiver are cadent or burned, and it will return to it what it received from it with its arrangement destroyed, on account of its condition of retrogradation or being under the rays: and the pushing one could not be able to advance with that matter. Then it signifies that there is neither a beginning nor end to that matter.[119]

[al-Qabīsī III.20] "Returning" follows this. This is when a planet is being connected to another planet which is being burned up or is ret-

---

[117] Or probably, "corruption" (Lat. *detrimento*).

[118] That is, the pushing planet will not be able to advance the matter properly because of its being cadent.

[119] The pushing planet represents the beginning of the matter, and the receiving one the end, but since both are in a bad condition, the matter never gets developed.

rograde, and it returns the virtue to it on account of its weakness. Then, if both planets were in an angle or in the succeedents to the angles, there will be a returning with profit. Likewise if only the one which is being connected to it were in an angle, and the one to which it is being joined, receives it. If however the planet which is being joined were cadent, and the one to which it is being joined [were] in an angle or in a follower to an angle, or if each were cadent, there will be returning with corruption.

[*BW* VIII.66] If the testimony of a significator were of the category of returning with corruption, it signifies the querent will regret the question.

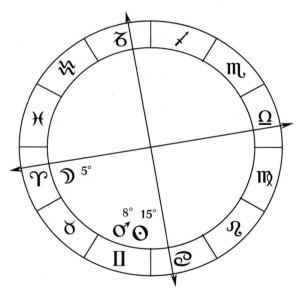

Figure 82: Returning with fitness or usefulness

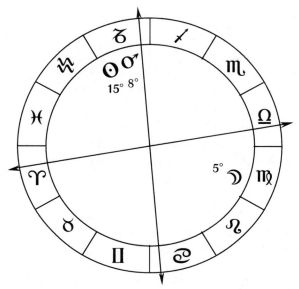

Figure 83: Returning with corruption or destruction

Comment by Dykes. The final stage of our "pushing" series is a description of situations where the pushing is unsuccessful: the pushing planet has attempted to push its nature, power, or management to another planet, but the one receiving the pushing cannot cope with the responsibility. Because the influence is returned, the pusher must handle matters on its own—which might not turn out so well. Returning always suggests some harm to the matter, and the question is whether or not the pusher has enough strength and fitness to advance the matter by itself. Thus one might regret the effort because of the missteps, but may still be able to make a good show of it.

The first figure above is one of returning with fitness. The Moon pushes nature to a burned and cadent Mars. He is harmed by the burning and is in a place of retreat (III.4), so cannot or will not cooperate with her, and sends her influence back somewhat worse for wear. However, because she is angular, she has the commitment to advance the matter (III.2) despite the rejection and whatever harm attends the matter due to Mars. The second figure is one of returning with unfitness or corruption. The Moon pushes management to a burned but angular Mars. He is harmed by the burning, such that even though he is angular he is too burdened and must return the influence to the Moon. But the Moon, being peregrine and cadent, finds herself too burdened as well, and cannot well manage the matter alone.

§III.20: Revoking

Arabic: Revoking (*'intikāth*)
John: Restraint (*refrenatio*)
Hermann: Objection (*contradictio*)
Adelard: Revoke, annul (*revocatio*)

[*Abbr.* III.43] Revoking is whenever, with planets prepared for application, the one of them[120] is not available for the application [because it is] made retrograde.

[*Gr. Intr.* VII.5.1059-61] "Restraint" is if a planet would be joined to another, but before it comes to it, the [first][121] one will go retrograde, and its conjunction will be annulled.

[al-Qabīsī III.21] Thence follows revoking, which comes to be when a planet wants to be connected to another, but, before it would complete the connection to it, retrogradation befalls it, and thus its connection is destroyed.

[*BW* VIII.67] If the testimony of a significator were of the category of revoking,[122] it denotes accidental circumstances[123] disturbing the matter.

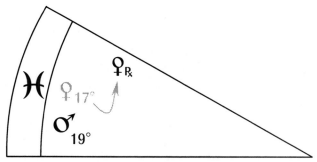

Figure 84: Revoking

---

120 That is, the lighter, applying one.
121 Reading for *alter*, which reverses the meaning of the sentence.
122 Reading for *refrenationis*.
123 *Res accidentes.*

Comment by Dykes. "Revoking" is one of the concepts which shows the failure of a connection, here by the retrogradation of the connecting planet. Traditional English texts transliterating directly from the Latin call this "refrenation," an unfortunate term that otherwise has no meaning in the English language. In my translation of Bonatti's *BOA*, I translated it accurately from the Latin as "restraint," but here I amend my views in light of the Arabic.

The Arabic *ʾintikāth* is based on the verb *nakatha*, which means to break or violate a promise or obligation, with some hint of disloyalty; it also means to untwist or unravel. The fact that this retrogradation concept was understood in terms of restraining or holding back (John) or calling back (Adelard) could reflect an earlier use of the Arabic verb to mean something like our "*going back* on one's word," but Adelard's *revocatio* is closest to the Arabic, with the notion of canceling, annulling, or revoking something done. Hermann's *contradictio* seems out of place, unless by it he means "saying the opposite of what one promised."

At any rate, the astrological meaning of this concept seems to be that some situation which seemed like it was going to complete, unravels—perhaps due simply to changing circumstances, but perhaps even due to dissuasion or a change of heart.[124] Like some other concepts in our list, it is of more immediate use in horary; but we must recall that in a nativity it might thematize a certain area of life as involving ongoing disappointments and difficulties in maintaining commitments.

---

[124] I myself have seen this in a horary chart in which someone who had agreed to go on a journey with someone else decided to decline due to changing circumstances and personal uncertainty.

§III.21: Obstruction

Arabic: Resistance, rebuttal (*i'tirad*)
John: Chance event (*accidens*)
Hermann: Hindrance, obstruction (*impeditio*)
Adelard: Interruption, breaking up (*interruptio*)

[*Abbr.* III.44] Interruption is whenever, with three of the planets being in order (the last one[125] of which seeking to apply itself to the middle one), the quickest one in front [is] made retrograde [and] breaks the application, running in between them.

[*Gr. Intr.* VII.5.1062-68] A "chance event" is if a light planet would have many degrees, and another one more weighty than it would be in fewer degrees, but [there is] a third one lighter than the aforesaid lighter one, wanting to be joined to that same weighty one, and the light one (namely the one which is in more degrees) will go retrograde and be joined to the weighty one through its own retrogradation. After this, it will cross over it and there will be a conjunction of the third one which is lighter than the lighter one, with the retrograde one weightier than it, not with the other weighty one.

[al-Qabīsī III.22] Obstruction follows this. This comes to be if some light planet had more degrees in a sign, and another more weighty than it in less degrees, [and] also a third one lighter than the first wanting to be connected to the weightier one—but, before it is connected to it, the lighter one which has more degrees becomes retrograde, and it is connected [instead] to the weightier one, and, passing over it, it is even connected to the other lighter planet: and thus the connection of the earlier one with the weighty one is destroyed.

[*BW* VIII.68] If the testimony of a significator were of the category of obstruction, it denotes an emerging matter[126] cutting off the thing he asked about.

---

125 That is, in an earlier degree than the rest.
126 Epstein reads, "something will happen," which exactly parallels John's use of *accidens*.

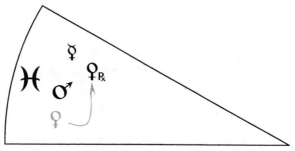

Figure 85: Obstruction

Comment by Dykes. Like revoking, obstruction[127] prevents the connection between two planets by retrogradation. But whereas revoking involves the applying planet breaking its own connection and going retrograde, here an otherwise uninvolved third planet goes retrograde and obstructs the connection. In the figure above, Mercury wants to connect with Mars; but before he can, Venus turns retrograde and completes a connection with Mars first, and then Mercury is forced into a connection with her.

The Arabic *ʾiʿtiraḍ* does mean "resistance," but also rebutting, protesting, and the legal power of veto; it comes from the verb *ʿaruḍa*, which refers to obstacles which become visible and hinder something from happening. The verb is the equivalent of the Latin *obsto*, which likewise means to stand in something's path, block the way, and object to something—and is the basis for the English "obstacle" and "obstruct."

Hermann's *impeditio* or "hindrance, obstruction" is the most literal of the Latin translations. Adelard's *interruptio* is also intriguing, as the verb *interrumpo* means to break in on something which is happening, or to cut short some ongoing action. And this seems to be what the retrograde planet does: it steps in from out of nowhere, stands in the way of an ongoing connection, and presents itself as an alternative connection. Astrologically, my sense is that obstruction refers either to a chance distraction for the applying planet, or else an intentional act by an unrelated and intrusive party. John's use of *accidens* suggests he understood it as a chance distraction, since *accido* means to "come about, arise, happen to, befall"—as though something accidental (i.e., not essentially related to the present situation) arises and obstructs the flow of things.

---

[127] Burnett *et al.* call this "resistance."

§III.22: Escape

Arabic: Escape (*fawt*)
John: Disappointment, failure (*frustratio*)
Hermann: Escape (*evasio*)
Adelard: Flight (*fuga*)

[*Abbr.* III.45] Flight is when, with a star being situated in some place, the one following it applies itself to it, but the leading one goes in haste from the place—whence the following one applies itself with another before it reaches it.[128]

[*Gr. Intr.* VII.5.1069-73] Disappointment is if there is a planet going toward the conjunction of another planet, but before it reaches it, the one to whom it was being joined will be changed to the next sign, and when the pusher was changed [into the next sign] there will be one of the planets closer to it than [the first one], and there will be a conjunction of it with that other planet, [and] its conjunction with the first [planet] will be disappointed.

[al-Qabīsī III.23] Escape follows. This, too, comes to be if some planet seeks the connection of another planet, but, before it reaches it, [the second planet] changes into another sign, and there will be some planet in few degrees aspecting the sign itself, and its rays will be at the beginning of the sign. And if the second[129] planet went out from the first sign, it will be connected to this aspecting one, and the connection which it was having with the first one will be annulled.

[*BW* VIII.36] If a planet seeks the conjunction of a second one, and before they are joined the second one crosses into the following sign and flees, [but] the first planet [follows] the one ahead of it, and it gets it in that [next] place, and another planet is not conjoined to it before [the first one] gets to it, the matter sought will be perfected after losing hope.[130]

---

[128] That is, when the applying planet follows the slower one into the next sign, it connects with a third planet before it can catch up to the one it originally wanted.

[129] Reading *secundus* for *sequens*.

[130] This is a case of recovering from escape.

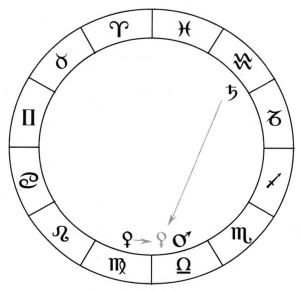

Figure 86: Escape

Comment by Dykes. The meaning of this term seems straightforward and clear. The Arabic *fawt* derives from the verb *fāta*, "to slip away, vanish, escape, leave behind." Hermann picks up on the notion of escape, and Adelard on leaving the applying planet behind, while John focuses on what it means for the planet left behind: *frustratio*, "disappointment, failure to achieve something."

Astrologically, escape refers to events or opportunities escaping or slipping out of one's grasp, fading away and disappearing. It seems to be an extension of the idea implicit in emptiness of course (III.9) and wildness (III.10), namely that new opportunities arise when planets enter new signs.

Although moving into another sign should be enough to show escape, the definitions go an extra step and describe how a different connection might take place in that next sign. In the figure above, Venus wanted to apply to Mars in Virgo, but Mars changed signs before she could make and complete a connection; once she followed him into Libra, she connected with the dexter trine of Saturn before she could catch up to Mars. Thus, the original intent of Venus is replaced by a new situation in which she applies to a different planet altogether.

This extra step may have been added for completeness: that is, to show that the opportunity to connect really is lost due to a connection with a third planet. Otherwise, one might still expect the connection to take place later in the next sign. And this is exactly what ibn Ezra envisions in his description of recovery from escape: if the connection does happen in the next sign before another planet interferes, the matter will finally be perfected after losing hope. On the other hand, the medieval authors might have insisted on it because it sets the stage for the second form of cutting the light below (III.23), which is essentially escape within the *same* sign.

§III.23: Cutting of light

Arabic: Cutting/sundering of light (*qaṭᶜ al-nūr*)
John: Cutting-off of light (*abscisio luminis*)
Hermann: Interception (*interceptio*)
Adelard: Hindrance (*impeditio*)

§III.23.1: Cutting of light #1

[*Abbr.* III.46] Hindrance comes to be in three ways. The first, when a following one is chasing after a middle one, but a leading one [in the following sign] becomes retrograde, and, applying itself to the middle one, it hinders the application of the following one. Which if [this] happened, an unexpected man will hinder the intention of the querent.

[*Gr. Intr.* VII.5.1074-84] The cutting of light comes to be in three ways. One, that there would be a planet wanting to be conjoined with another planet weightier than itself, and there would be another planet in the second sign from the lighter one, and before the lighter one would come to the conjunction of the weighty one, the planet which was in the second [sign] from it will go retrograde and will enter that sign, and it will be joined with [the weighty one] and will cut off [the lighter planet's] light from the planet to which it was wanting to be joined. And if that same conjunction signified the perfection of some matter, and the condition of the two planets were in this manner (concerning the cutting of the light of each of them from its companion), thus it will signify that a man will come up to[131] the Lord of the matter[132] unexpectedly, [and] he will destroy his matter and cut off his attainment [of it].

[al-Qabīsī III.24a] The cutting of light also follows this. This is that some planet would seek the connection of another, and another [third] planet would be in the second sign from the sign of the one to which it is being connected; but before the first one would be connected to it,

---

[131] *Occurret.* This can also indicate confrontation.
[132] That is, the querent or person represented by the first applying planet.

the [third] one which is in the second sign becomes retrograde and is connected to it, and it cuts off its light from the planet which was wanting to be connected to it.

[*BW* VIII.70] But if it were of the category of the cutting-off of light, it signifies [another] man destroying the thing he sought.

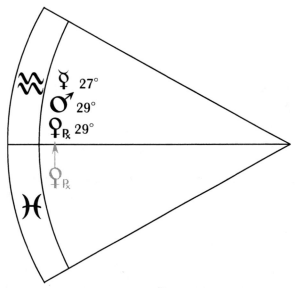

Figure 87: Cutting of light #1

§III.23.2: Cutting of light #2

[*Abbr.* III.47] The second [kind of hindrance]: whenever, with three planets being in order, and with the middle one chasing after the one first [in order], the one in the middle[133] runs past [the first one], and hinders the application of the [last] one in the rear by its own application. Which if [this]

---

[133] Reading with *Gr. Intr.* and al-Qabīsī for "rear." Adelard seems to have misunderstood the planetary scenario.

happened, the intention of the querent will be turned aside near its endpoint, by an intentional change of his will.[134]

[*Gr. Intr.* VII.5.1084-92] Secondly, that a light planet would be joined to a planet weightier than itself, and that planet would push to another weightier planet, and before the light planet would reach the degree of the one weightier than itself, that planet would be joined to the other weightier planet, and it would cross over it. And there will be a conjunction of the lighter one with that same weighty one, and its conjunction with the first one will be annulled. And this signifies that that man, in the seeking of the matter, will find something of the signification of the nature of that planet, and he will be eager in it until he reckons he will attain it, and then it will escape[135] and something else will come into his path.[136]

[al-Qabīsī III.24b] Likewise, if there were a planet going toward the connection of another planet, and that other planet to which it wants to be connected seeks the connection of [yet] another planet more weighty than itself; but, before the light one would reach the degree of the weightier one, the weighty one itself is connected to the other one more weighty than itself, and it cuts off its light from the first, lighter planet.

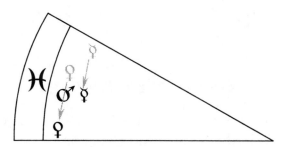

Figure 88: Cutting of light #2

---

134 Burnett says that this last sentence matches one of the Arabic manuscripts, though he did not use it in his critical edition of the Arabic.
135 *Frustrabitur* (Ar. *fātaha*), the technical word for "escape" (III.22).
136 *Accidet* (Ar. *fiaraθa*), the technical word for "obstruction" (III.21).

§III.23.3: Cutting of light #3

[*Abbr.* III.48] [The third kind of hindrance: that a planet would apply to a planet which is not the Lord of the topic, or a planet applies to it and it transfers its light to one other than the Lord of the topic.][137]

[*Gr. Intr.* VII.5.1092-95] Thirdly, that a planet would be joined to a planet which is not the Lord of the matter, or it would be joined to a planet which would transfer its light to another planet which is not the Lord of the matter.

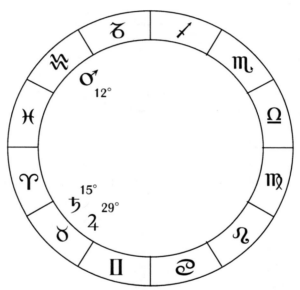

Figure 89: Cutting the light #3

Comment by Dykes. The meaning of "cutting" is relatively straightforward: *qaṭaʿa* means to cut something off (such as a limb), but has the more precise sense of sundering a connection in something or between two things: for example, it also means "to engage in highway robbery," which explains why Latin astrological texts often refer to robbers as "cutters of roads": obviously, they cut off a path and interrupt the flow of its traffic. Another

---

[137] Adding based on the Ar. and *Gr. Intr.* below. Al-Qabīsī does not include this type, probably because it does not really involve cutting off the light. It is puzzling that Abū Ma'shar felt the need to include it.

meaning of the verb is "to come to a standstill, to expire," which helps explain why planets and directions which signify death are sometimes called "cutters": they interrupt the flow of life and cut it short.

The Latin terminology is pretty accurate. Hermann's *interceptio* is absolutely precise: the verb *intercipio* means to intercept something and cut it off from its destination, to break the continuity of something, and also to cut something's life short. Adelard's *impeditio* only means to be hindered or obstructed. John's *abscisio* derives from *abscido*, which means to amputate or cut off (a straightforward meaning of *qaṭaʿa*), and, intriguingly, to banish hope. But he probably intended it to be derived from *abscindo*, to break something's continuous flow, to cleave: he might rather have coined a term such as *abscissus*.

The first two forms of cutting are variations on previous concepts. Cutting #1 is really obstruction (III.21) from the following sign. In the figure above, Mercury is connecting with Mars, but before he can complete the connection, the retrograde Venus enters from the next sign and blocks him. Since adjacent signs cannot aspect each other, which suggests a lack of awareness or constructive relationship between them, Abū Ma'shar says that a planet suddenly cutting the light from the next sign indicates that someone will appear *unexpectedly* and prevent the applying planet from completing its connection.

Cutting #2 is essentially escape (III.22) within the same sign. The middle planet escapes from the planet in the earlier degrees, continues past the planet in the later degrees, and ultimately the first and last planet come to be connected instead (just as in obstruction). In the figure above, Mercury wants to complete a connection with Venus. But Venus escapes from him (though still in the same sign), passing by Mars, and Mercury ends up connecting with Mars instead. Therefore, insofar as the earliest planet represents a person's intention, Abū Ma'shar says it will be disappointed (escape), and something else will befall or happen to him (obstruction).

Cutting #3 does not really fit well here as a combination of other definitions. It is closely focused on questions (horary), and simply refers generically to an applying planet (representing some issue) being prevented from connecting with some other desired planet. These are probably the reasons why al-Qabīsī omits it. In the figure above, Mars is the Lord of the Ascendant and represents the querent; we might imagine that it is a question about travel or religion (9th house), ruled by Jupiter the Lord of Sagittarius. But Mars instead connects with Saturn, whose body stands in the way.

§III.24: Largesse & Recompense

Arabic: Bestowing favors, recompense (na'mah, mukāfa'ah)
John: Largesse, repayment (largitio, retributio)
Hermann: Compassion, recompense (compassio, remuneratio)
Adelard: Patronage, paying back (patrocinium, mutuo reponere)

[Abbr. III.49-51] But patronage and lending are whenever, with a star situated in its own well or in its own humbleness,[138] a partner-star of its own proper quality[139] or its place (by domicile or kingdom or another kind of dignity) chases after it, and the chasing planet were in the domicile of the humbled planet (or in some dignity of it): whence it lifts it up from the well or humbleness. The one which is lifted up will be under [the other's] patronage until it pays it back in turn. [Sometimes the Lord of the kingdom of the planet's sign will be called the master of its patronage.][140]

[Gr. Intr. VII.5.1096-1107] Largesse and repayment is if a planet is in a well, or in its own descension, and a planet would be joined to it, or it would be joined to a planet friendly to it (or to the Lord of its triplicity, or to one of those which have some dignity in the sign), or it will be to one pushing or receiving testimony in its own sign. Then, [the second planet] will extract it and lead [it] out of the well or from its descension, and it will not cease to be its debtor until that planet which bestowed the largesse will fall into a well or into its own descension, and one of them would be joined to the other and lead it from the well or its own descension: and it will already be as though repaying it for its largesse, and as though observing faith to itself with respect to this. And perhaps the Lord of the exaltation of the sign of the planet will be called the master of his largesse.

[BW VIII.71] If the testimony of a significator were of the category of largesse, it signifies a man who does good for him.

---

138 That is, "descension" or "fall."
139 The Ar. reads "friendship," but Adelard might be thinking of friendship between planets, which is defined below in III.26 below as including planets which have one nature (such as being benefic).
140 Adding based on the Ar. and Gr. Intr.

[*BW* VIII.72] If however [it were of the category] of repayment, it signifies he will do good to others besides.

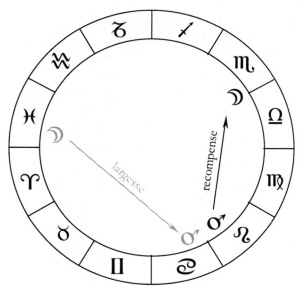

Figure 90: Largesse and recompense

Comment by Dykes. The Arabic *na'mah* has as its root verb *na'ama*, which on the one hand means to live in comfort and happiness and to be carefree, but also to be coddled, and to bestow favors upon someone and be graciously disposed towards them. The sense is obviously that the planet bestowing largesse is taking care of the planet in a welled degree or in its own fall. I have favored John's Latin in naming this concept rather than "favoring" or "bestowing favors" because his term is very close to the Arabic, and will not create confusion when other Latin authors like Hugo speak of planets treating each other well and bestowing "favors" upon them (*faveo*). Hermann's *compassio* shows the gracious disposition of the planet bestowing largesse, but does not actually suggest the bestowing itself. Adelard's "patronage" is intriguing because it comes from *patronus*, an influential person who takes another under his or her care or protection; but we normally think of patronage as ongoing employment, not something for which the patron needs to be recompensed. In the figure above, Mars begins in his fall, and the Moon (the domicile Lady of Cancer) applies to him, bestowing largesse so that he is lifted out of his fall. Later, Mars recompenses her when she is in her fall in Scorpio and applies to him again. Note that largesse can take place with either dignities or friendship (see III.26-17 below), and it does not matter who is applying to whom.

Largesse and recompense seem to be examples of pushing management involving one planet in fall. However, I am not exactly sure of their practical use. If largesse stood by itself, it might indicate in a nativity how one area of life indicating depression or obscurity (the planet in fall) is aided by another person or other area of life (the planet bestowing largesse). In that case, we might expect such situations of helplessness and aid to be activated when the relevant planets make certain transits or are activated by profection or another timing method.[141] But since largesse is paired with a later transit indicating recompense, it seems that it might have been used primarily for horary situations, when one might track the timing of a past or future situation.

---

[141] See VIII.2 below, and the guide to predictive techniques in Appendix F.

§III.25: Reception

Arabic: Reception (*qubūl*)
Latin authors: Reception (*receptio*)

[*Abbr.* III.52-55] Reception is whenever, with a star being situated [somewhere], and with another one in the domicile of [the first one] chasing after it, the one placed [there] receives, from the one chasing, what it conveys and offers.[142] For the other occupations of dignities are not very efficacious unless two [dignities] come together in one [planet]: like triangularity[143] and the bound, or the bound and face, or the like.

And there is another kind of reception: when some one of the planets occupies the trigon of the other, or the hexagon together with it, [but without an application, though reception with an application is stronger].[144]

And moreover, if one is arising by as many degrees as another, [or] even if the days of one sign were equal to those of another, or if even the two signs belonged to one Lord.[145]

[*Gr. Intr.* VII.5.1108-24] Reception is that a planet would be joined to a planet from the domicile of the one to which it is joined, or from its exaltation or bound, or from its triplicity or face, and it would receive it. Or, a planet would be joined to a planet, and the receiver of the conjunction is in the domicile of the pusher or in the rest of its dignities which we said before. And the stronger of these will be the Lord of the domicile or of the exaltation. However, if the conjunction were only with the Lord of the bound or the Lord of the triplicity, or with the Lord of the face, the reception will be weak, unless the bound and triplicity are being joined,[146] or the bound and the face, or the triplicity and the face: because then it will be a perfected reception.

---

[142] This is a case of pushing nature (III.15).
[143] Triplicity.
[144] Adding based on the Ar. and *Gr. Intr.* below.
[145] These are three types of agreement by sign from I.9.3 (equal daylight), I.9.5 (equal ascensions), and I.9.6 (same domicile Lord).
[146] That is, if the receiving planet is the Lord of at least two of these lesser dignities.

Also, the planets receive each other by aspect without a conjunction, but the reception of the conjunction is stronger.[147] Namely, if each one of the planets were unified in a trine or sextile aspect of the other, or in two signs of equal ascensions, or whose length by day were one [and the same], or in two signs which belonged to one planet: for each of them receives its companion through the concord of the nature of these signs to one another.

[al-Qabīsī III.19b] And this whole "pushing" is called "reception."

[*BW* VIII.39] If a received planet were a fortune, its strength is augmented; but if a bad one, it will be diminished from its evil.

[*BW* VIII.73] But if from the category of [mutual] reception of [each] significator to the other, it signifies the appearance of an unexpected thing.

[*BW* VIII.74] If however [the reception] were of the category of generosity,[148] it signifies the querent and sought thing are esteeming each other.

Comment by Dykes. The forms of reception described in these passages force us to take another look at the notion and language of "reception," since they do not all conform to classical or standard reception: when a planet applies to one of its dispositors. First of all, the text outlines three classes of reception: (1) by connection, (2) by whole sign, and (3) by alternative sign agreement. But we must also recognize that the term "reception" is fundamentally related to pushing generally: a receiving planet is archetypally the planet which gets influence pushed to it. Not all of these classes of reception involve pushing, and the language of domicile ownership adds an extra di-

---

[147] Abū Ma'shar means that reception can take place by whole sign configurations alone and not only by a connection by degrees. But note that he also suggests (perhaps as a last resort) planets whose signs agree in some way.

[148] That is, in a reception that does not involve a connection by degree. Ibn Ezra seems to have given the title "generosity" to this type of reception because of Abū Ma'shar's ambiguous use of the word "receive" in the next section, which deals with generosity proper (III.26).

mension to the idea of receiving another planet. Let us first describe the mechanics of reception and then look at its meaning.

(1) Reception by connection. This class has two types, and each involve one
planet in the dignities of the other. What I will call "classical" or "standard"
reception is simply pushing nature: if a planet applies to one of its dispositors
(preferably the Lord by domicile or exaltation). But the second type allows
the dispositor to apply to the other one. The following figure illustrates both
types:

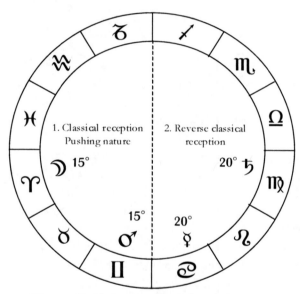

Figure 91: Two receptions by connection

On the left side of the figure is classical or standard reception (pushing
nature): the Moon is in the domicile of Mars, and is in an applying (actually,
exact) connection with Mars. On the right side is a similar situation but with
the pushing reversed: Mercury is completing a connection with Saturn, who
is in Mercury's domicile. In both cases, one of the planets is in the dignity of
the other, and they are in an applying connection.

(2) Reception by whole sign. As I read the texts, the second class of reception
still requires a proper dignity-relation between the two planets, but they may
be configured by a sextile or trine rather than an applying connection. The
figure below illustrates this:

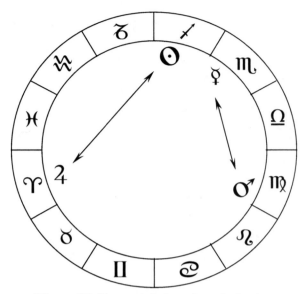

Figure 92: Two receptions by whole sign

On the right, Mars and Mercury are not in an applying connection, but they are in a whole-sign sextile and in each other's domiciles: this is a whole-sign mutual reception by sextile. On the left, the Sun is in the domicile of Jupiter, and Jupiter in the exaltation of the Sun: this is a whole-sign mixed reception by trine.

(3) Reception by alternative sign agreement. This class seems to expand or make more interesting some of the sign relationships described above in I.9 and as expounded by Porphyry and others.[149] As I read the texts, no dignity relationship is needed: the planets need only be in any of the signs which share the following agreements: by equal daylight (I.9.3), equal ascensions (I.9.5), or the same domicile Lord (I.9.6). Still, I must imagine that this—admittedly weaker—form of reception would be enhanced by dignity relationships. Certainly, reception by equal daylight and equal ascensions would be enhanced if the planets were in degrees which had precisely the same daylight or ascensions. The figure below illustrates these three types:

---

[149] See Schmidt 2009, pp. 275-78.

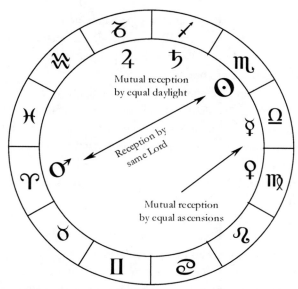

Figure 93: Three receptions by sign agreement

On the right, Mercury and Venus receive each other from their domiciles, because Virgo and Libra have equal ascensions; surely if they were in degrees which shared the same ascensions (such as 20° Virgo and 10° Libra), the reception would be enhanced. At the top, Saturn and Jupiter receive each other from their domiciles, because Sagittarius and Capricorn are signs of equal daylight. Again, if they were in degrees which shared the same hours of daylight, it would likely be enhanced. Finally, Mars receives the Sun in Scorpio, because both planets are in signs ruled by the same planet—namely, Mars himself.

My own sense is that reception by connection is the primary form of reception, particularly classical or standard reception (pushing nature), while all others are metaphorical and have been classed as reception for that reason. Let me say a few words about the Arabic term, and renew some comments I made about reception in my Introduction to *Works of Sahl & Māshā'allāh.*

The Arabic *qubūl* derives from the verb *qabila*, which encompasses the following meanings:

1.   To accept or receive something or someone (including abstract objects like requests), especially in a friendly or hospitable way.[150]
2.   To agree, yield, or consent to something or someone.[151]
3.   To vouch for someone.[152]
4.   To stand opposite something or someone, confronting, encountering, meeting, including receiving someone in audience.[153]
5.   To draw near something or someone, giving one's attention and showing interest, including applying oneself gladly to a task.[154]
6.   To kiss.[155]
7.   (Mixed form) To turn one's face towards something or someone or to receive a visitor or guest.

To my mind, these meanings really make the most sense for the first class of reception, either a planet applying to its dispositor (pushing nature) or the dispositor applying to it. I will assume it from this point forward.

The first and most important thing reception does is guarantee perfection of a matter.[156] This is so not only for the final dispositor of a matter,[157] but for any of the planets which must push management over the matter from one to another: if they receive each other, they help ensure the integrity and success of the matter. But if the management finally arrives at a bad final dispositor without reception, then the outcome will be unfavorable.[158]

Reception is said to provide these results in several ways. Generally speaking, received benefics produce a stronger good, while received malefics impede less.[159] Reception takes away the evil from a situation, so that a planet's signification will not suffer, even if it is in a bad place.[160] A received planet (or rather the person signified by it) will be able to bear its own problems more easily.[161] And one reason this seems to be so, is that the received planet is allowed to produce *itself*, despite bad circumstances. So for instance,

---

[150] Based on Arabic verb forms I and V.
[151] Based on Arabic verb form I.
[152] Based on Arabic verb form I.
[153] Based on Arabic verb forms III and VI.
[154] Based on Arabic verb forms IV and VIII.
[155] Based on Arabic verb form II.
[156] *OR* Ch. 5.
[157] See *OR* for Māshā'allāh's use of a final dispositor.
[158] *OR* Ch. 4.
[159] *Judgments* 25; *On Rev.* Ch. 23.
[160] *On Quest.* §10.3.
[161] *OR* Ch. 3.

in a question about illness and death, if the Lord of the 1st is received by the Lord of the 8th, the querent will live.[162] Although this aspect would normally be a classic sign of perfection—i.e., death—in such cases the Lord of the 1st is allowed to produce life. Likewise, if the Lord of the 1st received the Lord of the 8th, then although the Lord of the 8th is allowed to produce something like death and harm, the friendliness and benefic qualities conferred by reception will not allow the native to be destroyed.[163]

There are several qualities, including moral qualities, which reception is said to involve. Perfection with reception adds *esteem* (though whether this means one planet is esteeming the other in particular or not, is unclear);[164] planets in mutual reception will *make peace*, even if there is (or despite) a difficult aspect between them—so they will have good intentions and amenability toward one another;[165] a received planet's significations will be accompanied by *joy and security*;[166] a received planet has *allies*;[167] and *truth* and *knowledge* are involved: complete reception by domicile or exaltation involves truthful intentions, but a lack of reception can show a lack of knowledge, familiarity, or understanding.[168] Reception can take away someone's disgrace in a bad situation, or confer honor in a neutral one.[169] And in cases where a leader is deposed, if his significator is received (even if peregrine, which again means being a pilgrim or foreigner), it shows him returning home.[170]

If we put all these details together, I think we can see that reception is essentially about having a surrogate home—a form of support that does not depend on one's own ownership and responsibilities. Unlike being in one's own domicile, where one can rely on oneself, received planets have others helping and esteeming them; and it is as though the received planet is vouched for. This notion of a surrogate home explains why received planets have joy and security, can perfect reliably (because they have support), show a connection to home and returning home, have honor instead of disgrace, have allies, involve truthful intentions (as though they are trusted), and have peaceful relations with their receivers.

---

[162] *OR* Ch. 3.
[163] *OR* Ch. 4.
[164] *OR* Ch. 8.
[165] *OR* Ch. 1.
[166] *On Rev.* Ch. 19.
[167] *On Rev.* Ch. 25.
[168] *Introduct.* §§5.8-9.
[169] *On Quest.* §§10.3, 10.7.
[170] *On Quest.* §10.8.

Note the claim that received malefics impede less. One might question this—after all, why shouldn't they be able to harm more, since they are so supported in their efforts? I think we can understand this somewhat better if we think of medieval feudal relations.[171] In the medieval period, attachment to a lord or other institutional authority (with its own moral and legal standards of conduct) was an important way of establishing oneself as stable, loyal, and dependable. The modern idea of the unattached individual existing by himself would have struck traditional people as strange and suspicious. If we imagine the difference between a warrior who is unattached to any fixed purpose—and thereby is unpredictable and dangerous—and one who has become *domesticated* and *disciplined* through service to a Lord, I think we can see analogically why a received malefic would impede matters less than an unreceived one.

---

[171] Or medieval warrior culture in general, which might very well apply to the Islamic milieu in which Sahl and Māshā'allāh lived.

§III.26: Generosity and benefits[172]

[*Abbr.* III.56-57] But[173] all of the above-stated signs which belonged either to one Lord or one nature, are friendly to each other. Even all of the prosperous stars are generous between themselves, since their natures [are] similar; but the unprosperous ones are generous between *themselves*.

[*Gr. Intr.* VII.5.1125-28] But the fortunes receive each other on account of the proper mixture of their nature. Even Mars and Saturn: each of them receives the other from the conjunction and the sextile or trine aspect.

[al-Qabīsī III.31b] If however two planets agreed in [both] nature and substance[174] (like Jupiter and Venus), they are friends.

[*Abbr.* III.58-62] In generosity however, certain ones are found to be stronger, certain ones weaker, certain ones middling. But the greatest generosity is between the Sun and the Moon. For the Moon takes from the Sun in any sign except for the opposite (which is harmful). If therefore the Moon came into a sign in which the Sun enjoys some dignity, her benefit is doubled: for one favor is from the sign, the other from the nature. If another planet were in Virgo, Mercury presents two benefits to it. But a mediocre benefit is what any star receives from another, either from the domicile [alone] or from the kingdom or from the face or from the triplicity or from the bound—of which, if two [benefits] would be gifted, it will be greater. But anything other than the aforesaid will be weak.

[*Gr. Intr.* VII.5.1129-41] But of reception there is a strong reception, and a middle one and a lesser one. But strong reception more often comes to be from the Sun to the Moon, because he receives her from all the signs for the reason that her light is from him. But his reception from the opposition is horrible. If however her conjunction with him were from a sign in which he himself had dignity, there will be two receptions: namely reception of nature and reception of sign. Also, when

---

[172] This section should be read with reception (III.25).
[173] The rest of *Abbr.* III is only found in the Latin version.
[174] Or, "essence." This probably refers to their benefic-malefic qualities.

Mercury receives a planet in Virgo, the reception will even be strong (because it is his domicile and exaltation).[175]

But the middle reception is the reception of the planets to each other from domiciles, or from the exaltation or bound, or from the triplicity or face. Which if the two of these were collected, or all, and one of them received its companion, the reception will be strong. However, the rest which we stated are less than these.

---

[175] This comment was added by John.

§III.27: Friendship and enmity: al-Qabīsī

[al-Qabīsī III.30] And with the planets it is said that certain ones of them are esteeming or hating each other. But of the esteeming ones, certain ones of the ancients said that Jupiter esteems all planets, and that he is their friend, and they [are] his—except for Mars. All planets are friends of Venus, and all esteem her except for Saturn. But the friends of Saturn are Jupiter, the Sun and Moon; and his enemies [are] Mars and Venus, and she hates him more. And the friend of Mars is Venus, and the rest of the planets hate him, and Jupiter[176] hates him more. But the friends of the Sun are Jupiter and Venus, [and Saturn],[177] and [his] enemies Mercury and the Moon. The friends of Mercury are only Jupiter and Venus and Saturn; and his enemies the Sun, Moon, and Mars. But the friends of the Moon are Jupiter, Venus and Saturn, and her enemies Mercury and Mars. The friends of the Head of the Dragon are Jupiter and Venus, and [its] enemies Saturn and Mars. But the friends of the Tail of the Dragon are Saturn and Mars, and [its] enemies the Sun and Moon, Jupiter and Venus.

And another kind of enmity is if there were two planets having their domiciles as opposites.[178]

A third kind of enmity is if the exaltations of two planets were opposites.[179]

[al-Qabīsī III.31a] But a stronger friendship of the planets is that a planet would agree with a planet in nature and in common quality and substance and dignity: just as Mars agrees with the Sun, because each agrees in heat and dryness and sharpness and quickness, and [Mars] is the Lord of the exaltation of [the Sun], in which [the Sun's] strength appears; and as the Moon and Venus agree in cold and moisture, and [Venus] is the Lord of [the Moon's] exaltation.

---

[176] Omitting "and the Sun," as these two are said to be friendly below.
[177] Adding with the Ar.
[178] That is: Saturn-Moon (Capricorn-Cancer), Saturn-Sun (Aquarius-Leo), Jupiter-Mercury (Pisces/Sagittarius-Virgo/Gemini), Mars-Venus (Aries/Scorpio-Libra/Taurus).
[179] That is: Sun-Saturn (Aries-Libra), Venus-Mercury (Pisces-Virgo), Mars-Jupiter (Capricorn-Cancer).

§III.28: Bodyguarding or *dustūriyyah*

§III.28.1: Bodyguarding according to al-Qabīsī

[al-Qabīsī III.6] And from this the *dustūriyyah* of the planets. This is if a planet is in its own domain, and in some one of the angles of the Ascendant, and some one of the luminaries likewise in its own domain[180] [is] in its square, namely in an angle, so that [it is the Sun in the day and the Moon by night].[181]

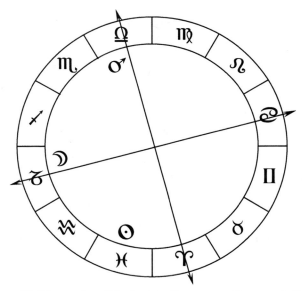

Figure 94: Example of bodyguarding according to al-Qabīsī

---

[180] See III.2, but here it seems to be a synonym for "sect." Thus, it may not require that the planet also be in a sign of its own gender, but possibly be (1) only a member of the sect of the chart, or (2) on the favored side of the horizon.

[181] Reading more closely with the Ar. for John's "a planet in the day is oriental of the Sun and in the night occidental of the Moon." Note that Al-Qabīsī's description does not mention any degree requirements for the aspects, and that the options for bodyguarding here are limited if both planets must be both in their own domains and in angles. I take it that only a luminary can be bodyguarded: thus in the figure above, the Moon in a nocturnal chart is being bodyguarded by Mars.

§*III.28.2: Medieval bodyguarding type 1*

[*BA* II.12a] Whenever any other [star] regarded a star placed in a pivot (in its own domicile, I say, or kingdom), from a pivot and domicile or kingdom. As, if Venus would be staying in the east (namely [in] Libra), under the aspect of Saturn from Capricorn, and [he] placed in the pivot of the earth; but if it would be traversing outside of the pivot, while however each [star] would be enjoying the mutual aspect from the trigon or hexagon or tetragon or opposition, *dustūrīyyah* would not be absent–of which manner is Venus being in an arising Libra, under the regard of Jupiter from the hexagon [in Sagittarius].

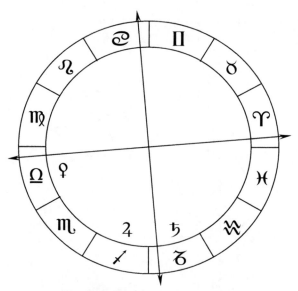

Figure 95: Medieval bodyguarding type 1

§III.28.3: Medieval bodyguarding type 2

[*BA* II.12c] Moreover, with the Sun and the Moon [in the Ascendant or the Midheaven, even if] established outside their own domiciles and kingdoms, but under the regard of the stars which we called "at rest" above, [such that the planet bodyguarding for the Sun aspects the degree rising before the Sun; but for the Moon, the degree after the Moon], another kind of *dustūrīyyah* occurs. [And the trigonal bodyguards are better than the tetragonal or oppositional ones, while the hexagonal ones are weakest.]

Indeed there is a *dustūrīyyah* of the Sun with him in Aries when it arises, or [with him] lingering in the Midheaven, while Saturn holds onto Capricorn or Aquarius. We call *dustūrīyyah* lunar while [the Moon] would be traversing in an arising Cancer, [and] Mercury would be staying in Virgo, Venus in Libra.[182]

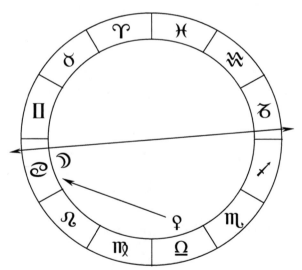

Figure 96: Medieval bodyguarding type 2 (nocturnal)

---

[182] This lunar example is only in Rhetorius, and the solar example must have been invented by Māshā'allāh or found in some other source.

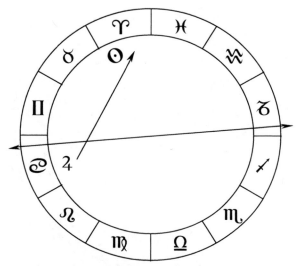

Figure 97: Medieval bodyguarding type 2 (diurnal)

§III.28.4: Medieval bodyguarding type 3

[*BA* II.12b] And there is another kind of *dustūrīyyah*, namely while any star occupies the east [or] holds onto the Midheaven, [but] any other–namely a diurnal one in a diurnal birth, a nocturnal one under a nocturnal one–[accompanies it as a bodyguard]. [The Sun will be accompanied by bodyguards which precede him, but the Moon by bodyguards following her within 7°. Bodyguards preceding the Sun by at least 15°, having come out of the rays, will not harm him. In the same way, the Sun and Moon can be bodyguards for a sect-mate which is in a pivot.]

Moreover, it was all right to be called "restlessness" or preferably anxiety[183] while diurnal [stars] aspect nocturnal ones, [and] nocturnal ones diurnal ones, from the [ones on the] right.[184]

---

[183] *Inquietas* and *sollicitas*, respectively. These referring to being contrary to sect.
[184] This statement by Māshā'allāh echoes *Gr. Intr.* VII.2. 175-96 and later texts like *BOA*, where Bonatti calls *dustūrīyyah* "dextration." Abū Ma'shar reduces bodyguarding to being part of the solar phase cycle, in which the superior planets engage in *dustūrīyyah* once they have emerged from the Sun's rays until they are about 90° away from him. But the third type of bodyguarding has sect and angularity requirements as well. See my comments below.

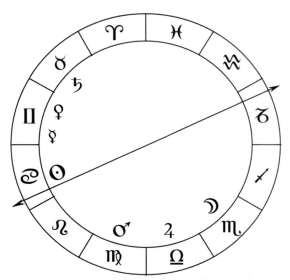

Figure 98: Medieval bodyguarding type 3 (diurnal)[185]

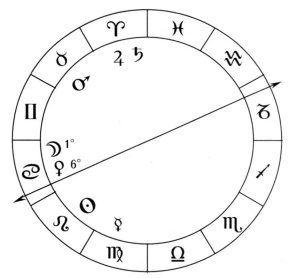

Figure 99: Medieval bodyguarding type 3 (nocturnal)[186]

---

[185] In this diurnal chart, Saturn and Mercury are diurnal bodyguards for the Sun because they rise before him. I take Venus to be a contrary-to-sect planet bodyguarding for the Sun, but the definitions might require that the bodyguards always be of the sect of the chart, while the protected planet may be of either: in that case, Venus would be irrelevant because nocturnal planets cannot be bodyguards in a diurnal chart. Jupiter, Mars, and the Moon do not fulfill any version of the definition and so are not part of the bodyguarding.

§III.28.5: Ptolemy's bodyguarding

[Latin *Tet.* IV.3] *On the native's prosperity and worth.*[187] But it is necessary to observe matters of worth, and his prosperity in social value,
from the qualities of the luminaries and of the stars surrounding[188]
them, and in the same way we attend to their likeness[189] in this.

(1) For if each of the luminaries were in masculine signs, and each
(or either of them) appeared in angles, but especially the one which was
the master of the sect,[190] and the five wandering stars surrounded
them, and the morning ones [were] surrounding the Sun, and the eve-
ning ones appeared to be encircling the Moon, we will not doubt that
the native will be a king.

(2) But if the stars which surround them likewise appeared in angles,
or they had fellowship in the figure with the angles appearing above
the earth, the native will be of great worth and most powerful, and a
king of the world. His fortune will even be increased if stars were surrounding on the right, and they were associated with the angles
appearing above the earth.

(3) If however the qualities of the rest of the stars were just like
these, and only the Sun turned in a masculine sign but the Moon in a
feminine one, and one of them were in the angles, the native will be
solely a governor,[191] and have the power over life and death.[192] Which
if in addition the surrounding stars did not appear in angles, nor did
they testify to them,[193] the native will only have a great name, and his
worth will appear just as that of one who rules one part [of the world],

---

[186] In this nocturnal chart, Venus bodyguards for the Moon because Venus is in a degree
rising after the Moon, within 7°.

[187] Lat. *valetudine*, "worth, social value," here translating the Gr. *axia* or "value, worth," i.e.,
eminence or social rank.

[188] I.e., bodyguarding.

[189] This probably refers to sect.

[190] *Haiz.* That is, the luminary of the sect of the chart. The Greek text focuses on the sect
light having the five planets as bodyguards, rather than as being angular—though being
angular would be a definite bonus.

[191] Reading with the Greek for *solius regiminis.*

[192] Reading with the Greek for *interfector.*

[193] The Greek apparently names the pivots as the places not being testified to; but it is
impossible that a planet could be anywhere and not aspect at least one of the pivots. My
sense is that this either means (a) that it does not aspect an axial degree within a few degrees, or else (b) it is not testifying to *the luminaries.*

or just like the dominion of a manager,[194] or dominion over an army, and not like the dominion of one[195] who manages the whole kingdom.

(4) And if most of those surrounding stars (but not the luminaries) appeared in angles, or if they had fellowship with them in the figure, he will not be of such worth, nor even of such a great name, and he will be ignored.[196] However, he will prevail in managing cities, and will be middling in managing the affairs of life.

(5) If however the stars which surrounded the luminaries had no likeness with the angles, the native will appear miserable and unlucky in his works.

(6) Which if the luminaries appeared neither in angles nor in masculine signs, nor even did the fortunes surround them, he will be at the lowest [level] of misery and improsperity.

(7) The path, therefore, by which one must advance in the investigation of these matters (concerning the increase and diminution of worth), is this one which we have shown. We must observe how many more qualities there are between increase and diminution, by means of those things which were found in that view of the particular alteration which the luminaries and the stars which surround them have, and the ones which manage the surrounding ones.[197] For if [the bodyguards] were masters of the sect or [they were] fortunes, the native will endure in great worth. If however they were masters of the contrary sect, or they were infortunes, his worth will appear weak, and will easily pass by.

(8) But one must observe the matters of future worth from the proper qualities of the stars which surround the luminaries. For if the manager of this matter were Saturn, the strength of the worth will be in the multitude of assets, and will persist in the gathering together of money. But if Jupiter or Venus appeared as it, his strength will be in favors and donations, and in honorifics and magnanimity. Which if it

---

[194] *Baiuli,* i.e. someone who manages or acts on behalf of a ruler.

[195] Omitting the unknown transliteration *alcaidis,* clearly a synonym for a governor or ruler.

[196] This is extremely close to Rhetorius Ch. 53, who probably took it from Ptolemy or Ptolemy's source. Rhetorius is a bit clearer that the bodyguarding stars are angular while the relevant luminary is actually cadent (probably in the 6th or 12th).

[197] This complicated sentence simply means that just as the luminaries and the bodyguards and their dispositors might be of varying sects, benefic/malefic qualities, in or out of angles, etc., so will the native's social worth be higher or lower.

were Mars, it will be in the dominion of expeditions and in victories, and in his subordinates' fear. And if it were Mercury, it will be in intellect and teaching, and in the managing of matters.

Comment by Dykes. The three "medieval" definitions above come from Māshā'allāh's *Book of Aristotle*, which relied on a version of Rhetorius for the formulations but not always for the actual examples. These definitions were based in turn on formulations in Antiochus and Porphyry (see Schmidt 2009), and I take them to be Hellenistic-era standards. But we can also see that Ptolemy felt justified in offering his own approach, as did al-Qabīsī.

The Greek word for this concept is *doruphoros*, which literally means "spear-bearer" but describes the function of a bodyguard and retinue (*doruphoria*). In modern dictionaries the Arabic means "constitutionality," but medieval Latin texts sometimes describe it as "security" (which is closer to the Greek), and it is clearly related to the Ar. *dast*, a place of honor or position of prestige, or being in "the front" of something, and *dustūr*, a rule or law or code. All of these words together suggest social value, command, and protection, and by extension eminence, power, and prosperity.

But there are several important unanswered questions about bodyguarding. For instance: (1) what exactly does bodyguarding contribute, as opposed to other eminence considerations;[198] (2) what is the difference in social impact between the three "medieval" types; and (3) do versions such as Ptolemy's rival more standard or legitimate types, or does bodyguarding simply come in many different and irreconcilable forms? Answering one of these questions might lead to answering all or many of them. I am not prepared to offer answers at this point, but Denningmann's work in German on this whole topic may be of use.[199]

Al-Qabīsī's version. Whatever the answers to these questions, by the end of the medieval period much of the Hellenistic and Ptolemaic definitions of bodyguarding had disappeared in favor of one or another version of al-Qabīsī's. Al-Qabīsī's version seems closest to Hellenistic Type 1, and seems to require that only the luminary of the sect can have a bodyguard. Although his definition uses "domain," which is a technical term in III.2, I could see it

---

[198] For those, see Appendix F below.
[199] See Denningmann 2005 in the Bibliography. I myself hope to translate or at least comment on major portions of this book in the future.

referring to dignities as well, as though al-Qabīsī is taking over a definition in which domain was originally equivalent to the domicile or exaltation mentioned in Type 1. Also, I can also imagine that "domain" here might not really require being in a sign of the same gender, but perhaps only on the favored side of the horizon (i.e., nocturnal planets above the horizon in a nocturnal chart, but below it in a diurnal one; and diurnal planets above the horizon in a diurnal chart, but below it in a nocturnal one). Finally, domain might simply be a synonym for being a member of the sect itself. This gives us several possibilities for what al-Qabīsī's definition really is:

- Both planets fully in their own domains as defined in III.2. I have crafted the example above to fit this version.
- Both planets only on the appropriate side of the horizon, and not necessarily also in a sign of the same gender (i.e., being in *ḥalb*).
- Both planets in their own domicile or exaltation, without regard to sect-based horizon placement or sign gender.
- Both planets being a member of the sect of the chart, without regard to dignity, sect-based horizon placement, or sign gender.

Hellenistic-medieval type 1. None of the Hellenistic-era astrologers require that both the protected planet and its bodyguard be pivotal (angular), though Antiochus does say that the protected or bodyguarded planet is preferred to be angular. Māshā'allāh wants both planets to be angular (perhaps for maximum effect), but immediately concedes that bodyguarding can still be present if they are not. In Porphyry's own definition, he underscores that this type of bodyguarding contributes to eminence, and he prefers that the bodyguards be members of the sect of the chart. One point of contention between Antiochus and Porphyry is whether or not the bodyguarding planet has to be aspecting a degree in front or behind, and indeed which planet it is in front of or behind (*viz.*, the bodyguarded planet or the bodyguard). In a future work I will state some of my own thoughts about this. At any rate, Māshā'allāh and his source in Rhetorius do not mention it.

Hellenistic-medieval type 2. In this type, only a luminary is bodyguarded, and without regard to dignities (unlike in type 1). I assume that we should prefer the luminary of the sect, but at any rate the bodyguards must belong to the sect of the chart. In addition, this type explicitly requires "striking with a ray" or "hurling a ray," which limits the location of the bodyguards. Although Schmidt[200] has developed his own position on what constitutes hurling a ray,

---

[200] Schmidt 2009, pp. 202ff and 254ff.

I will tentatively adopt the older assumption that it requires the hurling planet to be to the left of the other planet. Thus, the luminary must be in the Ascendant or Midheaven, and the bodyguard must be in a sign following it (see examples).

It is probably in reference to this and the first type of bodyguarding that Rhetorius Ch. 53 states that if planets bodyguard an angular Sun, it shows great eminence; but if they guard a cadent Sun, the native will only be a friend of eminent people. See the fourth paragraph of Ptolemy's treatment, which makes a similar point.

Hellenistic-medieval type 3. Here, just as in type 1, any planet may be guarded (although one should probably prefer a luminary), and like type 2 it must be in the Ascendant or Midheaven; likewise, as with type 2 the bodyguard must be of the sect of the chart even though it can guard one of the contrary sect. There seem only to be special rules for the luminaries: the Moon's body-guards must be in a later degree than her, but no more than 7° away; and the Sun's bodyguards must rise before him and thus be in an earlier degree. In examples by Antigonus,[201] it seems as though the Sun's bodyguards can rise before him anywhere up to approximately 90° before him. The statement about planets not harming the Sun may refer to the malefics: the idea seems to be that if malefics were under the Sun's rays, they would not be able to harm in any case, but that if they were assembled with him in the same sign outside of his rays, it might normally be harmful for him to be associated with them: but apparently if he is angular and they are rising before him, such is not the case.

Ptolemy's version. Ptolemy's instructions are helpful in pointing out that the identity of the bodyguard is important, but they are somewhat unhelpful by leaving it unclear how planets should be related to certain angles or houses, and which ones. Of greatest interest is his arrangement of bodyguarding into ranks, but here we must be careful. For on the one hand, he does give us helpful hints for comparing different scenarios; but on the other hand, he presents his types as though they describe a native's social position abso-lutely. This is contrary to other assumptions of his and is not exactly supported by the other texts. For instance, in *Tet.* I.2 Ptolemy argues (as do later astrologers) that the natal chart can only show relative types, not abso-lute ones. So we should expect that a native with an especially auspicious bodyguard situation might not be *the* king or queen in his or her country ab-

---

[201] Schmidt 2009, pp. 350-67.

solutely, but might be *king- or queen-like in his or her own environment*: if a beggar, then a king or queen of the beggars, and the consulting astrologer should have some biographical information about the native to begin with in order to make sound judgments. But even if Ptolemy does mean that the native may only be a relative king or queen (such as of the beggars), we must remember that the exact nature and contours and (in some cases) definitions of bodyguarding are still unclear. Ptolemy's ranking of different types of royalty, managers and generals may only be a convenient device, and we should beware of making definite judgments on the basis of it alone.

BOOK IV: PLANETARY CONDITIONS

[*Abbr.* IV.1] So much for these [aforementioned] things. But now the fourth promise must be fulfilled.

[al-Qabīsī III.25a] Also, these planets have places in which they are strengthened, and in which they are weakened, and places in which they become fortunes, and places in which they become bad ones.

§IV.1: The good fortune of the stars

[*Abbr.* IV.2-3] Therefore the good fortune[1] of the stars will be if a benevolent regards a benevolent[2] either from a hexagon or tetragon or a trigon or unification; or they would not be regarded by malevolents;[3] even to head from a benevolent to a benevolent; being well arranged between two good fortunes; but even if [they would be in the same degree or minute as the Sun],[4] and also if they should regard the Sun from a hexagon or trigon; [or in the aspect of the Moon, with the Moon being fortunate],[5] but even quick motion and an increase of light; even being in [their *ḥalb*, or being in][6] a place in which they enjoy either some dignity or a joy; but even being in bright degrees, or their own domains.[7]

[*Gr. Intr.* VII.6.1145-61] But the fortune of the planets is that planets would be in the aspects of fortunes from the sextile or from the square or trine aspect, or they would be joined to them. Or the bad

---

[1] Lat. *felicitas.* Ar. *saʿādah,* "happiness, bliss, prosperity, good fortune." This is the same Arabic word used for the Lot of Fortune.
[2] Or rather, that any planet would be in such an aspect of a benevolent: see below.
[3] I.e., that the malevolents would be cadent from them or in "aversion" to them, by whole sign.
[4] Reading with the Ar. and *Gr. Intr.* for "even if benevolents were in the same degree or minute."
[5] Adding with the Ar. and *Gr. Intr.*
[6] Adding with the Ar., and following *Gr. Intr.* below.
[7] Reading *ḥayyiz* with the Ar., for "places suited to their own sex."

ones would be cadent from them. Or they would be being separated from a fortune and be joined to a fortune. Or they would be besieged between two fortunes. Or united with the Sun or in his trine or sextile aspect. Or in the aspect of the Moon (with the Moon being fortunate). Or they would be quicker in course, increased in light and number. Or they would be in their goodnesses, that is, in their own domiciles or in their own exaltations or in the bounds or triplicities or faces, or in their joys. Or they would be in the bright degrees. Or they are received. Or they are in their domain: this is that a masculine[8] planet would be in a masculine sign and masculine degrees in the day above the earth and in the night under the earth, and a feminine one in a feminine sign and feminine degrees in the day below the earth and in the night above the earth. Also, if the luminaries were in the dignities of the fortunes, it would be practically as if they were in their own proper dignities. And each fortune becomes likewise if they were in the dignities of the luminaries.

[al-Qabīsī III.25b-26] But the places in which they become fortunes are these: namely that they are in the aspects of the good ones (naturally in the sextile or in the square or in the trine), or they are assembled with them, or the bad ones would be cadent from them; and they would be separated from a fortune and connected to a fortune, or they are besieged by fortunes. For this is a besiegement, that a planet would have a fortune or its rays in front of it, and another fortune or its rays after it. And certain people called this "being surrounded." Or, they would be united with the Sun in one degree, or they would be in his sextile or trine aspect, or in the aspect of the Moon (and the Moon then being made fortunate), and that they would be quicker in course, increased in light and number, or they would be in their own *halb* or in their own domain, or in signs in which they would have dignities, or in their own joys, or in the bright degrees, or received.

---

[8] See III.2: this should be a diurnal planet, and likewise a nocturnal planet in the last half of the sentence.

§IV.2: The power of the stars

[*Abbr.* IV.4-7] But the power[9] of the stars is if they should arise northern or be situated [there]; that they should be moved to apogee;[10] even being in the second station; going out from the rays of the Sun; being in a firm sign or one next to it;[11] of the three superiors, even to appear at daybreak; [it is] even stronger to have [a sextile] ray sent [to it];[12] even to be in male quarters. For if the Sun were in male quarters and male signs, he will be strong—with the exception of Libra, because even though it is masculine, still the Sun is in no way strong in it.[13] However, the power of the inferiors is if they should appear in the west[14] or in female quarters.

[*Gr. Intr.* VII.6.1182-91] Also, the strength of the planets is that they would be ascending in the north, or [simply] northern. Or they would be ascending in the circles of their apogees, or they would be in the second station, or going out from under the rays of the Sun, or they would be in an angle or in one following an angle. Or the three superior planets would be eastern from the Sun (and if [at the same time] he aspected them from a sextile aspect it will be stronger for them). And that they would be in the masculine quarters. Also, if the Sun were in these quarters or in the masculine signs he will even be stronger, unless he is in Libra. And, in terms of the strength of the three inferiors, it is that they would be western or in feminine quarters.

[al-Qabīsī III.27] And in terms of their power, that they would be ascending into the north or they would be northern, or they would be ascending in the circle of their apogee, or they would be in the second station (this is when they were in their station so that they would move forward from retrogradation), or they would be going out from under the Sun's rays, or in an angle or in the follower of it, or the three higher [planets] would be eastern of the Sun (which if they aspected him by a

---

[9] Lat. *potentia*. Ar. *quwwat'hā*, "power, strength, capacity."
[10] Reading with the Arabic for "being raised up" (*sublimationem*).
[11] That is, in an angular or succeedent sign.
[12] Reading with the Ar. and *Gr. Intr.* That is, to be a superior planet rising before the Sun, and in a sextile to the Sun.
[13] Libra is the sign of the Sun's fall.
[14] That is, to be setting after the Sun. See II.10.2 above.

sextile aspect this will be an increase of power for them), or [the supe-riors] would be in male quarters. And the Sun will even be powerful if he were in male quarters or in male signs, unless he is in Libra. And in terms of the power of the three inferiors, that they would be western of the Sun or in feminine quarters. And of the power of the Moon, that she would be above the earth in the night (and in the day below the earth) in a feminine place or in a feminine sign,[15] and if she were in the exaltation of the Sun, [or the Sun aspects the Moon's domicile].[16]

§IV.3: The impotence of the stars

[*Abbr.* IV.8-14] The impotence[17] of the planets is: walking slowly; being in the first station or turning backwards. But the worst [is] the retrogradation of Venus and Mercury, particularly if they are [also] being hidden by the Sun; or [planets are] found [under the rays of the Sun or] in dark degrees. Also, [a masculine planet][18] being in female signs or degrees under the earth in the day [but] above [it] in the night; [or a feminine planet in male signs or de-grees, above the earth by day or under it by night];[19] being in the sign of [its] slavery;[20] descending in the south [or being southern]; not being in either a firm [sign] or the one next to it; even being in the burnt place (that is, in Li-bra or Scorpio);[21] but even in [its own] estrangement;[22] even to be applying to a retrograde star. Of the three superiors, appearing in the west[23] or being in the female quarters. And the impotence of the Sun is to be in a female quarter or female signs [unless he is in the ninth place, his joy].[24] [For the

---

[15] That is, in her own domain (*ḥayyiz*).

[16] Adding with the Arabic. I take it this means the sign she is in, not simply Cancer.

[17] Lat. *impotentia.* Ar. *ḍuʿf*, "weakness, feebleness," related to the verb "become weak, frail, impotent, flabby, to slacken, abate."

[18] Again, here and below Abū Ma'shar and al-Qabīsī should be referring to "diurnal" and "nocturnal" planets, since Mars is a masculine but nocturnal planet. But they seem to want to use the gender of the planets as a shorthand for domain, since it is a gender-heightened condition of *ḥalb.*

[19] Adding the information for feminine planets to make the contrast complete.

[20] That is, its fall.

[21] That is, the burnt path or *via combusta*). Some texts define this as between 15° Libra and 15° Scorpio, others between the fall of the Sun in 19° Libra and the fall of the Moon in 3° Scorpio. See the *Gr. Intr.* excerpt.

[22] Or, detriment.

[23] That is, setting after the Sun (so that the Sun will overtake them).

[24] Adding with the Ar. and *Gr. Intr.*

inferiors, to be at the beginning of their easternness or in the masculine quarters.][25]

[*Gr. Intr.* VII.6.1192-1218] But in terms of the weakness of the planets, and their signification over the diminution of fortune, it is that they would be slow in course, or in the first station, or they would be retrograde. And the worse retrogradation is the retrogradation of the two inferior planets, and particularly if they would be burned up along with the retrogradation. Or, a planet would be under the rays or in the dark degrees. Or,[26] masculine [planets] in feminine signs or in feminine degrees, in the day under the earth and in the night above the earth. And that the feminine [planets] would be in masculine signs or in masculine degrees, in the night below the earth and in the day above the earth. Or, they would be in the sign of their own descension, or descending in the south or [be] southern, or cadent from an angle.[27] Or they would be in the burnt path (that is, in Libra and Scorpio), and more difficult than that if they were from the nineteenth degree of Libra to the third degree of Scorpio (because those are the descensions of the luminaries). And that they would be in the opposition of their own domiciles (because then they are inimical to them, and they are in their own detriment). And that they would be joined to a retrograde planet or to an impeded one, or one in its own descension, or cadent, or they were not received, or they were in peregrination—and more difficult than that if they were void [in course] and a fortune which esteems them, or, one from among the planets which agreed with them, did not aspect them. And that the three superior planets would be western of the Sun, or they would be in feminine quarters. And the weakness of the Sun is that he would be in feminine signs or even in feminine quarters, unless he is in the ninth house (which is his joy). And of the weakness of the three inferior planets, it is that they would be in the beginning of their [morning] arising, or they would be in masculine quarters.

---

[25] Adding with the Ar. and *Gr. Intr.*
[26] This is the opposite of being in one's domain; but see III.2 above.
[27] Omitting "or in a follower of the angles." This was a misread by John: see the wording in *Abbr.* above.

[al-Qabīsī III.29] And in terms of their weakness, that they would be slow in course or in the first station (this is when they are standing so that they would become retrograde), or they are retrograde, or they would be in dark degrees, or the masculine [planets] are in feminine signs and in feminine degrees in the day under the earth and in the night above the earth, or the feminine ones would be in masculine signs and in masculine degrees in the night below the earth and in the day above the earth; or they are in the opposition of their own dignities, or descending in the south or are southern, or cadent from the angles or from the succeedents of the angles (or: [that] they are in cadent houses), or they are in the burnt path (which is the last half of Libra and the first half of Scorpio), or they[28] would be connected to a retrograde planet or one impeded or cadent, or they are not received. Or, the three higher [planets] are western of the Sun or in feminine quarters. And the weakness of the Sun is that he would be in feminine signs or feminine quarters (unless he is in the ninth house). And in terms of the weakness of the three inferiors, that they would be eastern or in masculine quarters.

§IV.4.1: The misfortune of the stars

[Abbr. IV.15-18] The misfortune[29] of the stars is to be assembled with the malevolents; to be in the opposition of the malevolents [or in their square or trine or sextile, and there were less than a bound between them;[30] or if they were in the bound or domicile of a malevolent; or if a malevolent were overcoming them from the tenth or eleventh from their place].[31] But the greatest misfortune is applying themselves to a malevolent, [but] not being received by it.[32] [Or they are in the conjunction, square, or opposition of the

---

[28] Reading *iungantur* (pl.) for *iungatur*.

[29] Lat. *infortunium*. Ar. *nuḥūsa*, "bad luck, misfortune," related to the verb "be calamitous, ominous, unlucky, disastrous."

[30] I believe this means that the body of one planet is in a malefic bound, with the body or ray of another in it as well: the idea is that it would bring misfortune to the connection which they want to make.

[31] Reading with the Ar. and *Gr. Intr.*, and replacing Adelard's description of overcoming: "even for a malevolent to have arisen not a little amount at the hour of the chart."

[32] See below, where not being received worsens several of the conditions just mentioned, not just any aspect.

Sun.][33] Even to be in the Head or Tail of their Dragons; even if there were 12° or less between them and the Dragon;[34] but the worst [is] if the Moon were in these places. [For the Sun, to be within 4° of the Head or Tail.][35]

[*Gr. Intr.* VII.6.1219-33] Also, the misfortune[36] of the planets is that they would be conjoined to the bad ones in one sign, or in their opposition or in the square aspect, or in their trine or sextile aspect, and there were less than the bound of a planet between them and the bad ones. And that they would be in the bounds of the bad ones or in their domiciles. Or certain ones of the bad ones would be elevated over them from the tenth or eleventh [sign] from their place—and it will be more difficult than that in all of these places [if] the bad ones are not receiving them. Or, the bad ones would be in one sign with the Sun or in his square aspect or opposition. Or they are with the Heads or Tails of their own Node, or they would be with the Head or Tail [of the Dragon] and there were 12° or less between them and [the Nodes]: because then they will be in their Node. And [the Nodes] impede the Sun more severely if there were 4° between him and them, in front or behind. And they impede the Moon more severely if there were 12° between one of them and her, in front or behind.

[al-Qabīsī III.28a] But in terms of the misfortune of the planets and their destruction,[37] it is that they would be in the assembly of the bad ones or in their opposition, or in their tetragon or trigon or hexagon,[38] or if there were less than the bound of [the malefic][39] planet between them and the body or rays of a bad one,[40] or they would be in the bounds of the bad ones or in their domiciles, or [the bad ones] would be elevated[41] over them from the tenth or from the eleventh from their

---

[33] Adding based on the Ar. and *Gr. Intr.*

[34] Normally this is taken to mean the Moon's Nodes alone; but Abū Ma'shar may also mean this in relation to their own Nodes as well. See the table of planetary Node values in II.5.

[35] Adding based on the Ar. and *Gr. Intr.*

[36] Reading *infortunium* instead of *debilitas.*

[37] Al-Qabīsī uses *fasād,* indicating corruption.

[38] Omitting John's "by raying."

[39] Tentatively adding this clarification from Burnett.

[40] This would be approximately a connection.

[41] That is, "overcoming."

place; and much worse is if [the bad one] did not receive them. Or, they would be in the assembly of the Sun or his opposition, or in his tetragon,[42] or if they were with the Heads of their own Node, or with the Head of the Dragon [of the Moon] or its Tail, and there would be 12° or less between them and one of these; and especially if the Moon were likewise [that much] from any of them. And the Sun is impeded more by [the Nodes] if there were even 4° between him and one of them, before or behind. Or, were the planets besieged between the two bad ones.

[al-Qabīsī III.28c] And of this, that a planet would be retrograde or burned up under the Sun's rays, or cadent from the Ascendant.[43]

§IV.4.2: Enclosure or besieging

[Abbr. IV.21-25] And there is another kind of misfortune which is called "enclosure."[44] But this is twofold. First, with some star between two malevolents or between two rays of malevolents, or if it heads from a malevolent to a malevolent. And likewise concerning the rays.

The second kind of enclosure is if [a planet would be in a sign], with a malevolent [or its ray in the second sign from it, and] it finds a malevolent [or its ray] in the twelfth sign from it; or, if a [planet] were not found in it [but it were the Ascendant or some other sign,] that sign itself is enough for [having] enclosure.[45] If however the Sun or another prosperous one regarded it in this place, it releases [it] from the evil. Which if it occupied the seventh [degree] from the degree of the Sun, or if benevolent stars were in front of it or behind it [by that much], it will be liberated in the best way.

---

[42] Omitting John's "by raying."

[43] That is, being in aversion to it: in a sign which does not aspect the rising sign, particularly the twelfth, eighth, and sixth; the second sign is also cadent from the Ascendant but is not considered as difficult.

[44] I.e., "besieging." Lat. importunitas ("trouble"). Ar. ḥaṣr, "encirclement, confinement, besieging."

[45] Reading this second type with the Ar. and Gr. Intr. Adelard has switched a couple of key terms, making the condition barely recognizable: "it will be associated with a malevolent in the same sign or with its light; or if it finds a malevolent in twelfth sign from it; or, if a malevolent were not found in it, that sign itself is enough for trouble."

[*Gr. Intr.* VII.6.1244-60] Also, another impediment is what is called "besieging." And it comes to be in two ways. One, that a planet would be in some sign, and there is a bad one (or its ray) with it in the same sign, in front of it and[46] behind; or a planet would be separating from a bad one by the conjunction of one sign or by aspect, and it would be joined to another bad one in this condition.

The second manner of besieging is that a planet would be in some sign, and a bad one is in the second sign from it by its own body or its ray, and the other bad one also (or its ray) in the twelfth sign from it. Which if there were not a planet in it, and the condition of the Ascendant (or the rest of the signs) were thus, the Ascendant or that sign will be besieged.

And in [besieging by degree],[47] if the Sun or a certain one of the fortunes aspected the besieged planet by an aspect of friendship, and there were less than 7° between that planet and its rays, it signifies the loosening of that evil. And if the sign were besieged and a fortune or the Sun aspected it as above, they dissolve that impediment. And if a planet or sign were besieged by the fortunes, this will be of the more worthy fortunes.

[al-Qabīsī III.28b] This is if a planet is in some sign, and in addition a bad one or its rays is in front of it, and a bad one or its rays after it. Or, it would be diverted from a bad one by assembly or by aspect, and it would be connected in such a way to another bad one.

Or, a bad one or its rays would be in the sign which is in front of it, and another bad one or its rays was in the sign which is after it. It is said likewise about signs that they are besieged.

Which if a fortune or the Sun aspected that same besieged planet from a trine or sextile aspect, and there were less than 7° between it and the connection, the malice will be loosened.

[*BW* VIII.76] [But if a significator is] from the class of being-in-the-middle [between infortunes], it denotes [prison and torture; if between fortunes], a good condition is going to come.

---

[46] Reading *et* for *aut*.
[47] Reading instead of "in all of these."

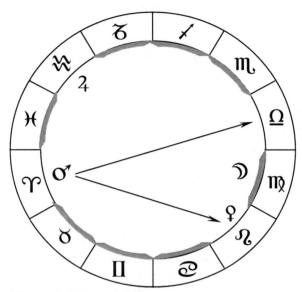

Figure 100: Malefic enclosure/besieging by sign

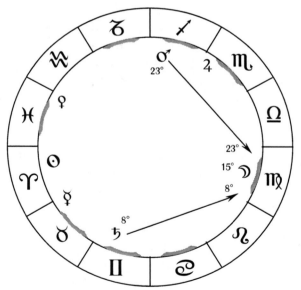

Figure 101: Malefic enclosure/besieging by degree

Comment by Dykes. Enclosure or besieging has two forms: by surrounding signs alone, or by degree. Both forms derive from Hellenistic practice, and our medieval sources preserve the basic descriptions well.[48] Enclosure is one of our 120° concepts, which we have already seen above, in assembly and regard (III.5-6), emptiness of course (III.9), and wildness (III.10). Let me explain the mechanics of enclosure and its relationship to other configurations, and then offer some ideas about its precise meaning.

Malefic enclosure by sign requires—at a minimum—that one malefic be aspecting the signs on either side of some sign or planet, with that malefic not aspecting the sign itself, and both benefic planets must be in aversion to that sign: that is, they must be in the 120° of the zodiac which forms the signs in aversion to it. In the above case, the Moon in Virgo is enclosed by sign by Mars in Aries:[49] the gray portions of the zodiac are forbidden to the benefics. But since the luminaries and Mercury can also be considered benefic in their actions and effects, in its maximal form this type of enclosure would require that *all* other planets be in aversion to the enclosed sign or planet. In its minimal form then, malefic enclosure is not as bad as wildness, since it restricts only the benefics to being in aversion. But in its maximal form, it would be identical to wildness: in the figure for wildness in III.10 above, the Moon is wild and in aversion to all other planets, but is being enclosed by the bodies of Mars and Saturn on either side of her sign.

Why do the texts not describe any benefic enclosure by sign? My conjecture is that astrology makes a default assumption: that planets will be able to move forward and perform their actions *until* something intervenes or restricts them. So for instance, we do not normally pay much attention to direct motion except as a counterpoint to retrograde motion: we assume that a planet's normal state is to move forward, *until* it is restricted and changed by retrogradation. Just so, we assume that planet have a general freedom and many relationships to others *until* they are enclosed by sign or encounter some other obstacle. Thus a benefic enclosure by sign is too general, and too much part of our default assumptions about planetary freedom, to be notable. Perhaps we should take more note of it?

---

[48] The only thing really missing is Porphyry's and Hephaistio's note that if the Ascendant or the Moon is enclosed by sign (i.e., with both benefics being in aversion), then the native will be poor and short-lived (Schmidt 2009, p. 195). This statement is probably meant in an "all other things being equal" way: surely if other features of the chart mitigate these problems, then it would not be so bad.

[49] This is in fact the example from Antiochus (Schmidt 2009, p. 195).

Just as our texts distinguish between aspects by sign alone and aspects by exact degree (III.6-7), so they distinguish between enclosure by sign and by degree. Malefic enclosure by degree requires that the body of a planet be enclosed between the body or ray of both malefics, up to 7° on either side, with no other planet casting a ray into one of those regions on either side. This too is one of our 120° concepts, because if we assume the greatest distance of 7°, then no planet can be within those degrees in any sign aspecting the besieged planet, effectively forbidding them from being in 120° of the zodiac. In the figure above, the Moon is in 15° Virgo, and is besieged on both sides by the squares of the malefics at the maximal distance of 7° on either side. Those degrees, plus the Moon's own, equal 15° total; in order for the enclosure to hold, there can be no planets in those degrees in the other signs configured to Virgo: that makes 8 forbidden regions of 15° apiece, or 120°.

However, enclosures or besiegings can be broken. In enclosure by sign, if a benefic moves into a sign which does aspect the enclosed planet, it breaks or prevents besieging. In enclosure by degree, a planet of opposite quality casting a ray into the region of enclosure will break or prevent it: a benefic planet will break or prevent a malefic enclosure by degree, and a malefic planet will break or prevent a benefic enclosure by degree. This breaking is nothing more than a version of barring (III.14), which is defined precisely as a planet's body or ray being in intervening degrees between two others: normally, it comes in between an applying planet and some other, but here it is broadened to include being on either side of the besieged planet. This kind of barring indirectly becomes part of the 120° group of concepts, since it falls into the forbidden range of degrees defined by enclosure. In the figure below I have put the ray of the breaking planet in front of the Moon in both cases:

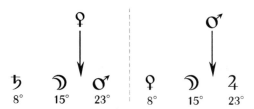

Figure 102: Breaking an enclosure by degree

As for what exactly enclosure or besieging and its breaking means, there are some clues in the passage by ibn Ezra above. I propose the following (omitting enclosure by sign as being very general):[50]

(a) Malefic enclosure by degree means: paralysis, fear, lack of hope, feeling kidnapped, being actively isolated and restricted, having one's efforts frustrated and destroyed—with all of the feelings of hopelessness and anger that may go along with that. But breaking such an enclosure means the introduction of hope, aid, liberation, especially by someone represented by the breaking planet.

(b) Benefic enclosure by degree means active support and protection, with all the feelings of ease and confidence one might expect from that; but breaking such an enclosure introduces doubt and skepticism, the poison of mistrust, and estrangement from one's helpers and friends.

From these considerations, I propose that the 120° concepts form something of a parallel series of configurations which illustrate a dialectical drama of closeness, loss, and recovery, each passing from a planetary relationship to passive isolation, to active isolation, to being freed—with perhaps the implication of later bodyguarding (III.28). That is, whether by whole sign or by degree, a planet can be dramatized as being in an active relationship, diverging or separating from it, finding itself alone, then finding itself trapped, then receiving aid and support again. As for the whole-sign series, it runs from aspect/assembly, through separation, to the passive isolation of wildness, to malefic enclosure by sign, to the breaking of enclosure. As for the degree-based series, it goes from a connection by degree, through separation, to the passive isolation of emptiness, to the malefic enclosure by degree, to the breaking of enclosure.[51]

---

50 These ideas were developed during a discussion with Chris Brennan and Demetra George.
51 I have illustrated this series in Appendix B.

§IV.5: The misfortunes of the Moon

[*Abbr.* IV.26-31] But the corruptions[52] of the Moon [are] eleven: the first [is] eclipse, especially if it were in the [sign it was in at the nativity][53] or in a trigonal or tetragonal [place] from it. The second, if she is hidden by the Sun. The third, when she is opposed to the Sun or is distant from [his] opposite by 12° before or behind, or she were in the square of the Sun.[54] The fourth, if she is with[55] the malevolents or is being regarded by them. The fifth, if she were in the twelfth-part of Saturn or Mars. The sixth, [being] in the Head or Tail of the Dragon. Seventh, [being] in the south, particularly if she were in the descending quarter.[56] The eighth, [being] in the burnt path. Ninth, [being] at the end of a sign, for there is the bound of an infortune. The tenth, [being] in the slowness of motion. The eleventh, [being] in the ninth sign from the horoscope.[57]

[*Gr. Intr.* VII.6.1261-77] Also, the impediment of the Moon comes to be in eleven ways. One, if she were veiled (that is, when she suffers eclipse)—and more difficult than that if she would be veiled in the sign in which she had been in the root of the nativity of a man, or in its triplicity or square aspect. Second, that she would be under the rays of the Sun and there would be 12° between her and [the Sun's] body, in front or behind. Third, if there would be an [amount] like these degrees between her and the minute of her opposition, while she goes toward his opposition, or while she is being separated from [the opposition]. Fourth, that she would be with the bad ones or they would aspect her. Fifth, if she were in the twelfth[-part] of Saturn or Mars. Sixth, if she were with the Head or Tail and there were 12° between her and one of

---

[52] Lat. *infortunium*, "misfortune. But Ar. *fasād*, "corruption, wickedness," what is usually translated as "detriment." Some of these correlate with the planets' impotence (IV.3) and misfortune (IV.4.1).

[53] Reading with the Ar. and *Gr. Intr.* for "Ascendant." Burnett notes that this comes from *Carmen* V.5.2 (which only mentions the trine). Perso-Arabic practice should also include the opposition.

[54] Neither the Ar. nor *Gr. Intr.* below add this.

[55] Reading with the Ar. for "being conjoined to."

[56] I.e., in the quarter of her circle which is where she actually descends in southern latitude. In the figure of the Moon's motion in II.5 above, that would be from the South Node in Cancer down to the lowest point in Libra.

[57] Perhaps because she will be in the opposite of her joy (which is in the third); but I am unaware of any technical term for that.

them. Seventh, if she were southern or descending in the south. Eighth, if she were in the burnt path (that is, in Libra and Scorpio). Ninth, if she were at the end of the signs, because there she will be in the bound of bad ones. Tenth, if she were slower in course, namely when she will go less than her average course. Eleventh, if she were in the ninth house from the Ascendant.

§IV.6: Twelfth-parts of the planets

[*Abbr.* IV.32-33] It is even appropriate for the twelfth-part of the stars to be known. Therefore, with a star appearing in any degree, [and] the number of its degree being multiplied by twelve and from thence being brought forth, distributed in the following signs, the last [sign] will be said to be the one receiving the twelfth-part of the star. If therefore the star were a benevolent, the twelfth-part will be good. But [if] malevolent, bad.

[*Gr. Intr.* V.18.1027-41] Because all those ancients wise in the stars divided each sign by twelve divisions, and each division will be 2 ½ degrees, and it is called "twelfth-part." And they did this for the reason that there would be the nature of the twelve signs in one sign. And the nature of its first division will be like the nature of that same sign; and the nature of the second division like that of the second sign from it, and the nature of the third division like the nature of the third sign— and likewise the rest of the twelve divisions.

And there is an abbreviated method for its numbering. This is that you should look to see how many degrees there are from the beginning of the sign up to the degree of and minute whose twelfth-part you want to know, and you would multiply that by 12, and whatever was collected, you will project it from the beginning of that same sign.[58] And where the number led you to, in that same sign is the nature of that same degree and its twelfth-part.

[al-Qabīsī IV.15] And among these is the twelfth-parts of the planets and houses. This is that you would look to see how much a planet will have walked in its own sign, or the degree of the house which you

---

[58] Omitting "giving two-and-a-half degrees to each sign."

wanted,[59] in terms of degrees and minutes, and you will multiply this by twelve. After this[60] you will project that from the beginning of that same sign, giving 30° to each sign: where the number were ended, there will be the twelfth-part of the planets and houses.

[BW VIII.46] If the strength of a planet's twelfth-part were in a good place, then the good will be increased.

	0°-2.5°	2.5°-5°	5°-7.5°	7.5°-10°	10°-12.5°	12.5°-15°	15°-17.5°	17.5°-20°	20°-22.5°	22.5°-25°	25°-27.5°	27.5°-30°
♈	♈	♉	♊	♋	♌	♍	♎	♏	♐	♑	♒	♓
♉	♉	♊	♋	♌	♍	♎	♏	♐	♑	♒	♓	♈
♊	♊	♋	♌	♍	♎	♏	♐	♑	♒	♓	♈	♉
♋	♋	♌	♍	♎	♏	♐	♑	♒	♓	♈	♉	♊
♌	♌	♍	♎	♏	♐	♑	♒	♓	♈	♉	♊	♋
♍	♍	♎	♏	♐	♑	♒	♓	♈	♉	♊	♋	♌
♎	♎	♏	♐	♑	♒	♓	♈	♉	♊	♋	♌	♍
♏	♏	♐	♑	♒	♓	♈	♉	♊	♋	♌	♍	♎
♐	♐	♑	♒	♓	♈	♉	♊	♋	♌	♍	♎	♏
♑	♑	♒	♓	♈	♉	♊	♋	♌	♍	♎	♏	♐
♒	♒	♓	♈	♉	♊	♋	♌	♍	♎	♏	♐	♑
♓	♓	♈	♉	♊	♋	♌	♍	♎	♏	♐	♑	♒

Figure 103: Table of twelfth-parts

---

[59] Obviously using quadrant houses.

[60] Omitting a redundant description: "on top of this [amount] which came out from the multiplication, you will add the degrees and minutes which you multiplied by twelve, and what was collected from that."

§IV.7: Times or changes

[*Abbr.* IV.34-36] And the changing of the planets must be understood, which has five parts: the first, if [a planet] were in the second or first station. The second, while it is being hidden by the Sun or goes out from being hidden; third, whenever a benevolent would apply itself to a bad one or neglect it.[61] The fourth, while it heads toward the degree of [its] slavery or the kingdom. Fifth, if it were in the last degree of a sign.[62]

[*BW* VIII.42] If a retrograde planetary significator of a matter goes direct, it signifies a portion of the matter [is completed]; and likewise if it were under the rays of the Sun and would go out from them.

---

[61] That is, "be separated" from it: see III.8 for this diversion or separation.
[62] For then it is about to enter a new situation.

BOOK V: PLANETARY NATURES

§V.0: Introduction

[*Abbr.* V.1-3] These things having been examined, even this should be attended to with no less diligence: because since the circles of the planets are placed some over the others, Saturn is found to be the highest of all. However, the second circle belongs to Jupiter; but the third to Mars; the fourth to the Sun; the fifth to Venus, the sixth to Mercury; the seventh to the Moon.

[*Gr. Intr.* VII.9.1383-88] In this section we want to describe the natures of the seven planets, and particularly their significations over existing things.[1] And not every thing which we describe in this section about the signification of each planet, is brought together in one [and the same] man, but perhaps much of those things are joined in him according to the extent of the condition of the planets in him, and [the planet's] condition in the houses of the circle.

[al-Qabīsī I.79-II.1] And because, with God assisting, we have already accomplished what we proposed to deal with regarding the circle of the signs and its accidents, let us continue and make mention of the seven planets and their natures, also their being and what they signify.

The second section, on the natures of the seven planets, and what proper [quality] they have, and what they signify about the being of things.

---

[1] Or perhaps, "over things we have discovered," which was how John read it.

§V.1: Saturn

[*Abbr.* V.4-7] But the nature of Saturn [is] malign, for he is cold and dry, melancholic, dim, stinking, gluttonous but still of good association, activities involving moist[2] things and waters and riverbanks and ploughing and plants and works of the hands; and when he shows provisions, he shows much; and when he takes away, he takes away much; greedy; a pilgrim in faraway and cold places; having one thing in his mouth, [but] another in his heart; occupied in evil; a traitor, solitary, a forcer, plunderer, torturer, jailer; but truthtelling, understanding, making things old,[3] deadly, an inheritor, chasing after old things; of grandfathers and great-grandfathers and fathers and full siblings born before [the native], and captives; occupied in knowledge, silent.

[*Gr. Intr.* VII.9.1390-1423] Therefore, the nature of Saturn is cold, dry, melancholic, dark, of heavy harshness. And perhaps he will be cold [and] moist,[4] heavy,[5] of stinking odor, and he is of much eating and true esteem. And he signifies works of moisture and the cultivation of land, and peasants, and village companions,[6] and the settlement of lands, also buildings and waters and rivers, and the quantities or measures of things, and the divisions of the earth, also affluence and a multitude of assets, and masteries which are done by hand, greed and the greatest poverty and the poor. And he signifies travel by sea, and

---

[2] Reading with the Ar. for Adelard's "moist."
[3] Or, making things last a long time (*inveterator*).
[4] For example, if he were eastern: see II.12. This is also used by Lilly in *Christian Astrology*, p. 533.
[5] Or perhaps, "oppressive."
[6] Or possibly, the "owners/lords" of villages.

foreign travel [that is] far away and at great length, and bad. And cleverness, envy and wits and seductions, and boldness in dangers and impediment, and hesitation, and being singular,[7] and a scarcity of association with men, and pride[8] and magnanimity and bluffing and bragging and the subjection of men, also the managers of a kingdom and of every work which comes to be with force and with evil and injuries and a tendency to anger, even warriors and fettering and prison, also truth in words, and esteem, and prudence and understanding, and experience, and offense, and obstinacy, and a multitude of thoughts and a depth of counsel, and insistence, and stubbornness in [his] method. He does not easily get angry, and if he were angry he would not be able to rule his own mind. He wishes good to no one. And he signifies old men[9] and weighty men and burdens and fear, griefs and sorrow and the complication of the mind. And fraud and affliction and difficulty and loss; also ancestors and what is left behind by the dead, mourning, and being orphaned, and old things. Even grandfathers and fathers and brothers, and senior people and slaves and mule drivers and men who are blamed, and robbers and those who dig up graves and who rob the garments of the dead. And fitters of leather and those who blame things. He signifies magicians and masters of discord,[10] and low-class men and eunuchs. And he signifies a great length of thought and a scarcity of speaking and the knowledge of secrets, and one does not know what is in his mind, nor does a wise person make disclosures to him about every obscure matter.[11] And he signifies austerity and the ascetics[12] of religions.

[al-Qabīsī II.2-7] Saturn is male, a bad one, diurnal. And he is a significator of fathers if the nativity were in the night. And he signifies the last [part of] old age if he were western, and the beginning of old age if he were eastern.[13] And he signifies the severity of cold and dryness.

---

[7] *Singularitatem.* This could mean either being alone, solitary, or else being strange or unusual.

[8] Or perhaps, "arrogance."

[9] The Ar. reads, "chieftains, senators, sheikhs."

[10] Or, "enticements" or "sedition."

[11] Reading with the Arabic. I believes this means one should hesitate because one does not know what he will do with the information.

[12] Or, "hermits."

[13] See VII.3 for what years each planet rules in the Ptolemaic Ages of Man.

And of the complexion of bodies, the melancholic—that is, its increase and disturbances.[14] And perhaps [the complexion] will be cold, moist, weighty, of a stinking odor. And he is of much eating and of true esteem.[15] And he signifies the depth of counsel and a multitude of silence.

And of masteries, watery things, valuable ones like the cultivation of fields, the population of lands and rivers (if he were fortunate), and low-class[16] ones if he were bad: like massaging in baths and fullers and sailors.[17] And if he were made fortunate, he will be of true esteem, taking time to do things;[18] and if he were bad, he will be obstinate,[19] unstable and sad and grieving, of bad suspicion, suspecting much, provoking men with whispers. And if he were fortunate, he signifies (of assets) ancient and lasting things, like real estate and the cultivation of the land; and if he were bad, he signifies [low-class property],[20] dirty waters and those with a bad taste, old and changeable.

And of illnesses, he signifies viscous phlegmatic and congealed melancholic diseases (like leprosy and cancers, morphew and gout and the rest of this kind).

And he signifies faraway[21] foreign travels, prison and fetters, also labor and delay and affliction and inheritance, even fathers and grandfathers and older brothers, eunuchs, slaves and low-class men.

And of works, he signifies the works of leather; if he were the sole significator, without the complexion of some one of the planets, he signifies the work of the common-laborer.[22] Which if Jupiter would be complected to him, it signifies the work of parchment in which divine books and those of judgments are written. And if Mars is complected to him, it signifies the sandals of shoemakers and their preparations. And if the Sun is complected, it signifies the work of sewn-up hides.[23]

---

14 Reading with the Ar. for "distillation" or "moistening, dripping."
15 Ar.: "trustworthy in friendship."
16 Or, "vile."
17 The Ar. adds: "serving drinks."
18 In the sense of taking a long time to do things. John adds: "and patient."
19 Reading with the Ar. for *indiscretus*.
20 Adding with the Ar.
21 Or, "long-lasting" (*longinquas*).
22 The Ar. reads "shoemaking," but perhaps John has generalized it because the Saturn-Mars combination below includes leather for footwear.
23 Ar.: "cobbler."

And if Venus is complected to him, it signifies the works of leathers from which drums and other instruments are made, which we use in entertainments. And if Mercury is complected to him, it signifies the work of leather in which wills and the accounts of taxes are written. And if the Moon is complected to him, it signifies the preparation of the hides of wild animals and what is like these.

And of sects, he signifies that which confesses unity, if he were fortunate; and if he were bad, it signifies belief in unity but with much hesitation. And Māshā'allāh said that he signifies the Jewish faith[24] and black clothing.

And certain others said that Saturn signifies the inner parts of the ear, and the spleen and the stomach; and of colors he has blackness, and of tastes the harsh and the acidic.[25] And of days, Saturday; and of nights, Wednesday night. And the quantity of his orb is 9°, and the years of his *firdārīyyah* are 11, but the greatest [years] 265, and the greater ones 57, and the middle ones 43 ½, and the lesser ones 30. His strength in the zones of the circle is to the right of the north.

And Māshā'allāh said that, of the figures of men, he signifies a black and orange[26] man who, when he walks, lowers his eyes; heavy in his tread, he attaches his feet,[27] and is one who is thin, stooped, having small eyes and dry skin, veiny, having a thin beard, thick lips, cunning, ingenious, a seducer and killer.

And Dorotheus said that he signifies a man very hairy in body, with joined eyebrows.

And of regions, he has Sind, Hind, and the whole land of the blacks.[28]

And of the Lots, he has the Lot of strength and of stability.[29]

---

[24] John of Seville adds: "and [Judaism] is of the more ancient [faiths], and all confess it but it [confesses] no other, just like Saturn, to whom all [planets] are joined and it to none." If one continued this logic, one would expect the Moon to be of a very flexible faith, accepting principles of all or many others; below, the Moon is linked with "Brahmanism": if this is a general term for Hinduism, the principle would seem to be correct.

[25] Or perhaps, "vinegary" (*acetosus*). These tastes are only in the Lat.

[26] This color usually means a kind of light saffron. The Ar. reads "brown-skinned."

[27] This either means that he is pigeon-toed or that he shuffles.

[28] The Ar. has Ethiopia and its mountains.

[29] This may indicate the Lot of Basis, but should probably be rather Hermetic Lot of Nemesis: see Book VI below.

And he signifies the causes of lands and real estate and those who are in charge of works, and boldness and labor and skills and the causes of death.

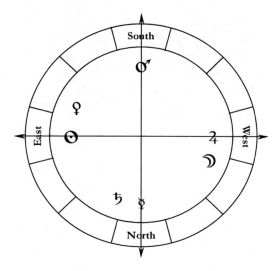

Figure 104: Strength of planets in cardinal directions: al-Qabīsī[30]

---

[30] These placements seem to be based on the relationship between benefic/malefic qualities, elemental natures, and other things, drawing on *Tet.* I.5: Mars is in the south to emphasize extreme hotness; Saturn in the north to emphasize extreme coldness; the Sun and Moon in the east and west to emphasize their moderate nature and relationship to the diurnal/nocturnal qualities; Venus in the east and west so that the implied heat and cold emphasizes their moderated natures. Mercury is often understood to be naturally cold and dry. But I do not understand why certain planets are to the right of the cardinal directions, nor why Mercury should be classed with the extreme of northern coldness.

§V.2: Jupiter

[*Abbr.* V.8-10] Jupiter however, [is] a prosperous one,[31] of a hot and moist nature, airy, moderate,[32] life-bringing, powerful in [signifying] children and philosophy and teachers,[33] explaining dreams, truth-telling, a giver of law, a medical doctor, constant,[34] a lover of women [and] pleasant to them, a solver of questions, a victor, generous, regal, powerful, rich, a patron,[35] alert, merciful, happy, humorous, clean.

[*Gr. Intr.* VII.9.1425-54] The nature of Jupiter is hot, moist, airy, temperate. And he signifies the nutritive soul and life and ensouled bodies.[36] Also children and the children of children, and beauty. And he signifies the wise and doctors of the law and just judges, and firmness and wisdom and intellect and the interpretation of dreams, truth and divine reverence, faith and the teaching of the law, religion, and the veneration and fear of God, charity, piety, also the unity of faith and its foresight, and the fitness of morals and responsibility. And he will be praiseworthy. And he signifies the observation of patience, and perhaps inconstancy will befall him, and hastiness, and lack of foresight[37] after being prudent. And he signifies blessedness[38] and

---

[31] I.e., a benefic.
[32] Reading more with the Ar.; the Lat. *medialis* really means "of the midday."
[33] *Magistros.* This can also mean advisors, guides, and leaders.
[34] I.e., trustworthy or faithful.
[35] This can also indicate a legal protector (*patronus*).
[36] See especially Abū Bakr I.2 for the operation of Jupiter and the soul during pregnancy.
[37] Or, "delusion, being led astray."
[38] Even in the conventional sense of happiness through wealth. But the Arabic seems to have "cultivation."

attainment and victory against one who seeks him. And respect and a kingdom, also the king and the rich, nobles and magnates, and good luck and hope and joy, and a passionate desire for assets (even the loftiness of fortune in the innovation of produce[39]), and the collections of assets, and enrichment, also a good condition in [his] aptitude, and enrichment and security in every matter. And the goodness of the moral habits of the mind, and the largesse of charity and generosity, comprehension and goodness, bragging and the sharpness of mind, and boldness, true esteem, and the esteem of an authority over the citizens of cities, and the esteem of powerful men and magnates, and his bending down[40] to them, and the assistance of men in matters. And he signifies a love of building and deluxe, flourishing residences, and compassion for people, and vision in matters, and bliss in knowledge, the fulfillment of promises, generosity, joking, banter, beauty, decoration, form. Also joy and laughter and a multitude of speaking and the keenness of the tongue. Whatever is joined to him, he is grateful for. And he signifies a multitude of sexual intercourse and the esteem of the good and hatred of evil, and making things right between people, and the commanding of what is known and the prohibiting of what is reprehensible.

[al-Qabīsī II.8-12] Jupiter: a fortune, male, diurnal. And he is a significator of assets and he works temperate heat and moisture; airy, sanguine. And regarding age he signifies youth up to the completion of that age.

And of masteries, those which pertain to the law,[41] like to judge just judgments, and to produce peace between men, and to study good things.

And he signifies an abundance of assets. And of business matters, those which come to be without seduction.[42] And he signifies the soul and life, happiness and truth, religion and patience and every beautiful and valuable precept, and an abundance of sexual intercourse.

---

[39] *Novitate frugum.* I am uncertain about this translation.
[40] *Declinationem.*
[41] The Ar. has "religious law," probably in accordance with Islamic concepts of law.
[42] Lit., "enticements" (*seductione*): that is, without corruption.

And of infirmities, whatever was from blood due to an increase of its quantity, [but] which was not overflowing beyond what is natural, nor from burning and changeable blood.

And he is a planet of wisdom and intellect and vision.[43] If Saturn is complected to him, it signifies black magic and incantations and exorcisms, and so on. And if Mars is complected to him, it signifies the science of medicine. And if the Sun is complected to him, it signifies the knowledge of sects and prudence in contentions and disputations. And if Venus is complected to him it signifies the composition of sounds and other delightful sciences. And if Mercury is complected to him, it signifies the knowledge of arithmetic and writing, also astronomy, philosophy and geometry. And if the Moon is complected to him, it signifies the knowledge of the disposition of waters and their measure, and also that of lands.

And in terms of the quality of the mind, he signifies generosity and modesty and justice.

And of sects, plurality and pretense.[44]

But certain people said that he signifies the liver and stomach and the left ear, and the arms and belly, also the lower parts of the navel [or] the pubic area, and the intestines.

And of colors, an ashen color and green and what is like these. And of tastes, the sweet.[45]

And the quantity of his orb is 9°. And of days, he has Thursday, and of nights Monday night. And the years of his *firdārīyyah* are 12, and his greatest years 427, and the greater ones 79, and the middle ones 45 ½, but the lesser ones 12. And his strength in the regions of the circle is in the west.

And Māshā'allāh said: of the figures of men, he signifies a white man having redness in the face, having eyes not altogether black, a nose uneven and short, bald, having blackness in one of his teeth, of beautiful stature, a good mind, good in morals, a beautiful body.

And Dorotheus said that he signifies one having big eyes and pupils, a broad beard, curly-haired.

---

[43] Reading *visus* for *usus*, following the Ar.
[44] Ar.: "polytheism and idolatry."
[45] The taste is only in the Ar.

And of regions, Iraq, Babylon, Isfahān and Persia, Ctesiphon and al-Ahwāz.[46]

[And he signifies wheat, barley, and glutinous grains; moderately sweet fruits; and natural medications appropriate to one's temperament.][47]

And of Lots, having the Lot of the blessedness of success.[48]

And he signifies faith and an appetite for good things, and the foundation of works, sound health and security and partnership.

---

[46] Following the Ar. The Ar. adds that Rome is sometimes attributed to Jupiter. This could be due to the known opulence and Christianity of Constantinople, the center of the surviving Roman Empire.

[47] Adding based on the Ar.

[48] The Hermetic Lot of Victory or Jupiter. See VI.1.7.

§V.3: Mars

[*Abbr.* V.11-14] Mars [is] malevolent, hot and dry, fiery, choleric, bitter [in taste], beautiful, strong, its part in a man the gallbladder,[49] kidneys, sinews, testicles; in [geographical] regions the fiery ones, things not hoped for; an overseer,[50] a plunderer, occupied in lawsuits and wars and hangings, a torturer, one who proscribes, a liar, of little libido, a killer of seed in the woman, expelling a premature embryo, occupying diverse lands, a foreigner, lying in ambush for travelers; [put] over middle siblings of full blood, a manager of horses, an excavator[51] of tombs, a hanger of dead men,[52] and the like.

[*Gr. Intr.* VII.9.1456-88] The nature of Mars is fiery, hot, dry, choleric, of a bitter taste. And he signifies youth and strength and the sharpness of the mind, also heats and fires and burning up, and everything which happens abruptly. And a king of power and cleverness, and the commands of leaders, and the army, and the companions of the king,[53] and over injustice and subjugation, and war, and killing and fighting, and courage,[54] and endurance, and the lust for glory and having his name be remembered, and being raised up high, and the instruments of war, and compatriots mobilized for wars, and an eagerness for wrongs and sowing discord, and drinking parties, and things

---

[49] Or, bile (*fel*).
[50] Or, "administrator" (*praefectus*).
[51] Reading with the Ar. for "scrutinizer."
[52] Ar.: "the crucifixion of the dead."
[53] In medieval times this included especially the *comites*, the king's personal military allies and those who would fight to support him.
[54] In Aristotelian ethics, courage is a virtue associated with the proper management of fear, another Martial characteristic.

breaking up, and fighting wars, and robberies and digging up of walls on account of stealing, and the cutting of roads and courage and a tendency to anger, and treating the unlawful as being lawful. And he signifies martyrdoms and being fettered, also whipping and prisons and restrictions,[55] fugitives and defection, captivity and prisoners, fear, lawsuits, injustice,[56] a tendency to anger, and violence, and recklessness, and harshness, and coarseness of emotion, and capacity and persistence, and a scarcity of foresight and quickness in matters and having preconceptions, bad eloquence and a ferocity of speech, foulness of words and the lack of self-control in the tongue. And the showing of esteem and friendship, and taking joy in beauty, economy of speech, strategem, regret in the promptness of [his] responses. And a scarcity of piety, and a scarcity of loyalty, and an abundance of lying and whispering, and immorality and wickedness, and the swearing of false oaths, and deception and double-dealing, and the committing of offenses and the scarcity of good, and the destruction of the good, and a multitude of worries in matters, and the instability or changing of counsel from condition to condition, and the quickness of [its] turning back. And a scarcity of modesty, also a multitude of labor and vexation. And foreign journeys and the condition of solitary people, and bad companionship. And fornication and the foulness of sexual intercourse, joking around,[57] being energetic.[58] And he signifies the menstruation of women, also divorce and loss in a conception, and the cutting of the child in the womb[59] and premature births.[60] And he signifies middle brothers and the managers of beasts and veterinary medicine, and the shepherds of sheep and the curing of wounds, and masteries of iron and its work. And the circumcisions of boys and the digging up of tombs and the plundering of the dead.

[al-Qabīsī II.13-17] Mars: male, nocturnal, a bad one; he works heat and dryness, and he is a significator of brothers and foreign travel. And

---

[55] Or, "difficulties, anxiety."

[56] Or more specifically, injuries done to someone.

[57] Or "banter," in a coarse and informal manner.

[58] *Impigritiam.* In the sense of being very active, the opposite of lazy (*pigritia*).

[59] I.e., abortions.

[60] Perhaps also miscarriages (*abortiva*).

of ages, he has youth up to the end of youth. And his nature [is] choleric, of a bitter taste.

And of masteries, every fiery mastery and what comes to be through iron, like the beating of swords with hammers. Which if Saturn is complected to him, it signifies the beating of iron. And if Jupiter is complected to him, it signifies the beating of copper. And if the Sun is complected to him, it signifies the beating of gold.[61] And if Venus is complected to him, it signifies the mastery of ornaments. And if Mercury is complected to him, it signifies the beating out of needles. And if the Moon is complected to him, it signifies the beating out of dishes and scales.[62]

And if he alone took up the signification, he even signifies the work of medicine. Which if no planet is complected to him, it signifies the withdrawing [of blood], and the opening of wounds,[63] and what is like these. And if Saturn is complected to him, it signifies (in terms of the works of medicine) the work of [curing] wounds.[64] And if Jupiter is complected to him, it signifies the work of natures.[65] And if the Sun is complected to him, it signifies the preparation of the eyes[66] and the cure of the eyes. Which if Venus is complected to him, it signifies the work of ornamentation, like cutting hair and beards, and the cutting of nails. And if Mercury is complected to him, it signifies the cutting of veins.[67] And if the Moon is complected to him, it signifies the pulling of teeth and the cleaning of ears.

And by himself he signifies injustice toward the wretched, and the shedding of blood, and oppressions by force and the cutting of roads, and a tendency to anger, and the leadership of armies, and hastening and lightness and shamelessness and foreign travel outside the fatherland, and the indulgence[68] in intercourse and the aborting of children,

---

[61] Or, gold coins (Ar.).
[62] Ar.: scales and weights.
[63] Ar.: cupping.
[64] Ar.: surgery.
[65] I.e., physics, in the sense of physics as "natural philosophy." This probably refers to Jupiter's role in moderate medicines suited to the patient's temperament, above.
[66] Omitting *et alcohol*.
[67] The Ar. has activities with cunning and intelligence and mathematics, which is out of place in this list of medical procedures. Another possibility is the restoration of dislocated limbs, which matches one of the Arabic manuscripts.
[68] Reading more with the Ar. for John's "foulness."

and middle brothers and sisters, and the knowledge and discernment of caring for beasts.

And of infirmities, hot fevers and maniacal behavior from the blood, and bloody pustules and anthrax, and the eating of flesh with rotting,[69] and a pain in half the head,[70] and the sacred fire and fear and horrible thoughts which make a man uneasy and provoke and impede, and render [men] useless, and whatever there was with an inflammation of heat.

And of qualities of the soul, provocation and disturbance. Which if Saturn aspected him, it signifies hatred and the greatest envy.

And of sects, one in which there was war[71] and unity[72] and the quickness of changing from faith, and a multitude of hesitation, and changing from testifying [to one] to testifying [to another]; but all of this will be under [a religion of] unity.

And certain people said that of limbs he has the gallbladder,[73] the kidneys and veins and the flowing out[74] of the sperm, and the back.[75]

And of colors he has redness, and of tastes the bitter.[76]

And the quantity of his orb is 8°. And of the days he has Tuesday, and of nights Saturday night. And his years of the *firdārīyyah* are 7, and his greatest years 284, and the greater ones 66, but the middle ones 40 ½, and the lesser ones 15. And his strength in the regions of the circle is in the south.

And Māshā'allāh said: of the images of men he signifies a man red in the face, having red hair on the head, and a round face, easily disrespecting men, having orange eyes, a horrible look, bold, having a sign or mark on his foot.[77]

And Dorotheus said: having a sharp look.

And of regions he has Jerusalem[78] and the land of the Romans up to the west, and the land of the Turks.

---

[69] Ar. "gangrene," but Burnett translates this as "cancer."
[70] I.e., migraines. The Ar. has hair loss (Burnett: "alopecia").
[71] Ar.: "fear."
[72] Burnett reads "monotheism," which is a valid translation.
[73] The Lat. suggests "gallstones."
[74] *Decursum.* Or, perhaps, spermatic vessels (Ar.) or ducts.
[75] Or perhaps the spine (*dorsum*).
[76] The taste is missing in the Ar.
[77] Ar.: "leg."
[78] Ar.: Syria.

Of Lots, the Lot of courage.

And he signifies perseverance and appropriateness, cunning in love, and pride and[79] lightness and mobility and boldness and denial and sharpness and hastening in all things.

---

[79] For the rest of this sentence up through "denial," the Ar. reads "arrogance, stubbornness, harshness, ingratitude."

§V.4: The Sun

[*Abbr.* V.15-18] However, the Sun [is] benevolent, hot and dry, choleric, life-bringing, gleaming, diurnal, a sensible person,[80] wise, understanding, subjugating,[81] ruler, a mediator, rich, worthy, eloquent, thinking things out beforehand, a philosopher, giver of law, religious, [put] over middle brothers, a socializer, [19] a hastener of good and giver of evil, supporting and pressing down.[82]

[*Gr. Intr.* VII.9.1490-1508] The nature of the Sun is hot, dry. He signifies the life-giving soul, and light and splendor, reason and intellect and knowledge and middle age. He even signifies the king and princes and generals, nobles and magnates, and the assembling of men. Strength, too, and victory[83] and fame, beauty[84] and greatness and the loftiness of the mind, and pride and good commendations, and the appetite for a kingdom and assets, and the greatness of esteem for gold. And he signifies a multitude of speaking and the valuing of cleanliness. And he impedes beyond measure one who is conjoined to him or approaches him. For he who was closer to him in place will be more full of labor than all men, and by how much more one will be elongated from him, he will be [that much] more fortunate. For he who is approaching [the Sun] will leave no memory, nor will a trace of him appear. He puts in order and destroys, profits and impedes, makes for-

---

[80] Or, "intellect" (Ar.).
[81] Reading with the Ar. for "dreamer" (or perhaps an interpreter of dreams).
[82] Or, raising up and bringing down (Ar.).
[83] The Ar. reads "struggle."
[84] Or, "brilliance."

tunate and unfortunate, sometimes raises up, sometimes puts down. And he signifies the matter of religion and the hereafter, also judges and the wise, fathers and middle brothers, and the crowd, and yellow bile: he is joined to men and [also] criticizes them, he provides every thing that [someone] asks for, is strong for revenge, punishing rebels and evildoers.

[al-Qabīsī II.18-24] The Sun: by aspect a fortune, and bad by assembly in one sign, and he is male, diurnal; he works heat and dryness. And he is the significator of fathers if the nativity were in the day. And he signifies the greatest kingdom and life-giving soul, and light and splendor, intellect and beauty[85] and faith. And in terms of age, the end of youth, [but] he partners with the rest of the planets in the arrangement of years.

And of masteries, supremacy and a position of first place, and he signifies the hurling of javelins and hunting and purging with every kind of purging by which bodies are purged inside and out.

And of infirmities, hot [and] dry infirmities appearing [externally] on bodies.

And of assets, much gold and all kinds of assets. And of the quality of his mind, the loftiness of the mind and prudence and what follows that: namely respectability and largesse and glory and broadness of mind.

And of sects, a good cult[86] and what is like it.

And he signifies the commanding of [the native's] voice, and the forcefulness of power.[87] Which if Saturn is complected to him, it signifies estate management and rulership of this kind. And if Jupiter is complected to him, it signifies a position of first place in faith or being a judge among men, judging the works of oppressors. And if Mars is complected to him, it signifies the leadership of an army and the rulership in wars.[88] And if Venus is complected to him, it signifies a kingdom through women and through the harem[89] of powerful people.

---

[85] Ar.: "cleanliness."
[86] Ar.: "the correct/orthodox religion." See below, where the correct religion is also Mercurial.
[87] Reading with the Ar. for "the strength of quickness."
[88] Reading partly with the Ar. for *investigator bellorum*.
[89] Reading with the Ar. for "allegiance" (*obsequium*).

And if Mercury is complected to him, it signifies the counselors of kings, and the work of books and real estate[90] and greater works. And if the Moon is complected to him, it signifies the work of legates and the revealing of counsels, and the rest suchlike.

And certain people said that the Sun signifies the image of a man's face, and particularly in men the right eye, and in women the left one.

And certain people said he has the heart and the marrow and thighs.

And of infirmities, the eating of the flesh[91] in the mouth, and the corruption of the mouth in particular, and the descending of water in the eye;[92] his power [is] in the head. And the Indians said if he were in the Ascendant, he will be burning, and [the native] has a sign in the face.[93]

And of colors he has whatever seems to be transparent[94] in color, and of tastes the sharp.[95]

The quantity of his orb [is] 15°. And of days, Sunday, and of nights Thursday night. The years of his *firdārīyyah* are 10, and his greatest years are 1,461, and the greater ones 120, but the middle ones 69 ½, but the lesser ones 19. His strength in the regions of the circle is in the east.

And Māshā'allāh said: of the figures of men he signifies him who had color between orange and black,[96] but covered with red, of a short stature, curly-haired, bald, with a beautiful body.

And Dorotheus said: the figure of the Sun and the Moon is the figure of the planets which were with them, and of that one which was more worthy in their place. If therefore you wanted the figure of the Sun, know that it is orange, having partly red hair on the head; his eyes a little bit orange.

And of regions he has Samarkand and Khurāsān, all Persia and the land of the Romans.[97]

And of the Lots, having the Lot of the Absent.[98]

---

[90] Ar.: "craftsmen."
[91] I.e., cancerous or other sores.
[92] I.e., cataracts.
[93] The Ar. omits this statement about the face.
[94] Reading with the Ar. for "exotic, strange" (*peregrinus*).
[95] Or, "acrid" (*acutus*).
[96] The Ar. reads, "brown-skinned."
[97] That is, of the Byzantine Empire.
[98] The Lot of Spirit: see Book VI.1.2.

And he is a significator of natures and spirit, wisdom and elation and perfection, also of faith and the sciences and praises.

[Of plants: those whose value is known and good to look at; with varied colors and red surfaces, like peaches, apricots, and dates.][99]

---

[99] Adding based on the Ar.

§V.5: Venus

[*Abbr.* V.20-23] Venus however [is] benevolent, cold and moist, phlegmatic, moderate,[100] [put] over [women and mothers],[101] waters and riverbanks and younger brothers, clean, showing necklaces and gold and silver and musical instruments and pleasures and joys. However, she is idle, drunk, fornicating with women, generous, sharing, a chaser of forms; not destroying the law.[102]

[*Gr. Intr.* VII.9.1510-39] The nature of Venus is cold, moist, phlegmatic, temperate, a fortune. And she signifies women and the mother and younger sisters, also beauty and clothing and ornaments, also gold and silver. And amiability toward friends, and admiration and elation, also pride and boasting, a love of singing and amusement and laughing, ornamentation and joy and happiness, dancing and playing the pipes, singing and plucking the strings of the lute. Even nuptials, and fragrances and what is pleasant, and amiability in the composing of songs, and the games of dice and chess. Also leisure and being dissolute and intoxication, and buffoonery, and resisting[103] the people, and the sons of fornication, and every male or female fornicator or singer or one having fun with different kinds of amusements. And she signifies a multitude of perjuries and lies. Also wine and honey and every intoxi-

---

[100] See parallel footnote for Jupiter above.
[101] Adding with the Ar.
[102] Venus is traditionally associated with religious observance and ritual cleanliness, which in ancient (Roman) times was a special role of women in the household.
[103] I think this is meant in the sense of irritating pranks; but it could also mean a blithe attitude towards social restrictions and norms.

cating drink, and a multitude of sexual intercourse of diverse kinds[104]...And she signifies the love of children and the love of people, and endearment towards them, and trust in everyone. And being dutiful and gracious, and generosity and liberality, and freedom, and the beauty of character, good looks and flirting, and receiving, and light and splendor, and the sweetness of speech, and femininity, and flirting and fondness and ridicule and rejection, and the strength of the body and weakness of the soul, and an abundance of flesh on the body, and multitude of pleasure in every matter. And she rejoices with every thing and seeks every thing and is eager for it. And she signifies types of masteries: the doing of clean and admirable things, also the arranging of wedding ceremonies and their decoration, and the wearing of crowns, and images and colors, and dyers and seamstresses. And houses of worship, and honesty, and adherence to religion, and becoming holy, and justice and fairness, and scales and measures, and the love of shopping[105] and clothing,[106] and commerce in it with pleasant things.

[al-Qabīsī II.25-30] Venus: a fortune, feminine, nocturnal. And she is a significator of women and wives and mothers if it were a diurnal nativity; and she works cold, temperate moisture. And of ages she has youth.

And of masteries, the instruments of games, ornaments too and beautiful shapes and the games of dice and chess, dancing and leisure and fornications and fornicators, and the children of fornication, and a multitude of sexual intercourse, and kinds of wantonness generally, and the putting-together of crowns and their use, and beauty and cleanliness, clothing and ornaments, gold and silver and esteeming games, laughter and joy and using different kinds of ointments, and intoxicating drinks; she believes everyone; she also signifies largesse and esteem and love, justice and houses of prayer; she also maintains the faith.

And she signifies the mastery of all sounds, like music and the rest. Which if Saturn is complected to her, it signifies the sound of singing by which the dead are mourned, or those which builders sing when

---

[104] The next phrases are missing in the Latin, and I cannot quite understand the Arabic, which seems to say "gathering in the rear, and a worn garment [or annihilation]."
[105] Lit., "markets."
[106] Reading *al-kuswah* for Lemay's *al-kuswabah*.

they build buildings. And if Jupiter is complected to her, it signifies the sound of recitation which the masters of sects use at altars and in the places of their prayer to God Omnipotent. And if Mars is complected to her, it signifies sounds which secular[107] people use, and the songs of the common masses in which there comes to be mention of battles or being bound[108] and labor and what is like these, such as song in which there is mention of capture and being bound up and the beating of whips. And if the Sun is complected to her, it signifies the sound of wood[109] by which one plays in the presence of kings and nobles. And if Mercury is complected to her, it signifies the sound which is used in the composition of verses. And if the Moon is complected to her, it signifies the sound of sailors on ships.

And of infirmities, cold [and] moist diseases which happen particularly and especially in the genital members.

And of assets, what is sought on account of beauty, as are the ornaments of women and their clothing, and pearls and paintings. [And of masteries, what pertains to ornamentation.][110]

And of the quality of the mind, sweetness and laughter and friendship and commingling in things like these, and passionate desire for eating, drinking, and sexual intercourse.

And of sects, the worship of idols and those especially in which they practice eating and drinking.

And certain people said that she signifies the hips and the spine of the back, and the sperm. And others said that she has signification over the fat and flesh and kidneys, the vulva and womb, the belly and the navel.

And of colors she has whiteness, and of tastes the greasy.

And the quantity of her orb is 7°. And of days she has Friday, and of nights Tuesday night. And the years of her *firdārīyyah* are 8. And her greatest years are 1,151, and her greater years 82, and the middle ones 45, but the lesser ones 8. Her strength in the regions of the circle [is] to the right of the east.

And Māshā'allāh said: of the figures of men she signifies a white man, tending towards blackness,[111] with a beautiful body and hair on

---

107 Ar.: "schemers and vagabonds."
108 Ar.: "killing."
109 Ar.: "the lute."
110 Reading from the Ar. in John's style.

the head, having a round face and small jaw; having beautiful eyes [and thighs],[112] the blackness of his eyes greater than the whiteness.[113]

And Dorotheus said: having a beautiful face and much hair on the head, and beautiful eyes; the blackness of his eyes more than what is good; the white finished with redness; plump, he shows benevolence.

And of regions she has the Hijāz and the Yemen and the south and the whole land of the Arabs.

And of the Lots she has the Lot of desire.[114]

She signifies friendship and play and esteem and patience[115] and conjoining [sexually] with males.

[Of grains: what is golden and delicious; all plants with a delicious smell; vines and grapes, delicious flavor, and tree oils.][116]

---

[111] Ar.: "white to brownish-red."
[112] Adding with the Ar.
[113] The Ar. reads "with a birthmark on his face."
[114] The Lot of Eros according to Valens: see VI.1.3. But of the Hermetic Lots, the Lot of Eros is calculated from the Lot of Spirit to Venus during the day, and the reverse by night (projected from the Ascendant).
[115] The Ar. lacks this, and I am not sure of its role here.
[116] Adding with the Ar., in John's style.

§V.6: Mercury

[*Abbr.* V.24-27] Mercury [is] of a nature open to all of the planets and the signs: male with male ones, female with female ones, nocturnal with nocturnal ones, diurnal with diurnal ones,[117] hot with hot ones, cold with cold ones; [put] over youths and younger brothers; loving and assembling together the children of the poor, seeking friends; clever, an interpreter, being superior in all arts, one making computations, a geometer, astrologer, augur, true expounder [of things]; an inventor of music and a scribe, a writer of history,[118] of little joy,[119] a loser of provisions, a giver and taker, malevolent, a deceiver, unstable, obedient, able to endure,[120] possessing little.

[*Gr. Intr.* VII.9.1541-80] Mercury bends with his nature toward the one who is complected to him, in terms of the natures of the planets and signs, on account of the mixing of dryness and cold in him. And he signifies youth and younger brothers and an affection for male and female servants,[121] and abundance from them. And he signifies divinity and the oracles of prophets, sense and reason, speech and conversations and stories and the committing of them to memory. Also wisdom, belief and the beauty of learning, sharpness of character. And

---

[117] This is an error I describe below in V.9 and V.11. Mercury is diurnal if rising before the Sun, nocturnal if setting after the Sun.

[118] Or of stories generally.

[119] Perhaps he is so busy working and calculating how to get his way, he cannot relax and enjoy life?

[120] Or, "patient" (*patiens*).

[121] Or perhaps more subservient males and females. John reads, "concubines," which is probably close.

intellect and literature and philosophy and a gift of knowledge, also arithmetic and geometry and the measure of higher and terrestrial things. Even the wisdom of the stars and prophecy and its declamation, and rebuking,[122] and a good omen, and hospitality, and knowledge in matters, and wisdom and obscure books. And rhetoric and eloquence or the sweetness of speech and its quickness, or the explanation of opinions and study in [types of] wisdom. And striving for a position of first place, and passionate desire in them, and praise and a memory because of it, and a beacon in all things, and he signifies haircuts. And writers and books and offices[123] and the assessing of land taxes, and colonies,[124] and slander and lying and false testimony, and fictitious books and the speculation of hidden secrets. And he signifies a scarcity of joy and the destruction of assets. He even signifies assets and distributions and merchandise and business deals, and buying and selling, giving and taking and partnering, affliction, burglaries and contentions, deception, lies, resentment, cunning, denials, and depth of counsel, and no one knows what he bears in his mind, nor does he disclose it to anyone. And he signifies combatants and hostility, and losses in [his] reckonings,[125] and a multitude of fears from them, slaves and assistants, and quickness in work, and crookedness of morals. And a multitude of color and charm, and gentleness of speech, and acquisition, and assistance, and willingness, and endurance, also an inclination to piety and mercy and calm, sobriety, and restraining the hands from [doing] evil. And the beauty of faith and obedience to God, the cause of truth, and the preservation of his brothers. Timid with diverse fears, beauty of voice, knowing melodies. And he signifies the precision of the hands in diverse masteries, and prudence in every matter which he takes on, having pleasure in every completed work. And he signifies bloodletters and those who work with razors and combs. And he signifies fountains of waters and rivers and wells and prisons and the dead, and mange in beasts.

---

[122] Probably in the sense that prophets often deliver a message of criticism and reform.
[123] Or, "agencies," such as government departments.
[124] Or perhaps, "wandering."
[125] Tentatively reading the Ar. 'i'dād for Lemay's 'i'dā'.

[al-Qabīsī II.31-35] Mercury: mixed,[126] male, diurnal; inclined by his own nature toward the one to which he is complected (from among the planets and signs). He himself is a significator of younger brothers, and he signifies slaves and the valuing of concubines,[127] and he signifies divinity and the oracles of prophets, and belief and [religious] work and oration. Which if he were in his own nature and no planet is being complected to him, he signifies earthy things and the increase of things by growing. And of ages, youth and advancement in it.

And of works, works which generate thought, preaching and rhetoric and works which were by [mathematics]:[128] like business deals and assessing and geometry and the managing and organization of a matter, and philosophy and augury and proverbs and writing and the knowledge of versifying, and especially the work of counting. Which if Saturn is complected to him, in terms of the work of number it signifies the work of measuring lands and real estate, and the calculation [involved in] building and looms.[129] And if Jupiter is complected to him, it signifies the counting involved in reciting psalms, and the numbers of divine books. And if Mars is complected to him, it signifies number which comes to be in the bonuses of armies and of those fighting, and numbering the striking with whips and cudgels. And if the Sun is complected to him, it signifies being in charge of counting for kings and the houses of assets. And if Venus is complected to him, it signifies the numbering of the chords of wooden [instruments], and the numbering of sounds and pipes. And if the Moon is complected to him, it signifies the numbering of dishes which come to be for the eating of those traveling outside their homes.[130]

And of infirmities, he signifies infirmities of the soul: that is, horrible thoughts and the disquiet of the mind and doubts and the rest-like. However, he signifies the quality of the mind according to his complexion and connection. If he were made fortunate, there will be goodnesses according to the kind of fortune which makes him fortunate, and according to the place in which he is made fortunate. And if

---

[126] That is, in benefic/malefic qualities.
[127] Ar.: "love for male and female servants."
[128] Reading with Ar. for "study."
[129] Ar.: "repairing."
[130] Ar.: "for instruments made for legations."

he were bad, there will be iniquities according to the bad one which makes him bad, and according to the place in which the bad one is.[131]

And of sects, he signifies the worship of unity[132] and of what is like these, and [what is] secret, with false sanctity and pretending.[133]

And certain people said that he signifies the thighs, the navel and the legs, also the nerves and veins.

And of colors he has every commingled color and azure,[134] and of tastes the acidic.[135]

And the quantity of his orb is 7°. And of the days he has Wednesday, and of nights Sunday night. And the years of his *firdārīyyah* are 13, and his greatest years 480, the greater ones 76, and the middle ones 48, but the lesser ones 20. His strength in the regions of the circle [is] in the north.

And certain people said that Mercury signifies childhood from the middle of his retrogradation up to the first station, and from the first station up to the assembly with the Sun [he signifies] youth, and from the assembly of the Sun up to the second station [he signifies] middle age, and from the second station up to the middle of retrogradation he signifies old age.

And[136] from the middle of his retrogradation he signifies contrariety,[137] and in his assembly in moving forward he signifies esteem and friendship. And from his [first] station, in moving direct up to assembly, he signifies esteem and the seeking[138] of love. And from his second station going toward assembly, he signifies searching for contrariety and dissimulation, and signifies delay and little cleverness and being occupied in matters (and in the middle of retrogradation he signifies a tempered quickness on account of a weakness of mind).

---

[131] Reading with the Ar. The Latin has it according to the place where Mercury is made bad.

[132] Again, as with the Sun, the Ar. reads "the correct/orthodox" religion. It is interesting that the true religion is Solar and Mercurial: it suggests Egyptian and Hermetic religion.

[133] Ar.: "secret monotheism and rational precepts."

[134] John says, "the color of a wild lily-flower."

[135] Or perhaps, the "vinegary" (*acetosus*).

[136] I have reworked this and the next paragraph based on al-Kindī's *The Forty Chapters* §§52-54, from which it is taken. Burnett's Arabic of al-Qabīsī tends to reverse the first and second stations.

[137] Omitting "decrepit old age" (Lat.).

[138] Reading with the Ar. for "change."

And within the first station he signifies being occupied in cleverness and delay [at first], and going out from this to quickness and the opening up to ingenuity. And in his assembly with the Sun by moving direct he signifies quickness and the expansion of ingenuity and its spread. It happens likewise to Venus in these places, and to the higher planets.

And Māshā'allāh said: of the figures of men, Mercury signifies a man having a color not very white nor black, having a high forehead, having length in the face and a long nose, having a thin [body] and [a thin] beard on his jaw, and beautiful eyes not totally black, also having long fingers.

And of regions, Daylam, Makrān, [Tibet][139] and the south, and all the regions of the Indians.

And of the Lots he has the Lot of business.[140]

And he signifies fear and harassment and war, enmities, seductions and contrarieties. He also signifies profit and mastery and subtlety in work and in inquiring, and in the rest of the things which come to be in men in terms of statements and contentions.

[And he signifies what is lacking in firmness and softness,[141] in mixed colors, and azure mixed with green; and it signifies a smell and taste like brackish water.][142]

---

[139] Adding with the Ar.
[140] Probably the Lot of necessity according to Valens: see VI.1.5. But the Hermetic Lot of Necessity is calculated from Mercury to the Lot of Fortune by day, the reverse by night (and projected from the Ascendant).
[141] This must be due to Mercury's ambiguous nature: neither too much this nor that.
[142] Adding based on the Ar.

§V.7: The Moon

[*Abbr.* V.28-31] The Moon [is] a benevolent, cold and moist, phlegmatic, moderate,[143] a little bit hot for the reason that her light is from the Sun; powerful over joy, clean, skilled in the inceptions of all duties, regal, increasing life, a dancer at the head of a procession,[144] a protectress[145] over countrysides and waters and their courses; marrying, [put] over sisters, creating embryos,[146] watching over mothers and likewise their sisters and [the sisters] of fathers; and legates and legations and false words[147] and the prosperities of fortune; not concealing secrets, abounding in the seeds of the earth.

[*Gr. Intr.* VII.9.1582-1602] The Moon is the luminary of the night, and her nature is cold, moist, phlegmatic, and there is accidental heat in her, because her light is from the Sun. And she is light, fit in every matter. She desires joy and beauty and being praised. And she signifies the beginning of every work, and the knowledge of riches and nobles, and fortune in the means of livelihood and the attaining of those things which she wanted. And poverty[148] in religion and the higher sciences,[149] also miracles and sorcery and a multitude of thoughts in

---

[143] See parallel footnotes for Jupiter and Venus above.
[144] *Praesul,* which Burnett reads as "bishop." The Ar. has "jurisprudence" and "religion."
[145] Reading *consultrix* for *consiliatrix.*
[146] Or, "births" (*partus*).
[147] The Latin reads "true words," but the Ar. has "lying."
[148] Ar. *al-faqr.* I am not sure if this means she lacks religion, or indicates religions where a lack of possessions is esteemed.
[149] Possibly because the Sun has his joy in the ninth, indicating priestly and learned religion, and higher learning; the Moon has her joy in the third, which would indicate more folk religion and magic.

matters. Also the inexperience[150] of the mind, and engineering and the science of lands and waters, and appraising them, and accounting and surveying, and weakness of one's sense.[151] And she signifies women who have nobility, and marriage-unions and every pregnant woman, and nourishment[152] and its condition, also mothers and maternal aunts, midwives and older sisters. And messengers and the postal service and reports, fugitives and lying and accusations. Also, she is a master with masters and a slave with slaves, and with every man she is just like his nature. A multitude of forgetting, timid, a flawless heart, cheerful to people, revered by them, flattered by them. She does not hide her secrets. And she signifies a multitude of infirmities and caring for the fitness of bodies, and the cutting of hair, also a bounty of foods and a scarcity of sexual intercourse.

[al-Qabīsī II.36-40] The Moon: a fortune, feminine, nocturnal; she works cold and moisture. And she is the significatrix of mothers if [someone's] nativity were nocturnal, and there is temperate phlegm in her. And she signifies the childlike age and the beginning of growing.

And of works she has legations[153] and commands and the works of waters and lands according to the greatness of fortune or evil. She even signifies a position of first place, if she were in charge over some matters pertaining to kings[154] and she were made fortunate and in a good aspect of the Sun. And of assets she signifies silver and the cultivation of the earth, if she had authority in the fourth.

And of faith, the religion [of Brahmanism].[155]

And of infirmities,[156] she signifies paralysis on one side of the body,[157] facial paralysis, the dislocation of the limbs, and whatever was in the likeness of cold and moisture.

---

[150] Ar. *ḥadīth*. But this can also mean "gossip, chit-chat." John reads, "sharpness," and in al-Qabīsī Burnett translates it as "premonition."
[151] That is, in terms of having good sense or being sensible.
[152] Or, "rearing" (*nutritionem*).
[153] The Ar. adds the postal service.
[154] Or, authorities. This undoubtedly refers to rulership over the tenth place or over the degree of the Midheaven.
[155] Adding with Ar.
[156] Following the Ar. for the first two illnesses.
[157] Ar. "hemiplegia."

And of the quality of the mind, according to her complexion with the planets. Which if a fortune is complected with her, and that fortune were Venus, it signifies courtliness and the sweetness of the mind, and the respectability of morals, and the quickness of motion. And if it were Jupiter, it signifies respectability and caution and the kindness of companionship, and divine obedience.[158] And if she were complected to the bad ones and it were Mars, it signifies an eagerness for whispering between men, and effort in such things. And if it were Saturn, hatred, faking, and envy. And if it were the Sun from a praiseworthy aspect, a regal disposition.[159] And if it were Mercury, it signifies rhetoric and the goodness of the tongue, and writing.

And certain people said that she signifies thinking and the inexperience of the mind,[160] and weakness of sense and the heaviness of the tongue and respectable women, and the nourishment of little ones, and mothers and maternal aunts and [wet-nurses and][161] the supplying of foods.

And others said she signifies the brain in particular, and the lungs.

And of colors she has the yellow,[162] and of tastes the salty.

And of men she signifies the left eye, and of women the right one.

And the quantity of her orb is 12°. And of days she has Monday, and of nights Friday night. And the years of her *firdārīyyah* are 9, the greatest ones 520, but the greater ones 108, and the middle ones 66 ½, but the lesser ones 25. And her strength in the regions of the circle [is] to the right of the west.

And Māshā'allāh said: of the figures of men she signifies a white man touched with redness, with joined[163] eyebrows, benevolent, having eyes not totally black, a round face and beautiful stature.

And of lands, she has that of the Turks, [al-Jīlān],[164] Armenia, and Daylam.

---

[158] Moving this phrase from the sentence on Moon-Venus here, and replacing "beauty of life" (which does not correspond to the Arabic, but does sound more like Venus).

[159] Or administrative authority (Ar.).

[160] Again, *ḥadīth* (see above). Burnett reads this as "innovation," which is another possibility.

[161] Adding with the Ar.

[162] Following the Ar. for "orange" or "saffron" (Lat. *croceum*).

[163] The Ar. reads "curved."

[164] Adding with the Ar.

And certain people said [the Moon] signifies childhood from the beginning of the [lunar] month up to seven days,[165] and from seven to fourteen days youth; and up to the twenty-first night she signifies the completion of middle age, and up to the conjunction [with the Sun], senility.

And if she were under the Sun's rays, she signifies secrets and hidden things (and thus with every planet).

And from the beginning of the month she signifies everything which is made, and from the opposition she signifies everything which is destroyed.[166]

And at the beginning of the [lunar] month she and the Sun signify accusers, and at the end of the month, the accused.

And at the beginning of the month she signifies profit and self-control, and at the end of the month taxes[167] and dispersing [of wealth].

And at the opposition, she signifies contrariety, and at the beginning of [her] change toward the opposition (which is when there would be 15° between her and the opposition) she signifies the beginning of contrariety and its cause. And when she is diverted,[168] she signifies the causes of being rescued from contrariety.

And in her going out from under the Sun's rays, she signifies going out from hiddenness and what is like this. And in her entrance under the rays, she signifies readiness for hiddenness. And at the hour of her division from the Sun she signifies readiness of her exit from hiddenness. And at the hour of her exit from under the rays she signifies appearance and arrival from absence.

And while she was in the square aspect of the Sun, she signifies diminution from a height into the lowest part; likewise in the second square aspect, but in the first square aspect she signifies the appearance of matters and profit and the increase of self-control, and in the second aspect of the Sun she signifies the opposites of these.

---

[165] The Ar. speaks of the seventh "night," the fourteenth "night," and so on.
[166] The Ar. only says that she signifies generation and corruption generally, but this fuller statement in the Latin makes sense.
[167] Or, "tribute" (*stipendia*). Obviously, a kind of spending.
[168] That is, "separated."

[al-Qabīsī II.41b] [Of plants: truffles, mushrooms, hashish, grass, the forest,[169] leeks, legumes and all herbs needing to be cut.]

---

[169] Reading instead of Burnett's "arable land" (Ar. *ḥirsh*).

§V.8: The Head and Tail of the Dragon

[*Abbr.* IV.19-20] But according to the most ancient of the philosophers, the nature of the Head of the Dragon is increasing; indeed if it were a lucky [planet], it adds to the good; but if there were a malevolent star in it, [it adds] to the bad; but on the contrary, the Tail [is] decreasing what it finds. However, the Head [is] good with a good one, bad with a bad one. But the Tail [is] bad with a good one, good with a bad one.

[al-Qabīsī II.45-48] The Head of the Dragon is male, and it is likewise a fortune, and its nature is composed of the nature of Jupiter and Venus. And this signifies a kingdom and fortune and assets. And certain people said that its nature is increase: that if it were with fortunes, it increases their fortune, and if it were with the bad ones, it increases their malice. And the years of its *firdārīyyah* are 3. But the Tail of [the Dragon] is bad, and its nature is composed of the nature of Saturn and Mars. It signifies depression, fall, and poverty. And certain people said that its nature is diminution, which if it were with the fortunes, it reduces their fortune; and if it were with the bad ones, it reduces their malice. And for that reason it was said that the Tail was a fortune with the fortunes and bad with the bad ones, and the Tail bad with the good ones and good with the bad ones. And the years of its *firdārīyyah* are 2.

§V.9: Benefic and malefic planets

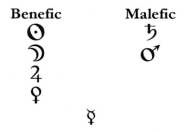

[*Gr. Intr.* IV.5.532-41] And we say that the composition of individuals comes to be through the tempering of natures. And the tempering of natures comes to be through the tempering of seasons, but the tempering of seasons is effected by the power of the motion of certain planets which are in that tempering. Therefore, any one of the planets which was of those from whom the signification over the tempering of the season and bringing [things] about and life in this world is taken, is a fortune. And whichever one was of those from which the signification over the corruption of the season by heat and cold is taken, and over destruction and loss and the rest of what is like these, is bad.

[*Gr. Intr.* IV.5.639-43] Since therefore the cold and heat from the works of Saturn and Mars in the seasons (when they are in charge of them) was found to be overflowing, and whenever these two elements were overflowing there will be loss with their overflowing, for this reason they made them bad ones.

[*Gr. Intr.* IV.5.652-54] But the proper quality of the Sun is the work of seasons, and the compositions and signification of universal life which is practically their type.[170] And so on account of these three reasons they made him a fortune.

[*Gr. Intr.* IV.5.655-58] Also the Moon, because in one month she walks through all the signs and moves the four seasons of the year, and tempers natures and strengthens them, and she operates in them what the Sun operates in one year, they made her a fortune.

[*Gr. Intr.* IV.5.661-64] And the proper quality of Jupiter in the seasons is tempering, and the blowing of the northern winds which

---

[170] I take this to mean that what seasons essentially do is to establish, compose and signify different features of biological life—and that the Sun is responsible for this.

temper natures; but the proper quality of the work of Venus in the seasons is tempering and moistening. And for this reason they made them
fortunes.

[*Gr. Intr.* IV.5.665-76] Also the proper quality of Mercury in the seasons is that he corrupts them moderately with respect to winds and
dryness, and he does not change them from a tempered nature, and for
that reason they make him a fortune. But on account of the multitude
of differences of his condition in retrogradation and directness and
quickness of motion, and that his work in the seasons is their corruption in terms of winds and moderate dryness, and winds have a quick
motion and corruption from condition to condition, but dryness is a
passive quality receiving a diversity of corruptions from the active
qualities (in the way we said once in Treatise II), they made him be
commingled with the one to which he is commingled, in terms of the
signs and planets, and he is corrupted toward their nature and is
changed to it, receiving and strengthening them.

[*Gr. Intr.* IV.5.679-85] And thus in every sign which he enters, and
with every planet (according to the likeness of the nature of that same
sign and planet), he operates its work. If however Mercury were alone
in a sign and one of the planets did not aspect him, then he shows his
own proper quality and is made a fortune, but he receives the nature of
the sign in which he was (in terms of heat and cold, dryness and moisture).

[*Gr. Intr.* IV.9.1338-41] And [the planets are] complected to the
[benefic] and [malefic] planets and [are] changed into their nature if
[they] were conjoined with them in one sign or from some aspect.[171]

---

[171] This statement originally appeared in Abū Ma'shar's material on the sect status of Mercury below, and originally read that *Mercury* was changed to be *diurnal or nocturnal* when
with or aspecting to other diurnal or nocturnal planets. But I believe this is an error the
Persians and Arabs picked up from Rhetorius (Ch. 2), and it was passed on via *BA* II.11
as well. The error arose like this. In *Tet.* I.7, Ptolemy reports the sect of all the planets
(including that Mercury is diurnal when rising before the Sun, and nocturnal when setting
after him), and then says that *all* planets become more benefic or moderated when with
benefic planets, and the contrary with malefic planets: he specifically describes Saturn and
Mars as being tempered in this way. Then Paul of Alexandria, following this sort of passage, included the rising/setting rule for Mercury, but made the benefic/malefic rule apply
to *Mercury alone*, for the specific reason that he has a "common nature." Rhetorius, picking
up on the notion of Mercury being common, *includes* the Mercury-specific benefic/malefic
rule from Paul, but *omits* the rising/setting rule. So, when astrologers like Māshā'allāh
relied on Rhetorius, they saw that Mercury was common both in sect status and in ben-
efic/malefic status, but the only guidance for making decisions about him was based on

[*Judgments* 2] The malefic planets signify detriment and evil on account of the excessiveness or overflowing of the power of cold and heat conquering and impeding in them. But if a benefic planet were in the domicile of a malefic (or in its exaltation), [the malefic] receives [the benefic] and restrains its own malice from him; or if there were an aspect of the malefics by a trine or sextile aspect, it would even be restrained by that, because it would be an aspect of friendship without any enmity. Indeed the benefics, because they are of a temperate nature and equal complexion (that is, because they are temperated from heat and cold), always profit and perform, were they to receive or not—but reception with them is more useful and better.[172]

[*Judgments* 4] And a planet is called "impeded" while a malefic is projecting rays over its light according to the quantity which I told you concerning their orbs. And if it transited a bound of the malefics it is called "looking at the malefic," and [the malefic] would not be able to impede. And if a malefic transited a planet[173] by a complete degree, it sends in fear without the impediment of the body, and the malefic planet would not be able to act because it is separated from it. Likewise if a benefic transited a planet and were separated from it by a full degree,[174] he has hope, but the matter is not perfected. And every impeding [planet], if it were cadent from the Ascendant, sends fear and does not impede. Likewise if benefics were cadent from the Ascendant: it is hoped for, but the matter is not perfected.

[*Judgments* 5] If a planet were in the angles of the malefics (that is, if it were with one, or in the fourth from him, or in the seventh or in the tenth), it will be like one who fights on his own behalf[175] against the tribulation and evil which descends upon him. And if [the malefic]

---

the Mercury-specific benefic/malefic rule: they had no choice but to apply the benefic/malefic logic to the sect case, and said that Mercury is diurnal with diurnal planets and nocturnal with nocturnal planets. Luckily, Abū Ma'shar also had access to the original rising/setting rule, which I have preserved below.

[172] *Cf. Tet.* I.5.

[173] Reading *planetam* for *planeta*, in parallel with the following sentence.

[174] *Per gradum integrum. Integer* suggests that the degree itself is counted as a whole: so if the malefic were transiting a planet at 25° 57', it would be separated by a full degree as soon as it enters 26°, only 3' away.

[175] *Pro semetipso.*

transited it, and it were separated from it by a full degree (as I said to you before), he has already escaped the impediment of that malefic, and the malefic would be able to do nothing besides sending in fear. Therefore, observe these chapters: because they are of the secrets of questions.

[*Judgments* 12] The malefics signify difficulty, and pressure, and haste in work.

[*Judgments* 18] If a malefic planet were oriental (that is, if it were to appear in the east in the morning), in its own domicile or in its own exaltation, and it was not joined to a malefic who would impede him, it is better and more worthy than a retrograde and impeded benefic.

[*Judgments* 19] If malefics were the Lords of purposes,[176] and the Lord of the Ascendant or the Moon were joined to them from a square aspect or the opposition (that is, from the fourth sign or from the seventh one),[177] they make the purpose but destroy it in the end. And if the malefics were those who are joined to benefics (that is, if the malefics would push and be joined to them), it will be better than if they were the ones receiving the arrangement.

[*Judgments* 22] When the benefics aspect the malefics, they decrease [the malefics'] impediment.

[*Judgments* 23] When the malefics aspect the benefics from a square aspect or from the opposition, they decrease [the benefics'] fortune.

[*Judgments* 24] If the benefics were cadent from the Ascendant,[178] or retrograde, they will be impeded [and be] like the malefics.

[*Judgments* 25] When planets are received, and they are benefics, their good will be stronger; and if they were malefics, their impediment will be less.

---

[176] That is, they rule the houses of the quaesited or the topic of an election.
[177] Again, this also includes the tenth sign from it.
[178] I.e., not aspecting the rising sign.

[*Judgments* 26] If the malefic planets were in a peregrine sign, and if they were not in their own domiciles (nor in the exaltation, nor in triplicity), they increase evil and their impediment is made greater; and if they were in signs in which they have testimony, they are restrained from evil, and altogether there will not be an impediment.

[*Judgments* 27] If the malefics were in their own domiciles (or in the exaltations or in triplicities or in their own bounds), and in the angles or in the followers of the angles, and they were the Lords of matters, their strength will be like the strength of benefics. Understand what I have said.

[*Judgments* 28] If the benefics were in a sign in which they do not have testimony, their fortune and good is decreased; and if they were in a sign in which there is testimony for them (that is, in their own domiciles or exaltations or triplicities or bounds), their fortune is made greater, and the matter is perfected, and good is increased.

[*Judgments* 29] If the benefics and malefics were in a malign place (that is, in one of the domiciles which I have said before), or they were under the rays, combust, they signify small and despicable things,[179] and the planets would not be able to signify good or evil on account of the weakness which is in them. Because if a planet were under the rays, combust, or in the opposition of the Sun, it will be weak, since in this place there is no usefulness nor anything of the good for benefic planets, nor anything of evil for the malefic ones: because the benefics signify a modicum of the good if they were under the rays, and likewise if the malefics were under the rays their impediment will be less.

[*Judgments* 30] And every benefic planet (or malefic), if it were in its own domicile or in the exaltation or in its own triplicity, and so on— whatever is in them of evil is turned away into the good. Marvel therefore at what I have told you, and take your measure of judging from it.

[*Judgments* 31] If the malefics were in the angles of the Ascendant, and they impeded from the square aspect or the opposition, the

---

179 This is an arresting phrase.

malefics will be strong at harming, and their affliction will be greater, and especially and most particularly if they were stronger than the planet whom they oppress or impede (that is, if they were in a stronger place, that is, if they were to have some dignity); but if they aspected from a trine or from a sextile aspect, they are restrained from evil and their impediment is decreased.[180]

[*Judgments* 32] Always, a benefic does not signify except for fortune, and a malefic always signifies nothing except for evil (on account of the overflowing of its nature and the malignity of its complexion). Therefore it is necessary to look at the places of the planets—that is, their places from the Ascendant, and the signs in which they are: because even though a planet may be malefic, if it were in its own likeness, or in its own light,[181] or in its own domicile or exaltation or triplicity, or in a good place from the Ascendant, it signifies good.

[*Judgments* 33] If a benefic were not in its own light[182] (that is, if it were of the planets of the night, and it were a significator in the day, or it were of the planets of the day and were a significator in the night), or were it peregrine[183] from its own sign, or cadent from the Ascendant or under the rays, it impedes and is not profitable.[184]

---

[180] Trines and sextiles are likened to Jupiter and Venus, so indicating friendship; squares and oppositions are likened to Mars and Saturn, and indicate enmity. This correspondence is based on the relation of the domiciles to one another.

[181] My sense is that these are synonyms for domain (III.2), not to being separated from another planet (II.9).

[182] *Lumine.* That is, if it is not a member of the sect of the chart.

[183] *Peregrinus*, literally, "a foreigner, foreign."

[184] *Non proficit.*

§V.10: Masculine and feminine planets

Masculine   Feminine

☉   ☽
♄   ♀
♃
♂
☿

[*Gr. Intr.* IV.8.1273-1310] Generation comes to be through a conjunction of the male and female, for the nature of the male is hot, and he is active, but the nature of the female is moist, and she is passive. And the planets have a signification over masculinity and femininity: therefore the hot planets signify masculinity, and the moist planets signify femininity.

Therefore the nature of Jupiter and Mars and the Sun is hot, for that reason they are male. Also, Saturn's nature is practically inseparable to him: it is cold (namely an active quality), but another one is dryness, and dryness is a quality agreeing with heat: for this reason Saturn signifies masculinity on account of these two natures. And because there is no heat in his nature, his signification over masculinity is weaker than the significations of the three planets which we stated before. On account of this reason, in terms of masculinity he may perhaps signify eunuchs and the effeminate, and males who do not have sex with women, nor those who have seed. But dryness conquers in Mercury, and dryness agrees with heat: therefore Mercury is male. And since there is no heat in his nature, for that reason he signifies boys who [are not yet mature],[185] and eunuchs. And because dryness is a passive quality, it signifies that he receives the nature of the [other] planets in terms of masculinity and femininity.

Venus signifies temperate moisture, and on account of this reason she is feminine. Also the Moon is made feminine on account of the multitude of her moisture.

Moreover the nature of the Head is hot and masculine, but the nature of the Tail is cold and feminine.

---

[185] My tentative addition, replacing John's "have not yet suffered frailty."

But these things which we have said (in terms of the masculinity or femininity of the planets) are things which are referred to the planets; but perhaps their conditions will be different, and the male ones will signify femininity, and the feminine ones masculinity, on account of the diversity of their conditions: because planets appearing eastern (those which arise before the Sun) signify masculinity, and the western ones (namely those which set after the Sun) signify femininity. And if the planets were from the Ascendant to the Midheaven, or from the west to the angle of the earth, they signify masculinity in these eastern quarters; but in the remaining, western ones, they signify femininity. Also, their conditions become different in masculinity and femininity in their own places of the signs, and the houses of the circle. And we will describe these things.

[*BA* II.15] But of those which are transformed from females into the male sex, a three-fold manner is observed: firstly indeed when they become eastern [within 15°],[186] secondly while they linger between the fourth and the seventh, thirdly when they traverse through from the Midheaven to the east. [Fourthly, when in masculine or northern signs.][187]

However, those male ones which cross over to the female nature are divided into three parts: for instance firstly when they become western [within 15°], but secondly when they are moved from the east toward the fourth, thirdly when they walk through from the Midheaven to the seventh. [Fourthly, when in feminine or southern signs.]

Therefore, whenever an eastern star should happen to be found in a male sign or between the fourth and the seventh, let a judgment be advanced about what is male; but while in the rest of the places which we have called female, the judgment should be advanced about a female nature.

If therefore it happens otherwise, it is necessary for the [star] which is supported by more testimony to earn the judgment.

---

[186] Adding with Rhet. Ch. 2, here and below.
[187] By the "northern" and "southern" signs he probably means northern and southern in declination (Aries through Virgo, and Libra through Pisces, respectively).

§V.11: Diurnal and nocturnal planets

Diurnal	Nocturnal
☉	☽
♃	♀
♄	♂

☿

[*Gr. Intr.* IV.9.1312-1338] Of the planets, certain ones are diurnal and certain ones nocturnal. And they gave them these significations because they looked at a planet whose nature is more temperate in the day than in the night, and they made this a diurnal one; but they made a planet nocturnal whose nature is more temperate in the night than in the day.

For, concerning Saturn, we have already stated that his nature is tempered in the day, and for that reason he is diurnal; but Jupiter is made diurnal on account of the temperedness of his nature, because the day is more tempered than the night. Moreover, the nature of Mars is in overflowing heat and dryness, but the overflowing of his heat and dryness is tempered in the night, on account of the cold of the night and its moisture: therefore Mars is nocturnal. But the Sun is a diurnal planet.

And Venus is a planet in which there is moisture, and her nature is moist, agreeing with the nature of the night: and for that reason she is nocturnal. And if she were western, she will be stronger in signification and her good fortune will appear more, because [westernness] agrees with the nature of the night and making feminine. But if she were eastern and she were above the earth in the day, in masculine signs, her good fortune and her temperateness is diminished because she is inclined toward the nature of the diurnal planets, and a little bit toward masculinity.

Also, dryness conquers in Mercury, and dryness agrees with heat, but the day is hot: therefore when Mercury takes up a signification alone the signification of the day will be more conquering in him. And if is arising [before the Sun] he becomes diurnal, but when he sets [after the Sun] he will be nocturnal.[188] And while he was [in his] setting [phase] his work will appear more and be stronger than while he is eastern, because he will be direct in his setting [phase], and he will be retrograde in his arising.[189]

[Gr. Intr. IV.9.1341-52] And the Moon signifies the night on account of her own cold and moisture, and she is nocturnal on account of these reasons.

Moreover, the Head is diurnal and the Tail nocturnal. And likewise the Heads of the Nodes of the planets, and their Tails.

And these natures which the planets have, in terms of the diurnal and nocturnal [natures] are practically inseparable from them. But the arising of the planets [before the Sun] strengthens the signification of the diurnal planets, and weakens the signification of the nocturnal planets—except for Mercury, about whom we have said that if he were western, his nature signifies more good fortune. And the western-ness[190] of the planets strengthens the signification of the nocturnal planets and weakens the signification of the diurnal planets.

§V.12: Additional notes on the planets: al-Qabīsī

[al-Qabīsī II.43] And certain people said that the Sun signifies spirit, and the Moon thought; and Saturn grief and sorrow and labor and evil; and Jupiter wisdom and reason; Mars anger, theft and quickness; Venus play and joy; Mercury rationality and teaching.[191] And we have stated certain things in our book about the signification of a planet while another one is being complected to it; likewise one must even consider what the planets signify in the rest of things.[192]

---

[188] This is the view of Paul of Alexandria (Ch. 6) and Ptolemy (*Tet.* I.7).

[189] That is, when making an appearance from out of the Sun's rays on the setting or western side, he will be direct; but when doing so on the arising or eastern side, he will be retrograde.

[190] Reading for John's "setting."

[191] Reading with the Latin for Burnett's "speech and culture."

[192] That is, not only in professions but in all topics.

§V.13: Planetary days and hours

[*Abbr.* V.32-35] Now however we must state which is in charge over the day, and which the night. The first [day] of the week belongs to the Sun, the second to the Moon, the third to Mars, the fourth to Mercury, the fifth to Jupiter, the sixth to Venus, the seventh to Saturn. Of the individual days,[193] the first hour will even be that of the Lord of the day[194] itself. But the rest are given to them according to the order of the planets, namely so that it would be given to Saturn after the Moon, then to the others.

[*Gr. Intr.* VI.33.1947-61] And know that the beginning of the hours of the day is from the beginning of the rising of the Sun in the eastern hemisphere, but the beginning of the hours of night is from the setting of the body of the Sun in the western hemisphere.[195]

[al-Qabīsī II.49] A chapter begins [on] what (from among the days) each planet would have. If it were some day[196] belonging to some one of the planets, its first hour[197] will belong to that planet, and the second hour to the next planet which comes after this one, and so on. For example, Friday belongs to Venus, and its first hour belongs to Venus, the second one to Mercury, the third to the Moon, the fourth to Saturn, [and so on until the end of the day and night].[198]

---

[193] Note: "day" means the period of daylight when the Sun is above the horizon, not our 24-hour standardized day. Likewise, "night" means the period of darkness when the Sun is below the horizon.

[194] Reading with the Ar. for "holiday"(i.e., Sunday).

[195] This still leaves it unclear whether the body of the Sun must only touch the horizon, or be completely below it.

[196] Omitting John's "or night."

[197] Traditionally, the day begins at daybreak, not at midnight as we consider it today.

[198] Al-Qabīsī adds that these are seasonal hours, not the regular 60-minute hours (equinoctial hours) we standardly use today.

	Sunday	Monday	Tuesday	Wednesday	Thursday	Friday	Saturday
1	☉	☽	♂	☿	♃	♀	♄
2	♀	♄	☉	☽	♂	☿	♃
3	☿	♃	♀	♄	☉	☽	♂
4	☽	♂	☿	♃	♀	♄	☉
5	♄	☉	☽	♂	☿	♃	♀
6	♃	♀	♄	☉	☽	♂	☿
7	♂	☿	♃	♀	♄	☉	☽
8	☉	☽	♂	☿	♃	♀	♄
9	♀	♄	☉	☽	♂	☿	♃
10	☿	♃	♀	♄	☉	☽	♂
11	☽	♂	☿	♃	♀	♄	☉
12	♄	☉	☽	♂	☿	♃	♀

Figure 105: Planetary hours from sunrise

	Sunday	Monday	Tuesday	Wednesday	Thursday	Friday	Saturday
1	♃	♀	♄	☉	☽	♂	☿
2	♂	☿	♃	♀	♄	☉	☽
3	☉	☽	♂	☿	♃	♀	♄
4	♀	♄	☉	☽	♂	☿	♃
5	☿	♃	♀	♄	☉	☽	♂
6	☽	♂	☿	♃	♀	♄	☉
7	♄	☉	☽	♂	☿	♃	♀
8	♃	♀	♄	☉	☽	♂	☿
9	♂	☿	♃	♀	♄	☉	☽
10	☉	☽	♂	☿	♃	♀	♄
11	♀	♄	☉	☽	♂	☿	♃
12	☿	♃	♀	♄	☉	☽	♂

Figure 106: Planetary hours from sunset

§V.14: Masculine and feminine hours: al-Qabīsī

[al-Qabīsī II.50] The hours are even said to be masculine and feminine: because the first hour of each day and night is masculine and the second one feminine, also the third masculine and the fourth feminine, and they follow each other thus in order, namely with one masculine and the next feminine, up to the end of the day and night.

[al-Qabīsī II.51] And since (with God assenting) we have already finished the being of the planets in themselves and what they signify, let us go on by describing what happens to them in themselves and with each other.[199]

---

[199] Al-Qabīsī's text now moves on to what are Books III-IV above.

BOOK VI: LOTS

[*Abbr.* VI.1-2] The order of treatment invites us to name the Lots.

[al-Qabīsī V.1-2] On the recollection of all the Lots. And when we have noted in the place of the Lots, "take from that place to that place, and project from the Ascendant or from some other place," we are saying that you should add the degrees of the Ascendant on top of what there was between each place, and to project from the Ascendant or from the beginning of the sign from which you are projecting.[1]

§VI.1: The seven planetary Lots

§VI.1.1: The Lot of Fortune or the Moon

[*Abbr.* VI.3] First therefore, is [the one] called the Lot of Fortune and prosperity, which is found in this way: in the day the degrees are counted from the Sun up to the Moon, but by night from the Moon to the Sun; however, the degrees of the horoscopic sign are added to these, from the first degree of the sign up to the horoscope itself. The sum, however, is distributed through the rest of the signs, beginning from the [sign of] horoscope itself. For the last [degree] receiving [the numbering] signifies the Lot of Fortune. But if the Sun and the Moon were in one degree, the Lot of prosperity will be in the horoscope itself.

[*Gr. Intr.* VIII.3.279-309] And because the Sun is the luminary of the day, and the Moon the luminary of the night, they began this Lot in the day from the diurnal fortune (which is the Sun), up to the nocturnal fortune (which is the Moon), by equal degrees;[2] and in the night from the nocturnal Moon to the diurnal Sun. After this, they added on top of what ascends from the beginning of the ascending sign, up to the ascending degree, by equal degrees. Then they projected this from the beginning of the ascending sign, giving 30° to each sign. And where the number reached, they said that there was this Lot. Which if both

---

[1] See example by Dykes below.
[2] That is, zodiacal or ecliptical degrees.

luminaries were in one minute, the Lot will be in the minute of the Ascendant.

And this Lot is called the Lot of Fortune. And it signifies according to what the luminaries signify. And the proper quality of its signification is to signify the soul and its fortune and its strength. And it signifies life and bodies and assets and success and fortune, also enrichment and poverty, gold and silver, also the ease and severity of [the prices of] goods of exchange, also praise and a good reputation, and the loftiness of the native and of [his] kingdom and position of first place. And it signifies riches and honor, also loftiness and good and evil [both] present and absent, also appearing and hidden. It also signifies intention, and the beginning of works and matters.

And this Lot is put before all the Lots in the way that the Sun is put before the other planets through his gleaming. And it is more sublime and valuable than all the Lots. And as—among the planets of the circle—it is not more gleaming nor more beautiful then them, nor more notable, and it has its own being individually apart from the rest of the stars, likewise if they were in a good condition or place and they signified good fortune individually, such as rulership and power and assets, so will he be famous and renowned, precious [and] dear. And they do not use it except for those who individually exceed the being of the rest through their own being. And it is they for whom the luminaries and the Lot of Fortune is in the optimal and praiseworthy places in their nativities.[3]

[al-Qabīsī V.3] An example of which is the work of the Lot of Fortune: because you take whatever is between the Sun and Moon in terms of degrees, and you add on top of them the degrees of the ascending sign, and you will project what was collected, 30° by 30°. And you will begin to project from the beginning of the ascending sign, and where the number is ended, there is the Lot of Fortune; and in the night the contrary: from the Moon to the Sun, and you will add from above the degrees of the ascending sign, and you project this, 30° by 30°.

---

[3] This last paragraph is a bit confusing, but the point near the end is that the Lot of Fortune (along with the luminaries) is used in determining eminence. For more on eminence, see Appendix F.

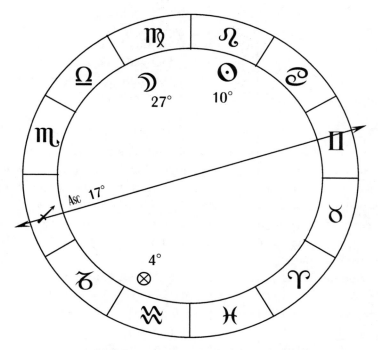

Figure 107: Lot of Fortune calculation: Dykes

Comment by Dykes. All Lots begin by measuring the longitude between two points, and then projecting that distance from a third point (usually the degree of the Ascendant). But Abū Ma'shar and al-Qabīsī also suggest what they believe is an easier method: adding the degrees already arisen to that distance, and projecting the sum from the beginning of the *rising sign* itself. Take the example of the Lot of Fortune in a diurnal chart, above. The Ascendant is at 17° Sagittarius (or 257° absolute degrees if we count from 0° Aries). First, measure the distance forward in zodiacal order from the Sun, up to the Moon: in this case, the distance from 10° Leo (the Sun) to 27° Virgo (the Moon) is 47°. The more common method nowadays would be to add 47° to 257°, which puts the Lot at 304° or 4° Aquarius. But Abū Ma'shar recommend that we add 47° to the number of degrees actually arisen in Sagittarius (17°), yielding 64°. If we then count out this 64° in 30° increments from the beginning of Sagittarius, then 30° goes to Sagittarius and 30° to Capricorn, with 4° left over: the Lot is at 4° Aquarius.

§VI.1.2: The Lot of Spirit or the Sun

[*Abbr.* VI.4] But the Lot of Absence:[4] in the day from the Moon to the Sun, but by night from the Sun to the Moon; and the addition being made just as we said before, the last [degree] of those receiving [the counting] shows the place sought.[5]

[*Gr. Intr.* VIII.3.323-36] They began the Lot of the Absent in the day from it (namely, from the Moon) to the Sun by equal degrees, and in the night from the Sun to the Moon. And on top of this is added what was collected from what is ascending, from the beginning of the ascending sign up to the ascending degree and its minute, by equal degrees, and it is projected from the beginning of the ascending sign, by giving 30° to each sign. And where the number reached, the Lot will be in that same place.

And this Lot is called the Lot of the Absent, and it comes after the Lot of Fortune. And its proper quality is to signify the soul and body and its being. And it signifies faith and prophecy, religion and the honoring of God, and secrets and thoughts and intentions and hidden and concealed matters, and everything of matters which is absent. And praise and a good reputation and courtliness and generosity, also heat and cold.

[al-Qabīsī V.4a] And so, after the Lot of Fortune, let us begin the Lots of the twelve houses, and we should begin from the Ascendant.[6]

[al-Qabīsī V.4d] The Lot of the Absent[7] is taken in the day from the Moon up to the Sun, and conversely in the night, and it is projected from the Ascendant.

---

[4] The Lot of Spirit. In Perso-Arabic astrology it is often called the Lot of Absence or the Lot of Hidden. "Absence" could be related to the fact that it was also used anciently to study travel (*Anth.* I.30); the "hidden" could also relate to the inner mind, as opposed to external and physical fortune signified by the Lot of Fortune.

[5] The Ar. continues: "This agrees with the Lot of Religion." But it does not (see below), nor does *Gr. Intr.* include this line. It must be an error.

[6] Al-Qabīsī wants to treat some of the planetary Lots as belonging to the first house.

[7] Reading for John's "things to be" (*futurorum*), here and throughout al-Qabīsī below.

§VI.1.3: The Lot of Eros or Venus (Valens)

[*Abbr.* VI.6] The Lot of appetite and companionship is found in this way: the degrees being taken from the Lot of Fortune up to the Lot of Non-Appearance,[8] the degrees from the first [degree] of the rising sign up to the horoscope itself will be added, and, by distributing the sum as was stated, the last [degree] receiving [the numbering] will indicate the Lot of appetite and companionship. This, however [is] in the day; but by night from the Lot of Non-Appearance up to the Lot of Fortune. Carry out the rest as above.

[*Gr. Intr.* VIII.3.428-437] The Lot of Venus, which is that of love and concord, is taken in the day from the Lot of Fortune to the Lot of the Absent, and in the night conversely, and from above it is increased [by] what ascends from the beginning of the ascending sign, [and it is projected from the Ascendant], and where the number reaches, the Lot will be in that same place.

And this signifies pleasure and passionate desire in sexual intercourse, and cherishing and the seeking of those things which the mind desired, and in which it rejoices and is strengthened; also love and all matters of sexual intercourse, and marriage-unions and concord and happiness and games and delights.

[al-Qabīsī V.4e] The Lot of esteem and concord is taken in the day from the Lot of Fortune to the Lot of the Absent, and conversely in the night, and you project from the Ascendant.

§VI.1.4: The Lot of Basis

[*Abbr.* VI.7] The Lot of [stability, abiding, support of the Ascendant, and the][9] form and perfection of the native, follows the Lot of Venus.[10]

[*Gr. Intr.* VIII.3.560-78] The Lot of durability and stability, which is the Lot of the trust[11] of the Ascendant, and of the native's looks and

---

[8] The Lot of Spirit.
[9] Adding and following the Ar.
[10] That is, the Lot of Eros according to Valens immediately above.
[11] *Fiduciae.* "trust, confidence, security" (including financial deposits).

his beauty, is taken in the day from the Lot of Fortune to the Lot of the Absent, and conversely in the night, and the degrees of the Ascendant are added on top of what was collected, and it is projected from the beginning of the ascending sign.

And this Lot matches the Lot of Venus.[12] And it signifies the native's facial appearance and his likeness to the father or mother. And it signifies the fitness of the native's body, and his soundness at the hour of the nativity, and [also] foreign travel. And if this Lot and its Lord were of a good condition, the native will have a beautiful facial appearance, and a perfected body in [his] limbs, and sound in frame, of balanced form, sound in his limbs and with a sound body for his whole life. He profits on foreign travels and will acquire many profits in them. But if they were impeded, they signify the foulness of the body and shabbiness and a disgusting form and facial appearance, and a multitude of infirmities. And if they declined towards the significator of the father, the native will be like the father and the household members of his father; but if they declined to the significator of the mother, the native will be like the mother and her household members.

[al-Qabīsī V.4f] The Lot of stability and duration and the trust of the Ascendant, and the duration of the native,[13] is just like the Lot of esteem and concord.

§VI.1.5: The Lot of Necessity or Mercury (Valens)

[Abbr. VI.8] The Lot of ineffective worry[14] thusly: in the day it will be numbered from the Lot of Non-Appearance up to the Lot of Fortune; but by night, conversely. The rest as above.

[Gr. Intr. VIII.3.439-49] The Lot of Mercury, which is the Lot of poverty and middling wit, is taken in the day from the Lot of the Absent up to the Lot of Fortune, and conversely in the night, and from above it is increased [by] what ascends from the beginning of the as-

---

[12] That is, the Lot of Eros according to Valens, above.
[13] The Ar. adds language similar to Abū Ma'shar's about the native's appearance and growth.
[14] The Ar. reads: "poverty."

cending sign, and it is projected from the beginning of the ascending sign, and where the number reached, the Lot will be in that same place.

And this signifies poverty and war and fear, also hatred and a multitude of contention, and enemies, and anger and contentions in an hour of anger, and business dealings, buying and selling, also worries and cleverness, and writings and number and the seeking of diverse sciences and astronomy.

[al-Qabīsī V.5b] The Lot of poverty and smallness of mind[15] is taken in the day from the Lot of the Absent to the Lot of Fortune, and conversely in the night, and it is projected from the Ascendant.

§VI.1.6: The Lot of Courage or Mars

[*Abbr.* VI.9] The Lot of dispute and disagreement thusly: in the day from Mars up to the degree of the Lot of Fortune; but conversely by night. The rest as above.

[*Gr. Intr.* VIII.3.410-19] The Lot of Mars, which is of courage and boldness, is taken in the day from Mars up to the degree of the Lot of Fortune, and conversely in the night, and from above are increased the degrees of the Ascendant, and it is projected from the beginning of the Ascendant, and where the number reaches, the Lot will be in that same place. And this Lot signifies management and assistance and boldness and courage, also strength and harshness and rudeness and coarseness, and haste, also killing and robbery and foul and horrid works, and lewdness and seductions and cunning things.

[al-Qabīsī V.4g] The Lot of courage and boldness is taken in the day from Mars to the degree of the Lot of Fortune, and conversely in the night, and project from the Ascendant.

---

[15] The Ar. reads, "lack of means." This could be an implicit criticism of people who are mentally focused on money instead of more exalted mental states.

§VI.1.7: The Lot of Victory or Jupiter

[*Abbr.* VI.10] [The Lot of prosperity and assistance and victory: by day from the Lot of Spirit to Jupiter, conversely by night, projected from the Ascendant.][16]

[*Gr. Intr.* VIII.3.390-404] The Lot of Jupiter, which is that of blessedness[17] and assistance, is taken in the day from the Lot of things to be (which signifies fortune) up to Jupiter (which signifies blessedness and assistance), and conversely in the night. And from above are increased the degrees of the Ascendant, and it is projected from the beginning of the Ascendant; and where the number reaches, the Lot will be in that same place.

And its signification is over honor and achievement and assistance and blessedness and kindness, also praiseworthy ends, and fitness and the seeking of faith and whatever is of its being. And belief in God and study in every good work, and the esteeming of it. And the seeking of justice, and of a just judgment between men. And the building of places of oratory, and wisdom and the wise and the loftiness of the wise. Also trust and hope, and every thing a man enjoys in terms of goods, and the partnership of men with each other.

[al-Qabīsī V.5c] The Lot of blessedness and triumph and victory is taken in the day from the Lot of the Absent to Jupiter, and conversely in the night, and it is projected from the Ascendant.

§VI.1.8: The Lot of Nemesis or Saturn

[*Abbr.* VI.11] [The Lot of bonds and imprisonment and [whether] he [will] escape: by day from Saturn to the Lot of Fortune, conversely by night, projected from the Ascendant.][18]

[*Gr. Intr.* VIII.3.371-86] The Lot of Saturn, the heavy one, should be taken in the day from the degree of Saturn up to the degree of the Lot

---

[16] Adding and adapting from the Ar.; missing in Adelard.
[17] In the sense of being supremely happy, blissful, and also blessed with riches.
[18] Adding and adapting from the Ar.; missing in Adelard.

of Fortune, and conversely in the night, and from above is added what is ascending from the degrees of the ascending sign, and it is projected from the beginning of the ascending sign; and where this number reaches, the Lot will be in that same place.

But its signification is over memory and the depth of counsel, also over faith and religion and self-control in faith. And over every matter which is lost or was stolen, or fled or fell into a well or in the sea, or were dead. And over the condition of the dead, and what kind of death it is. Also, the condition of lands and his harvests, and over buildings and shipyards, and anxiety and avarice, and over praise or blame, and over middle age and malice and old age, and what is weighty, and over every thing fettered or put in prison, and the condition of his liberation from that same prison or fetters.

[al-Qabīsī V.11d] The Lot of bonds and prison and whether he would be liberated from it or not, is taken in the day from Saturn to the Lot of Fortune, and conversely in the night, and it is projected from the Ascendant.

§VI.2: Lots of the houses

§VI.2.1: The Lot of life

[*Abbr.* VI.12] [The Lot of life: by day from Jupiter to Saturn, conversely by night, projected from the Ascendant.][19]

[*Gr. Intr.* VIII.4.541-50] And they took it up in the day from the diurnal fortune: this Lot in the day is taken from Jupiter to Saturn, and conversely in the night, and from above is added what ascends of the ascending sign; then it is projected from the beginning of the ascending sign, and where it reaches, the Lot of life will be in that same place.

And this is a Lot of the Ascendant, and it signifies natural life and the condition of the body and [its] sustenance. Which if it were of a good condition, it signifies a great length of life, and the soundness of the body and the joy of the soul. But if it were impeded, it signifies a scarcity of life and a multitude of infirmities, also the grief of the soul.

[al-Qabīsī V.4b] The Lot of life is taken in the day from Jupiter to Saturn, and conversely in the night, and it is projected from the Ascendant.

§VI.2.2: The Lot of the releaser or hīlāj

[*Abbr.* VI.13] The Lot of the observation of life,[20] thusly: it will be numbered from the degree of the conjunction of the Sun and Moon up to the place of the Moon, and this number will be joined with the number of the horoscope. The rest as above. This however [is] from the New Moon up to the Full Moon.[21] But from the time of the Full Moon, the computation must be begun from the degree of the Full Moon itself.[22] The rest as above.

---

[19] Adding and adapting from the Ar.; missing in Adelard.

[20] The Ar. reads "of the *hīlāj*," i.e., the "releaser."

[21] That is, if the birth were conjunctional (following a New Moon).

[22] This calculation is different from that found in Valens (*Anth.* III.7), and is probably wrong. According to Valens, in conjunctional births (after a New Moon) we count from the conjunction to the natal Moon; in preventional births (after a Full Moon) we count

[*Gr. Intr.* VIII.5.1533-52] For the Lot of the releaser, look at the nativity. Which if it were conjunctional, take it from the degree and minute of the conjunction which was before the native's birth, up to the Moon; and if the nativity were preventional, take it from the degree and minute of the prevention which was before the birth of the native, up to the Moon, and project from the Ascendant (and where the number were finished, there will be the Lot).

And this Lot is directed in the way a releaser is directed, by degrees, and its advancement is led through the signs (in the way it happens with a releaser). And when its advancement reached the bad ones, it signifies disaster.

And there were many of the wise astrologers, when they found a man suffering the greatest in certain times, and they did not find that the releasers[23] had arrived at the places of the bad ones in that same time, nor did they find an evident signification of that same impediment in the revolution of that year, they did not know the reason of this matter, and therefore this was hidden from them: because they did not direct this Lot. And if they had directed it, they would have found this evil happening in that same time in which this Lot had reached certain places signifying the danger. Because with respect to signification over matters, this Lot has something near to the signification of the other releasers in its motion through the signs.

[al-Qabīsī V.4c] The Lot of the releaser is taken from the degree of the conjunction or prevention which was before the nativity, to the degree of the Moon, and it is projected from the Ascendant.

---

from the natal Moon to the next Full Moon. The amount is projected from the Ascendant.

[23] That is, the other points which are usually directed for longevity and other matters: see VIII.1.3 and VIII.2.2*f* below.

§VI.2.3: The Lot of origins and condition

[*Abbr.* VI.41] [The Lot of the oppressive place below[24] is like the Lot of character.][25]

[*Gr. Intr.* VIII.4.747-59] The Lot of origins and condition is taken in the day from Saturn to Mars and conversely in the night, and from above are increased the degrees which Mercury walked through in the sign in which he was, and it is projected from the beginning of that same sign; and where it reached, the Lot will be in that same place.

After this, look: if this Lot were in an angle and some one of the Lords of its dignity aspected it, or it was the Sun or the Lord of the Midheaven or some one of the Lords of the angles aspecting it by an aspect of friendship, the native will be of a noble lineage and respectable kinship. For he would not be able to be blamed in his kinship. But if this Lot were cadent from the angles and joined to the bad ones, or no Lord of its dignity or of the Lords of the angles aspected it, he will be blameworthy and dejected in his origin and condition.

§VI.2.4: The Lot of assets

[*Abbr.* VI.14] The Lot of resources thusly: in the day it will be computed from the place of the Lord of the domicile of resources up to [the degree of the place of resources, and projected from the Ascendant].[26]

[*Gr. Intr.* VIII.4.607-17] The Lot of assets is taken in the day and in the night from the Lord of the house of assets to the degree of the house of assets by equal degrees, and from above are increased the degrees of the Ascendant, and it is projected from the Ascendant.

And this Lot signifies profit and the means of livelihood and food by which bodies are sustained for their whole life. Which if it were in a good place, it signifies a good condition in assets and food and the

---

[24] In VI.2.30.

[25] Adding with the Ar.; missing in Adelard. Burnett has this Lot being projected from the Ascendant, not Mercury; but we can see that Abū Ma'shar does project from Mercury.

[26] Adding and adapting from the Ar. Adelard's text combines the first part of the Lot of money with the last part of the Lot of grandfathers, which I have moved to its proper place below.

means of livelihood. And if it were impeded, it signifies a bad condition in these things which we have said. But the rest of the significators of assets and fortune signify the rest of the kinds of fortunes [which] appear in terms of assets, namely what is treasured and watched over.

[al-Qabīsī V.5a] The second house. The Lot of assets is taken in the day and night from the Lord of the house of assets to the degree and minute of the house of assets, and it is projected from the Ascendant.

§VI.2.5: The Lot of brothers

[*Abbr.* VI.15] [The Lot of brothers: by day and night from Saturn to Jupiter, projected from the Ascendant.][27]

[*Gr. Intr.* VIII.4.646-57] Hermes and all the ancient sages said that the Lot of brothers is taken in the day and night from Saturn to Jupiter by equal degrees, and from above are increased the degrees of the Ascendant, and it is projected from the Ascendant.

And al-Andarzaghar said (relating this to Valens)[28] that the Lot of brothers is taken in the day and night from Mercury to Jupiter, and from above are increased the degrees of the Ascendant, and it is projected from the Ascendant. But what Hermes said is more true: because the signification of Saturn and Jupiter over brothers is closer on account of the closeness of their circles and complexion, and they have a signification over brothers and childbirth. And for this reason the ancients sometimes called Saturn the "brother" of Jupiter; and in certain places Jupiter is called the brother of Saturn.

[al-Qabīsī V.6a] The third house. The Lot of brothers is taken in the day from Saturn to Jupiter, and in the night likewise,[29] and it is projected from the Ascendant.

---

[27] Adding and adapting from the Ar.; missing in Adelard.
[28] This is a misattribution which was current among the Arabs and Persians. See the parallel discussion in *BA* III.3.2.
[29] That is, without reversing the calculation.

§VI.2.6: The Lot of the death of the brothers

[Abbr. VI.16] The Lot of the death of the brothers thusly: in the day from the Sun up to the southern degree,[30] by night the converse. The rest as above.

[Gr. Intr. VIII.4.685-695] The Lot of the death of brothers and sisters is taken in the day from the Sun to the degree of the Midheaven by equal degrees, and conversely in the night, and from above are increased the degrees of the Ascendant, and it is projected from the Ascendant: and where it reached, the Lot will be in that same place.

And this Lot signifies the cause of the brothers' and sisters' death. And whenever this Lot reached the significators of the brothers and sisters according to the turning of the signs, [giving] one year to each sign, or according to the number of degrees (namely one year to each degree)—when the significators of the brothers and sisters reached it in the way we said, the brothers and sisters will find mishaps.

§VI.2.7: The Lot of the father

[Abbr. VI.17] The Lot of fathers thusly: in the day from the Sun to Saturn; by night conversely. The rest as above. Which if Saturn were with the Sun, Jupiter will be put down instead of [Saturn].[31]

[Gr. Intr. VIII.4.703-26] And therefore they said, for the Lot of fathers, that it is taken in the day from the Sun to Saturn, and conversely in the night, and from above are increased the degrees of the Ascendant, and it is projected from the Ascendant. If however Saturn were under the rays, it is taken in the day from the Sun to Jupiter, and conversely in the night, and from above are increased the degrees of the Ascendant, and it is projected from the Ascendant; and where it reached, the Lot of the father will be in that same place.

And certain people said that if Saturn were under the rays, the Lot of the father is taken in the day from Mars to Jupiter and conversely in

---

[30] That is, the degree of the Midheaven.
[31] The next sentence [Abbr. VI.18] refers to a tenth-house Lot, so I have moved it to that section below.

the night, and it is projected from the Ascendant. But what Hermes said is more true, because the signification of Jupiter is more valid over fathers than that of Mars; also, if the signification of Saturn is annulled because he is under the rays, still the signification of the Sun remains, and for that reason it is good that if Saturn is under the rays it should be taken in the day from the Sun to Jupiter, and conversely in the night, and it is projected from the Ascendant—in the way Hermes said.

And[32] this Lot signifies the being of the father, and his nobility and lineage. Also, the Lord of the domicile of the Lot signifies the good fortune of the father in assets and labor. Which if the Lot were of a good condition in the circle, his father will be noble; and if it contradicts this, [there will be] controversy. And if its Lord were of a good condition, he will be fortunate. But if it were of a bad condition and place, he will be full of labor. And if it[33] were fortunate, it signifies a long length of life. And if it were impeded, it signifies a scarcity of life. Also, this Lot and its Lord signify the native's kingdom and his honor and strength.[34]

[al-Qabīsī V.6b-7a] The Lot of [the father][35] is taken in the day from the Sun to Saturn, and conversely in the night, and it is projected from the Ascendant; and while Saturn was under the rays, it is taken in the day from the Sun to Jupiter, and conversely in the night, and it is projected from the Ascendant.

§VI.2.8: The Lot of the death of the parents

[al-Qabīsī V.7b] The Lot of the death of fathers is taken in the day from Saturn to Jupiter, and conversely in the night, and it is projected from the Ascendant.[36]

---

32 For this paragraph, cf. *BA* III.4.3.

33 Here and in the next sentence, I am not sure what "it" refers to.

34 Reading *honor atque fortitudo* for *honoris atque fortitudinis*.

35 In both the Arabic and Latin, al-Qabīsī mistakenly describes this as the Lot of the death of the brothers. After that, he says "the fourth house," and repeats this first sentence with the correct title, so I omit it here.

36 This Lot is not in *Abbr.*, but since it is in al-Qabīsī I follow it with the excerpt from *Gr. Intr.* below.

[*Gr. Intr.* VIII.4.728-33] The Lot of the death of fathers is taken in the day from Saturn to Jupiter, and conversely in the night, and from above are increased the degrees of the Ascendant, and it is projected from the Ascendant. And this Lot signifies the cause of the death of fathers. And whenever the profection of the year reached this Lot or its Lord, it signifies the father's danger. And likewise if one of them reached the significators of the father.

§VI.2.9: The Lot of grandfathers

[*Abbr.* VI.19] The Lot of grandfathers thusly: in the day from the Lord of the sign in which the Sun was, up to Saturn; but by night to the contrary, and so on. But if the Sun were in his own domicile or in the domicile of Saturn, it will be computed from the Sun to Saturn in the day, but by night from Saturn to the Sun, wherever Saturn was. [Do not care whether Saturn is under the rays or appearing.][37]

[*Gr. Intr.* VIII.4.735-45] The Lot of grandfathers is taken in the day from the Lord of the house of the Sun to Saturn, and conversely in the night, and it is projected from the Ascendant; and where it reached, this Lot will be in that same place. Which if the Sun were in his own domicile, it is taken in the day from the first degree of Leo to Saturn, and conversely in the night, and it is projected from the Ascendant. And if the Sun were in a domicile of Saturn, you will take it in the day from the Sun to Saturn, and conversely in the night, and you will project from the Ascendant. And you will not care if Saturn were under the rays or appearing [from out of them].

And this Lot and its Lord signify the condition of the grandfathers. And whenever it were joined to the bad ones, dangers will find the grandfathers. And whenever it were joined to the fortunes, good and fortune and abundance in assets will find them.

[al-Qabīsī V.7c] The Lot of grandfathers is taken in the day from the Lord of the house of the Sun to Saturn, and conversely in the night, and it is projected from the Ascendant. And if the Sun were in

---

[37] Adding with the Ar., and with *Gr. Intr.* below.

his own domicile or in one of the domiciles of Saturn, take it in the day from the Sun to Saturn, and conversely in the night, and project from the Ascendant; and you should not consider whether Saturn is appearing or under the rays.

§VI.2.10: The Lot of real estate

[*Abbr.* VI.20-21] The Lot of open fields and thickets thusly: it will be numbered from Saturn to the Moon by day or night. The rest as above. [The Lot of real estate is like the Lot of what work the native does.][38]

[*Gr. Intr.* VIII.4.761-71] The Lot of real estate according to Hermes is taken in the day and night from Saturn to the Moon, and the degrees of the Ascendant are increased from above, and it is projected from the Ascendant; and where the number were ended, this Lot will be in that same place. And this Lot agrees with the Lot of the king and what kind of work the native does.

But if this Lot and its Lord were suitable in condition and place, the native will have real estate and villages, and he will be made fortunate because of it, and because of the cultivation of the earth and sowing, and he will acquire assets from that. But if they were of a bad condition and place, they signify griefs and afflictions and something horrible because of real estate.

[al-Qabīsī V.7d] The Lot of real estate and possessions[39] is taken in the day and night from Saturn to the Moon, and it is projected from the Ascendant.

---

[38] Adding and adapting from the Ar., and with *Gr. Intr.* See the Lot of authority and what a native does, in VI.2.40 below.
[39] Perhaps even "holdings" (*possessionum*)?

§VI.2.11: The Lot of cultivation

[*Abbr.* VI.33] [The Lot of women's marriage according to Hermes agrees with the Lot of cultivation.][40]

[*Gr. Intr.* VIII.4.778-83] This [Lot of the cultivation of the earth and sowing] is taken in the day and night from Venus to Saturn,[41] and is projected from the Ascendant; and where it reached, this Lot will be in that same place.

After this, look at this Lot and at its Lord: if they were made fortunate, he will have success from the cultivation of the earth and sowing and planting. But if they were impeded, he will not see good from them, and he will suffer horrible loss because of them.

§VI.2.12: The Lot of the end of matters

[*Abbr.* VI.39] But this Lot [of a year suspected of death or illness][42] is like the Lot of ending business matters.

[*Gr. Intr.* VIII.4.785-95] It is taken in the day and night from Saturn to the Lord of the house of the conjunction (if he were born conjunctional) or to the Lord of the house of the prevention (if he were born preventional), and from above is increased the degrees of the Ascendant, and it is projected from the Ascendant. Which if this Lot and the Lord of its house were in signs of straight ascension, or made fortunate, the ends of matters will be good. But if they were in signs of crooked ascension or impeded, the ends of his matters will be bad. And if they were different, that is, if one of them were in a straight sign and the other in a crooked sign, there will be diversity and a commingling in the ends of his matters; after this, the matter will revert to that which the sign in which the Lord of the Lot is, signifies.

---

[40] Adding with the Ar., and moving up from VI.2.23 below.
[41] I note that Venus and Saturn are the domicile and exalted Lords of the fourth (Libra) in the Greek *Thema Mundi*.
[42] See VI.2.29 below.

[al-Qabīsī V.7f] The Lot of the end of things is taken in the day and night from Saturn up to the Lord of the house of the conjunction or the prevention, and the degree of the Ascendant is added from above, and it is projected from the Ascendant.

§VI.2.13: The Lot of children

[*Abbr.* VI.22-23] The Lot of children thusly: it will be computed from Jupiter[43] up to Saturn in the day, but from Saturn to Jupiter in the night. The rest as above. And this Lot is like the Lot of life.

[*Gr. Intr.* VIII.4.799-820] It is taken in the day from Jupiter to Saturn and conversely in the night, and from above will be added the degrees of the Ascendant, and it is projected from the Ascendant; and where it reached, the Lot of the child will be in that same place. And this Lot matches the Lot of life. But at night, the Lot of children and the Lot of brothers meet in one place.[44] And Theophilus thought that the Lot of children is taken in the day and night from Jupiter to Saturn, but the first [version of the] Lot which Hermes and all the ancients described is more true.

And through this Lot is signified whether a man will have a child or not. Which if this Lot and its Lord were in a sign of many children, he will have many children. And if it were in a sterile sign, he will not have a child. But if it were in a sign of few children, he will have few children. If however this Lot signified the production of children and it were made fortunate, they will be [live and be] preserved; but if it were impeded, it signifies the child's death. It also signifies the child's general condition, and how his being will be with the father in concord and diversity, and in esteem or hatred. One even takes what there was between this Lot and its Lord, or what was between its Lord and it (in terms of signs), and a child is put down for every sign. If however there were a common sign between them, the number of that sign will

---

[43] Reading with the Ar. and *Gr. Intr.* for "the Sun," here and in the next clause.
[44] Assuming, that is, that Abū Ma'shar is correct about the Lot of brothers not being reversed at night.

be doubled; and if there were a planet between them, one child will be counted for it.

[al-Qabīsī V.8a] The fifth house. The Lot of children is taken in the day from Jupiter to Saturn, and conversely in the night, and it is projected from the Ascendant.

§VI.2.14: The Lot of the time of children

[*Abbr.* VI.24] The Lot of the time of children[45] is shown thusly: it will be numbered by day and night from Mars up to Jupiter.[46] The rest as above.

[*Gr. Intr.* VIII.4.829-41] They said that the Lot which judges children for him, and their number, and whether they are male and [whether they are] daughters, is taken in the day and night from Mars to Jupiter, and from above are increased the degrees of the Ascendant, and it is projected from the Ascendant; and where it reached, the Lot will be in that same place. Then, look to see if the first Lot which Hermes described,[47] and the rest of the significators, signified that the native will have a child. Which if this were [the case], it signifies their number.

And in addition, if Jupiter reached this Lot by his bodily conjunction, or he aspected it by a strong aspect, it will reaffirm a child for him in that same hour—if however the man were already of such an age that he could procreate.

Also, if it were in a masculine sign, his children will be more male; and if it were in a feminine sign, they will be more female.

[al-Qabīsī V.8b] The Lot which signifies the time in which he will have children, and their number (namely of masculine ones or feminine ones, and what a woman will give birth to), is taken in the day and night from Mars to Jupiter, and is projected from the Ascendant.

---

[45] The Ar. adds that it also predicts the sex of the children, as with al-Qabīsī and *Gr. Intr.*
[46] Again, reading with the Ar. and *Gr. Intr.* for "the Sun."
[47] I.e., the Lot of children immediately above.

[al-Qabīsī V.8e] The Lot signifying a child when Jupiter reaches it, is taken in the day and night from Mars to Jupiter, and it is projected from the Ascendant.[48]

§VI.2.15: The Lot of male children

[Abbr. VI.25] The Lot of knowing the proper qualities of male children thusly: it must be numbered by day and night from the Moon to Jupiter.[49] The rest as above.

[Gr. Intr. VIII.4.852-67] The Lot of masculine children is taken in the day and night from the Moon to Jupiter, and from above are increased the degrees of the Ascendant, and it is projected from the Ascendant.

And certain Persians said that the Lot of masculine children is taken in the day from the Moon to Saturn, and conversely in the night, and it is projected from the Ascendant. And Theophilus thought that it is taken in the day and night from the Moon to Saturn and projected from the Ascendant.[50]

Also, certain ones of the Persians, not to mention Theophilus, said that these two Lots which they described assist the fortune of the one born[51] in the way that it does with the Lot of Fortune. And they spoke something true in this, because this Lot has a signification over fortune.

But what Hermes described in the drawing out of the Lot of masculine children is more true, and that is that it is taken from the Moon to Jupiter: because Jupiter has a greater signification over masculine children than Saturn does.

---

[48] Al-Qabīsī or later editors have presented this as though it is a separate Lot, but it is clearly a continuation of the Lot of the time of children.

[49] Reading with the Ar. and Gr. Intr.

[50] Despite his favoring of Hermes in the next paragraph, Abū Ma'shar obviously prefers Theophilus, since he used his formula in Abbr.

[51] But wouldn't this Lot say something about the children's good fortune, just as it does for the female children in the Lot below? Or perhaps the children themselves are also being considered a blessing to the parents.

[al-Qabīsī V.8c] The Lot of the knowledge of a male child[52] is taken in the day and night from the Moon to Jupiter, and it is projected from the Ascendant.

§VI.2.16: The Lot of female children

[Abbr. VI.26] The Lot of the condition of daughters thusly: it must be numbered from the Moon to Venus in both the day and night. The rest as above.

[Gr. Intr. VIII.4.871-85] Hermes said: the Lot of female children is taken in the day and night from the Moon to Venus, and on top of that are added the degrees of the Ascendant, and it is projected from the Ascendant. And Theophilus said: it is taken in the day from the Moon to Venus and conversely in the night, and it is projected from the Ascendant. But what Hermes said is more correct, because each star is nocturnal, and the signification of the Moon over women is stronger in the day and night than that of Venus. Therefore, it is good that one should begin with it.

However, this Lot signifies the dispositions of female children, and their marriage-unions, and fluctuations in their conditions. Therefore, if it were of a suitable disposition, they will come to praiseworthy fortunes and will be successful with a marriage-union. And if it were the contrary of this, then it will be to the contrary. And if this Lot is made unfortunate, then it obtains a mishap for the female children.

[al-Qabīsī V.8g] The Lot of the knowledge of the condition of daughters is taken in the day and night from the Moon to Venus, and it is projected from the Ascendant.

---

[52] Omitting et feminae.

§VI.2.17: The Lot of a child's sex[53]

[*Abbr.* VI.27] The Lot of the discrimination of birth before its emergence (namely whether it is male or female) thusly: it will be numbered in the day from the Lord of the domicile in which the Moon was, up to the Moon, by night to the contrary. The rest as above.

[*Gr. Intr.* VIII.4.898-902] It is taken in the day from the Lord of the domicile of the Moon to the Moon, and to the contrary in the night, and it is projected from the Ascendant. If therefore it fell in a masculine sign, then the native or the one about whom it is asked (or the fetus) will be male. And if it fell in a feminine sign, then it will be female.

[al-Qabīsī V.8d] The Lot through which a native is known (about which there is an interrogation), whether it is male or female, is taken in the day from the Lord of the house of the Moon to the Moon, and conversely in the night, and it is projected form the Ascendant.

§VI.2.18: The Lot of delight

[al-Qabīsī V.8f] The Lot of delight is taken in the day and night from Venus to Saturn, and it is projected from the Ascendant.[54]

§VI.2.19: The Lot of chronic illness

[*Abbr.* VI.28] The Lot of illness and old age and death thusly: it will be numbered in the day from Saturn to Mars, by night to the contrary. The rest as above.[55]

[*Gr. Intr.* VIII.4.905-08] The first Lot: of disease and defects and chronic illness according to Hermes. And it was [over] pains and ill-

---

[53] This is a horary Lot.
[54] This is the same as Abū Ma'shar's Lot of women's marriage according to Hermes (see below). It does not appear in the Ar.
[55] For this Lot, cf. *BA* III.6.3, topic 2.3.

nesses and chronic illness from excessive heat and dryness and cold and moisture, and their overwhelming [the native]. Head and dryness belong to Mars, and moisture and cold to Saturn—and these illnesses. They attribute all illnesses and diseases to these two planets, and they said the Lot of disease and defects and chronic illness is taken in the day from Saturn to Mars and conversely in the night, and it is projected from the Ascendant. And this Lot and its Lord, if they were in an [un]supportive or unlucky condition, they signify over what strikes one down and prolonged and chronic illnesses; and if they were fortunate, they signify safety.

[al-Qabīsī V.9a] The sixth house. The Lot of infirmity and chronic illness[56] is taken in the day from Saturn to Mars, and conversely in the night, and it is projected from the Ascendant.

§VI.2.20: The Lot of slaves

[Abbr. VI.29] The Lot of his slaves thusly: by day or night from Mercury to the Moon. The rest as above.

[Gr. Intr. VIII.4.916-27] Hermes and the ancients said: the Lot of slaves is taken in the day and night from Mercury to the Moon, and it is projected from the Ascendant; and where it reached, this Lot will be in that same place.

However, if this Lot and its Lord were made fortunate, he will enjoy good from slaves. But if they were impeded, he will enjoy evil from them. And if this Lot were of a good condition and its Lord of a bad condition, he will enjoy good from his slaves [but] then he will enjoy hindrance from them. And if they were different, it will be according to its difference. And if this Lot were in a sign of many children, he will be the master of many female and male slaves, also of underofficials and attendants. And if it were different from this, it will be according to its difference.

---

[56] Ar. zamānah, often called azamena in Latin texts.

[al-Qabīsī V.9b] The Lot of slaves is taken in the day from Mercury to the Moon, and conversely in the night, and it is projected from the Ascendant. And al-Andarzaghar said it is taken in the day from Mercury to the Lot of Fortune,[57] and conversely in the night, and it is projected from the Ascendant. And he said: it is good that we should use both Lots at the same time.

§VI.2.21: The Lot of men's marriage (Hermes)

[*Abbr.* VI.30] [The Lot of the marriage of men according to Hermes: by day and night from Saturn to Venus, projected from the Ascendant.][58]

[*Gr. Intr.* VIII.4.949-65] Hermes numbered the Lot of men's marriage in the day and night from Saturn to Venus, and from above he added the degrees of the Ascendant, and he projected from the Ascendant. And certain people said that it should be taken conversely in the night and projected from the Ascendant. But what Hermes said is more fitting.

And this Lot which Hermes described, and its Lord, signify the being of men's marriage. Which if they were of a good condition, they signify a fit marriage-union and good fortune, and benefit because of it, and they signify that he will be joined to a beautiful and suitable woman. But if they were impeded, they signify a bad marriage-union, and disasters because of marrying women, and he will marry corrupted women.

And whenever Jupiter reached this Lot or aspected it by a strong aspect, there will be a marriage-union in that same hour. Also, if this Lot were with the Lord of its sign, or the Sun or Moon aspected this Lot and the Lord of its house, by a strong aspect, he will be joined to one of his own relations.

[al-Qabīsī V.10e] The Lot of [men's] nuptials is taken in the day and night from Saturn to Venus, and is projected from the Ascendant.

---

[57] This is the same as the Hermetic Lot of Necessity.
[58] Adding and adapting from the Arabic. Note that this Lot is really supposed to be reversed at night: *Carmen* II.2.2

§VI.2.22: The Lot of men's marriage (Valens)

[*Abbr.* VI.31] The Lot of nuptials for men [according to Valens][59] thusly: by day or night from the Sun to Venus. The rest as above.[60]

[*Gr. Intr.* VIII.4.967-70] Another Lot of men's marriage, from those which Valens described, is taken in the day and night from the Sun to Venus, and the degrees of the Ascendant are increased on top of what was collected, and it is projected from the Ascendant; and where it reached, this Lot will be in that same place.

[al-Qabīsī V.10a] The seventh house. The Lot of men's betrothal is taken in the day and night from the Sun to Venus, and it is projected from the Ascendant. And this Lot is like the Lot of rumors.[61]

§VI.2.23: The Lot of women's marriage (Hermes)

[*Abbr.* VI.32] The Lot of nuptials for women thusly, according to Hermes: by day and night from Venus to Saturn.[62] The rest as above.

[*Gr. Intr.* VIII.4.995-1003] The situation in the marriage-union of women is like the situation of men's marriage-union. But in the marriage-union of women Hermes counted in the day and night from Venus to Saturn, and he increased from above the degrees of the Ascendant, and he projected from the Ascendant. And this Lot matches the Lot of the cultivation of the earth.[63]

Which if this Lot and its Lord were of a good condition, they will signify the fortune of women through a marriage-union. But if they were corrupted, they will signify sorrow and afflictions which they will find because of the marriage-union, and the woman will be wanton.

---

[59] *Anth.* II.38, p. 6. Valens gives the planets but does not actually specify anything about nocturnal charts.
[60] Omitting "But according to Hermes, from Venus to the Sun."
[61] Omitting "commands or," following the Arabic. But see VI.2.35, which is a Mercury-Moon Lot.
[62] Again, this Lot is supposed to be reversed at night.
[63] See VI.2.11 above.

[al-Qabīsī V.10b] The Lot of women's betrothal or marriage-union by Hermes is taken in the day and night from Venus to Saturn, and it is projected from the Ascendant; and this Lot matches the Lot of the cultivation of the earth.

§VI.2.24: The Lot of women's marriage (Valens)

[*Abbr.* VI.34] The Lot of [women's marriage according to Valens][64] thusly: by day and night from the Moon to Mars.

[*Gr. Intr.* VIII.4.1005-09] Another one of women's marriage, from those which Valens described. It is taken in the day and night from the Moon to Mars, and from above are increased the degrees of the Ascendant, and it is projected from the Ascendant. And certain ones of the Persians said that it is taken conversely in the night. But the first one which Valens described is more fitting.

[al-Qabīsī V.10c] Moreover, the Lot of women's betrothal according to Valens is taken in the day and night from the Moon[65] to Mars, and it is projected from the Ascendant.

§VI.2.25: The Lot of the time of marriage

[*Abbr.* VI.35] [The Lot of the time of marriage according to Hermes: by day and night from the Sun to the Moon, projected from the Ascendant.][66]

[*Gr. Intr.* VIII.4.1056-66] The Lot of the hour of a marriage-union, which Hermes recalled, is taken in the day and night from the Sun to the Moon, and from above are increased the degrees of the Ascendant, and it is projected from the Ascendant.

---

[64] Reading with the Ar. and *Gr. Intr.* for "the Lot of knowing when a daughter ought to be given by the parents." See *Anth.* II.38: Valens does list these planets, but omits any mention of nocturnal charts.

[65] Reading for "the Sun." Neither the Arabic nor the Latin has this correct.

[66] Adding with the Ar.; missing in Adelard.

And when Jupiter reached this Lot or aspected it by a strong aspect, a man will marry a beautiful and clean and respectable and desirable woman in that same hour. However, this Lot will be used if the root of the nativity of a man signifies that he will marry. The reason for this matter is because one luminary is hot [and] masculine, and the other moist [and] feminine. However, all generation in this world happens through the conjunction of heat and masculinity with moisture and femininity. Because of this, they counted this Lot from the luminaries.

[al-Qabīsī V.10c] [...from the Sun to the Moon, and it is projected from the Ascendant.][67]

§VI.2.26: The Lot of delight and pleasure

[al-Qabīsī V.10d] The Lot of delight and pleasure is taken in the day and night from Venus to the degree of the seventh, and it is projected from the Ascendant.[68]

[*Gr. Intr.* VIII.4.1049-54] This Lot of Hermes is taken in the day and night from Venus to the degree and minute of the angle of nuptials, and it is projected from the Ascendant. Which if this Lot were assembled with[69] the bad ones or they aspected it, [disgraceful things][70] will be exposed in his marriage-union. And if its Lord were in a malign place and Venus impeded by Saturn or under the rays, he will not marry, forever.

§VI.2.27: The Lot of death

[*Abbr.* VI.36] The Lot of death thusly: by day and night from the Moon up to the eighth sign from the horoscope, with the number of the degrees of

---

[67] This Lot was merged with that of women's marriage according to Valens in the Arabic, and does not appear in the Latin.
[68] This Lot does not appear in *Abbr.* Note that neither al-Qabīsī nor Abū Ma'shar reverse the Lot by night, though it should be: see *Carmen* II.5.4.
[69] That is, in the same sign, especially within 15° (see III.5 above).
[70] Adding based on *BA* III.7.6.

Saturn added on top, in whatever sign he was. But this sum will be distributed by beginning from the first degree of the sign in which Saturn was, and
the last [degree] receiving [the counting] shows the Lot.

[*Gr. Intr.* VIII.4.1098-1106] Hermes put it...[that] the Lot of death
is taken in the day and night from the degree of the Moon to the degree of the eighth house by equal degrees, and from above is increased
what Saturn had walked through in the sign in which he is, and it is
projected from the beginning of that same sign; and where it reached,
this Lot will be in that same place. Which if this Lot and its Lord were
impeded and the fortunes did not aspect them, the native will be killed
by a most foul death. But if the fortunes did aspect, it will be conversely.

[al-Qabīsī V.11a] The eighth house. The Lot of death is taken in the
day and night from the Moon to the degree and minute of the eighth
house, and from above is added what Saturn will have walked through
in his own sign, and it is projected from the beginning of Saturn's sign.

§VI.2.28: The Lot of the killing planet

[*Abbr.* VI.37] The Lot of the killing star thusly: in the day from the degree
in which the Lord of the horoscopic sign was, up to the Moon; but by night
the contrary. The rest as above.

[*Gr. Intr.* VIII.4.1117-25] The Lot of the killing planet is taken in the
day from the degree of the Lord of the Ascendant to the degree of the
Moon, and conversely in the night, and it is projected from the Ascendant; and where the number were ended, this Lot will be in that same
place.
Which[71] if the Moon alone aspected the Lord of this Lot,[72] and the
Moon were impeded in a sign of severed limbs, he will be killed by undergoing [that]. And if she were not impeded, some limb of his limbs
will be cut off. But if the Lord of this Lot and the Lord of the eighth

---

[71] For this paragraph, cf. Rhetorius Ch. 77 (esp. pp. 125 and 128).
[72] Rhetorius has the Moon aspecting the Lot, not its Lord.

were making each other unlucky, then he will be killed by undergoing [that].

[al-Qabīsī V.11b] The Lot of the planet which kills is taken in the day from the degree of the Lord of the Ascendant to the degree of the Moon, and conversely in the night, and it is projected from the Ascendant.

§VI.2.29: The Lot of the suspected year

[*Abbr.* VI.38] The Lot of a year suspected of death or illness, thusly: by day and night from Saturn up to the Lord of the sign of the conjunction of the Sun and Moon, if the Moon will appear waxing. But if she will appear waning, from Saturn to the Lord of the sign of the Full Moon. The rest as above.

[*Gr. Intr.* VIII.4.1130-46] The Lot of the year in which death will be feared for the native, and affliction and exhaustion, also impediment and severity, is taken in the day and night from Saturn to the Lord of the house of the conjunction, or to the Lord of the house of the prevention (if it were before the nativity), and from above are increased the degrees of the Ascendant, and it is projected from the Ascendant; and where it reached, this Lot will be in that same place. And this Lot agrees with the Lot of the end of matters.[73]

However, if this Lot and its Lord were impeded with the Lord of the Ascendant, the native will have many infirmities and afflictions in his body and assets, and often he will see the ruin of his body and the loss of assets. And whenever the year reached this Lot, or this Lot reached the Ascendant or its Lord, [either] through the profections which give a year to each sign, or by direction, the native will find dangers in the body from infirmities and diseases, and he will find difficulty and something horrible in assets and so on; he will also fear death from diverse directions.

---

[73] See above.

[al-Qabīsī V.11c] The Lot of the year in which death is feared for the native, and poverty and impediment and destruction, is taken in the day and night from Saturn to the degree of the Lord of the house of the conjunction or prevention which was before the nativity, and it is projected from the Ascendant.

§VI.2.30: The Lot of the oppressive[74] place

[*Abbr.* VI.40] The Lot of most serious illness and suffering in a limb, thusly: in the day from Saturn to Mars, but by night to the contrary, [and it is projected from Mercury].[75]

[*Gr. Intr.* VIII.4.1148-66] The Lot of the weighty place is taken in the day from Saturn to Mars and conversely in the night, and from above are increased what Mercury walked through in the sign in which he is, and it is projected from the beginning of that same sign, and where the number were ended, the Lot will be in that same place. And this Lot is like the Lot of origins.[76]

Which if this Lot were impeded with the Lord of the Ascendant, the native will have an inseparable illness in [that limb] of his body which the sign in which the Lot was, signifies; and his matters and his inquiries will slow down, and he will be worried in them.

And if the year arrived from the Ascendant to this Lot, or this Lot arrived to the Ascendant or to its Lord through the profections by which one year is given to each sign, or by direction, it signifies that the native's matters will be overtaken, and his works will slow down, and griefs and sorrows and afflictions will find him, and he will begin nothing in that same year which will not be overtaken and slow down. And whenever the year reached this Lot, he will find an infirmity in the limb which the sign in which the Lot was, signifies. And if the bad ones aspected [the sign], difficulties and ruin will find him.

---

[74] Following the Ar.
[75] Adding with the Ar. and *Gr. Intr.*
[76] The Lot of character, in VI.2.3 above.

§VI.2.31: The Lot of travel

[*Abbr.* VI.42] The Lot of travel thusly: by day and night from the Lord of the ninth sign up to the degree of the ninth, and so on.

[*Gr. Intr.* VIII.4.1184-86] It is taken in the day and night from the Lord of the ninth sign to the degree of the ninth house by equal degrees, and it is projected from the Ascendant. And this Lot and its Lord signify the native's foreign travel and his condition in it.

[al-Qabīsī V.12a] The Lot of foreign travel is taken in the day and night from the Lord of the ninth house to the degree and minute of the ninth house, and it is projected from the Ascendant.

§VI.2.32: The Lot of navigation

[*Abbr.* VI.43] The Lot of navigation thusly: in the day from Saturn up to the fifteenth degree of Cancer, by night to the contrary. Which if Saturn were in the fifteenth of Cancer, the leaders[77] of this Lot will be Saturn and the horoscope.

[*Gr. Intr.* VIII.4.1188-96] This is taken in the day from Saturn to the fifteenth degree of Cancer, and in the night from the fifteenth degree of Cancer to Saturn, and it is projected from the Ascendant. Which if this Lot fell with the fortunes in watery signs, he will see good proficiency in travel by sea, and success, also profit and good health. And if it were otherwise, the converse. If however Saturn were in the fifteenth degree of Cancer, that degree itself in which Saturn was, and the degree of the Ascendant, will be the significators. Look at them and their condition, also at the aspect of the planets to them. Then reckon it according to what you see.

[al-Qabīsī V.12b] The Lot of travel by water is taken in the day from Saturn to the fifteenth degree of the sign of Cancer, and conversely in the night, and it is projected from the Ascendant; which if Saturn were

---

[77] That is, "significators."

in the fifteenth degree of Cancer, the degree of the Lot will be the degree of the Ascendant.

§VI.2.33: The Lot of intellect and profound thought

[*Abbr.* VI.44] The Lot of sense and foresight thusly: from Saturn to the Moon in the day, but by night to the contrary (from the Moon to Saturn), and so on; and this Lot is like the one which is [the Lot of] offices.[78]

[*Gr. Intr.* VIII.4.1206-12] This is taken in the day from Saturn to the Moon, and conversely in the night, and it is projected from the Ascendant. And this Lot signifies reason and thinking and the depth of counsel, also the consideration of matters, and search for and scrutiny of obscure things, and the conclusions of the sciences, praiseworthy counsels. And particularly if Saturn were eastern [and] above the earth in the day, aspecting the Lot and receiving it, or [if] the Moon aspected it from an optimal place.

[al-Qabīsī V.16c] The Lot of reason and the depth of sense is taken in the day from Saturn to the Moon, and conversely in the night, and it is projected from the Ascendant.

§VI.2.34: The Lot of wisdom

[al-Qabīsī V.16d] The Lot of wisdom[79] is taken in the day and night from Saturn to Jupiter, and it is projected from Mercury.[80]

---

[78] See the Lot of authority and what a native does, in VI.2.40 below; this latter Lot is not reversed at night, according to Abū Ma'shar.

[79] Omitting "and teaching" from the Lat., following the Arabic.

[80] This Lot did not appear in *Abbr.* and was categorized by al-Qabīsī as one of the non-topical Lots, but it evidently belongs here. I have changed the calculation of the Lot because I believe the Arabic copyist made a mistake. Originally, this Lot read as though it is projected from the Ascendant, but two Lots later is the Lot of the peace and concord of armies, which incorrectly reads as though it is projected from Mercury. Therefore I believe the Arabic scribe switched the two projection points: I have restored this text to read "Mercury," and the other Lot to read "Ascendant."

[*Gr. Intr.* VIII.4.1219-27] The Lot of wisdom and judgment is taken in the day from Saturn to Jupiter and conversely in the night, and it is projected from Mercury. And this Lot signifies wisdom and judgment and patience and expansiveness.[81] Which if this Lot were in the aspect of Saturn and Jupiter, received by them or by one of them, and the Lord of the Ascendant were in its aspect, the native will be expansive and tolerant and rational and patient. And if Mercury aspected it, he will be knowledgeable and experienced in matters, and searching and scrutinizing in obscure matters, and handling proverbs.[82]

§VI.2.35: The Lot of the truth and falsity of rumors

[*Abbr.* VI.45-46] The Lot of the truth and falsity of messengers thusly: in the day and night from Mercury to the Moon, and so on;[83] and this is like the one which is [the Lot of] slaves [according to Hermes].

[*Gr. Intr.* VIII.4.1239-43] This is taken in the day and night from Mercury to the Moon, and it is projected from the Ascendant. And this Lot is like the Lot of slaves.

[al-Qabīsī V.16b] Of them is a Lot which signifies the lying of rumors, if it fell into a crooked or movable sign, or the Lord of its domicile were retrograde or impeded, or the bad ones aspected it[84] or were assembled with it. And it signifies their truth if it fell with fortunes or in their domiciles or bounds, or they aspected it or it were in a sign of straight ascension. It is taken in the day from Mercury to the Moon,[85] and conversely in the night, and it is projected from the Ascendant.

---

[81] This must mean either speaking at length, or taking a long, considered time in making decisions.

[82] This word in Arabic has a broader connotation of understanding how things are alike and different: in other words, he will have words of wisdom.

[83] I would follow Māshā'allāh (*BA* III.11.1) and al-Qabīsī below, and reverse it by night.

[84] John's Latin suggests that this aspecting and assembling is with the Lord of the Lot, but the Arabic does not seem to indicate whether the Lot or the Lord is meant.

[85] Reading with the Arabic and Abū Ma'shar. The Latin had "Venus" here, and so John of Seville or a later scribe then wrote: "And according to Abū Ma'shar, it is taken in the day from Mercury to the Moon, and conversely in the night, and it is projected from the Ascendant."

§VI.2.36: The Lot of religion[86]

[al-Qabīsī V.12c] The Lot of religion is taken in the day from the Moon to Mercury, and conversely in the night, and it is projected from the Ascendant.

[Gr. Intr. VIII.4.1198-1204] The Lot of religion is taken in the day from the Moon to Mercury, and conversely in the night, and it is projected from the Ascendant. Which if this Lot and its Lord fell with the Lord of the Ascendant or with the significators of the Ascendant, the native will be pious and virtuous. And likewise if the significators of the Lot aspected it and the Lord of the Ascendant. But if it were otherwise, that is, if the Lot were impeded, it will be conversely.

§VI.2.37: The Lot of nobility[87]

[Abbr. VI.47] The Lot of the nobility or ignobility of birth thusly: in the day from the Sun up to his kingdom;[88] but by night from the Moon up to her kingdom. Which if [either] were in its own kingdom, the Lot will be in the horoscope itself.

[Gr. Intr. VIII.4.1253-68] The Lot of nobility is taken in the day from the Sun to the degree of his exaltation, which is the fulfillment of the nineteenth degree of Aries, and in the night from the degree of the Moon to the fulfillment of three degrees of the sign of Taurus, and from above is increased what ascended, and it is projected from the Ascendant; and where it reached will be the Lot of the native's nobility.[89]

Therefore, look at this Lot: which if it fell in the Midheaven or with planets which were of a good condition and place, the native will achieve nobility and value and importance, and the rank of kings; and

---

[86] The Arabic word of this Lot really means "piety, being virtuous, God-fearing." It does not appear in Abbr.

[87] Also known as the Hellenistic Lot of exaltation. Here it is also made to indicate whether the native has the father people think he does.

[88] That is, to the degree of his exaltation (according to the Ar.); likewise for the Moon in the next clause.

[89] Or, "exaltation."

if he were of those whom a kingdom is owed, he will get it. But if the Sun were in the nineteenth degree of Aries in the day, or the Moon in the third degree of Taurus in the night, the signification will belong to those degrees and the degree of the Ascendant.

Which if the significators of this Lot aspected it or they were in certain good complexions with it, the native will be the son of the father to whom he is imputed. And if were to the contrary, it would change his legitimacy.

[al-Qabīsī V.7e] The Lot of the native's nobility and of him about whom there is doubt whether he is the son of that father (in whose charge he is put) or that of another, is taken in the day from the degree of the Sun to the degree of his exaltation, and in the night from the Moon to the degree of her exaltation. Which if the Sun in the day were in the degree of his exaltation, or the Moon in the night in the degree of her exaltation, the Lot will be in the degree of the Ascendant, and the signification will belong to [the luminary's] degree and to the degree of the Ascendant.

§VI.2.38: The Lot of the kingdom and authority

[*Abbr.* VI.48] The Lot of the kingdom and authority thusly: in the day from Mars up to the Moon, but by night to the contrary, and so on.

[*Gr. Intr.* VIII.4.1270-73] It is taken in the day from Mars to the Moon and conversely in the night, and is projected from the Ascendant. And this Lot and its Lord, if they were if a good condition and were complected with the Lord of the 10th or of the Ascendant, the native will be a king or leader,[90] and he will be with rich people who will receive his words and listen to him.

[al-Qabīsī V.13b] The Lot of the king and the kingdom is taken in the day from Mars to the Moon, and conversely in the night, and it is

---

[90] Or, "general" (*dux*). Clearly the Mars represents powerful authority, and the Moon the people.

projected from the Ascendant. And it has another Lot like the Lot of fathers.[91]

§VI.2.39: The Lot of power or kingdom or supremacy

[*Abbr.* VI.18] [The Lot of fathers is like the Lot of power.[92]][93]

[*Gr. Intr.* VIII.4.1290-97] The Lot of the kingdom[94] is taken in the day from the Sun to Saturn, and conversely in the night, and it is projected from the Ascendant. And this Lot matches the Lot of fathers if Saturn were not under the rays. And this Lot signifies authority and rank and renown, and value for the native. Which if it had a complexion with the Lord of the Midheaven and the Lord of the Ascendant, he will attain a kingdom and honor and exaltation.

And if it were in a sign in which the Lord of the Ascendant had testimony,[95] it will signify victory for him against those who contend with him.

§VI.2.40: The Lot of authority and what a native does

[*Abbr.* VI.49-50] The Lot of the office of a child[96] thusly: by day or night from Saturn to the Moon, and so on. [The Lot of a child's office like that of real estate and villages.][97]

[*Gr. Intr.* VIII.4.1331-46] And they said: the Lot of the kingdom and what work the native does is taken in the day and night from Saturn to the Moon, and it is projected from the Ascendant. And this Lot signi-

---

[91] The Lot of power or kingdom or supremacy (see the next Lot).

[92] Or, "authority" (Ar. *sulṭān*).

[93] Adding and adapting from the Ar.; missing in Adelard. I have moved this section from its earlier place in order to emphasize its tenth-house nature.

[94] Or perhaps, "supremacy" (*regnum*).

[95] This probably means that the Lord of the Ascendant is the domicile or exalted Lord of it.

[96] Omitting "royal" from the Lat.

[97] Adding and adapting from the Ar.; missing in Adelard. See the Lot of real estate in VI.2.10 above.

fies a kingdom and honor and grandeur, and what kind of work the native will do, and what kind of mastery he will practice with his own hand, and whether he will acquire it and be fortunate in acquiring from the works of a kingdom and masteries, or not.

Which if this Lot and its Lord were of a good condition, he will acquire a kingdom and power; and if it were in Gemini or Virgo, or in signs of arts and masteries, he will be raised up through the works of his hands which are necessary for the rich, by which they are adorned and made brilliant, and he will be with rich people because of [his] subtlety and his experience in masteries. And if it were commingled with the significators of assets, he will acquire assets of great quantity from his mastery. But if it were to the contrary to what we have said, he will be poor and unfortunate in his mastery, acquiring only enough for a day [at a time.]

[al-Qabīsī V.13a] The Lot of the kingdom and what work the native would do, is taken in the day and night from Saturn to the Moon, and it is projected from the Ascendant.

§VI.2.41: *The Lot of the mother*

[*Abbr.* VI.51] The Lot of the mother[98] thusly: by day from Venus to the Moon, by night to the contrary, and so on.

[*Gr. Intr.* VIII.4.1384-87] This Lot is taken in the day from Venus to the Moon, and conversely in the night, and is projected from the Ascendant. And this Lot signifies the condition of mothers. However, we have put the Lot of the mother in the tenth sign for the reason that the tenth sign signifies the condition of mothers, because it is opposed to the house of fathers.

[al-Qabīsī V.13e] The Lot of the mother is taken in the day from Venus to the Moon, and conversely in the night, and it is projected from the Ascendant.

---

[98] Reading with the Ar. for "pride" (*superbiae*).

§VI.2.42: The Lot of a job and authority (Valens)[99]

[al-Qabīsī V.13c] The Lot of positions of first place and work and a kingdom according to Valens is taken in the day and night from the Sun to the degree of the Midheaven, and it is projected from the Ascendant.

§VI.2.43: The Lot of the cause of a kingdom[100]

[al-Qabīsī V.13d] The Lot signifying whether there is a cause of a kingdom or not,[101] is taken in the day and night from the Sun to the degree of the Midheaven, and it is projected from Jupiter.

§VI.2.44: The Lot of hope

[Abbr. VI.52] The Lot of hope thusly: whether by day or night from Saturn up to Venus,[102] and so on, as they are determined above.

[Gr. Intr. VIII.4.1449-56] This Lot is taken in the day from Saturn to Venus and conversely in the night, and is projected from the Ascendant. However, certain people thought that the Lot of hope was extracted in the way the Lot of men's marriage-union according to Hermes is extracted: and these people went astray.[103]

However, this Lot (which is the Lot of hope), if it and its Lord were made fortunate in an optimal place, he will attain everything which he was hoping for and in which he had trust. But if it were of a bad condition and place, he will not attain it.

---

[99] I do not currently know the source of this Lot, though al-Qabīsī certainly got it from al-Andarzaghar or Buzurjmihr.

[100] This is a natal version of al-Qabīsī's mundane Lot of the kingdom and command #3 in VI.4.3 below.

[101] That is, whether someone will gain a position of authority.

[102] Reading with the Ar. for "Mars."

[103] Because Abū Ma'shar believes the Hermetic Lot of men's marriage should not be reversed at night. See VI.2.21 above.

§VI.2.45: The Lot of friends

[*Abbr.* VI.53] The Lot of companions thusly: by day and night from the Moon to Mercury, and so on.[104]

[*Gr. Intr.* VIII.4.1464-69] The Lot of friends is taken in the day and night from the Moon to Mercury, and is projected from the Ascendant. And if this Lot and its Lord were of a good condition and place, in movable signs, the native will have many brethren[105] and friends. Which if they were made fortunate, they will be useful to him, and he will be useful to them, and they will enjoy the good with each other. And if they were received, he will be praiseworthy among them and esteemed by them.

[al-Qabīsī V.14a] The eleventh house. The Lot of friends is taken in the day and night from the Moon to Mercury, and it is projected from the Ascendant. And al-Andarzaghar said it is taken conversely in the night.

§VI.2.46: The Lot of making friends and enemies

[al-Qabīsī V.14b] The Lot signifying the bringing about of friends and enmity is taken in the day from the Lot of Fortune to the Lot of the Absent, and conversely in the night, and it is projected from the Ascendant.[106]

---

[104] This should be reversed at night, as al-Qabīsī credits al-Andarzaghar with this instruction: see also *BA* III.12.1.

[105] Lit. "brothers," but in the sense of comrades.

[106] This is the same as the Lot of Eros or Venus according to Valens, in VI.1.3 above.

§VI.2.47: The Lot of enemies (certain ancients)

[*Abbr.* VI.54] [The Lot of enemies according to some: by day and night from Saturn to Mars, projected from the Ascendant.][107]

[*Gr. Intr.* VIII.4.1511-12] The Lot of enemies [according to certain ancients] is taken in the day and night from Saturn to Mars and is projected from the Ascendant.

[al-Qabīsī V.15b] And according to certain ones of the ancients it is taken in the day and night from Saturn to Mars, and is projected from the Ascendant. And these are the Lots of the twelve houses.

§VI.2.48: The Lot of enemies (Hermes)

[*Abbr.* VI.55] The Lot of enemies [according to Hermes] thusly: by day and night from the Lord of the domicile of enemies up to the degree of the domicile itself, and so on.[108]

[*Gr. Intr.* VIII.4.1514-19] Hermes thought about the Lot of enemies that it is taken in the day and night from the Lord of the house of enemies to the degree of the house of enemies, and is projected from the Ascendant.

And these two Lots[109] should each be used. Which if they were in the square aspect or in the opposition of the Lords of their own houses or of the Lord of the Ascendant, the native will have many enemies. And if it were otherwise, it will be to the contrary.

[al-Qabīsī V.15a] The twelfth house. The Lot of enemies according to Hermes is taken in the day and night from the Lord of the house of enemies to the degree[110] of the house of enemies, and it is projected from the Ascendant.

---

[107] Adding and adapting from the Ar.; missing in Adelard.
[108] Adelard got the calculation backwards; reading with the Ar.
[109] That is, both Lots of enemies.
[110] Omitting "and minute," following the Ar.

§VI.3: Other miscellaneous Lots: al-Qabīsī

[al-Qabīsī V.16a] And here are other Lots which the masters of the judgments of the stars use much:[111]

§VI.3.1: The Lot of knowledge

[al-Qabīsī V.16e] The Lot of knowledge is taken in the day from the Moon to Jupiter, and conversely in the night, and it is projected from the Ascendant.

§VI.3.2: The Lot of heroism and bravery[112]

[al-Qabīsī V.16f] The Lot of war and fighting is taken in the day and night from Saturn to the Moon, and it is projected from the Ascendant.

[*Gr. Intr.* VIII.5.1563-69] The Lot of heroism and bravery is taken in the day from Saturn to the Moon, and conversely in the night, and it is projected from the Ascendant. And this Lot is like the Lot of reason and the depth of counsel, and the Lot of the king and what a native does.[113]

And if this Lot were in the sextile aspect of Mars or Jupiter, in signs of animals, it signifies that the master of [the chart] is a brave knight, and he will deal with riding animals, and be active, and he will be a master of swordplay,[114] and work with weapons, and play with spears and swords.

---

[111] Some of the Lots which followed in al-Qabīsī's own text matched those in Abū Ma'shar and clearly belonged in the lists for the houses, so I have moved them there.

[112] *Militiae*, favoring "war" rather than "military." This is probably the Lot described by Abū 'Alī in *JN* Ch. 34.

[113] For both of these Lots, see VI.2.33 and VI.2.40 above.

[114] Reading a variant on the Ar., which technically means "culture" or "training."

§VI.3.3: The Lot of peace among soldiers

[al-Qabīsī V.16g] The Lot of the peace and concord of armies is taken in the day and night from the Moon to Mercury, and it is projected from the Ascendant.[115]

§VI.3.4: The Lot of the revolution of the year

[al-Qabīsī V.16h] The Lot of looking into the revolution of the year is taken in the day from the Moon to Venus, and conversely in the night, and it is projected from the Sun.[116]

---

[115] The Arabic has "from Mercury," but as explained in VI.2.34 I believe this is an error, with an Arabic scribe switching the projection points between this and the Lot of wisdom. Note that this Lot is identical to the Lot of friends, suggesting that perhaps this Lot was simply retitled and re-used by an astrologer in a horary or mundane context.

[116] I take this Lot to refer to revolutions of nativities and not mundane revolutions, else al-Qabīsī would have classified it with the next group.

§VI.4: Mundane Lots: al-Qabīsī

[al-Qabīsī V.17a] And since, with God aiding, we have introduced these Lots which fall in particular matters, let us follow it up by dealing with the Lots which fall in the revolutions of the years of the world and of conjunctions signifying the causes of a kingdom and its stability:

§VI.4.1: The Lot of the kingdom and command #1

[al-Qabīsī V.17b] Of which there is a Lot which is called the Lot of the kingdom and command, which is used in the revolution of the years of the world: and it is taken from Mars to the Moon, and it is projected from the Ascendant of the conjunction which signifies a changing of the religion.[117]

§VI.4.2: Lot of the kingdom and command #2

[al-Qabīsī V.17c] It also happens in another way: namely it is taken from the degree of the Ascendant of the conjunction to the degree of the conjunction, and it is projected from the degree of the Ascendant of the revolution.[118]

---

[117] This is the same as the natal Lot of the kingdom and authority (see VI.2.38 above), except that the projection is made from the Ascendant for the moment of a Saturn-Jupiter conjunction which has shifted into a new triplicity. It is reversed at night. See *BRD* I.4.6.

[118] That is, cast a chart for the moment of the exact Saturn-Jupiter conjunction (apparently during a shift of triplicities), measure the distance from that Ascendant to the conjunction, and project the result from the Ascendant of the Aries ingress earlier in that year. See *BRD* I.4.8.

§VI.4.3: The Lot of the kingdom and command #3

[al-Qabīsī V.17d] It also happens in another way: it is taken [by day and night] from the degree of the Sun up to the degree of the Midheaven of the revolution,[119] and it is projected from the degree of Jupiter.[120]

§VI.4.4: The Lot of the duration of the kingdom #1

[al-Qabīsī V.17e] The Lot of the duration[121] of the kingdom is taken at the hour of the accession[122] of the king, from the Sun to the fifteenth degree of the sign of Leo, and it is projected from the Moon; then [by night] it is taken from the Moon to the fifteenth degree of the sign of Cancer, and it is projected from the Sun.[123]

§VI.4.5: The Lot of the duration of the kingdom #2[124]

[al-Qabīsī V.17f] Another Lot of the time of the duration of the accession of the king[125] is taken at the hour of the accession of the king in the day from Jupiter to Saturn, and conversely in the night, and it is projected from the Ascendant of the revolution of the year in which the king stood up [to take power]. Which if Jupiter were in a common sign and it were a diurnal revolution, and[126] Jupiter were cadent from

---

[119] Presumably this is particularly for a year in which there will be a shift of triplicities.

[120] The natal version of this is the Lot of the cause of a kingdom, above; it is found in *BRD* I.4.8.

[121] Reading with the Ar. for "time."

[122] Or rather, at the revolution of the year *in which* the king actually accedes and takes charge (reading the Ar. *qiyām* for "choosing"). See the next Lot in VI.4.5.

[123] According to *BRD* II.4.12, this is really two Lots, and they indicate the types of activities the king is involved in—not the duration of rule. One calculates both (whether by day or night), and their domicile Lords indicate the types of activities (Abū Ma'shar assumes they will fall into the domiciles of the same planet): for example, if they fall into the domiciles of Mars, he will be interested in the military and wars.

[124] This is based on *BRD* II.5.14.

[125] Again, reading with the Arabic. Al-Qabīsī's Arabic makes this a Lot about the length of the kingdom or dynasty. But Abū Ma'shar speaks of this in terms of the king's lifespan, which probably assumes that the rulership will last until the king dies or is killed.

[126] The Ar. reads "or."

the angles, it should then be taken from Saturn to Jupiter, and on top of that should be added 30°, and it should be projected from the Ascendant. But if Saturn and Jupiter were opposite each other, and[127] both were cadent from the Ascendant, one should halve what came out between them, and it is projected from the Ascendant. And if Jupiter were in his own exaltation and the revolution were in the night, it is counted from him to Saturn, and it is projected from the Ascendant.[128]

§VI.4.6: The two "greatest Lots" #1[129]

[al-Qabīsī V.18a] The two greatest Lots, from which is extracted the time of the choosing of the king and his duration. The first of them is that, at the hour of the choosing[130] of the king, you should look to see where the advancement of the year arrived[131] from the conjunction of the triplicity which signified the sect, from which number a year is given to every 30°, and one month to every 2 ½ degrees. And when you know in which sign or degree this happens, keep it [in your mind]: because this is the place from which you will calculate the first Lot. And if you wanted to calculate it, you will calculate the Ascendant of the revolution of the year in which the one who was chosen stood up [to take power]. After this, take (of [either] Saturn or Jupiter) the planet [which is] eastern of the Sun in that year, up to the degree of the calculation of the first degree which you saved, and project from the Ascendant of the revolution: and where it reached, that is the place of the first Lot.[132]

---

[127] The Ar. reads "or."

[128] The rest of *BRD* II.5.14 gives some instructions on how to use the Lot.

[129] This and the next Lot are two additional lifespan Lots, again under the assumption that the king will rule until he dies. See *BRD* II.5.15, which then gives (rather turgid) instructions on how to use the Lots.

[130] Or rather, at the revolution of the year *in which* the king actually takes power.

[131] That is, by profection.

[132] See *BRD* II.5.15. In other words, (1) profect from the Ascendant of the triplicity shift which indicated a new religion or dynasty, up to the date of the revolution in which a new king will take power (or perhaps to the date of the accession itself?)—at a rate of one year for every 30° (taking into account fractions of a year); (2) of Saturn and Jupiter, take whichever is eastern and measure from it to the degree of the profection; (3) project the result from the Ascendant of the year in which the king takes power. If both Saturn and Jupiter are eastern, use Saturn.

§VI.4.7: The two "greatest Lots" #2

[al-Qabīsī V.18b] The second Lot of these. Look, in the month and day in which the king stood up or began [his] rule,[133] to see what sign or degree the profection of the year reached [from the smaller Saturn-Jupiter][134] conjunction, from which number one year is given to every 30°, and this is the place of the calculation of the second Lot: keep it [in mind] as well. After this, take it (of [either] Saturn or Jupiter) from the planet western of the Sun up to the place of the calculation of the second degree which you have kept [in mind], and project it from the Ascendant of the revolution; and where it reached, there will be the place of the second Lot.[135]

These, therefore, are the Lots which signify the strength of the kingdom and its duration.

---

[133] Again, this is actually at the revolution of the year in which the king actually takes power.

[134] Adding with *BRD* II.5.15.

[135] See *BRD* II.5.15. In other words, go back to the time of the most recent Saturn-Jupiter conjunction, and profect in 30° to the day the king actually takes power, and determine what degree the profection from the Ascendant of that conjunction comes to. Then measure from Saturn or Jupiter (whichever is western) up to that degree, and project the result from the Ascendant of the revolution of the year in which the king takes power. If both Saturn and Jupiter are western, use Jupiter.

§VI.5: Lots for Commodities: al-Qabīsī

[al-Qabīsī V.19] Moreover, these are other Lots which we use in a revolution of the years of the world, and through them is known what would be more burdensome in [the price of] marketplace goods or what will be easier in price.[136]

And this is that you should look to see where the Lot fell—that is, into whose domicile or exaltation or bound or triplicity. Which if the planet were retrograde or burned up or in a malign place, that thing will become cheaper.[137] But if it were in a place of strength[138] or in an angle, and especially in the Midheaven, that thing will become more burdensome and will be of a greater price.[139] And if the Lord of that house arrived at the place of its own descension,[140] that thing will become more cheap.[141]

And look at the aspects of the fortunes and the bad planets to [the Lot], and also the Moon and her Lord.[142] If the fortunes and the Moon aspected the Lot, that thing will be multiplied; and if the bad ones aspected it, it will suffer detriment.[143]

The Lot of food:[144] from the Sun to Mars.[145]

The Lot of water: from the Moon to Venus.

The Lot of barley: from the Moon to Jupiter.

The Lot of chickpeas: from Venus to the Sun.

The Lot of lentils: from Mars to Saturn.

The Lot of Egyptian beans: from Saturn to Mars.

The Lot of Indian peas: from Saturn to Mars.

---

[136] Omitting a comment by John of Seville or a scribe: "and what is expensive or cheap, much or little.

[137] Omitting the comment: "and it will be of a small price."

[138] This could indicate some of the places of a planet's power as described in Book IV above.

[139] The Ar. explicitly appeals to supply and demand, i.e., it will become more burdensome precisely because it is scarce.

[140] I.e., by transit. I assume that the transit could also be followed throughout the year and not only at the revolution.

[141] Omitting the comment: "and it will be of an easier price."

[142] Omitting the comment: "and see which one aspects the Lot itself, and how."

[143] I have deferred to Burnett in the translation of some of the following commodities terms.

[144] The Latin and one Arabic manuscript read: "wheat."

[145] I assume all of these are projected from the Ascendant of the revolution.

The Lot of dates: from the Sun to Venus.

The Lot of honey: from the Moon to the Sun.

The Lot of rice:[146] from Jupiter to Saturn.

The Lot of olives: from Mercury to the Moon.

The Lot of grapes: from Saturn to Venus.

The Lot of cotton: from Mercury to Venus.

The Lot of sesame:[147] from Saturn to Jupiter or to Venus.

The Lot of watermelons:[148] from Mercury to Saturn.

The Lot of acidic foods: from Saturn to Mars.

The Lot of sweet foods: from the Sun to Venus.

The Lot of pungent[149] foods: from Mars to Saturn.

The Lot of bitter foods: from Mercury to Saturn.

The Lot of purgative and sweet medicines: from the Sun to the Moon.

The Lot of purgative and acidic medicines: from Saturn to Jupiter.

The Lot of purgative and salty medicines: from Mars to the Moon.

The Lot of poisons: from the Node to Saturn.[150]

And all of these are projected from the Ascendant of the revolution.

[al-Qabīsī V.20] These are all of the Lots which have fallen to us. We have also introduced the latter Lots even though the description of them is weak, lest we omit something which could be an introduction to the mastery of the judgments of the stars by not mentioning it. With praise to God and for his support.

---

[146] Omitting the comment: "which is a certain type of grain."

[147] Omitting the comment: "which is a certain kind of white seed like flaxseed, and medical doctors use it, and from it comes an ointment useful in medicine."

[148] Omitting the comment: "which are great and ripe orange melons."

[149] This Arabic word can also mean "spicy" (*ḥarrīfah*). The Latin has "of the taste of celery [or parsley], or of herbs having a taste of this kind."

[150] Burnett notes here that other Arabic and Latin manuscripts contain other Lots as well: see Bonatti's *BOA* Tr. 8.2 for some of these.

BOOK VII: DEGREES OF THE SIGNS

[*Abbr.* VII.1-2] These things having been determined thus far, next one must deal with the gifts of times, but even the bounds according to the philosophers of the Egyptians,[1] and even the ninth-parts and the dark and shadowy degrees and the bright and empty ones, finally even the masculine and feminine ones, and the differences of the degrees.

Therefore, the planets decree certain years:

[*Gr. Intr.* VII.8.1358-61] For the planets have known numbers, of which certain ones are called *firdārīyyāt*, and certain ones "years," which we will describe briefly and in an unqualified way. But we have described the reason for them in a book in which it is necessary that it be described...

§VII.1: The planetary *firdārīyyāt*[2]

[*Abbr.* VII.3] For instance, the years of the Sun are 10, the years of Venus 8, the years of Mercury 13, of the Moon 9, of Saturn 11, of Jupiter 12, of Mars 7; however, of the Head of the Dragon 3, but of the Tail 2. And all the years come to be 75.[3]

[*Gr. Intr.* VII.8.1362-64] Of course, the *firdārīyyah* of the Sun is 10 years, and the *firdārīyyah* of Venus 8, and that of Mercury 13, and of Jupiter 12, and of Mars 7, and of the Moon 9,[4] and of Saturn 11, and of the Head 3, but of the Tail 2. These are 75 years.

[al-Qabīsī IV.20] And from this, the management of the *firdārīyyāt*. This is that if the nativity were diurnal, the Sun is in charge of the management of that *firdārīyyah* at the beginning of life, according to the quantity the years of his *firdārīyyah* (which are 10). After this, the planet

---

[1] Lit., "of the Medes" (*Medorum*).
[2] See PN3 and its introduction for a lengthy discussion of the *firdārīyyāt*.
[3] Reading instead of "lxxvii."
[4] Reading for "8."

which succeeds the Sun, which is Venus (whose years of the *firdārīyyah* are 8); and after Venus, the planet which succeeds her, which is Mercury (and the years of his *firdārīyyah* are 13); then the Moon (and the years of her *firdārīyyah* are 9); then Saturn (and the years of his *firdārīyyah* are 11); then Jupiter (and the years of his *firdārīyyah* are 7); then the Head (whose years of the *firdārīyyah* are 3); and after that the Tail (and the years of its *firdārīyyah* are 2). The years all collected together come to be 75 years. After this, the management reverts to the Sun, and likewise up to the last of the planets.

If however the nativity were nocturnal, the management will begin from the Moon, and she will manage the years of her *firdārīyyah* (which are 9); likewise planet after planet, just as we said for the Sun.

And if a planet managed the years of its *firdārīyyah*, it will manage the first one-seventh in particular alone—that is, one-seventh of its *firdārīyyah* —then in the second one-seventh the second planet which succeeds it [will] partner with it; after this, the third planet (which succeeds the second one) [will] partner with it in the third one-seventh, and thus until the one which is before it would partner with it in the last one-seventh of the years of its *firdārīyyah*. And for each one of them which partners with the other, there is a judgment with respect to the nativity.

§VII.2: The planetary years

[*Abbr.* VII.4-7] However, these [planetary] years are divided into three donations, the greater[5] and the middle and the least.

[*Gr. Intr.* VII.8.1365-80] But their years are of four kinds: namely the greatest, the greater, the middle, and the lesser.

	Lesser	Middle	Greater	Greatest
♄	30	43 ½	57	265
♃	12	45 ½	79	427
♂	15	40 ½	66	284
☉	19	69 ½	120	1,461
♀	8	45	82	1,151
☿	20	48	76	480
☽	25	66 ½	108	520

Figure 108: Table of planetary years

[*Abbr.* VII.8-9] However, these many [greater] years are given to the planets[6] according to the [number of] bounds which they hold onto in the signs,[7] but the small ones according to the lesser circle,[8] but the middle ones partly according to [the greatest], partly according to [the least].[9] And so, the many [greater] years of the Sun and the Moon [are] according to the greater circle, but fewer according to the lesser, the middle ones according to the middle.[10]

---

[5] Reading for "greatest," which the *Abbr.* does not include but appear below in *Gr. Intr.* and the table.

[6] Or rather, to the non-luminaries.

[7] For instance, if we add up the number of degrees allotted to Mercury in VII.4 below, they equal 76—the number of his greater years.

[8] Based on planetary returns to the natal degree or the natal sign.

[9] That is, they are an average of the greater and lesser years.

[10] There is some controversy over exactly how some of the years for the luminaries are derived.

§VII.3: Planets and the ages of man: al-Qabīsī[11]

[al-Qabīsī II.44b] Also, the rule of the planets in human life is distributed thusly: the Moon begins from the fetus's going out [from the womb], and she manages according to the quantity of the years of nourishment, which are 4 years; then Mercury for 10 after this; then Venus for 8, the Sun for 19, after this Mars for 15, after this Jupiter for 12, after this Saturn up to the end of life.

§VII.4: The Egyptian bounds

[*Abbr.* VII.10-21] However, the bounds according to the Egyptians are distinguished thusly:[12]

[al-Qabīsī I.19a] On the bounds. The planets also have bounds in the signs,[13] wherefore in every sign the five planets have bounds arranged throughout different degrees. For from the beginning of Aries up into the sixth degree of that same Aries is the bound of Jupiter; and from the sixth up to in the twelfth, the bound of Venus; and from the twelfth up to in the twentieth, the bound of Mercury; and from twenty up to twenty-five the bound of Mars, and from twenty-five up to the thirtieth the bound of Saturn.[14] And on account of the diversity of their degrees, and the difficulty of remembering them, we have written them down in a table so that the work was easier:

---

[11] For more on the ages of man, see Appendix F.
[12] Both the Arabic *Abbr.* and *Gr. Intr.* contain tables as well as texts. Therefore I have substituted tables here and below, and put the actual texts in Appendix A.
[13] Omitting the addition: "or 'ends'."
[14] Note the ambiguity between cardinal and ordinal numbers.

♈	♃ 0°-5°59'	♀ 6°-11°59'	☿ 12°-19°59'	♂ 20°-24°59'	♄ 25°-29°59'
♉	♀ 0°-7°59'	☿ 8°-13°59'	♃ 14°-21°59'	♄ 22°-26°59'	♂ 27°-29°59'
♊	☿ 0°-5°59'	♃ 6°-11°59'	♀ 12°-16°59'	♂ 17°-23°59'	♄ 24°-29°59'
♋	♂ 0°-6°59'	♀ 7°-12°59'	☿ 13°-18°59'	♃ 19°-25°59'	♄ 26°-29°59'
♌	♃ 0°-5°59'	♀ 6°-10°59'	♄ 11°-17°59'	☿ 18°-23°59'	♂ 24°-29°59'
♍	☿ 0°-6°59'	♀ 7°-16°59'	♃ 17°-20°59'	♂ 21°-27°59'	♄ 28°-29°59'
♎	♄ 0°-5°59'	☿ 6°-13°59'	♃ 14°-20°59'	♀ 21°-27°59'	♂ 28°-29°59'
♏	♂ 0°-6°59'	♀ 7°-10°59'	☿ 11°-18°59'	♃ 19°-23°59'	♄ 24°-29°59'
♐	♃ 0°-11°59'	♀ 12°-16°59'	☿ 17°-20°59'	♄ 21°-25°59'	♂ 26°-29°59'
♑	☿ 0°-6°59'	♃ 7°-13°59'	♀ 14°-21°59'	♄ 22°-25°59'	♂ 26°-29°59'
♒	☿ 0°-6°59'	♀ 7°-12°59'	♃ 13°-19°59'	♂ 20°-24°59'	♄ 25°-29°59'
♓	♀ 0°-11°59'	♃ 12°-15°59'	☿ 16°-18°59'	♂ 19°-27°59'	♄ 28°-29°59'

Figure 109: Egyptian bounds

[al-Qabīsī I.19b] But certain people put the triplicities before the bounds, because the Lords of the triplicities are stronger in nourishment,[15] and the Lords of the bounds are stronger in directions.[16]

---

[15] Or, "rearing" (*nutritionem*). Omitting the comment: "because they signify nourishing, and because there is no disagreement in the triplicities as there is in the bounds."

[16] This comment refers to certain predictive techniques. The idea is that it is useless to predict for a child who will not survive or be reared: since triplicity Lords are used for determining nourishing or rearing (see *TBN* I.3 and Abū Bakr I.12), but directing through the bounds is for predicting things later in life, triplicities should be introduced first.

§VII.5: The ninth-parts

[*Abbr.* VII.22-23] However, it is called a "ninth-part" when any sign is divided according to nine, and from thence they relate 3 1/3 degrees to every distributing [planet]. And so, beginning from Aries, the first ninth-part will be given to Mars, but the second one to the Lord of Taurus (that is, to Venus), the third to the Lord of Gemini (that is, to Mercury); the same order in the rest, too, according to the position of the signs and Lords and ninth-parts.[17]

[al-Qabīsī IV.16-17] And from this, the *nawbahrāt*, which are the ninth-parts. The knowledge of which is that you should know how far a planet has walked in its own sign, in terms of degrees and minutes, or the degree of the house whose ninth-part you want to know. After this, you will divide the sign into nine divisions, and each division is 3 1/3 degrees. After this, you will look to see in which ninth-part of the ninth-parts the degree of the planet or the degree of the house fell. After this, you will give the first ninth-part of the signs to the Lord of the movable sign of that same triplicity, and the second ninth-part to the Lord of the sign which succeeds that one, until you come to the ninth-part in which the degree is: and it will be the planetary Lord of that ninth-part.

For example, [suppose] the sign in which the degree was, was of the triplicity of Aries. Therefore, the first ninth-part of that same sign will belong to Mars (the Lord of Aries), and the second ninth-part to Venus (the Lady of Taurus), and the third ninth-part to Mercury (the Lord of Gemini)—likewise up to the ninth ninth-part. And if the sign were of the triplicity of Cancer, its first ninth-part will belong to the Moon, and the second ninth-part to the Sun (the Lord of Leo), and the third to Mercury (the Lord of Virgo). And if the sign were of the triplicity of Libra, its first ninth-part will belong to Venus (the Lady of Libra), and the second to Mars (the Lord of Scorpio), and the third to Jupiter (the Lord of Sagittarius). Likewise in the triplicity of Capricorn, its first ninth-part belongs to Saturn (the Lord of Capricorn), and the second one to Saturn (the Lord of Aquarius), and the third to Jupiter

---

[17] See *PN3* III.9-10 for instructions on how to use directions with the ninth-parts.

(the Lord of Pisces); then the ones which follow according to the order of the succession of signs.

For example, a planet or some house (of the houses) will be in the nineteenth degree of Aquarius. And when the sign is divided by the nine divisions, the nineteenth degree will be in the sixth division. And since the sign of Aquarius is of the triplicity of Libra, its first ninth-part is put as belonging to Venus (the Lady of Libra), and the second one to Mars (the Lord of Scorpio), and the third to Jupiter (the Lord of Sagittarius), and the fourth to Saturn (the Lord of Capricorn), and even the fifth to Saturn (the Lord of Aquarius), and the sixth to Jupiter (the Lord of Pisces). And the ninth-part of the nineteenth degree of Aquarius will belong to Jupiter.

	0°00'- 3°20'	3°20'- 6°40'	6°40'- 10°00'	10°00'- 13°20'	13°20'- 16°40'	16°40'- 20°00'	20°00'- 23°20'	23°20'- 26°40'	26°40'- 30°00'
♈	♂	♀	☿	☽	☉	☿	♀	♂	♃
♉	♄	♄	♃	♂	♀	☿	☽	☉	☿
♊	♀	♂	♃	♄	♄	♃	♂	♀	☿
♋	☽	☉	☿	♀	♂	♃	♄	♄	♃
♌	♂	♀	☿	☽	☉	☿	♀	♂	♃
♍	♄	♄	♃	♂	♀	☿	☽	☉	☿
♎	♀	♂	♃	♄	♄	♃	♂	♀	☿
♏	☽	☉	☿	♀	♂	♃	♄	♄	♃
♐	♂	♀	☿	☽	☉	☿	♀	♂	♃
♑	♄	♄	♃	♂	♀	☿	☽	☉	☿
♒	♀	♂	♃	♄	♄	♃	♂	♀	☿
♓	☽	☉	☿	♀	♂	♃	♄	♄	♃

Figure 110: Ninth-parts[18]

[*Abbr.* VII.24] However, according to others [it is] otherwise: for, the signs being divided according to nine, the first ninth-part [is] to Mars, the second to the Sun, and likewise they will be distributed to the rest, so that Saturn is put after the Moon.[19]

---

[18] Table by Dykes, not in text.
[19] This is just like the order of the decans or faces, but put into the smaller increments of the ninth-parts.

[*Gr. Intr.* V.17.1011-24] They even put down the Lords of the ninth-parts in another way. This is that the signs would be divided by nine divisions according to the first working [above], then the Lords of the ninth-parts would be put down by the succession of the circles of the planets. And let it be put that the first ninth-part of Aries belongs to Mars, and the second one to the Sun, the third to Venus, the fourth to Mercury and the fifth to the Moon, the sixth to Saturn, the seventh to Jupiter, the eighth to Mars, and the ninth to the Sun. Also the first ninth-part of Taurus is that of Venus, and the second of Mercury, and the third of the Moon, up to where its nine ninth-parts would be ended. Then the beginning of Gemini will belong to the Moon, and the beginning of Cancer to Jupiter, and the beginning of Leo to the Sun, and the beginning of Virgo to Mercury, and the beginning of Libra to Saturn, and the beginning of Sagittarius to Venus, and the beginning of Capricorn to the Moon, and the beginning of Aquarius to Jupiter, and the beginning of Pisces to the Sun. And there is no agreement over these. But the first [type of ninth-parts] is more certain.

§VII.6: The *darījān*: al-Qabīsī[20]

[al-Qabīsī IV.18] And from this, the *darījān*. This is that you would divide the Ascendant into three parts, and let every division be one of 10°. And you will give the first division to the Lord of the Ascendant, and the second to the Lord of the fifth sign, and the third to the Lord of the ninth sign. For the Ascendant and the fifth and the ninth are a triplicity. For example, Aries was the Ascendant: from the beginning of Aries up to in its tenth degree, its *darījān* is Mars. And if it were ascending from 10° up to 20°, its *darījān* will be the Sun, the Lord of Leo. And if it were from 20° up to its end, its *darījān* will be Jupiter, the Lord of Sagittarius.

[*Gr. Intr.* V.16.950-70] The Indians agreed with the rest in the division of each sign into three parts according to the method of the faces, and they named every division of these "*darījān*," and they called their Lords the "Lords of the *darījān*." But they did not agree with the rest in terms of their Lords. And they make the first Lord of the *darījān* of the signs (namely the Lord of the first face), the Lord of that same sign. And the Lord of the second *darījān* the Lord of the fifth sign…and the Lord of the third *darījān* the Lord of the ninth sign from it.

For example, Aries: since the first 10° of it are the *darījān* of Mars (the Lord of Aries), and the 10° of the second *darījān* belong to the Sun (the Lord of Leo), and the 10° of the third *darījān* of it belong to Jupiter, the Lord of Sagittarius…and likewise the *darījān* of each sign: namely the first of it will belong to its Lord, the second to the Lord of the sign of its triplicity which succeeds [it], which is the Lord of the fifth sign [from it]. And the third one of it to the Lord of the sign of its triplicity which is after that (which is the Lord of the ninth sign [from it]).

And they put it in this way because they think that there were three faces to each sign, and three signs to each triplicity. Therefore, the Lords of these triplicities are more worthy…in every face of them, than the rest are.

---

[20] This is a decan or face system attributed to the Indians.

And the division of the others (with respect to the Lords of the faces), about which mention by us came earlier,[21] is more certain, if God wills.

---

[21] See the standard "Chaldean" order in I.5 above.

§VII.7: Degrees in the signs

[*Abbr.* VII.25-37] But next one must speak about the degrees:[22]

[*Gr. Intr.* V.20.1104-07] The degrees of the signs are in four orders, in this way: first, the degrees which are called "bright." Second, the gloomy degress, [which] they also say are "shadowy" and "smoky." Third, the degrees of "emptiness," I mean the blank zero. Fourth, they are called "dark."

♈	S 3	D 5	S 8	B 4	D 4	B 5	D 1
♉	S 3	D 7	E 2	B 8	E 5	B 3	S 2
♊	B 7	S 3	B 5	E 2	B 6	S 7	
♋	S 7	B 5	S 2	B 4	D 2	B 8	D 2
♌	B 7	S 3	D 6	E 5	B 9		
♍	S 5	B 4	E 2	B 6	D 4	B 7	E 2
♎	B 5	S 5	B 8	S 3	B 7	E 2	
♏	S 3	B 5	E 6	B 6	D 2	B 5	S 3
♐	B 7[23]	S 3	B 7	D 4	S 7		
♑	S 7	B 3	D 5	B 4	S 2	E 4	B 5
♒	D 4	B 5	S 4	B 8	E 4	B 5	
♓	S 6	B 6	S 6	B 4	E 3	B 3	S 2

Figure 111: Degrees in the signs according to *Gr. Intr.*

[al-Qabīsī I.50] And in every one of these signs are degrees which in particular are said to be bright, and degrees which are said to be dark, and degrees which are called smoky, and degrees which are called empty. For certain people even said that from the beginning of Aries up to the third degree they are dark, and from the three to the eighth bright, and from the eighth to the sixteenth dark, and from the sixteenth up to the twentieth bright, and from the twentieth to the twenty-fourth empty, and from the twenty-fourth to the twenty-ninth

---

[22] Note that there is disagreement between *Abbr.*, *Gr. Intr.*, and al-Qabīsī. I reproduce the tables from *Gr. Intr.* and al-Qabīsī here. In the tables below, B = bright, D = dark, E = empty, S = shadowy or smoky.

[23] This should read 9, to equal 30° total.

bright, and from the twenty-ninth to the end of Aries empty—of which we will make a table, if God wills:

♈	D 3	B 5	D 8	B 4	E 4	B 5	E 1
♉	D 3	B 7	E 2	B 8	D 5	B 3	E 2
♊	B 7	D 3	B 5	E 2	B 6	D 5	E 2
♋	B 12	D 2	E 4	S 2	B 8	E 2	
♌	D 10	S 6	E 5	B 9			
♍	D 6	B 3	E 2	B 6	S 4	E 5	D 4
♎	B 5	D 5	B 8	D 3	B 6	E 3	
♏	D 3	B 5	E 6	B 6	S 2	E 5	D 3
♐	B 9	D 3	B 7	S 4	B 7		
♑	D 7	B 3	S 5	B 4	D 2	E 4	D 5
♒	S 4	B 5	D 4	B 8	E 4	B 5	
♓	D 6	B 6	D 6	B 4	E 3	B 3	D 2

Figure 112: Degrees in the signs according to al-Qabīsī

[*Abbr.* VII.38] Therefore it must be known that the power of a planet is increased to the good in the bright degrees. But in the dark ones it harms and takes away. In the empty ones neither this nor that. But in the shadowy ones it is inclined to little harm.

[*Gr. Intr.* V.20.1108-14] And if planets fell into the bright degrees, it will be stronger for them in the signification of the good, and they will signify beauty and brilliance and fortune. And if they fell into the dark degrees, they signify difficulty and mishaps and the bitter darkness of ruin. And if they fell into the gloomy or shadowy degrees, or in the empty degrees, they signify a small mishap.

§VII.8: Masculine and feminine degrees

[*Abbr.* VII.39-50] Finally however, it remains to discuss which degrees are called masculine and which feminine.

[*Gr. Intr.* V.19.1057-58] That there are masculine degrees and feminine degrees in the twelve signs.

[*Gr. Intr.* V.19.1062-66] For instance, from the first degree of the sign of Aries up to the completion of the seventh degree, they are masculine, and up to the completion of the ninth degree, feminine; and up to the completion of the fifteenth degree, masculine, and up to the completion of the twenty-second, feminine, and up to the thirtieth, masculine. And for the rest of the signs, just as you see in the table:

[al-Qabīsī I.49] There are also degrees in each sign which are said to be particularly masculine and feminine. For from the beginning of Aries up to eight degrees they are said to be masculine, and from the eighth to the ninth feminine, and from the ninth to the fifteenth masculine, and from the fifteenth up to the twenty-second feminine, and from the twenty-second up to the end of Aries masculine—which we have determined to describe just as we have described the bounds, and in this way we have depicted [them] in a table so that the work might be rendered easier, with God aiding:

♈	M 7[24]	F 2[25]	M 6	F 7	M 8		
♉	M 7[26]	F 8[27]	M 15				
♊	F 6	M 11	F 6	M 4	F 3		
♋	M 2	F 5	M 3	F 2	M 11	F 4	M 3
♌	M 5	F 2	M 6	F 10	M 7		
♍	F 7	M 5	F 8	M 3[28]	F 7[29]		
♎	M 5	F 5	M 11	F 7	M 2		
♏	M 4	F 6	M 4	F 5	M 8	F 3	
♐	M 2	F 3	M 7	F 12	M 6		
♑	M 11	F 8	M 11				
♒	M 5	F 7	M 6	F 7	M 5		
♓	M 10	F 10	M 3	F 5	M 2		

Figure 113: Masculine and feminine degrees according to *Gr. Intr.*

[*Gr. Intr.* V.19.1079-99] Also, certain people of the ancients used to look in the masculine signs, and they put the male ones from the beginning of them up to 12 ½ degrees, and 12 ½ degrees feminine ones, and 2 ½ degrees male, and 2 ½ degrees feminine. But in the feminine signs they put it as feminine from the beginning up to the 12 ½ degree, then 12 ½ degrees masculine, after that 2 ½ degrees feminine, then 2 ½ degrees masculine.

And certain people made the degrees of each sign in masculinity and femininity to be in twelve parts according to the number of the signs. And they said that the masculine signs, each of them from its beginning up to 2 ½ degrees, [was] masculine according to the nature of that sign, then 2 ½ degrees feminine according to the nature of the second sign from it. Afterwards, 2 ½ degrees masculine according to the nature of the third sign from it, and likewise feminine on top of that up to the completion of the signs. But the feminine signs [would be] feminine from the beginning of each one of them up to 2 ½ degrees, then 2 ½ degrees masculine, then likewise feminine.

---

24 Al-Qabīsī has 8.
25 Al-Qabīsī has 1.
26 Al-Qabīsī has 8.
27 Al-Qabīsī has 7.
28 Al-Qabīsī has 10, and no further degrees in this sign.
29 Al-Qabīsī has no further degrees in this sign.

And so, they related the masculinity and femininity of the degrees of the signs according to these three methods.

[*Abbr.* VII.51-53] But we have carried out these [lists] for the reason that if, in a chart of males, a degree fell into the masculine ones, and one of females into the feminine ones, they turn out prosperously. But if the converse, the contrary.[30] However, even though they may make partitions in different ways, we have followed this teaching as a most potent one.

[*Gr. Intr.* V.19.1059-61] …this will be stronger for them; and if it were a nativity and interrogation by feminine people, and the planets fell in feminine degrees, it will be stronger for them.
[*Gr. Intr.* V.19.1099-1101] And whenever two of three of these significations in masculinity or femininity were gathered together in one place, it will be stronger for them.

---

[30] See a related discussion in V.10 above.

§VII.9: Welled, increasing fortune, eminent degrees

[*Abbr.* VII.54] But near the end of [this] instruction, it seems we must speak about the wells and the eminences.

§VII.9.1: Welled degrees

[*Abbr.* VII.55] Therefore, in the signs there are certain degrees which are called "wells,"[31] for the reason that if prosperous stars fell into them, they wholly lose [their] virtue. [56] Even the malevolents are changed [there] so that they would not have the power to harm, [but rather] they benefit. [57] But, however, in certain hours their malice is increased in that same place.[32]

[*Gr. Intr.* V.21.1129-44] Wherefore in the signs are degrees which are called "wells." And if some one of the planets fell into those degrees of a sign (that is, so that it does not fall in front of or behind it, but in it), its beauty and look will disappear, and it will be made weak by its signification. In fact, if fortunes fell into them, their being will be in the way we have described in terms of weakness.[33] But if the bad ones fell into them, their signification will be weakened, and perhaps it will have signified accidental fortune on account of its weakness over evil, and perhaps the nature of that malice will be strengthened. And the ancients have already described the places [of the planets] in which it signifies fitness and destruction, and we will describe it in its own place (if God wills).[34]

But in truth, with the degrees of the wells of the signs there was disagreement between them; for this reason we have avoided making mention of their disagreement, and we have described the degrees of their signs according to what the generality of the sages of Egypt and Persia have agreed upon.

[*Gr. Intr.* V.21.1158] If there were planets in these degrees which we have said, they will be in wells.

---

[31] Often called "pitted" degrees in English, after the English astrologers of the 17th Century.

[32] *Abbr.* VII.58-69 are represented in the table below.

[33] See perhaps IV.3 above.

[34] See for example IV.3 above.

♈	6th	11th	17th	24th	29th	
♉	5th	13th	18th	24th	25th	26th
♊	2nd	13th	17th	22nd	30th	
♋	12th	17th	22nd	23rd	28th	30th
♌	6th	13th	15th	22nd	23rd	28th
♍	8th	13th	16th	21st	25th	30th
♎	1st	7th	20th	23rd	27th	30th
♏	9th	10th	17th	22nd	23rd	27th
♐	7th	12th	15th	23rd	27th	30th
♑	2nd	17th	22nd	29th		
♒	1st	12th	17th	22nd	29th	
♓	4th	9th	24th	27th	28th	

Figure 114: The welled degrees according to *Gr. Intr.*

[al-Qabīsī I.51] And in the signs are degrees which are said to be wells: if a planet were in some one of them, it is said to be in a well.[35]

♈	6th	9th	11th	17th	24th	29th
♉	5th	13th	18th	24th	25th	29th[36]
♊	2nd	12th	17th	26th	30th	
♋	12th	17th	23rd	26th	30th	
♌	6th	13th	15th	22nd	23rd	28th
♍	8th	13th	16th	21st	25th	
♎	1st	7th	20th	30th		
♏	9th	10th	22nd	23rd	27th	
♐	7th	12th	15th	24th	27th	30th
♑	2nd	7th	17th	22nd	24th	28th
♒	1st	12th	17th	23rd	29th	
♓	4th	9th	24th	27th	28th	

Figure 115: The welled degrees according to al-Qabīsī

---

[35] Omitting the rest of the list of degrees, as they appear in this table based on the Ar.
[36] According to one Ar. manuscript.

§VII.9.2: Degrees increasing fortune

[*Abbr.* VII.70] But the places of the eminences are these: of Taurus, the 15th, 27th and 30th; of Leo, the 3rd and 5th; of Scorpio the 7th; of Aquarius the 20th.

[*Gr. Intr.* V.22.1160-61, 1166] The ancients thought that there were degrees increasing fortune in the circle…And these are the degrees, namely:

♉	15th	27th	30th
♌	3rd	5th	
♏	7th		
♒	20th		

Figure 116: The degrees of eminences according to *Gr. Intr.*

[*Abbr.* VII.71] And so these degrees, if the planetary Lord of anyone's chart fell into them, or if the horoscope of the chart did so, they surpass unexpected luckiness.

[*Gr. Intr.* V.22.1162-5] And they said that if planets receded from their places signifying the native's fortune, and the Moon or the Lot of Fortune were in these degrees, or the degree of the Ascendant,[37] they increase the native's fortune. And if they were signifying his fall, these degrees move him to loftiness by some quantity.

---

[37] Reading for *fuerint ipsi per semetipsos gradus ascendens.*

§VII.9.3: Degrees of personal eminence[38]

[*Abbr.* VII.72] But the personal eminences, whence even ignoble people are promoted to kingdoms, are these:

[*Gr. Intr.* V.22.1169-74] And certain people said that if some one of these degrees which we will [now] describe were ascending, or the Sun were in certain ones of them in the day, and the Moon in the night, and they were in an optimal place of the circle, and the planets of the root of the nativity signified fortune, it will lead the native through to loftiness and the seat of nobility and a kingdom, and he will rule over lands and cities, and he will possess many riches:

♈	19th				
♉	8th				
♊	11th				
♋	1st	2nd	3rd	14th	15th
♌	5th	7th	17th	20th	
♍	2nd	13th	20th		
♎	3rd	5th	21st		
♏	12th	20th			
♐	13th	20th			
♑	12th	13th	14th	20th	
♒	7th	16th	17th	20th	
♓	12th	20th			

Figure 117: The degrees of personal eminence according to *Gr. Intr.*

---

[38] These degrees in *Abbr.* and al-Qabīsī were probably the locations of eminent fixed stars which show great personal fortune and eminence. For such stars and their use, see the references for eminence in Appendix F. (Abū Bakr spreads his fixed stars throughout his material on profession, as well.)

[al-Qabīsī I.53] And in the circle are certain degrees which are said to be increasing fortune, and they are these:[39]

♈	19th				
♉	3rd	15th	27th		
♊	11th				
♋	1st	2nd	3rd	14th	15th
♌	3rd	5th	7th	17th	
♍	3rd	12th	20th		
♎	3rd	5th	21st		
♏	7th	12th	20th		
♐	13th	20th			
♑	12th	13th	14th	20th	
♒	7th	17th	20th		
♓	13th	20th			

Figure 118: The degrees of increasing fortune according to al-Qabīsī

[*Abbr.* VII.73] These are the places of the eminences with which we will make the end of [this] instruction.

[*Gr. Intr.* V.22.1182-93] And these things of which mention came before, are the partnerships of the planets with the signs, and these are general things on which all of the ancients of the sages of the stars agree. And they have particular partnerships from the proper quality of their complexion with one another, which we will describe in their own places in every book.[40]

Also, the Indians and certain individuals of the sages of the stars, gave other partnerships to the stars with the signs apart from these which we have stated, memory of which we have omitted. But in this treatise we will describe everything which agrees with the complexions of the natures of the planets with the signs, in a natural order, from those things on which all the sages of the science of the stars agreed.

---

[39] Omitting the list in Latin as they appear in this table based on the Ar.
[40] Primarily in *Gr. Intr.* VII, and all of III above.

§VII.10: Degrees of chronic illness: al-Qabīsī

[al-Qabīsī I.52] And in the signs are certain degrees which are said to be degrees of chronic illness. These are:

♉	6th, 7th, 8th, 10th
♋	9th to 15th
♌	18th, 27th, 28th
♏	19th and 29th
♐	1st, 7th, 8th, 18th, 19th
♑	26th, 27th to 29th
♒	10th, 18th, 19th

Figure 119: The degrees of chronic illness (al-Qabīsī)

Constellation in *BA*	Name of stars/clusters	Modern zodiacal positions (2010)
Taurus	Pleiades	29° ♉ 26' (Alcyone)
Cancer	Praesepe (nebula in Cancer)	About 7° ♌
Leo	Coma Berenice	Around 8° ♎ (Diadem)
Scorpio	Face and sting of Scorpio	Face: around 2° ♐ (Graffias) Sting: around 25°-28° ♐ (Aculeus, Acumen)
Sagittarius	Point of Arrow in Sagittarius	About 0° 30' ♑ (al Nasl)
Capricorn	Spine (ε, κ) of Capricorn[41]	Around 13° ♒ (Dorsum, θ Cap.)
Aquarius	Pitcher of Aquarius	Around 6° ♓

Figure 120: Fixed star degrees of chronic illness (*BA*)[42]

---

[41] That is, according to Burnett and Pingree.
[42] These positions derive from *Carmen* IV.1.108-11 and Rhetorius Ch. 61.

BOOK VIII: SPECIAL TECHNIQUES

§VIII.1: Pregnancy, birth, longevity: al-Qabīsī

[al-Qabīsī IV.1] The fourth section, on the exposition of the [technical] terms of the astrologers.

§VIII.1.1: Pregnancy[1]

[al-Qabīsī II.44a] But concerning the order of the planets in the conception of children, one must know that the first month, namely from the hour of conception, belongs to Saturn; the second to Jupiter; the third to Mars, the fourth to the Sun, the fifth to Venus, the sixth to Mercury, the seventh to the Moon, the eighth to Saturn, but the ninth to Jupiter.

§VIII.1.2: Birth: determining a more exact Ascendant

[al-Qabīsī IV.3] And from this the *namūdār*.[2] And many of the astrologers think that the [exact] degree of the Ascendant of some native itself would be found through it, but this is false. And I have already made this clear in the book which I wrote about the indicator. But through it is found the more worthy of [the rest] of the degrees of the circle after the ascending degree in that same hour according to the natural course.[3] And it is often agreed that the ascending degree itself would be found through it.

The understanding of which matter is that the degree of the conjunction or degree of the prevention[4] which was before the nativity should be considered: because if it were the conjunction which was be-

---

[1] For more on pregnancy, see Appendix F.
[2] Or, "indicator." John adds: "which is the investigation of the degree of the Ascendant of some nativity." There are several methods for determining a more exact birth Ascendant: see Appendix F.
[3] That is, the Ascending degree in the approximate hour of birth, as the heavens turn.
[4] The New Moon or Full Moon, respectively.

fore the nativity—[that is,] closer to the nativity than the past prevention—the nativity is called "conjunctional." And if there were a
prevention closer to it, it is called "preventional." And since the degree
of the conjunction is the same degree in which the luminaries are
joined, there is no [need to] search [for it] there. But in the prevention,
since each luminary is in its own degree, it is necessary for us to know
which of these degrees want s to be understood as the degree of the
prevention. And Ptolemy has already said[5] that the degree of the luminary which was above the earth [at the time of the prevention] is the
degree of the prevention. And certain ones of the sages said: if it came
about in a prevention that one of the luminaries is in the degree of the
east and the other in the degree of the west, then the degree of the east
is the degree of the prevention. And Valens said[6] that the degree of the
prevention is the degree in which the fullness is—wanting the degree
of the Moon to be understood [as being that]. But since this method is
Ptolemy's,[7] it is good for us to return to his opinion in it.

If therefore the degree of the conjunction or the degree of the prevention were made perfectly clear, you will establish the ascending
degree by estimation at the hour of the nativity, and [then establish] the
four angles at the hour of the nativity.[8] Then, you will look at the degree of the conjunction or the degree of the prevention which was
before the nativity, and see which of the planets is more worthy or
stronger in it at that same hour of the conjunction or the prevention,
by a multitude of dignities.[9] Therefore, you will calculate that planet for
the hour of the nativity. Then, you will look to see whether the degree
of that planet (in the sign in which it is [at the nativity]) is closer to the
degree of the [estimated] tenth house or to the degree of the Ascendant: and the one to which it is closer, you will make that [degree] the
angle, in the image of the degree of that planet itself and its minute,
and you will distribute the twelve houses through it.

---

[5] *Tet.* III.3.

[6] Cite uncertain, but this is also 'Umar's opinion in *TBN* I.4.1.

[7] That is, al-Qabīsī is about to teach us Ptolemy's method rather than that of Hermes or another (see footnote above).

[8] That is, based on that approximate time.

[9] Ptolemy (*ibid.*) lists the following as relevant: a planet aspecting by a trine, and rulership by domicile, exaltation, bound, and "phase or configuration." It is unclear exactly what this latter means, but very possibly being in a station or making an appearance from out of or going under the rays. See the passage below in al-Qabīsī IV.6.

Ptolemy said:[10] if many planets agreed in the rulership of that same place, and they were equal in strength, you will establish the one which was the Lord of the sect[11] as the Lord of that place.[12] Which if they even agreed in this, you will establish the one which should be changed more quickly from its own being to one which was better.[13]

§VIII.1.3: Longevity[14]

[al-Qabīsī IV.4] And from this, the *hīlāj* [15] in nativities, the knowledge of which is that you should look at the hour of the nativity. Which if it were in the day, you will begin from the Sun—which, if he were before[16] the degree of the ascending sign by 5° or less, or he were in the tenth or in the eleventh (whether that sign were masculine or feminine), he will be fit to be the releaser. But if he were in the seventh or in the eighth or in the ninth in a masculine sign, he will likewise be fit to be the releaser. If however he were in a feminine sign in these three [latter] places, he will not be fit to be the releaser.

Then you will look at the Moon. Which, if she were in the Ascendant or in the second or in the third, also in the seventh or eighth, she will be fit to be the releaser, were the sign masculine or feminine. And if she were before the degree of the ascending sign by 5° or less, or she

---

[10] There is some understandable confusion about what Ptolemy was saying, since Ptolemy spoke both about the number of degrees, and planets with greater numbers of dignities or relationships. But according to Schmidt's Ptolemy, it is the following: if there is one planet with all or most of these dignities or relationships, then use its degree; if there are two or more (with roughly equal amounts of relationships, it seems), then use the one which is closer in *ascensional* degrees (though why not zodiacal degrees?); but if these two or more should be very close in distance by degrees, then use the one which has more of a "relationship" with the angles and the sect.

[11] Ar. *hayyiz*, "domain," but here clearly a synonym for sect.

[12] The Ar. instructs us to make some planet the Lord of the sect, but doesn't tell us which; at any rate, both the Arabic and Latin texts depart from Ptolemy.

[13] This last part is not in Ptolemy. But for examples of planetary "changes," see IV.7 above.

[14] For more on the longevity techniques of the releaser and *kadukhudhāh*, see Appendix F below and my Appendix B in *PN1*.

[15] A Persian word meaning "releaser" (because it is used in primary directions, usually glossed as "releasing" in traditional astrology), often spelled *hyleg* by Latin authors. I will translate it as "releaser" from now on.

[16] That is, in an earlier zodiacal degree. He is "before" or "in front of" the ascending degree only by the primary motion of the heavens.

were in the tenth or in the eleventh or in the fourth or in the fifth in a feminine sign, she is made fit to be the releaser. If however she were in a masculine sign in some one of these places, she will not be fit to be the releaser, if the nativity were in the day.

But if the nativity were nocturnal, we begin from the Moon. Which, if she were in some one of the aforesaid places according to what we have said before, she will be fit to be the releaser. If however the Moon were not in them, you will look after this to the Sun. Which, if he were before the degree of the seventh by 5° or less, or he were in the fourth or in the fifth, he will be in a fit place to be the releaser, were the sign masculine or feminine. But if he were in the Ascendant or in the second, in a masculine sign, he will even be made fit to be the releaser. If however he were in a feminine sign in some one of these places, he will not be fit to be the releaser.

Which if the luminaries were not fit to be the releaser, you will look after this to the nativity to see if it is conjunctional or prevential. Which if the nativity were conjunctional and the degree of the conjunction were in some one of the angles or in the succeedents of the angles, it will be in a fit place to be the releaser. But if the aforesaid degree were cadent from these eight places, it will not be the releaser. Then look at the degree of the Lot of Fortune. Which, if it were in some one of the angles or in their succeedents, it will be in a fit place to be the releaser. But if it were cadent from these eight places, it will not be fit to be the releaser. After this, you will look at the degree of the Ascendant, and establish it as the releaser.

But if the nativity were prevential, you will begin from the degree of the prevention, and you will look in it just as you did before with the degree of the conjunction; and after this at the Lot of Fortune, and after that to the degree of the Ascendant, in the order in which we said before with the degree of the conjunction.

You will look to see whether the signs are masculine or feminine only in the case of the luminaries. But for the degree of the conjunction and the prevention and the Lot of Fortune, you should not consider whether they are in masculine signs or in feminine signs: these three will only be fit to be the releaser if they were in these eight places, namely in the angles or their succeedents. But if they were in the places receding from the angles, they will not be fit to be the releaser.

And so it appears that the Sun is fit to be the releaser in the day and night above the earth and under the earth in eleven places: namely in six places above the earth and in five below the earth. Also, the Moon is made fit to be the releaser in the day and night above the earth and likewise under the earth in eleven places: above the earth in five places and below the earth in six. And in addition, if the Moon were under the rays of the Sun in these places, she will not be fit to be the releaser.

However, you will look for the releaser in the angles and in their followers according to how the twelve houses of the circle are calculated through the degrees of the hours of the Ascendant, according to how its work is laid out in the canon of the planets.[17] And once you have calculated the houses in this way, every planet which was before the degree of the Ascendant or any house by five equal degrees and less, its strength will be valid in the house which follows it. And every place (from among the places which we said before) will be fit to be the releaser, if the Lord of the domicile or of the exaltation or of the rest of the dignities aspected it.[18] But if some one of its Lords did not aspect it (which are the Lord of the domicile or the Lord of the exaltation or the Lord of the bound or the Lord of the triplicity or the Lord of the face), it will not be fit to be the releaser.

[al-Qabīsī IV.5] And from this the kadukhudhāh,[19] which is the significator of [the length of] life. Which if you wished to know [it], and you have already known the releaser beforehand by means of the order which we said before, you will look at the Lord of the domicile of the releaser, or at the Lord of its exaltation or the Lord of its bound or the Lord of the triplicity or the Lord of the face. The one of these which was stronger and more authoritative in the place of the releaser, and aspected the releaser, will be more worthy to be the kadukhudhāh. Which if the one which had more authority did not aspect, you should look at one which had lesser authority, until you find the one of them which does aspect. Which if they did not aspect the releaser, that place

---

[17] Nowadays we would call this a "table of houses." Al-Qabīsī is telling us to use quadrant-style houses, (such as Porphyry or Alchabitius Semi-Arc) for this longevity method.

[18] Note that, if we keep strictly to the vocabulary of configurations, the Lord does not need to be connected to the releaser itself (which would require orbs or at least a very close aspect), suggesting that only a whole-sign aspect to the releaser's sign is needed.

[19] An Arabic rendering of a Pahlavi word meaning "domicile master" or "Lord of the domicile." I will continue to use kadukhudhāh, since an accurate translation could be confused with a normal Lord of a sign.

would not be able to be the releaser,[20] and then you will seek the releaser from another, and again you will seek a *kadukḫudhāh* from that
second releaser, in the order in which we said before. Which if two or
three planets were equal in authority in the degree of the releaser, and
each one aspected [it], the one which was stronger in [its own] place
will be more worthy of being the *kadukḫudhāh*. But if they were equal in
the strength of [their own] place, the one which was closer to the degree of the releaser will be the *kadukḫudhāh*.

And to some it seemed better to begin from the Lord of the domicile: which if it aspected the releaser, they made it the *kadukḫudhāh* and
did not consider another. Which if they did not find the Lord of the
domicile to be aspecting the releaser, they looked at the Lord of the
exaltation: which if they saw it to be aspecting the releaser, they make it
the *kadukḫudhāh*, and they did not consider another besides it. They did
likewise with the Lord of the bound and the triplicity and the face, in
order. [But] Dorotheus used to put the Lord of the bound before the
Lord of the domicile in this.[21]

[al-Qabīsī IV.6] And certain people said: if two or three or more
planets were equal in worthiness and the nearness of the aspect, the
one which was with the Sun in one minute will be the one (and this is
if it were united to the Sun), or [is nearest the center of the Sun or else
is already][22] in its easternness or is in the beginning of its arising [out of
the rays] or is in its second station or in some praiseworthy relationship
from the Sun just as we said before: it will be the *kadukḫudhāh*.

But if the degree of the Sun were the releaser, and he were in Aries
or in Leo, the Sun will be the releaser and the *kadukḫudhāh* together,
and another will not be considered as the *kadukḫudhāh* besides him.
Likewise, if the degree of the Moon were the releaser and she were in
Taurus or in Cancer, have her as the releaser and the *kadukḫudhāh* together, and you will not consider another besides her as the
kadukḫudhāh.

---

[20] This is stated ambiguously. Technically, all of these candidates (depending on the author) are still releasing places and can be directed through the bounds using the method of
distribution (see *Persian Nativities III* for a full exposition of this). The point is that they
will not be the predominating releaser for the purposes of longevity. But al-Qabīsī intriguingly says that such a situation is "incomplete" to play the role of the longevity releaser.
[21] *Carmen* III.2.5-6. This does in fact seem to have been the preferred and older approach.
[22] Adding based on the Ar.

§VIII.1.4: The victor over the native[23]

[al-Qabīsī IV.7] But the victor[24] which is in charge of the nativity signifies the being of the native after the releaser and the *kadukhudhāh*. And it has more authority than the other planets in the Ascendant and in the places of the luminaries and in the place of the Lot of Fortune, and also in the place of the degree of the conjunction or prevention which is before the nativity. Which if some planet were in charge of two or three or four places or more, by the multitude of its power in them, it will be the victor, that is the master, and significator of life after the releaser and the *kadukhudhāh*, and the being of the native is signified through it. And certain people take it instead of the *kadukhudhāh* for giving life.

---

[23] For a much more elaborate medieval formula for determining the victor or *mubtazz*, see ibn Ezra's *The Book of Nativities and Revolutions.* For a Hellenistic version reported by Porphyry, Schmidt 2009 pp. 321-22. Cf. al-Qabīsī's victor for a topic in I.18, above.
[24] *Mubtazz.*

§VIII.2: Annual techniques: al-Qabīsī[25]

§VIII.2.1: Natal profections[26]

[al-Qabīsī IV.8] And from this, profection[27] in the years of nativities and the world.[28] And in the years of nativities, the knowledge is that you should look to see how many years have passed for the native in terms of completed solar years, and you will take one sign for every year, beginning from the native's Ascendant through the succession of signs: where the number were ended, the sign which follows is the sign of the profection of the Ascendant, namely the sign of the entering year which you do not put forth in the counting.[29] And this will be in such a degree as it was in the Ascendant of the nativity,[30] and the Lord of its sign is called the *sālkḥudāy*, the interpretation of which is "Lord of the Year."[31]

Likewise, you will count from the sign of the Sun, one sign for each year, and it will go out through this sign of the profection from the Sun; likewise from the sign of the Moon and from the Midheaven and from the Lot of Fortune, in a likeness of the degree of the root.

An example of which is that the native was born with Capricorn arising under the seventeenth degree,[32] and the Sun in Pisces in the fifteenth degree, and the Moon in Libra in the fifteenth degree, and the Midheaven in the eighth degree of Scorpio, and the Lot of Fortune in

---

[25] I have put the material on *firdārīyyāt* earlier in VII.1, corresponding to Abū Ma'shar's treatment. See also *PN3*.

[26] For more on profections, see Appendix F.

[27] The Arabic specifies the *endpoint* of the profection, i.e., the point to which the profection has arrived. John simply glosses this as the profection itself. I follow John's Latin, but the reader should keep in mind that he means both the process and its endpoint.

[28] See mundane profections in VIII.3.2 below.

[29] This simply means that since the native is 0 years old at birth, age 1 begins with the next sign. So, if the native is 1 year old, we do not count the Ascendant itself as "1," but rather the second sign as "1."

[30] Like 'Umar al-Tabari (see *TBN*), al-Qabīsī uses 30° increments in his profections instead of whole-signs.

[31] I will translate *sālkḥudāy* as "Lord of the Year" in what follows.

[32] The Ar. has cardinal numbers ("*seventeen* degrees," etc.).

Leo in the seventeenth degree.[33] And three completed years have already passed for the native, and the fourth year from the Ascendant arrived in Aries, which is the fourth [place] from Capricorn, to the seventeenth degree. And Mars will be the Lord of the Year.[34]

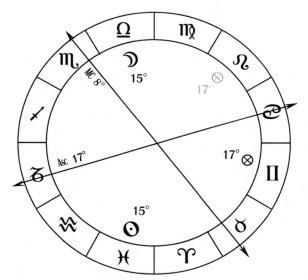

Figure 121: Example of profections: Abū Ma'shar

And the profection of the place of the Sun reached Gemini, to the fifteenth degree of that same sign, and the profection of the Moon reached Capricorn, to the fifteenth degree of it, and the profection from the Midheaven to the eighth degree of the sign of Aquarius, and the profection from the Lot of Fortune reached the seventeenth degree of Scorpio.[35]

And when the year reached the degree of a profection, and there was a planet or its rays after that degree [up to the equivalent degree in the next sign],[36] and you wanted to know when the profection would

---

[33] This is incorrect, as Leo would be the diurnal calculation and al-Qabīsī employs reversals at night. The Lot should be in Gemini, and I have indicated it in black in the diagram below, with the incorrect value in gray.

[34] The native is three years old, which makes the profection of the Ascendant reach Aries, ruled by Mars.

[35] Again, with the proper nocturnal calculation this should read "Virgo."

[36] Reading with the Ar. for John's "in the same house."

reach that planet or its rays, you will look to see what there is between the degree which the profection of the year reached and the planet or rays, in terms of degrees and minutes, and you will multiply that by 12 1/6: and what it was, will be the days from [the beginning of] that year in which you were, after which the profection of that planet comes to be.

Comment by Dykes. The annual profection method outlined here is the same as 'Umar al-Tabari's "greater condition" of the native in *TBN*, which treats the 30° span of the profection as equivalent to an entire year of about 365.25 days: this means that every zodiacal degree will amount to 12.175 (or about 12 1/6) days. Any body or ray or Lot falling in that 30° is supposed to be activated at the time proportionate to its position in those degrees. For example, let us profect the above native's Midheaven to age 28: this advances the Midheaven to 8° Pisces, and so anything between 8° Pisces and 8° Aries will pertain to age 28. The natal Sun is 7° away, at 15° Pisces: so something solar will be manifested at a date proportionate to the Sun's position. Multiply 7° by 12.175 days = 85.225 days. The solar event should manifest or be relevant about 85 days after the native's birthday.

§VIII.2.2: Directions[37]

[al-Qabīsī IV.11a] And from this, direction. This is that you should direct some significator to some place of the signs, and you should know what there is between them in terms of the [equatorial] degrees of the direction, and you should take one year for every [equatorial] degree.

§VIII.2.2a: Directions from the angles

[al-Qabīsī IV.11b] If therefore you wanted this, and the significator which you want to direct to some part of the circle were on the Ascendant, you will subtract the [oblique] ascensions of the degree in which the significator which you wished to direct by the ascensions of the re-

---

[37] Readers are referred to Gansten 2009 for the best current guide to directions.

gion was, from the [oblique] ascensions of the degree to which you wished to direct it, and what remained will be the degrees of direction. Which if the significator were in the degree of the seventh, you will subtract the [oblique] ascensions[38] of the nadir, [namely opposite] the degree in which the significator is,[39] from the [oblique] ascensions of the nadir of the degree to which you wished to direct it in that region.

But if the significator were on the Midheaven or on the angle of the earth, you will subtract the [right] ascensions of the significator from the [right] ascensions of that degree to which you wished to direct it, by ascensions of the right circle: and what remained will be the degrees of direction.

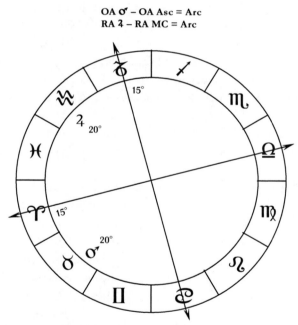

Figure 122: Directions from the degrees of the angles

---

[38] Normally these are called the oblique "descensions" because they are on the descending side of the chart.

[39] By the "nadir," al-Qabīsī means the ascensions of the opposite degree. Astronomical tables listed the ascensions of the degrees in the eastern hemisphere, so for points on the western side of the chart they simply used the opposite degrees.

§VIII.2.2b: Directions outside the angles[40]

[al-Qabīsī IV.11c] But if the significator which you wished to direct were in another place outside the four angles, you will look at its distance from one of these angles: which are the angle of the Midheaven and the angle of the earth.

§VIII.2.2c: Directions on the eastern side of the chart

[al-Qabīsī IV.11d-12a]
[Meridian distance (upper)] That is: you will look at the significator. Which, if it were between the Ascendant and the Midheaven, you will subtract the ascensions of the degree of the Midheaven by the right circle, from the [right] ascensions of the degree of the significator. And if it were between the seventh and the Midheaven, you will subtract the [right] ascensions of the degree of the significator from the ascensions of the degree of the Midheaven by the right circle. And you will divide what remained (of whatever one of these places it was) by the parts of the hours of the day belonging to that degree in which the significator was: and what came out will be the hours of the distance from the angle.

[Meridian distance (lower)] And if it were between the Ascendant and the angle of the earth, you will subtract the ascensions of the degree of the significator by the right circle from the [right] ascensions of the degree of the angle of the earth. Again, if the significator were between the angle of the earth and the seventh, you will subtract the ascensions of the degree of the angle of the earth by the right circle from the [right] ascensions of the degree of the significator. And you will divide what remained (of whatever one of these places it was) by the times of the hours of the day of the nadir-degree of the significator: and what came out will be the hours of the distance from the angle.

[Significator of the right circle] And if you knew the hours of the distance from the angle, and you wished to direct a significator to some place in the circle of the signs, and the significator were in the eastern

---

[40] See Appendix E for a fully worked-out example using both al-Qabīsī's method and the formula as described by Martin Gansten.

half of the circle (which is from the Midheaven up to the angle of the earth, of those [degrees] which come after the Ascendant), you will subtract the [right] ascensions of the degree in which the significator is, from the ascensions of the degree of the one to which you wished to direct it, by the right circle, and what remained will be the "significator of the right circle." Save this [value].

[Significator of the region] After this, subtract the ascensions of that degree in which the significator is, by ascensions of the region,[41] from the ascensions of that degree to which you wished to direct it, by ascensions of the region: and what it was, will be the "significator of the region."

[Equation] After this, you will take the remainder which was between the significator of the right circle and the significator of the region, and you will take one-sixth of it, and multiply it by the hours of the distance from the angle: and what there was, will be the "equation."

[Degrees of direction] And if the significator of the right circle were less than the significator of the region, you will add the equation on top of the significator of the right circle; and if the significator of the right circle were more, you will subtract the equation from it: and what remained will be the degrees of direction.[42]

§VIII.2.2d: *Directions on the western side of the chart*

[al-Qabīsī IV.12b][43]

[Significator of the right circle] Likewise, if the significator which you wished to direct were in the western hemisphere (which is from the angle of the earth up to the Midheaven, in what comes after the seventh), you will subtract the [right] ascensions of the nadir of the degree of the significator which you wished to direct, from the ascensions of the nadir of the degree to which you wished to direct it, by the right circle: and what remained will be the significator of the right circle.

---

[41] That is, in oblique ascension.
[42] That is, the arc of degrees which are converted into years of life. A common conversion key is: 1° = 1 year of life.
[43] Al-Qabīsī assumes we have already determined the upper or lower meridian distance for the points on the western hemisphere of the chart, as above.

[Significator of the region] After this, you will even subtract the ascensions of the nadir of the degree of the significator by ascensions of the region, from the [oblique] ascensions of the nadir of that degree to which you wished to direct it: and what remained will be the significator of the region.

[Equation] Then you will take the remainder which was between the significator of the right circle and the significator of the region, and you will take 1/6 of it and you will multiply [it] by the hours of the distance from the angle: and what there was, will be the "equation."

[Degrees of direction] After this, you will look at the significator of the right circle. If it were less than the significator of the region, you will add the equation on top of the significator of the right circle; and if the significator of the right circle were more than the significator of the region, you will subtract the equation from the significator of the right circle; and what came out from that will be the degrees of direction.

§VIII.2.2.e: Directions across quarters

[al-Qabīsī IV.12c] Which if the significator were in one quarter, and the place to which you are directing it in another quarter, you will direct the significator to the angle which comes after it; after this, you will direct from the angle to the place, in the way which I showed you the direction from an angle, and you will join both [of the arcs of the] directions together.

§VIII.2.2f: Directions and distributions[44]

[al-Qabīsī IV.12d] Which if you knew the significator and you wanted to know where in the circle of signs it will arrive in any of the years, and the significator were on the Ascendant, you will add the number of years on top of the [oblique] ascensions of the degree of the

---

[44] In this sections, al-Qabīsī introduces the method of distributions or directing through the bounds. Unlike older authors who simply used tables of ascensional times to map out these periods of life (which had close but approximate values), al-Qabīsī applies the general directional method above to get a more exact value. For more on distributions, see Appendix F, and the simpler method of ascensions in Appendix E.

Ascendant, and you will make an arc in the ascension of the region: and where the arc came out in the circle of the signs, the direction will arrive there in that same year.[45]

But if the significator were on the seventh, you will add the number of years on top of the ascensions of the nadir of the degree of the significator, and you will make it arc in the ascensions of the region: and where it came out in the circle of signs, the direction will arrive to its nadir in that same year.

Which if the significator were on the tenth or on the fourth, you will add the number of years on top of the ascensions of the degree of the significator in the right circle, and you will make it arc in the ascensions of the right circle: and what came out in the circle of signs, the direction will arrive there in that same year.

If however the significator were outside the four places which are the angles, you will know the hours of distance from the angle, just as I have told you before. Which if the significator were in the eastern half, you will add the number of the years which you wanted on top of the ascensions of the degree of the significator by the right circle, and you will make this arc in the ascensions of the right circle: and what came out will be the significator of the right circle. Save it. After this, you will add the number of years even on top of the ascensions of the degree of the significator in the region, and you will make it arc in the ascensions of the region: and what came out will be the significator of the region. After this, you will take 1/6 of the remainder between the significator of the right circle and the significator of the region, and you will multiply it by the hours of distance from the angle: and what there was, will be the equation. Which if the significator of the right circle were less than the significator of the region, you will add the equation on top of the significator of the right circle; and if it were more, you will subtract it from it; and what remained, the direction in the circle of the signs will arrive there in that same year.

Which if the significator were in the western half, you will do with the nadir of the degree of the significator just as you did with the degree of the significator in the work which was before this: and what

---

[45] This requires that we convert the oblique ascensions back into zodiacal degrees: a table of ascensional times can do this rather well.

there was, the direction in the circle of the signs will arrive there in that same year.

And the place to which the direction arrives is called the "place of distribution," and the Lord of the bound of that place is called the "distributor." Which if there were a planet or its rays in the degree of the distribution, or near the place in front of it, this planet or the Lord of its rays is said to be the "partner" of the distributor in the distribution.

But[46] the significators which are directed are: the degree of the Ascendant, and the degree of the Sun, and the degree of the Moon, also the degree of the Lot of Fortune and the degree of the Midheaven. Therefore, the degree of the Ascendant is directed for distinguishing the accidents which happen in the body; and the Sun for the causes of dignity and exaltation, also honor and kingdom; and the Moon on account of the being of the soul and body[47] and marriage-union; and the Lot of Fortune on account of acquisitions and success, also scarcity and bounty; and the Midheaven on account of mastery and the rest of the particular managements, and their being.[48]

[al-Qabīsī IV.14] And from this, the *jārbakhtār*[49] in nativities: and it is the direction of the degree of the Ascendant.[50] This is that you would look at the degree of the Ascendant to see what planet's bound it is in, and you subtract the ascensions of the Ascendant in the region[51] from the [oblique] ascensions which are at the end of the bound of that planet: and for what remained, you will take one year for every degree, and a month for every five minutes, and six days for every minute, and the Lord of the bound will be the manager of the years, which is called the "distributor."

---

[46] See *Tet.* IV.10 and *PN3*.

[47] In Ptolemy, "passions" of the soul, which are usually considered to be linked to physiology.

[48] Ptolemy lists several general types of activities and ways of spending time: in friendships, actions, and having children.

[49] Pahlavi: "distributor of time, time lord." I will call it this below when al-Qabīsī uses the Pahlavi again.

[50] Or rather, the *jārbakhtār* is the distributor, the bound Lord of any directed releaser. It just so happens that some authors like al-Qabīsī and Abū Ma'shar (*PN3*) prefer the Ascendant as the releaser, while others like Māshā'allāh (*BA*) prefer the releaser for longevity as determined in VIII.1.3 above.

[51] I.e., in oblique ascension.

After this you will take the degrees of the bound which succeeds it, and you will turn even those into degrees of ascensions, and what there was, you will take one year for every degree and a month for every five minutes, and six days for every minute, and the Lord of the bound will be the distributor and manager of those years.

Likewise, you will enter [thusly] with every Lord of a bound, by succession, up to the end of life. And if, in the bound of some planet, there were a planet or its rays, it will be [the distributor's] "partner" in the distribution. And this distribution is called the distribution of the distributor of time.[52]

[al-Qabīsī IV.13b] And in a revolution of the years of nativities, for knowing the condition of the native beforehand, [it is directed] from the degree of the Ascendant of the revolution, one day for every 59' 08" by the ascensions of the region.[53]

♈	♃ 0°-5°59'	♀ 6°-11°59'	☿ 12°-19°59'	♂ 20°-24°59'	♄ 25°-29°59'
♉	♀ 0°-7°59'	☿ 8°-13°59'	♃ 14°-21°59'	♄ 22°-26°59'	♂ 27°-29°59'
♊	☿ 0°-5°59'	♃ 6°-11°59'	♀ 12°-16°59'	♂ 17°-23°59'	♄ 24°-29°59'
♋	♂ 0°-6°59'	♀ 7°-12°59'	☿ 13°-18°59'	♃ 19°-25°59'	♄ 26°-29°59'
♌	♃ 0°-5°59'	♀ 6°-10°59'	♄ 11°-17°59'	☿ 18°-23°59'	♂ 24°-29°59'
♍	☿ 0°-6°59'	♀ 7°-16°59'	♃ 17°-20°59'	♂ 21°-27°59'	♄ 28°-29°59'
♎	♄ 0°-5°59'	☿ 6°-13°59'	♃ 14°-20°59'	♀ 21°-27°59'	♂ 28°-29°59'
♏	♂ 0°-6°59'	♀ 7°-10°59'	☿ 11°-18°59'	♃ 19°-23°59'	♄ 24°-29°59'
♐	♃ 0°-11°59'	♀ 12°-16°59'	☿ 17°-20°59'	♄ 21°-25°59'	♂ 26°-29°59'
♑	☿ 0°-6°59'	♃ 7°-13°59'	♀ 14°-21°59'	♄ 22°-25°59'	♂ 26°-29°59'
♒	☿ 0°-6°59'	♀ 7°-12°59'	♃ 13°-19°59'	♂ 20°-24°59'	♄ 25°-29°59'
♓	♀ 0°-11°59'	♃ 12°-15°59'	☿ 16°-18°59'	♂ 19°-27°59'	♄ 28°-29°59'

Figure 123: Egyptian bounds

[52] Again, all of this is the same method of distribution, but al-Qabīsī and others (perhaps not understanding the Pahlavi) tend to use *jārbakḫtār* as a special technical term.

[53] This is 'Umar al-Tabarī's method for finding the "lesser condition" of the native, where the Ascendant of the revolution is directed around the whole revolutionary chart over the course of the year: it is an annual version of natal distributions.

§VIII.2.3: The Lord of the turn

[al-Qabīsī IV.19] And from this, the Lord of the "turn"[54] in nativities. This is that you should look at the Lord of the hour in which the native arose, and you will give the Ascendant and the Lord of the hour to the first year of his nativity, and the good health or infirmity of the native's body will be signified through its being, just as it is signified by the Lord of the Ascendant of the root. And you will give the Lord of the second hour from [the nativity] to the second house from the Ascendant in the second year, and the being of assets and so on will be signified through its being in that same year, just as it is signified through the being of the Lord of the house of assets. And you will give the Lord of the third hour to the third house from the ascendant of the root in the third year, and the being of brothers and sisters and the rest will be signified through its being in that same year, just as it is signified through the being of the Lord of the third house. And you will give the Lord of the fourth hour to the fourth house from the Ascendant of the root in the fourth year, and the being of parents will be signified through its being in that same fourth year, and [also] that of those [others] who are signified through the fourth house.

You will do likewise with the Lords of the hours by succession: namely, you will give the Lord of each hour to a house (from among the rooted houses). And the Lord of the twelfth hour from the hour of the nativity will belong to the twelfth house from the Ascendant of the root, and the Lord of the thirteenth hour from the nativity will belong to the Ascendant[55] of the root and the thirteenth year, and the Lord of the fourteenth hour from it will belong to the house of assets and the fourteenth year.

And the Lord of the first hour is called the "Lord of the hour of the Ascendant," and the Lord of the second hour the "Lord of the hour of the house of assets," and the Lord of the third hour the "Lord of the hour of the house of brothers," and through this is signified the being of the boy and [his] brothers, and thus with the rest.

---

[54] Ar. *dawr*, in the sense of a cyclical taking of turns or roles. Burnett calls this the Lord of the "period."

[55] Omitting *dominus*.

Likewise the Lord of each one of these hours is called by the name of the house and is even called the "Lord of the period," and through it is signified in every year just as it is signified by the Lord of the Year.

And certain ones of the astrologers gave the Lord of the period (namely the Lord of the Ascendant of the root) to the first year, and the planet which succeeds this one to the second year, and the planet which succeeds that one to the third year, just as was said about the Lord of the hour.[56]

§VIII.2.4: Transits[57]

[al-Qabīsī IV.21] And from this, transit: because it is said that a planet passes over a planet. This is that you should look at the average course of a planet and at its calculated place:[58] and its calculated place were less than its average course, it will be ascending in the middle of its circle to the summit of its [epicyclic] circle; and if its calculated place were more than its average course, it will be descending from the middle of its circle to its lowest part; and if its calculated place were equal to its average course, it will be in the middle of its circle. After you knew this most certainly, subtract the lesser of these from the greater, and you will multiply what remained by 7, and you will divide by 22,[59] and what came out from the division will be the amount (for every planet) of its ascent and descent.

Concerning Venus and Mercury, we take what there is between each place (that is, between the place of the Sun and that of Venus and Mercury), and we do as above, because through this we know which if them is stronger in the circle of the apogee. But Venus and Mercury, if each one of them were eastern and its calculated place were less than the place of the Sun, you will take the remainder which is between its

---

[56] By the planet "succeeding" it, al-Qabīsī could mean in astronomical order (Saturn, Jupiter, Mars, etc.), or whichever one comes next in zodiacal order by transit at the nativity. The text does not make this clear.

[57] For more on transits, see PN3.

[58] Ar.: "corrected place." See II.1 above: traditional astronomers calculated both the expected place of a planet based on average speed (measured by the equant circle) and the exact position (measured from the center of the earth), to determine exactly where a planet was on its epicycle.

[59] 22/7 is a close rational approximation for pi (3.14159).

place and the place of the Sun, and you will do with it just as you with the higher planets, in terms of multiplication and division.

And the signification of the planets is stronger if they passed over each other in a conjunction. However, in the opposition and in the square aspect their signification will be less in [its] appearance, and weaker.

And if one of them were ascending [in its circle] and the other descending, then the ascending one of them goes over the descending one. But if they were [both] descending, the one which had less descension goes over the one which had more descension. And if they were [both] ascending, the one which had greater ascension goes over the one which had less ascension.

It is also said in another way: that is, that you should know the latitude of each of the planets, because the northern one of them goes over the southern one. And if they were both northern, the one which had more latitude goes over the one which had less latitude. But if they were both southern, the one which had less latitude goes over the one which had greater latitude: therefore it is said that the Moon goes over Jupiter in these two workings. Likewise, if some one of the two planets were in the middle of its circle, or having no latitude, then the one of them ascending in its own circle and being northern goes over the one which lacks latitude, and he goes over the southern one and over the descending one.

§VIII.3: Mundane astrology: al-Qabīsī

§VIII.3.1: Conjunctions

[al-Qabīsī IV.2] The beginning of these is conjunction[60] and the things signifying the changes which come to be in this world from the conjunction—the number of which is six.[61]

But greater than all the [other] conjunctions is the conjunction of Saturn and Jupiter at the beginning of Aries, and this comes to be [every] 960 years.[62]

The second of them is the conjunction in the beginning of each triplicity, and this comes to be [every] 240 years. For [Saturn and Jupiter] are joined twelve times in every triplicity, then their conjunction is changed to the triplicity which comes after it.

The third is the conjunction of Saturn and Mars at the beginning of Cancer, which comes to be every 30 years.

Also, the fourth is the conjunction of Saturn and Jupiter in every sign, which comes to be every 20 years.

The fifth is the settling of the greater luminary into the point of the time of the vernal equinox,[63] which comes to be every year.

The sixth is the conjunction of the luminaries and their opposition, which comes to be at one-half of each lunar month.

And when the "ascendant of the conjunction" is said, they do not want it [to be understood as anything] other than the Ascendant at the hour of the entrance of the Sun into the point of the vernal equinox— namely at the beginning of the year in which a conjunction is supposed to take place.

---

[60] Ar. *qiran*, "connection, marriage." Since this refers only to bodily conjunctions and is not the same word for "connection" in the list of planetary configurations in III.7 above, I will continue to say "conjunction" here.

[61] Al-Qabīsī's list is based on *BRD* I.1.12-20.

[62] The frequency of these and the following years is approximate.

[63] The Sun's annual ingress into Aries.

§*VIII.3.2: Mundane profections*

§*VIII.3.2a: Profecting from the conjunction of 571 AD to the Hijra (622 AD)*

[al-Qabīsī IV.9a] But the profection from the years of the world: al-Kindī said there were 52 solar years between the year of the conjunction which signified the sect of the Muslims and the year of the Hijra.[64]

[al-Qabīsī IV.9b] And the Ascendant of the year of the conjunction of the sect [and the sign of the turn itself] was the sign of Gemini, and the profection of that same year [to the year of the Hijra] reached Virgo.[65]

§*VIII.3.2b: Profecting from the Hijra to the accession of Yazdigird (632 AD)*

[al-Qabīsī IV.9c] And between that first year of the years of the Arabs[66] and the first of the years of Yazdigird were 3,624 days.[67] If therefore you wanted to have knowledge of this matter, take the years of Yazdigird and turn them into days just as is laid out in the *Zij*, and add on top of that the days which are between the first of the years of the Arabs and that of Yazdigird, and divide this by 365 ¼ days, and how many divisions came out will be that many solar years; and what remained in terms of months and days will be of an incomplete year;

---

[64] That is, between the Saturn-Jupiter conjunction in Scorpio in 571 AD (heralding Islam) and the Hijra or Muhammad's flight to Medina in 622 AD. Al-Kindi probably meant that it was the 52nd year of the shift, not that there were 52 complete years between the two dates: really, there are only 51 complete years and some months.

[65] This requires some explanation. Al-Qabīsī's source is claiming that Gemini shows up two times in this period. First, Gemini was the sign of the "turn" (Ar. *dawr*), a time-lord system which lasts for 360 years: around the time of the shift, the turn went to Gemini-Venus for the whole world, so the key moments of the Islamic religion have a special relationship to Gemini and Venus. Second, the source claims that Gemini was also the Ascendant of the year in which the Saturn-Jupiter conjunction took place. Other authors say that Ascendant was Libra (below), but the Arabic version of al-Rijāl in *BRD* p. 561 seems to say Gemini was the Ascendant at the time of the conjunction itself. Whichever Ascendant it was, if the conjunction was in 571, then profecting from the Ascendant of the shift to the Hijra in 622 would correspond to age 51 in a nativity: profecting from Gemini for 51 years leads to Virgo.

[66] I.e., the Hijra.

[67] This is about 10 years. Yazdigird III was the last king of the Sassanid Persians, ascending the throne on June 16, 632 AD. The Sassanids were overthrown by the Muslims in 651 AD.

and what came together in terms of years will be the solar years from the beginning of the years of the Arabs. Therefore, project one sign for every year, and begin from Virgo.[68] And to whatever sign the number will have led you, that will be the sign which the year of the world has reached, from the ascending of the conjunction of the aforesaid sect.

§VIII.3.2c: Profecting from the conjunction of 571 AD to the accession of Yazdigird

[al-Qabīsī IV.10a] But to others besides al-Kindī, it seems that they should add 61 years and 2 months and 12 days and 16 hours (in the years of the Persians) on top of the completed years of Yazdigird,[69] and they turned these years into days and turned the days into solar years just as we said before, and they began to project from the beginning of Libra.[70]

[al-Qabīsī IV.10b] Which if you wanted the profection from the sign of the conjunction of the sect, let the projection be from Scorpio.[71]

§VIII.3.2d: Profecting from the accession of Yazdigird to the 'Abbasid dynasty (750 AD)

[al-Qabīsī IV.10c] But if you wanted the profection from the ascent of the ['Abbasid] kingdom,[72] subtract 117 complete Persian years from the [complete] years of Yazdigird, and turn them into solar years just as we said, and begin to project from Virgo.[73]

---

[68] See above: if the profection from Gemini (the Ascendant in 571) had reached Virgo in the time of the Hijra (622), then if we profect from the Hijra to the accession of Yazdigird we must continue from Virgo.

[69] Actually, this is from the conjunction signifying Islam (571 AD) to the beginning of Yazdigird's reign (632 AD).

[70] Māshā'allāh and Abū Ma'shar report that the Ascendant of the year in which the conjunction of 571 happened, was Libra. So, despite the backwards-seeming calculation, they are profecting forward in time from the Ascendant of the year in 571 (Libra) to the year of the accession of Yazdigird in 632.

[71] The Saturn-Jupiter conjunction in 571 occurred in Scorpio. Thus, another option is to profect from the sign where the conjunction took place.

[72] The 'Abbasid dynasty began in 750 AD.

[73] If we compare this paragraph with the next, al-Qabīsī's source probably means that the Ascendant of the year in which the 'Abbasid dynasty began, was Virgo. But the instruc-

§VIII.3.2e: Profecting from the conjunction of 571 AD to the shift into the fiery triplicity (809 AD)

[al-Qabīsī IV.10d] Moreover, if you wanted the profection from the Ascendant of the revolution of the conjunction of the change from the watery triplicity to the fiery triplicity,[74] subtract 176 completed years from the years of Yazdigird, and turn those which remain into solar years, and begin to project from Leo.[75]

[al-Qabīsī IV.10e] And where the number reached, in that same sign will be the profection of each beginning (of those which we said before).

§VIII.3.3: Mundane directions

[al-Qabīsī IV.13a] If however it were the Ascendant of the revolution of some one of the years of the world or of nativities, its significators will be directed according to this direction, namely one day for every degree. And to certain people it seems that the significators of the year should be directed in this way: namely on day for every 59' 08".

But the direction of the kingdom and kings is directed for them thus: namely from the degree of the Midheaven by ascensions of the right circle,[76] one year for every 59' 08", until it reaches the good or bad planets.

And for the being of the bodies of kings (namely for soundness or infirmity), it is directed from the degree of the Ascendant to the good or bad planets, one day for every 59' 08" by the ascensions of the region.[77]

---

tions do not really make sense, and both this paragraph and the next seem to suggest a backwards profection.

[74] That is: profecting from the Ascendant of the mundane ingress, in which there was a conjunction that shifted from one triplicity to another.

[75] This does not seem right. The shift (809 AD) did take place 176 years (and some months) after the accession of Yazdigird (632 AD). And the Ascendant of the year in which the shift to fire took place was indeed Leo, according to Abū Ma'shar and others. But the paragraph reads as though we are profecting *backwards* from the Ascendant of the shift, which does not make sense.

[76] That is, by right ascension.

[77] That is, by oblique ascension.

And for knowing beforehand the condition of the common masses in a revolution of the years of the world, the direction [is] likewise from the degree of the Ascendant.

And for knowing beforehand the condition of the king, from the degree of the Midheaven.

§VIII.3.4: Weather

[al-Qabīsī IV.22] And from this, the opening of the portals. For it is said when an inferior planet is connected to a superior planet and in addition their domiciles were opposites.[78]

---

[78] This is also the opening line of a Latin work on astrometeorology, *The opening of the portals*, which was also used by John of Spain. The text goes on to include connections between a luminary with Saturn, Mercury with Jupiter, and Mars with Venus. The "doors" seem to be the opposed domiciles which symbolize changes in the atmosphere from above to below, as though weather is unleashed onto the earth. Rain of some type is indicated if such planets are connected in a chart of a New or Full Moon, and planets aspecting the superior-inferior combination tell what type. Mars, for instance, adds lots of lightning and thunder. See Bos and Burnett (2000), pp. 385ff.

§VIII.4: Elections: al-Qabīsī

[al-Qabīsī IV.23] And from this the *bust*,[79] which is a thing the Indians very much used to observe. For they counted 12 hours after the conjunction [of the Sun and Moon], and they apply them to the Sun, and they divide the 12 hours in the domain[80] of the Sun into three, and they judge, with respect to every 4 hours, according to the judgment of the Lords of the triplicity of the Sun at the hour of the conjunction. Then they even give Venus 12 hours after the 12 hours of the Sun, and they divide them again into three, and they judge over every one-third division according to the Lords of the triplicity of Venus at the hour of the conjunction. After this, they do likewise with Mercury and the rest of the planets through their successions, until the orb reverts back to the Sun after 84 hours, and they do not cease to do thus frequently until it comes to the following conjunction.

[al-Qabīsī IV.24] And certain people said that the *bust* is this: that after the conjunction there are 12 unequal hours[81] which are called "burnt," and it is not good to undertake some work in them; and after these 12 are 72 "unburnt" hours, in which the undertaking of works is useful; and after the 72 unburnt hours, 12 burnt ones,[82] up to the conjunction which comes after. After this, they divide these 12 hours into 3 divisions, and they said that one who undertakes to wage war in the first four hours will have to fear the loss of his own soul; and one who undertook it in the second 4 hours will have to fear the corruption of his own body without the loss of his soul; and he who undertook it in the last four hours will have to fear the corruption of his assets and companions.

---

[79] A transliteration of the Sanskrit *bhukti*, the ecliptical distance traveled in a particular time. See al-Biruni, §§197-98. In *BA* II.4 it is defined as 12°, roughly the average distance traveled by the Moon in one day. But here it is defined in terms of seasonal hours, such as the first 12 seasonal hours after the New Moon.

[80] *Hayyiz*, here being roughly synonymous with sect.

[81] I.e., seasonal hours (sometimes called planetary hours): the period of daylight or night divided by 12, which gives hours of more or less than the standardized or equinoctial sixty minutes.

[82] These correspond to the hours belonging to the Sun and his triplicity Lords in the previous paragraph.

[al-Qabīsī IV.25] And since we have completed the exposition of those things which are known from among the names of the astrologers, let us follow [it with] the relating of all of the Lots.[83]

---

[83] Al-Qabīsī now proceeds to the material on Lots in Book VI above.

GLOSSARY

- **Advancing**. When a planet is in an **angle** or succeedent. See III.3 and the Introduction §6.
- **Ages of man**. A division of a typical human life span into periods ruled by planets as **time lords**. See VII.3.
- **Agreeing signs**. Groups of signs which share some kind of harmonious quality. See I.9.5-6.
- *Alcochoden*. Latin transliteration for *Kadukhudhāh*.
- **Alien** (Lat. *alienus*). See **Peregrine**.
- *Almuten*. A Latin transliteration for *mubtazz*: see **Victor**.
- **Angles, succeedents, cadents.** A division of houses into three groups which show how powerfully and directly a planet acts. The angles are the 1st, 10th, 7th and 4th houses; the succeedents are the 2nd, 11th, 8th and 5th; the cadents are the 12th, 9th, 6th and 3rd. But the exact regions in question will depend upon whether and how one uses **whole-sign** and **quadrant houses**, especially since traditional texts refer to an angle or pivot (Gr. *kentron*, Ar. *watad*) as either (1) equivalent to the whole-sign angles from the **Ascendant**, or (2) the degrees of the **Ascendant-Midheaven** axes themselves, or (3) quadrant houses as measured from the degrees of the axes. See I.12-13 and III.3-4, and the Introduction §6.
- **Antiscia** (sing. *antiscion*), "throwing shadows." Refers to a degree mirrored across an axis drawn from 0° Capricorn to 0° Cancer. For example, 10° Cancer has 20° Gemini as its antiscion. See I.9.2.
- **Apogee**. Typically, the furthest point a planet can be from the earth on the circle of the **deferent**. See II.0-1.
- **Applying, application**. When a planet is in a state of **connection**, moving so as to make the connection exact. Planets **assembled** together or in **aspect** by sign and not yet connected by the relevant degrees, are only "wanting" to be connected.
- **Arisings**. See **Ascensions**.
- **Ascendant**. Usually the entire rising sign, but often specified as the exact rising degree. In **quadrant houses**, a pace following the exact rising degree up to the cusp of the 2nd house.
- **Ascensions**. Degrees on the celestial equator, measured in terms of how many degrees pass the meridian as an entire sign or **bound** (or other spans of zodiacal degrees) passes across the horizon. They are often used in the

predictive technique of ascensional times, as an approximation for **directions**. See Appendix E.

- **Aspect/regard**. One planet aspects or regards another if they are in signs which are configured to each other by a **sextile**, **square**, **trine**, or **opposition**. See III.6 and **Whole signs**.
- **Assembly**. When two or more planets are in the same sign, and more intensely if within 15°. See III.5.
- **Aversion**. Being in the second, sixth, eighth, or twelfth sign from a place. For instance, a planet in Gemini is in the twelfth from, and therefore in aversion to, Cancer.
- *Azamene*. Equivalent to **Chronic illness**.
- **Bad ones**. See **Benefic/malefic**.
- **Barring**. When a planet blocks another planet from completing a **connection**, either through its own body or ray. See III.14.
- **Benefic/malefic**. A division of the planets into groups that cause or signify typically "good" things (Jupiter, Venus, usually the Sun and Moon) or "bad" things (Mars, Saturn). Mercury is considered variable. See V.9.
- **Benevolents**. See **Benefic/malefic**.
- **Besieging**. Equivalent to **Enclosure**.
- **Bicorporeal signs**. Equivalent to "common" signs. See **Quadruplicity.**
- **Bodyguarding**. Planetary relationships in which some planet protects another, used in determining social eminence and prosperity. See III.28.
- **Bounds**. Unequal divisions of the zodiac in each sign, each bound being ruled by one of the five non-**luminaries**. Sometimes called "terms," they are one of the five classical **dignities.** See VII.4.
- **Bright, smoky, empty, dark degrees**. Certain degrees of the zodiac said to affect how conspicuous or obscure the significations of planets or the Ascendant are. See VII.7.
- **Burned up** (sometimes, "combust"). Normally, when a planet is between about 1° and 7.5° away from the Sun. See II.9-10, and **In the heart.**
- **Burnt path** (Lat. *via combusta*). A span of degrees in Libra and Scorpio in which a planet (especially the Moon) is considered to be harmed or less able to effect its significations. Some astrologers identify it as between 15° Libra and 15° Scorpio; others between the exact degree of the **fall** of the Sun in 19° Libra and the exact degree of the fall of the Moon in 3° Scorpio. See IV.3.

- **Bust**. Certain hours measured from the New Moon, in which it is considered favorable or unfavorable to undertake an action or perform an **election**. See VIII.4.
- **Cardinal.** Equivalent to "movable" signs. See **Quadruplicity.**
- **Cazimi:** see **In the heart.**
- **Celestial equator**. The projection of earth's equator out into the universe, forming one of the three principal celestial coordinate systems.
- **Choleric**. See **Humor.**
- **Chronic illness (degrees of)**. Degrees which are especially said to indicate chronic illness, due to their association with certain fixed stars. See VII.10.
- **Collection**. When two planets **aspecting** each other but not in an applying **connection**, each apply to a third planet. See III.12.
- **Combust**. See **Burned up.**
- **Commanding/obeying.** A division of the signs into those which command or obey each other (used sometimes in **synastry**). See I.9.
- **Common signs.** See **Quadruplicity.**
- **Conjunction (of planets)**. See **Assembly** and **Connection.**
- **Conjunction/prevention.** The position of the New (conjunction) or Full (prevention) Moon most immediately prior to a **nativity** or other chart. For the prevention, some astrologers use the degree of the Moon, others the degree of the luminary which was above the earth at the time of the prevention. See VIII.1.2.
- **Connection**. When a planet applies to another planet (by body in the same sign, or by ray in **aspecting** signs), within a particular number of degrees up to exactness. See III.7.
- **Convertible signs**. Equivalent to "movable" signs. See **Quadruplicity.**
- **Corruption**. See **Detriment.**
- **Crooked/straight.** A division of the signs into those which rise quickly and are more parallel to the horizon (crooked), and those which arise more slowly and closer to a right angle from the horizon (straight or direct). The signs from Capricorn to Gemini are crooked; those from Cancer to Sagittarius are straight.
- **Crossing over.** When a planet begins to **separate** from an exact **connection**. See III.7-8.

- **Cutting of light**. Three ways in which a **connection** is prevented: either by **obstruction** from the following sign, **escape** within the same sign, or by **barring**. See III.23.
- *Darījān*. An alternative **face** system attributed to the Indians. See VII.6.
- **Decan**. Equivalent to **face**.
- **Deferent**. The circle on which a planet's **epicycle** travels. See II.0-1.
- **Descension**. Equivalent to **fall**.
- **Detriment** (or Ar. "corruption," "unhealthiness," "harm."). More broadly (as "corruption"), it refers to any way in which a planet is harmed or its operation thwarted (such as by being **burned up**). But it also (as "harm") refers specifically to the sign opposite a planet's **domicile**. Libra is the detriment of Mars. See I.6 and I.8.
- **Dexter**. "Right": see **Right/left**.
- **Diameter**. Equivalent to **Opposition**.
- **Dignity** (Lat. "worthiness"; Ar. *ḥazz*, "good fortune, allotment"). Any of five ways of assigning rulership or responsibility to a planet (or sometimes, to a **Node**) over some portion of the zodiac. They are often listed in the following order: **domicile, exaltation, triplicity, bound, face/decan**. Each dignity has its own meaning and effect and use, and two of them have opposites: the opposite of domicile is **detriment**, the opposite of exaltation is **fall**. See I.3, I.4, I.6-7, VII.4 for the assignments; I.8 for some descriptive analogies; VIII.2.1 and VIII.2.2*f* for some predictive uses of domiciles and bounds.
- **Directions**. A predictive technique which is more precise than using **ascensions**, and defined by Ptolemy in terms of proportional semi-arcs. There is some confusion in how directing works, because of the difference between the astronomical method of directions and how astrologers look at charts. Astronomically, a point in the chart (the significator) is considered as stationary, and other planets and their **aspects** by degree (or even the **bounds**) are sent forth (promittors) as though the heavens keep turning by **primary motion**, until they come to the significator. The degrees between the significator and promittor are converted into years of life. But when looking at the chart, it seems as though the significator is being **released** counterclockwise in the order of signs, so that it **distributes** through the bounds or comes to the bodies or aspects of promittors. Direction by **ascensions** takes the latter perspective, though the result is the same. Some later astrologers allow the distance between a significa-

tor/releaser and the promittor to be measured in either direction, yielding "converse" directions in addition to the classical "direct" directions. See VIII.2.2, Appendix E, and Gansten.

- **Disregard**. Equivalent to **Separation**.
- **Distribution**. The **direction** of a **releaser** (often the degree of the **Ascendant**) through the **bounds**. The bound **Lord** of the distribution is the "distributor," and any body or ray which the **releaser** encounters is the "**partner**." See VIII.2.2f, and *PN3*.
- **Distributor**. The **bound Lord** of a **directed releaser**. See **Distribution**.
- **Diurnal/nocturnal**. See **Sect**.
- **Domain**. A **sect** and **gender**-based planetary condition. See III.2.
- **Domicile**. One of the five **dignities**. A sign of the zodiac, insofar as it is owned or managed by one of the planets. For example, Aries is the domicile of Mars, and so Mars is its domicile **Lord**. See I.6.
- **Doryphory** (Gr. *doruphoria*). Equivalent to **Bodyguarding**.
- **Dragon**: see **Node**.
- **Dodecametorion**. Equivalent to **Twelfth-part**.
- *Duodecima*. Equivalent to **Twelfth-part**.
- *Dustūrīyyah*. Equivalent to **Bodyguarding**.
- **Eastern/western**. A position relative to the Sun, in which a planet either rises before the Sun (eastern) or sets after him (western). Usually called "oriental" and "occidental." Different astrologers have different definitions for exactly what counts as being eastern or western. See II.10.
- **Ecliptic**. The path defined by the Sun's motion through the zodiac, defined as having 0° ecliptical latitude.
- **Election** (lit. "choice"). The deliberate choosing of an appropriate time to undertake an action, or determining when to avoid an action; but astrologers normally refer to the chart of the time itself as an election.
- **Element**. One of the four basic qualities. fire, air, water, earth) describing how matter and energy operate, and used to describe the significations and operations of planets and signs. They are usually described by pairs of four other basic qualities (hot, cold, wet, dry). For example, Aries is a fiery sign, and hot and dry; Mercury is typically treated as cold and dry (earthy). See I.3, I.7, and Book V.
- **Emptiness of the course**. Medievally, when a planet does not complete a **connection** for as long as it is in its current sign. In Hellenistic astrology,

when a planet does not complete a connection within the next 30°. See III.9.

- **Enclosure**. When a planet has the rays or bodies of the **malefics** (or alternatively, the **benefics**) on either side of it, by degree or sign. See IV.4.2.
- **Epicycle.** A circle on the **deferent**, on which a planet turns. See II.0-1.
- **Equant.** A circle used to measure the average position of a planet. See II.0-1.
- **Escape**. When a planet wants to **connect** with a second one, but the second one moves into the next sign before it is completed, and the first planet makes a **connection** with a different, unrelated one instead. See III.22.
- **Essential/accidental.** A common way of distinguishing a planet's conditions, usually according to **dignity** (essential, I.2) and some other condition such as its **aspects** (accidental). See IV.1-5 for many accidental conditions.
- **Exaltation.** One of the five **dignities**. A sign in which a planet (or sometimes, a **Node**) signifies its matter in a particularly authoritative and refined way. The exaltation is sometimes identified with a particular degree in that sign. See I.6.
- **Face**. One of the five **dignities**. The zodiac is divided into 36 faces of 10° each, starting with the beginning of Aries. See I.5.
- **Facing**. A relationship between a planet and a **luminary**, if their respective signs are configured at the same distance as their **domiciles** are. For example, Leo (ruled by the Sun) is two signs to the **right** of Libra (ruled by Venus). When Venus is **western** and two signs away from wherever the Sun is, she will be in the facing of the Sun. See II.11.
- **Fall**. The sign opposite a planet's **exaltation**. See I.6.
- **Feminine**. See **Gender**.
- **Feral**. Equivalent to **Wildness**.
- *Firdārīyyah* (pl. *firdārīyyāt*). A **time lord** method in which planets rule different periods of life, with each period broken down into sub-periods. See VII.1.
- **Firm**. For firm signs, see **Quadruplicity**. For the houses, see **Angles**.
- **Fixed**. See **Quadruplicity**.
- **Foreign** (Lat. *extraneus*). Usually equivalent to **peregrine**.
- **Fortunes**. See **Benefic/malefic**.

- **Gender.** The division of signs, degrees, planets and hours into masculine and feminine groups. See I.3, V.10, V.14, VII.8.
- **Generosity and benefits**. Favorable relationships between signs and planets, as defined in III.26.
- **Good ones.** See **Benefic/malefic.**
- **Greater, middle, lesser years**. See **Planetary years.**
- **Ḥalb.** Probably Pahlavi for "sect," but normally describes a rejoicing condition: see III.2.
- **Ḥayyiz.** Arabic for "domain," normally a gender-intensified condition of *ḥalb.* See III.2.
- **Hexagon**. Equivalent to **Sextile.**
- **Hīlāj** (From the Pahlavi for "releaser"). Equivalent to **Releaser**.
- **Horary astrology**. The branch of astrology concerned with asking and answering questions.
- **Hours (planetary)**. The assigning of rulership over hours of the day and night to planets. The hours of daylight (and night, respectively) are divided by 12, and each period is ruled first by the planet ruling that day, then the rest in descending planetary order. For example, on Sunday the Sun rules the first planetary "hour" from daybreak, then Venus, then Mercury, the Moon, Saturn, and so on. See V.13.
- **Humor.** Any one of four fluids in the body (according to traditional medicine), the balance between which determines one's health and **temperament** (outlook and energy level). Choler or yellow bile is associated with fire and the choleric temperament; blood is associated with air and the sanguine temperament; phlegm is associated with water and the phlegmatic temperament; black bile is associated with earth and the melancholic temperament. See I.3.
- **In the heart.** Often called *cazimi* in English texts, from the Ar. *kaṣmīmī.* A planet is in the heart of the Sun when it is either in the same degree as the Sun (according to Sahl bin Bishr and Rhetorius), or within 16' of longitude from him. See II.9.
- **Indicator**. A degree which is supposed to indicate the approximate position of the degree of the natal **Ascendant**, in cases where the time of birth is uncertain. See VIII.1.2.
- **Inferior**. The planets lower than the Sun: Venus, Mercury, Moon.
- **Infortunes**. See **Benefic/malefic.**
- **'Ittiṣāl**. Equivalent to **connection**.

- **Joys.** Places in which the planets are said to "rejoice" in acting or signifying their natures. Joys by house are found in I.16; by sign in I.10.7.
- *Jārbakhtār* (From the Pahlavi for "distributor of time"). Equivalent to **Distributor**; see **Distribution.**
- *Kadukhudhāh* (From the Pahlavi for "domicile master"). One of the Lords of the longevity **releaser**, preferably the **bound Lord**. It is also equivalent to the **distributor** when directing any releaser through the bounds. See VIII.1.3.
- *Kaṣmīmī*: see **In the heart**.
- **Kingdom**. Equivalent to **exaltation**.
- **Largesse and recompense**. A reciprocal relation in which one planet is rescued from being in its own **fall** or a **well**, and then returns the favor when the other planet is in its fall or well. See III.24.
- **Leader** (Lat. *dux*). Equivalent to a **significator** for some topic. The Arabic word for "significator" means to indicate something by pointing the way toward something: thus the significator for a topic or matter "leads" the astrologer to some answer. Used by some less popular Latin translators (such as Hugo of Santalla and Hermann of Carinthia).
- **Lord of the Year.** The **domicile Lord** of a **profection**. The Sun and Moon are not allowed to be primary Lords of the Year, according to Persian doctrine. See VIII.2.1 and VIII.3.2, and Appendix F.
- **Lord.** A designation for the planet which has a particular **dignity**, but when used alone it usually means the **domicile** Lord. For example, Mars is the Lord of Aries.
- **Lot**. Sometimes called "Parts." A place (often treated as equivalent to an entire sign) expressing a ratio derived from the position of three other parts of a chart. Normally, the distance between two places is measured in zodiacal order from one to the other, and this distance is projected forward from some other place (usually the Ascendant): where the counting stops, is the Lot. Lots are used both interpretively and predictively. See Book VI.
- **Luminary**. The Sun or Moon.
- **Malefic**. See **Benefic/malefic.**
- **Malevolents**. See **Benefic/malefic.**
- **Masculine**. See **Gender**.
- **Melancholic**. See **Humor**.

- **Midheaven**. Either the tenth sign from the **Ascendant**, or the zodiacal degree on which the celestial meridian falls.
- **Movable signs**. See **Quadruplicity.**
- *Mubtazz.* See **Victor.**
- **Mutable signs**. Equivalent to "common" signs. See **Quadruplicity.**
- *Namūdār.* Equivalent to **Indicator.**
- **Nativity**. Technically, a birth itself, but used by astrologers to describe the chart cast for the moment of a birth.
- **Ninth-parts**. Divisions of each sign into 9 equal parts of 3° 20' apiece, each ruled by a planet. Used predictively by some astrologers as part of the suite of **revolution** techniques. See VII.5.
- **Nobility.** Equivalent to **exaltation.**
- **Node.** The point on the ecliptic where a planet passes into northward latitude (its North Node or Head of the Dragon) or into southern latitude (its South Node or Tail of the Dragon). Normally only the Moon's Nodes are considered. See II.5 and V.8.
- **Northern/southern.** Either planets in northern or southern latitude in the zodiac (relative to the ecliptic), or in northern or southern declination relative to the celestial equator. See I.10.1.
- **Oblique ascensions**. The **ascensions** used in making predictions by ascensional times or primary **directions**.
- **Obstruction**. When one planet is moving towards a second (wanting to be **connected** to it), but a third one in a later degrees goes **retrograde**, connects with the second one, and then with the first one. See III.21.
- **Occidental**. See **Eastern/western.**
- **Opening of the portals/doors**. Times of likely weather changes and rain, determined by certain **transits**. See VIII.3.4.
- **Opposition**. An **aspect** either by **whole sign** or degree, in which the signs have a 180° relation to each other: for example, a planet in Aries is opposed to one in Libra.
- **Orbs/bodies**. Called "orb" by the Latins, and "body" (*jirm*) by Arabic astrologers. A space of power or influence on each side of a planet's body or position, used to determine the intensity of interaction between different planets. See II.6.
- **Oriental**. See **Eastern/western.**
- **Overcoming**. When a planet is in the eleventh, tenth, or ninth sign from another planet (i.e., in a superior **sextile**, **square**, or **trine aspect**), though

being in the tenth sign is considered a more dominant or even domineering position. See IV.4.1 and *PN3*'s Introduction, §15.

- **Part.** See **Lot.**
- **Partner.** The body or ray of any planet which a **directed releaser** encounters while being **distributed** through the **bounds.**
- **Peregrine.** When a planet is not in one of its five **dignities.** See I.9.
- **Phlegmatic.** See **Humor.**
- **Pitted degrees.** Equivalent to **Welled degrees.**
- **Pivot.** Equivalent to **Angle.**
- **Planetary years.** Periods of years which the planets signify according to various conditions. See VII.2.
- **Prevention.** See **Conjunction/prevention.**
- **Primary directions.** See **Directions.**
- **Primary motion.** The clockwise or east-to-west motion of the heavens.
- **Profection** (Lat. *profectio,* "advancement, setting out"). A predictive technique in which some part of a chart (usually the **Ascendant**) is advanced either by an entire sign or in 30° increments for each year of life. See VIII.2.1 and VIII.3.2, and the sources in Appendix F.
- **Prohibition.** Equivalent to **Barring.**
- **Promittor** (lit., something "sent forward"). A point which is **directed** to a **significator,** or to which a significator is **released** or directed (depending on how one views the mechanics of directions).
- **Pushing.** What the planet making an applying **connection** does to the one **receiving** it. See III.15-18.
- *Qasim/qismah*: Arabic terms for **distributor** and **distribution.**
- **Quadrant houses.** A division of the heavens into twelve spaces which overlap the **whole signs,** and are assigned to topics of life and ways of measuring strength (such as Porphyry, Alchabitius Semi-Arc, or Regiomontanus houses). For example, if the Midheaven fell into the eleventh sign, the space between the Midheaven and the Ascendant would be divided into sections that overlap and are not coincident with the signs. See I.12 and the Introduction §6.
- **Quadruplicity.** A "fourfold" group of signs indicating certain shared patterns of behavior. The movable (or cardinal or convertible) signs are those through which new states of being are quickly formed (including the seasons): Aries, Cancer, Libra, Capricorn. The fixed (sometimes "firm") signs are those through which matters are fixed and lasting in their character:

Taurus, Leo, Scorpio, Aquarius. The common (or mutable or bicorporeal) signs are those which make a transition and partake both of quick change and fixed qualities: Gemini, Virgo, Sagittarius, Pisces. See I.10.5.

- **Quaesited/quesited**. In **horary** astrology, the matter asked about.
- **Querent**. In **horary** astrology, the person asking the question (or the person on behalf of whom one asks).
- **Reception.** What a planet does when another planet **pushes** to it, but especially when they are related by **dignity** or by a **trine** or **sextile** from an **agreeing** sign of various types. See III.25.
- **Reflection.** When two planets are in **aversion** to each other, but a third planet either **collects** or **transfers** their light. If it collects, it reflects the light elsewhere. See III.13.
- **Refrenation**. See **Revoking.**
- **Regard**. Equivalent to **Aspect.**
- **Releaser**. The point which is the focus of a **direction**. In determining longevity, it is the one among a standard set of possible points which has certain qualifications (see VIII.1.3). In annual predictions one either directs or **distributes** the longevity releaser, or any one of a number of points for particular topics, or else the degree of the **Ascendant** as a default releaser. Many astrologers direct the degree of the Ascendant of the **revolution** chart itself as a releaser.
- **Remote**. Equivalent to **cadent**: see **Angle.**
- **Retreating**. When a planet is in a cadent place. See III.4 and the Introduction §6, and **Angle.**
- **Retrograde.** When a planet seems to move backwards or clockwise relative to the signs and fixed stars. See II.8 and II.10.
- **Return**. Equivalent to **Revolution.**
- **Returning**. What a **burned up** or **retrograde** planet does when another planet **pushes** to it. See III.19.
- **Revoking**. When a planet making an applying **connection** stations and turns **retrograde**, not completing the connection. See III.20.
- **Revolution.** Sometimes called the "cycle" or "transfer" or "change-over" of a year. Technically, the **transiting** position of planets and the **Ascendant** at the moment the Sun returns to a particular place in the zodiac: in the case of nativities, when he returns to his exact natal position; in mundane astrology, usually when he makes his ingress into 0° Aries. But the

revolution is also understood to involve an entire suite of predictive techniques, including **distribution**, **profections**, and *firdārīyyāt*. See *PN3*.

- **Right ascensions**. Degrees on the celestial equator, particularly those
  which move across the meridian when calculating arcs for **ascensions** and
  directions.
- **Right/left.** Right (or "dexter") degrees and **aspects** are those earlier in
  the zodiac relative to a planet or sign, up to the **opposition**; left (or "sinister") degrees and aspects are those later in the zodiac. For example, if a
  planet is in Capricorn, its right aspects will be towards Scorpio, Libra, and
  Virgo; its left aspects will be towards Pisces, Aries, and Taurus. See III.6.
- **Root**. A chart used as a basis for another chart; a root particularly describes something considered to have concrete being of its own. For
  example, a **nativity** acts as a root for an **election**, so that when planning
  an election one must make it harmonize with the nativity.
- *Sālkhudhāy* (from Pahlavi, "Lord of the Year"). Equivalent to the **Lord of
  the Year**.
- **Sanguine**. See **Humor**.
- **Scorched**. See **Burned up**.
- **Secondary motion**. The counter-clockwise motion of planets forward in
  the zodiac.
- **Sect**. A division of charts, planets, and signs into "diurnal/day" and "noc-
  turnal/night." Charts are diurnal if the Sun is above the horizon, else they
  are nocturnal. Planets are divided into sects as shown in V.11. Masculine
  signs (Aries, Gemini, *etc.*) are diurnal, the feminine signs (Taurus, Cancer,
  etc.) are nocturnal.
- **Seeing, hearing, listening signs**. A way of associating signs similar to
  commanding/obeying. See Paul of Alexandria's version in the two figures attached to I.9.6.
- **Separation**. When planets have completed a **connection** by **assembly** or
  aspect, and move away from one another. See III.8.
- **Sextile**. An **aspect** either by **whole sign** or degree, in which the signs
  have a 60° relation to each other: for example, Aries and Gemini.
- **Significator**. Either (1) a planet or point in a chart which indicates or signifies something for a topic (either through its own character, or house
  position, or rulerships, *etc.*), or (2) the point which is **released** in primary
  directions.
- **Sinister**. "Left": see **Right/left**.

- **Slavery.** Equivalent to **fall**.
- **Spearbearing**. Equivalent to **Bodyguarding.**
- **Square.** An **aspect** either by **whole sign** or degree, in which the signs have a 90° relation to each other: for example, Aries and Cancer.
- **Stake.** Equivalent to **Angle.**
- **Sublunar world.** The world of the four **elements** below the sphere of the Moon, in classical cosmology.
- **Succeedent.** See **Angle.**
- **Superior.** The planets higher than the Sun: Saturn, Jupiter, Mars.
- **Synastry.** The comparison of two or more charts to determine compatibility, usually in romantic relationships or friendships. See *BA* Appendix C for a discussion and references for friendship, and *BA* III.7.11 and III.12.7.
- *Tasyīr* (Ar. "dispatching, sending out"). Equivalent to primary **directions**.
- **Temperament.** The particular mixture (sometimes, "complexion") of **elements** or **humors** which determines a person's or planet's typical behavior, outlook, and energy level.
- **Tetragon.** Equivalent to **Square.**
- **Time lord.** A planet ruling over some period of time according to one of the classical predictive techniques. For example, the **Lord of the Year** is the time lord over a **profection**.
- **Transfer.** When one planet **separates** from one planet, and **connects** to another. See III.11.
- **Transit.** The passing of one planet across another planet or point (by body or **aspect** by exact degree), or through a particular sign (even in a **whole-sign** relation to some point of interest). In traditional astrology, not every transit is significant; for example, transits of **time lords** or of planets in the **whole-sign angles** of a **profection** might be preferred to others. See VIII.2.4 and *PN3*.
- **Translation.** Equivalent to **Transfer.**
- **Trigon.** Equivalent to **Trine**.
- **Trine.** An **aspect** either by **whole sign** or degree, in which the signs have a 120° relation to each other: for example, Aries and Leo.
- **Turn** (Ar. *dawr*). A predictive term in which responsibilities for being a **time lord** rotates between different planets. See VIII.2.3 for one use of the turn.

- **Twelfth-parts.** Signs of the zodiac defined by 2.5° divisions of other signs. For example, the twelfth-part of 4° Gemini is Cancer. See IV.6.
- **Under rays.** When a planet is between approximately 7.5° and 15° from the Sun, and not visible either when rising before the Sun or setting after him. Some astrologers distinguish the distances for individual planets (which is more astronomically accurate). See II.10.
- *Via combusta*. See **Burnt path**.
- **Victor** (Ar. *mubtazz*). A planet identified as being the most authoritative either for a particular topic (I.18) or for a chart as a whole (VIII.1.4).
- **Void in course**. Equivalent to **Emptiness of the course.**
- **Well.** A degree in which a planet is said to be more obscure in its operation. See VII.9.
- **Western**. See **Eastern/western.**
- **Whole signs.** The oldest system of assigning house topics and **aspects**. The entire sign on the horizon (the **Ascendant**) is the first house, the entire second sign is the second house, and so on. Likewise, aspects are considered first of all according to signs: planets in Aries aspect or regard Gemini as a whole, even if aspects by exact degree are more intense. See I.12, III.6, and the Introduction §6.
- **Wildness.** When a planet is not **aspected** by any other planet, for as long as it is in its current sign. See III.10.

APPENDIX A: TEXTS FOR TABLES OF DEGREES

I. Planetary periods

[*Abbr.* VII.5] And so the greatest years of the Sun are 120, but of Venus 82 years, of Mercury 76, of the Moon 108, of Saturn 57, of Jupiter 79, of Mars 66. [6] But the middle [period] of the Sun is 39 ½ years,[1] of Venus 45, of Mercury 48, of the Moon 39 ½,[2] of Saturn 43 ½, of Jupiter 45 ½, of Mars 40 ½. [7] But the least ones of the Sun [are] 19, of Venus 8, of Mercury 20, of the Moon 25, of Saturn 30, of Jupiter 12, of Mars 15.

II. Egyptian bounds

[*Abbr.* VII.10-21][3] In Aries, Jupiter holds onto 6 degrees, Venus the same amount, Mercury 8, Mars 5, Saturn the same amount. In Taurus, Venus [holds onto] 8, Mercury 6, Jupiter 8, Saturn 5, Mars 3. In Gemini, Mercury [holds onto] 6, Jupiter 6, Venus 5, Mars 7, Saturn 6. In Cancer, Mars [holds onto] 7, Venus 6, Mercury 6, Jupiter 7, Saturn 4. In Leo, Jupiter [holds onto] 6, Venus 5, Saturn 7, Mercury 6, Mars 6. In Virgo, Mercury [holds onto] 7, Venus 10, Jupiter 4, Mars 7, Saturn 2. In Libra, Saturn [holds onto] 6, Mercury 8, Jupiter 7, Venus 7, Mars 2. In Scorpio, Mars 7, Venus 4, Mercury 8, Jupiter 5, Saturn 6. In Sagittarius, Jupiter 12, Venus 5, Mercury 4, Saturn 5, Mars 4. In Capricorn Mercury [holds onto] 7, Venus 7,[4] Jupiter 8,[5] Saturn 4, Mars 4. In Aquarius, Mercury [holds onto] 7, Venus 6, Jupiter 7, Mars 5, Saturn 5. In Pisces, Venus [holds onto] 12, Jupiter 4, Mercury 3, Mars 9, Saturn 2.

---

[1] This is not correct, it should be 69 ½ as in the table.
[2] *Gr. Intr.* VII.8.1376-77 says this is only according to "certain people." The value above is the standard one.
[3] *Gr. Intr.* V.9.811-23 contains this same list as a table.
[4] Reading instead of "8."
[5] Reading instead of "7."

III. Degrees in the signs

[*Abbr.* VII.26-37][6] Therefore in Aries the first 3 degrees [are] shadowy, but 5 dark, 8 shadowy, 4 bright, 4 dark, 5 bright, 1 dark. In Taurus, 4 shadowy, 7 dark, 3 shadowy, 3 empty, 3 bright, 5 empty, 3 bright, 2 empty. In Gemini, 7 bright, 3 shadowy, 5 bright, 2 empty, 6 bright, 7 shadowy. In Cancer, 12 bright, 2 dark, 4 shadowy, 2 indifferent, 8 bright, 2 shadowy. But Leo has the first 10 as dark, 10 empty, 5 shadowy, 5 bright. However, Virgo [has] 6 dark, 3 empty, 2 shadowy, 6 bright, 6 indifferent, 5 empty, 2 black. Libra [has] 5 bright, 5 empty, 8 bright, 3 dark, 6 bright, 3 empty. Scorpio [has] 3 dark, 5 bright, 6 empty, 6 bright, 2 indifferent, 5 empty, 3 dark. Sagittarius [has] 9 bright, 3 dark, 7 bright, 4 indifferent, 7 bright. Capricorn [has] 7 dark, 3 bright, 5 indifferent, 4 bright, 3 dark, 3 empty, 5 dark. Aquarius [has] 4 dark, 5 bright, 4 shadowy, 8 bright, 4 empty, 5 bright. Pisces [has] 6 shadowy, 6 bright, 6 shadowy, 4 bright, 3 empty, 3 bright, 2 shadowy.

IV. Masculine and feminine degrees

[*Abbr.* VII.39-50] Therefore Aries has the first 7 masculine, 2 feminine, 6 masculine, 7 feminine, 8 masculine. Taurus: 7 masculine, 8 feminine, 15 masculine. Gemini: 6 feminine, 11 masculine, 6 feminine, 4 masculine, 3 feminine. Cancer: 2 masculine, 5 feminine, 3 masculine, 2 feminine, 11 masculine, 4 feminine, 3 masculine. Leo: 5 masculine, 2 feminine, 6 masculine, 10 feminine, 7 masculine. Virgo: 7 feminine, 5 masculine, 8 feminine, 10 masculine. Libra: 5 masculine, 5 feminine, 11 masculine, 7 feminine, 2 masculine. Scorpio: 4 masculine, 6 feminine, 4 masculine, 5 feminine, 8 masculine, 3 feminine. Sagittarius: 2 masculine, 3 feminine, 7 masculine, 12 feminine, 6 masculine. Capricorn: 11 masculine, 8 feminine, 11 masculine. Aquarius: 5 masculine, 7 feminine, 6 masculine, 7 feminine, 5 masculine. Pisces: 10 masculine, 10 feminine, 3 masculine, 5 feminine, 2 masculine.

---

[6] This corresponds to al-Qabīsī I.50 and *Gr. Intr.* V.20.1115-26.

V. The welled degrees

[*Abbr.* VII.58-69] Therefore, the wells of Aries are the 6th degree and the 11th and 17th, 28th, and 29th. Of Taurus, the 5th degree and the 13th and 18th and 24th and 25th and 26th. Of Gemini, the 8th and 13th and 17th and 26th and 30th. Of Cancer, the 12th and 17th and 23rd and 26th and 30th. Of Leo, the 6th and 13th and 15th and 22nd and 23rd and 28th. Of Virgo, the 8th, 13th, 16th, 21st, 25th. Of Libra, the 1st, 27th, 30th. Of Scorpio, the 19th, 17th, 22nd, 23rd, 27th. Of Sagittarius, the 7th, 12th, 15th, 24th, 27th, 30th. Of Capricorn, the 2nd and 7th, 17th, 22nd, 29th. Of Aquarius, the 1st, 12th, 17th, 23rd, 29th. Of Pisces, the 4th and 9th, 24th, 27th, 28th.

VI. The degrees of personal eminence

[*Abbr.* VII.72] …those of Aries, the 19th; of Taurus the 8th, of Gemini the 11th, of Cancer the 1st and 2nd and 3rd and 14th and 15th; of Leo the 5th and 7th and 17th and 20th; of Virgo the 2nd and 13th and 20th; of Libra the 3rd and 5th and 21st; of Scorpio the 2nd, 5th and 20th; of Sagittarius the 13th and 20th, of Capricorn the 12th, 13th, 14th and 20th, of Aquarius the 7th and 17th and 27th; of Pisces the 12th and 20th.

APPENDIX B: RELATIONSHIPS BETWEEN CONFIGURATION DEFINITIONS (BOOK III)

The following arrangements of definitions from Book III are my own, and are explained in greater detail in my comments in each section.

Fitness group:
Domain
Advancement
Retreat

Relationship group:
Assembly
Regard
Connection

Solitude group:
Disregard/separation
Emptiness
Wildness

Connection group
Connection
Transfer (incl. Reflection #2)
Collection (incl. Reflection #1)

Pushing group
Nature
Power
Two natures
Management
Returning

120° group
Emptiness
Wildness
Reflection
Enclosure/besieging

Isolation and Rescue series

Whole signs	*Degree-based*
Aspect/Assembly	Connection
(Separation)	Separation
Wildness	Emptiness of course
Enclosure by sign	Enclosure by degree
Barring by aspect	Barring by degree

Prevented connections

By blocking	*By failure*
Barring	Revoking
Obstruction	Escape
Cutting #1	Cutting #2

Constituents of prevented connections:

	Blocking/failure	*Direct/retrograde*	*Same/next sign*
Barring:	Blocking	Direct	Same
Obstruction:	Blocking	Retrograde	Same
Cutting #1:	Blocking	Retrograde	Next
Escape:	Failure	Direct	Next
Revoking:	Failure	Retrograde	Same
Cutting #2	Failure	Direct	Same

APPENDIX C: RELATION BETWEEN ANTIOCHUS/PORPYHRY AND ARABIC AUTHORS

In 2009, Robert Schmidt of Project Hindsight released a new set of translations of Antiochus of Athens, Porphyry, and others on basic concepts in Hellenistic astrology. In Book III I have already begun to indicate how our Persian and Arabic and Latin authors include material on planetary configurations. Here I offer basic correspondences between the material in Antiochus/Porphyry and *ITA*, supplemented by material in other authors where necessary. Although I translate some of the Greek terms differently in Book III above, I have retained Schmidt's translations here for those consulting his text. Please note that these are primary correspondences only; there may be some differences in detail between the Hellenistic and Arabic passages.

Antiochus/Porphyry	*ITA* References
1. Planets and significations	V.1-V.11
2. Phases of Moon	II.10.3
3. Sun and seasons	I.10.4-5
4. Sect	V.11
5. Sign classifications	I.9-10
6. Sign gender	I.3
7. Signs and winds	I.7, *On Rev.* Ch. 2[7]
8. Planetary domiciles	I.6
9. Exaltations and depressions	I.6
10. Bounds	VII.4
11. Spiral motion in latitude	II.5
12. Signs/planets and limbs	I.3
13. Joint domicile masters	
14. Testimony (*marturia*)	III.6
15. Right/left figures	III.6
16. Transposition (*parallagê*)	III.8
17. Connection by aspect (*sunaphê*)	III.7
18. Adherence (*kollêsis*)	III.7
19. Concourse (*sunodos*)	III.5
20. Flowing forth (*aporroia*)	III.8
21. Decimation, overcoming (*epidekateia, kathuperterêsis*)	IV.4.1, *BA* II.11
22. Neighboring (*homoroêsis*)	See III.8, IV.4
23. Emptiness in course (*kenodromia*)	III.9

---

[7] Māshā'allāh's *On Rev.*, in *WSM.*

24. Containment (*perischesis*)	IV.1, IV.4
25. Enclosure (*emperischesis*)	IV.1, IV.4
26. Intervention (*mesembolēsis*)	III.14
27. Striking with a ray (*aktinobolia*)	
28. Chariots (*lampēnē*)	III.16?
29. Solar phases	II.10
30. Participation (*metochē*)	III.17
31. Counteraction (*antanalusis*)	
32. Spearbearing 1-3 (*doruphoria*)	III.28
33. Maltreatment (*kakōsis*)	IV.3-4
34. Non-figural relations	I.9, III.6, III.25
35. Conducive to business (*chrēmatizō, kentra, epanaphora, apoklimata*)	I.12, III.3-4
36. Slopes (*klima*)	I.11
37. Sowing with the Sun	Cf. Abū Bakr I.3-I.4
38. Sowing with the Moon	Cf. Abū Bakr I.3-I.4
39. Lords of nativity	Cf. Abū Bakr I.3-I.4
40. Asc. of conception	Cf. Abū Bakr I.3-I.4
41. Twelfth-parts of Moon, Sun, Asc	IV.6
42. Climes & Ascensions	I.9.1
43. System of 12 houses	I.13
44. System of 8 houses	
45. Fortune and Spirit	Cf. VI.1
46. Fortune and places	Cf. *BA* III.2.1, pp. 83-84
47. Predominator, domicile master	VIII.1.3
48. Lord of nativity	Cf. VIII.1.4
49. Nativity of Cosmos (*Thema Mundi*)	See III.6.2
50. Luminaries	Perhaps VIII.2.2f
51. Lord & domicile master of nativity	Perhaps VIII.2.2f; cf. *PN3*
52. Commixture and testimony	

APPENDIX D: LOTS

The following two tables present all of the natal Lots found in *Abbr.*, al-Qabīsī, and *BA*. (No mundane Lots are included.) The first table organizes the Lots by the first two points in descending astronomical order: for instance, any Lot using Mercury and the Moon is listed in Mercury's row. The second table presents the Lots by the first point in the diurnal calculation: so Mercury-Moon Lots are listed separately from Moon-Mercury Lots. In each table, Lots which employ other Lots, or rulers, or special degrees, are listed first. Finally, since there is some dispute over which Lots are reversed, no reversals are indicated.

I. Lots by abstract combination

Fortune	Spirit	Eros (Valens), Basis, Necessity (Valens), Making friends and enemies
Fortune	♄	Nemesis
Fortune	♂	Courage
Fortune	☿	Necessity (Hermes), Slaves (al-Andarzaghar)
Spirit	♃	Victory
Lord ☉	♄	Grandfathers
Lord ☽	☽	Child's sex
Lord ASC	☽	Killing planet
Lord 2nd	2nd	Assets
Lord 9th	9th	Travel
Lord 12th	12th	Enemies (Hermes)
☉	MC	Death of brothers, Job and authority (Valens), Cause of a kingdom[8]
♀	DSC	Delight and pleasure
☽	8th	Death[9]
☉/☽	19° ♈/3° ♉	Nobility
♄	15° ♋	Navigation

---

[8] This Lot is projected from Jupiter.
[9] This Lot is projected from Saturn.

Prenatal ♂/ ☽	☽/Next ♂	Releaser
Lord PNL	♄	Suspected year, End of matters
♄	♃	Life, Brothers, Death of parents, Children, Wisdom[10]
♄	♂	Origins,[11] Chronic illness, Oppressive place,[12] Enemies (alternative)
♄	☉	Father, Power or kingdom or supremacy
♄	♀	Cultivation, Women's marriage (Hermes), Delight, Men's marriage (Hermes), Hope
♄	☽	Real estate, Intellect and profound thought, Authority and what a native does, War and fighting, Male children (Theophilus)
♃	♂	Time of children
♃	♀	Brothers (alternative)
♃	☽	Male children, Knowledge
♂	☽	Women's marriage (Valens), Kingdom and authority
♂	♀	Work
☉	♀	Men's marriage (Valens)
☉	☽	Fortune, Spirit, Time of marriage (Hermes), Wedding[13]
♀	☽	Female children, Mother, Revolution of year[14]
☿	☽	Slaves, Truth/falsity of rumors, Religion, Friends, Peace among soldiers

---

[10] This Lot is projected from Mercury.
[11] This Lot is projected from Mercury.
[12] This Lot is projected from Mercury.
[13] This Lot is projected from Venus.
[14] This Lot is projected from the Sun.

II. Lots by beginning point (diurnal)

Fortune	Spirit	Eros (Valens), Basis, Making friends and enemies
Spirit	Fortune	Necessity (Valens)
Spirit	♃	Victory
Prenatal ♂/ ☽	☽/Next ♂	Releaser
♄	Lord PNL	Suspected year
Lord 2nd	2nd	Assets
Lord ☉	♄	Grandfathers
Lord ☽	☽	Child's sex
Lord ASC	☽	Killing planet
Lord 9th	9th	Travel
Lord 12th	12th	Enemies (Hermes)
♄	15° ♋	Navigation
♄	Lord PNL	Suspected year, End of matters
♄	Fortune	Nemesis
♄	♃	Brothers, Death of parents, Wisdom[15]
♄	♂	Origins,[16] Chronic illness, Oppressive place,[17] Enemies (alternative)
♄	♀	Men's marriage (Hermes), Hope
♄	☽	Real estate, Intellect and profound thought, Authority and what a native does, War and fighting
♃	♄	Life, Children
♂	Fortune	Courage
♂	♃	Time of children
♂	☽	Kingdom and authority

---

[15] This Lot is projected from Mercury.
[16] This Lot is projected from Mercury.
[17] This Lot is projected from Mercury.

☉/☽	19° ♈/3° ♉	Nobility
☉	MC	Death of brothers, Job and authority (Valens), Cause of a kingdom[18]
☉	♄	Father, Power or kingdom or supremacy
☉	♀	Men's marriage (Valens)
☉	☽	Fortune, Time of marriage (Hermes), Wedding[19]
♀	DSC	Delight and pleasure
♀	♄	Cultivation, Women's marriage (Hermes), Delight
♀	☽	Mother
☿	Fortune	Necessity (Hermes), Slaves (Al-Andarzaghar)
☿	♃	Brothers (alternative)
☿	♂	Work
☿	☽	Slaves, Truth/falsity of rumors
☉/☽	19° ♈/3° ♉	Nobility
☽	8th	Death[20]
☽	♄	Male children (Theophilus)
☽	♃	Male children, Knowledge
☽	♂	Women's marriage (Valens)
☽	☉	Spirit
☽	♀	Female children, Revolution of year[21]
☽	☿	Religion, Friends, Peace among soldiers

---

[18] This Lot is projected from Jupiter.
[19] This Lot is projected from Venus.
[20] This Lot is projected from Saturn.
[21] This Lot is projected from the Sun.

APPENDIX E: ASCENSIONAL TIMES & PRIMARY DIRECTIONS

Many Hellenistic and Perso-Arabic astrologers used ascensional times as their preferred form of directions, the most important application of which was directing or distributing significators through the bounds (see VII.4 and VIII.2.2f above). Ascensional times convert the number of degrees of right ascension (RA) passing across the Midheaven as a single sign crosses the horizon, into years of life: 1° of RA = 1 year. A table of ascensional times and instructions for using it may be found at my website, www.bendykes.com.

Not all astrologers agreed in using ascensional times: al-Qabīsī follows Ptolemy in preferring an astronomically more accurate method, which I will explain here. The best book on primary directions is by Martin Gansten (2009), and anyone interested in learning how to understand and calculate them is referred there. I greatly appreciate his personal help in making sense of al-Qabīsī's method, and all of my values below were calculated using the formulas in his book and a calculator that performs trigonometric functions.

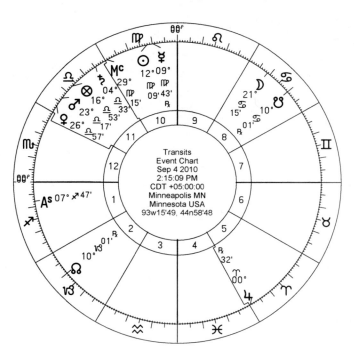

In primary directions, we choose a significator which means something in the chart, and keep it stationary as we move other planets and points clockwise (in diurnal or "primary" motion) to it. The planets and points we move toward the significator are called "promittors," which in Latin means something that is "sent forward." The distance between these points and the significator are turned into years of life, normally at a rate of 1° per year of life—with the understanding that these degrees are measured using the celestial equator, not the zodiac, just as with ascensional times.[22]

Directing planets or points or aspects to the degrees of the angles is conceptually simple: when directing a planet or point to the Midheaven or IC, the difference between them in RA is the arc or time; when directing a planet or point to the Ascendant or Descendant, the difference in oblique ascension (OA) is the arc or time. But directing to planets or points which are not on the angles becomes more tricky.

In my example, we will treat Saturn as the significator and stationary point, and the body of Venus as the promittor or moving point: thus our direction will involve sending the body of Venus forward by diurnal motion (i.e., clockwise) to the body of Saturn. In the zodiac, there are only 22° 24' between them. But because degrees move by diurnal motion at different rates depending on the sign and the birth latitude, the actual arc measured on the celestial equator might be larger or smaller. Moreover, since significators and promittors are not all exactly on the zodiac or the celestial equator, we have to ask, "how can Venus really come *to* the place of Saturn?" For we can turn the heavens by diurnal motion, but unless she is exactly at his latitude and declination, she cannot really come to his exact place (or rather, to his exact *virtual* place, since he will no longer really be there).

The solution to this problem (as expressed by Ptolemy and al-Qabīsī) involves proportional semi-arcs. A semi-arc (SA) is simply the number of degrees or time it takes for a planet or point to move clockwise in primary motion from the circle of the horizon to the circle of the meridian[23] or vice versa. This arc is "proportional," because we will calculate how much it takes

---

[22] There is some confusion in traditional and modern texts over which planet is the significator and which is the promittor. One reason for this is a holdover from the use of ascensional times, and because astrologers are used to thinking about motion through the zodiac. In the example below, it is easier to imagine directing Saturn forward in the zodiac to Venus, rather than that Venus moves by diurnal motion to Saturn.

[23] That is, the north-south circle which determines where the Midheaven and Imum Coeli are.

for Venus to move to a position in *her* semi-arc, *proportional to* where Saturn is in *his* semi-arc. The size of their semi-arcs are different precisely because they are in different areas of the zodiac and at different zodiacal latitudes, so they will rise at different rates. So, the direction of Venus to Saturn involves finding out when she will come to a place proportionate to his. If Saturn had traveled 50% of the way to the Midheaven in his own semi-arc, we would want to know how much it would take for Venus to come to 50% of *her* semi-arc. But we have some choices to make: for instance, are we finding the proportional semi-arc for the bodies of Venus and Saturn themselves (directing with latitude), or only for the zodiacal degrees on the ecliptic which correspond to their positions (directing without latitude)?

Let me explain in general terms how we will find this value, and introduce you to some terminology. As I said before, Saturn is our stationary significator (Sig) and Venus is the moving promittor (Prom). Each of them is in a *diurnal* semi-arc (DSA): that is, in a semi-arc during the day:[24] in this case, the semi-arc which reaches from the horizon in the east to the meridian. Since we want to know when Venus will reach a place in her own DSA, proportional to where Saturn is, we must first know where he is.

To find out how far he is from the meridian, we must subtract his right ascension (RA) from the RA of the Midheaven (RAMC):[25] this gives us his meridian distance (MD). Then, we must find out his entire diurnal semi-arc. If we divide his MD by his entire DSA, we essentially get how much of his DSA he has traveled and how much he has left. If we then know the MD and DSA of Venus, we can figure out how much she must travel to get to a proportional place in her own DSA. Following is the basic formula:

$$\text{PromMD} - [(\text{SigMD}/\text{SigSA}) * \text{PromSA}] = \text{Arc}$$

That is, divide the significator's MD by its SA to get the proportion already traveled by the significator, and multiply the result by the promittor's entire SA. Then subtract this result from the promittor's MD to yield the distance between the promittor and where the proportional place is: this is the arc of direction, the number of years before the direction takes effect.

---

[24] If the planets were below the horizon, they would be in one of the two nocturnal semi-arcs, between the Descendant and the IC or the IC and the Ascendant.
[25] Right Ascension (RA) is exactly like zodiacal longitude or earthly longitude, except that it is measured on the celestial equator. Likewise, declination is the equatorial equivalent to zodiacal latitude or earthly latitude.

Al-Qabīsī's method is essentially the same as this, except that he (like others in his day) divided the significator's SA and another value[26] by 6. But the final calculation essentially cancels the 6 out, making it unnecessary.

In what follows I will direct Venus to Saturn, first using the planets' own ecliptical latitude (i.e., their very bodies), and then using only their zodiacal degrees.[27] In each case, I first give the values we need for the formulas (calculated using Gansten's book), then I give Gansten's own formula, followed by al-Qabīsī's slightly more complicated one. Readers should compare the al-Qabīsī calculation below to his own descriptions in VIII.2.2.*b-f*.

---

[26] The difference between the "significator of the right circle" and the "significator of the region."

[27] Gansten (private communication) says that al-Qabīsī probably would have used tables giving the values without planetary latitude. Modern computer programs tend to use calculations only with planetary latitude.

A. Directing using planetary latitude:

Problem: to direct ♀ (promittor) to ♄ (significator):

RAMC: 179° 19' 33"	MD ♀: 24° 23' 27"	DSA ♀ = 75° 57' 21"
RA ♀: 203° 43' 00"	MD ♄: 05° 43' 16"	DSA ♄ = 90° 10' 46"
RA ♄: 185° 02' 49"		

A1. Gansten's formula:

24° 23' 27 − [(05° 43' 16"/90° 10' 46") * 75° 57' 21"] = **Arc 19° 34' 20"**

A2. Al-Qabīsī method:

Al-Qabīsī's method requires the following additional values:

Oblique Ascension (OA) ♀: 217° 45' 39"
Oblique Ascension (OA) ♄: 184° 52' 03"

Significator (♄) DSA/6: 15° 01' 48"

Sig. of Right Circle (♀ RA − ♄ RA) = 18° 40' 11"
Sig. of Region (♀ OA − ♄ OA) = 32° 53' 36"
Difference: 14° 13' 25"
Diff./6: 02° 22' 14"

Now the formula is, first:

$$[SigMD / (SigDSA/6)] * Diff./6$$

$$(05° 43' 16" / 15° 01' 48") * 02° 22' 14" = 00° 54' 09"$$

Since the Sig. of Right Circle is less than the Sig. of Region, we add it to the result:[28]

$$18° 40' 11" + 00° 54' 09" = \textbf{Arc } \textbf{19° 34' 20"}$$

This procedure cancels out the 6 by which we divided two values above, yielding the same result as Gansten's shorter method.

---

[28] As al-Qabīsī explains, if it were less we would subtract it from the Significator of the Right Circle.

B. Directing using zodiacal degrees only (no latitude):

Problem: to direct ♀ (promittor) to ♄ (significator):

RAMC: 179° 19' 33" MD ♀: 25° 41' 18" DSA ♀ = 79° 26' 40"
RA ♀: 205° 00' 51" MD ♄: 04° 51' 37" DSA ♄ = 88° 11' 16"
RA ♄: 184° 11' 10"

B1. Gansten's formula:

PromMD − [(SigMD/SigDSA) * PromDSA] = Arc

25° 41' 18" − [(04° 51' 37"/88° 11' 16") * 79° 26' 40"] = **Arc 21° 18' 36"**

B2. Al-Qabīsī method:

Al-Qabīsī's method requires the following additional values:

Oblique Ascension (OA) ♀: 215° 34' 11"
Oblique Ascension (OA) ♄: 185° 59' 54"

Significator (♄) DSA/6: 14° 41' 53"

Sig. of Right Circle (♀ RA − ♄ RA) = 20° 49' 41"
Sig. of Region (♀ OA − ♄ OA) = 29° 34' 17"
Difference: 08° 44' 36"
Diff./6: 01° 27' 26"

Now the formula is, first:

[SigMD / (SigDSA/6)] * Diff./6

(04° 51' 37" / 14° 41' 53") * 01° 27' 26" = 00° 28' 55"

Since the Sig. of Right Circle is less than the Sig. of Region, we add it to the result:

20° 49' 41" + 00° 28' 55" = **Arc 21° 18' 36"**

This procedure cancels out the 6 by which we divided two values above, yielding the same result as Gansten's shorter method.

APPENDIX F: STUDY GUIDE TO *PERSIAN NATIVITIES*

This guide will help students compare the natal teachings of the five astrologers in all three volumes of *Persian Nativities* (*PN1-3*). References are listed by chapter based on their main content, so not every possible reference to every topic is listed. The division of questions for each topic is based mainly on those found in *BA*.

Book Abbreviations

Abū Bakr	Abū Bakr, *On Nativities* (in *PN2*)
BA	Māshā'allāh bin Atharī, *The Book of Aristotle* (in *PN1*)
JN	Al-Khayyāt, Abū 'Ali, *The Judgments of Nativities* (in *PN1*)
Nativities	Māshā'allāh bin Atharī, *On Nativities* (in *WSM*)
On Rev. Nat.	Abū Ma'shar al-Balhi, *On the Revolutions of the Years of Nativities* (=*PN3*)
TBN	Al-Tabarī, 'Umar, *Three Books on Nativities* (in *PN2*)

1. Overview of questions and methods: Abū Bakr I.1

2. Rectification/namūdārs ("indicators")

	BA	*TBN*	*Abū Bakr*
1. Ptolemaic		I.2	
2. Hermetic	III.1.10		I.4.1-2
3. Other			I.4.3

3. Conception, pregnancy and birth

	TBN	*Abū Bakr*
1. Conception		I.2
2. Gestation	I.1	I.2-3, I.5
3. Birth		I.7
4. "Monsters"	I.3.1	I.8

4. Rearing/nourishment

	BA	*Nativities*	*JN*	*TBN*	*Abū Bakr*
1. Survival	III.1.2	§1	Ch. 1		I.12.0, I.14
2. No survival	III.1.3	§1	Ch. 1		I.12.0
3. Exposure	III.1.4				I.13
4. Birth type 1				I.3.1	I.12.1
5. Birth type 2				I.3.2	I.12.2
6. Birth type 3				I.3.3	I.12.3
7. Birth type 4				I.3.4	I.12.4
8. Prediction		§1	Ch. 1	I.3.1-3	I.12.2, 12.5-6

5. Longevity

	BA	*Nativities*	*JN*	*TBN*	*Abū Bakr*
1. *Hīlāj* ("releaser")	III.1.5	§2	Ch. 2	I.4.1	I.15
2. *Kadukḫudhāh*	III.1.6	§3-4	Ch. 3	I.4.2-4	I.15
3. Prediction	III.1.7-10.	§4	Ch. 4	I.4.5-8	I.15

6. Character

	Nativities	*JN*	*Abū Bakr*
1. Overview			II.1
2. Lord 1st/Mercury	§5	Ch. 5	
3. Fear			II.1.1
4. Aggression		Ch. 34	II.1.2-3
5. Shame/modesty			II.1.4-5
6. Happy/sad			II.1.6, 1.25-27
7. Truthfulness			II.1.7-8, 1.17
8. Intellect/knowledge			II.1.12-16
9. Faithfulness			II.1.18-19
10. Taking/giving			II.1.20-24
11. Greed			II.1.28
12. Discord			II.1.29-30
13. Beauty			II.1.31
14. Calm/quick			II.1.32-33

7. Body/physiognomy

	Abū Bakr
1. Face	I.9-10
2. Body type	I.10
3. Family resemblance	I.11

8. Prosperity

	BA	Nativities	JN	TBN	Abū Bakr
1. Always high	III.2.1	§6	Chs. 6-7, 30-32	III.1.1, III.9	II.2.0-2
2. Always middle	III.2.3		Ch. 7		II.2.3
3. Always low	III.2.6	§6	Ch. 7	III.1.1	II.2.4-7
4. Rising	III.2.4	§6	Ch. 7	III.1.1	II.2.9
5. Sinking	III.2.2		Ch. 7	III.1.1	II.2.8
6. When	III.2.6	§6	Ch. 8	III.1.2	
7. Other			Chs. 10, 30-32		II.2.10

9. Wealth

	JN	TBN	Abū Bakr
1. Source	Chs. 9, 11	III.2	II.3.2-11
2. Abundance	Ch. 11	III.2	II.3.1
3. Scarcity	Ch. 11	III.2	
4. When	Ch. 11	III.2	

10. Siblings

	BA	JN	TBN	Abū Bakr
1. Older/younger	III.3.3	Ch. 13	III.3	II.4.1
2. Number	III.3.2-3	Ch. 12	III.3	II.4.1-2
3. Sex	III.3.2	Ch. 13	III.3	II.4.1
4. Half-siblings		Ch. 12		II.4.5
5. Concord	III.3.5-6	Chs. 13, 15-16	III.3	II.4.1, 4.3-4
6. Status		Chs. 12, 14	III.3	II.4.5
7. Death	III.3.4, 3.7			

11. Parents

	BA	JN	TBN	Abū Bakr
1. Legitimacy	III.4.2		III.4.1	I.6, II.5.10
2. Lineage	III.4.3-4			II.2.10, II.5.1
3. Status/when	III.4.1	Ch. 16	III.4	II.5.1-2, 5.6-7, 5.10-11
4. Love between			III.4	
5. Love with native	III.1.4, 4.5, 12.7		III.4, III.9	II.5.3-4
6. Death	III.4.6-4.7, 4.9	Chs. 17-19	III.4	II.5.8-13
7. Inherit?	III.4.8	Ch. 16		II.5.5

12. Children

	BA	*JN*	*TBN*	*Abū Bakr*
1. Fertility	III.5.2	Ch. 20	III.6	II.6.1-3
2. Number	III.5.3-4	Ch. 20	III.6	II.6.1-2, 6.4
3. Sex	III.5.5			II.6.1
4. Death	III.5.3	Ch. 20		II.6.10
5. Status				II.6.8-9
6. Love for native		Ch. 21	III.6	II.6.1, 6.6-7
7. When	III.5.3, 5.5	Ch. 21	III.6	II.6.1, 6.5

13. Illness

	BA	*JN*	*TBN*	*Abū Bakr*
1. Signs of illness				II.7.1-2
2. Eyes	III.6.2	Ch. 24	III.7	II.7.3-8
3. Various	III.6.3	Ch. 24	III.7	II.7.9-13, 7.15-22, 7.24, 7.28, 7.31-36, 7.38
4. Mind	III.6.4	Ch. 24		II.7.14
5. Sociality	III.6.5			
6. Sexual	III.6.6		III.5, III.7	II.7.23, 7.25-27
7. Height	III.6.7			II.7.11, 7.29-30
8. When	III.6.8	Ch. 24		II.7.37

14. Slaves/servants

	BA	*JN*	*Abū Bakr*
1. Concord	III.11.1	Ch. 22	II.8
2. Benefit/harm		Ch. 22	II.8

15. Animals

	JN	*Abū Bakr*
1. Benefit/abundance	Ch. 23	II.3.6
2. Loss/scarcity	Ch. 23	

16. Marriage

	BA	JN	TBN	Abū Bakr
1. Marry?	III.7.2	Chs. 25-26	III.5	II.9.2-3
2. Spouse age	III.7.4-5	Ch. 26		II.9.6
3. Appropriate/type	III.7.4, 7.6, 7.11	Chs. 25-26	III.5	II.9.0, 9.4-8
4. Benefit/harm	III.7.3	Ch. 25		II.9.13-14
5. Incest	III.7.7			II.9.6
6. Sexual misbehavior	III.7.8	Ch. 25	III.5	II.9.1, 9.5, 9.8-9, 9.15
7. Number	III.7.9	Ch. 25		II.9.17
8. Death	III.7.12	Ch. 25		II.9.16
9. Homosexuality	III.7.13	Ch. 25	III.5	II.9.1, 9.10-12
10. When	III.7.2, 7.10	Chs. 25-26	III.5	II.9.18

17. Death

	BA	JN	TBN	Abū Bakr
1. Cause	III.8.1	Ch. 37	III.13	II.10.2-12, 10.14
2. Suicide	III.8.1			II.10.13
3. Where		Ch. 37		II.10.15-17
4. Easy		Ch. 37		II.10.2
5. Violent	III.8.1	Ch. 37	III.13	II.10.3, 10.5, 10.8-12

18. Faith/Law

	JN	TBN	Abū Bakr
1. Type of law	Ch. 29		II.1.9, 1.11
2. Changes	Ch. 29	III.12	
3. Honesty	Ch. 29	III.8, III.12	II.1.10
4. When	Ch. 29	III.12	

19. Travel

	BA	JN	TBN	Abū Bakr
1. Travel?	III.9.2	Ch. 27	III.8	II.11 passim
2. Benefit	III.9.2	Chs. 27-28	III.8	II.11.1
3. Harm	III.9.2	Chs. 27-28	III.8	II.11.2, 11.4

20. Profession/trades[29]

	BA	JN	TBN	Abū Bakr
1. Unskilled?	III.10.2, 10.6		III.9	
2. Three sigs.	III.10.2	Ch. 33	III.9	II.12.2, 12.5, 12.46
3. Moon's application	III.10.3-4	Ch. 33		II.12.7
4. Lot of Work	III.10.4, 10.7			
5. Success	III.10.5	Ch. 33	III.9	II.12.1, 12.3, 12.6, 12.8
6. Misc. indications	III.10.8	Ch. 33	III.9	II.12.4, 12.9-45

21. Friends

	BA	JN	TBN	Abū Bakr
1. Synastry	III.12.1, 12.4, 12.8		III.10	
2. Prediction	III.12.3, 12.6			
3. Types	III.12.2	Ch. 35	III.10	II.13.1-2
4. Strength	III.12.3, 12.5	Ch. 35	III.10	II.13.3-5
5. Election	III.12.9			

22. Enemies

	JN	TBN	Abū Bakr
1. Have enemies?	Ch. 36	III.11	II.14.1
2. Status	Ch. 36	III.11	II.14.1
3. Who prevails	Ch. 36	III.11	II.14.2

---

[29] In the Persian method, one should determine first the level of prosperity, and thus whether the native will actually practice a trade.

23. Annual Methods

	BA	TBN	Abū Bakr	On Rev. Nat.	Al-Qabīsī
1. Ages of Man				I.7-8	
2. Profection	IV.1-7	II.4-6		II.1-22, II.24	IV.8
3. Distributor-partner	III.1.10, IV.8-13	II.2	I.17	III.1-8	IV.14
4. Solar revolution	IV.14-15			I.6, II.23	
5. Firdāriyyāt	III.17-25		I.16	IV.1-8	IV.20
6. Ingresses, returns	IV passim			V.1-9	IV.21
7. Moon	IV.1			II.22, III.8, V.10	
8. Directions in the revolution		II.3, II.5-6		II.1, III.1	IV.13
9. Ninth-parts				III.9-10	IV.16-17
10. Monthly, daily, hourly rulers	IV.16			IX.7	
11. Natal directions	II.17, III.1.10	I.4, II.1, II.5-6	I.15		IV.11-12

APPENDIX G: THE ESSENTIAL MEDIEVAL ASTROLOGY CYCLE

The *Essential Medieval Astrology* cycle is a projected series of books which will redefine the contours of traditional astrology. Comprised mainly of translations of works by Persian and Arabic-speaking medieval astrologers, it will cover all major areas of astrology, including philosophical treatments and magic. The cycle will be accompanied by compilations of introductory works and readings on the one hand, and independent monographs and encyclopediac works on the other (including late medieval and Renaissance works of the Latin West).

I. Introductions
- *Introductions to Astrology*: Abū Ma'shar's *Abbreviation of the Introduction*, al-Qabīsī's *The Introduction to Astrology* (2010)
- Abū Ma'shar, *Great Introduction to the Knowledge of the Judgments of the Stars* (2011-12)
- *Basic Readings in Traditional Astrology* (2012-13)

II. Nativities
- *Persian Nativities I*: Māshā'allāh's *The Book of Aristotle*, Abū 'Ali al-Khayyāt's *On the Judgments of Nativities* (2009)
- *Persian Nativities II*: 'Umar al-Tabarī's *Three Books on Nativities*, Abū Bakr's *On Nativities* (2010)
- *Persian Nativities III*: Abū Ma'shar's *On the Revolutions of Nativities* (2010)

III. Questions (Horary)
- Hermann of Carinthia, *The Search of the Heart* (2011)
- Various, *The Book of the Nine Judges* (2011)
- Al-Kindī, *The Forty Chapters* (2011)

IV. Elections
- *Traditional Electional Astrology*: Abū Ma'shar's *On Elections* and *Flowers of Elections*; other minor works (2011-12)

V. Mundane Astrology
- *Astrology of the World*: Abū Ma'shar's *On the Revolutions of the Years of the World*, *Book of Religions and Dynasties*, and *Flowers*, Sahl bin Bishr's *Prophetic Sayings*; lesser works on prices and weather (2011-12)

VI. Other Works

- Bonatti, Guido, *The Book of Astronomy* (2007)
- *Works of Sahl & Māshā'allāh* (2008)
- *A Course in Traditional Astrology* (TBA)
- Al-Rijāl, *On the Judgments of the Stars* (TBA)
- *Astrological Magic* (TBA)
- *The Latin Hermes* (TBA)
- Firmicus Maternus, *Mathesis* (TBA)

BIBLIOGRAPHY

Abū Ma'shar al-Balkhi, *Liber Introductorii Maioris ad Scientiam Iudiciorum Astrorum*, vols. IV, V, VI, IX, ed. Richard Lemay (Naples: Istituto Universitario Orientale, 1995)

Abū Ma'shar al-Balkhi, *The Abbreviation of the Introduction to Astrology*, ed. and trans. Charles Burnett, K. Yamamoto, and Michio Yano (Leiden: E.J. Brill, 1994)

Abū Ma'shar al-Balhi, *On Historical Astrology: The Book of Religions and Dynasties (On the Great Conjunctions)*, vols. I-II, eds. and trans. Keiji Yamamoto and Charles Burnett (Leiden: Brill, 2000)

Al-Bīrūnī, Muhammad ibn Ahmad, *The Book of Instruction in the Elements of the Art of Astrology*, trans. R. Ramsay Wright (London: Luzac & Co., 1934)

Al-Qabīsī, *The Introduction to Astrology*, eds. Charles Burnett, Keiji Yamamoto, Michio Yano (London and Turin: The Warburg Institute, 2004)

Bonatti, Guido, *Book of Astronomy*, trans. and ed. Benjamin N. Dykes (Golden Valley, MN: The Cazimi Press, 2007)

Brady, Bernadette, *Brady's Book of Fixed Stars* (Boston: Weiser Books, 1998)

Burnett, Charles ed., *Adelard of Bath: An English Scientist and Arabist of the early Twentieth Century* (London: Warburg Institute Surveys and Texts 14, 1987).

Burnett, Charles and Gerrit Bos, *Scientific Weather Forecasting in the Middle Ages* (London and New York: Kegan Paul International, 2000)

Crofts, Carole Mary, "*Kitāb al-Iktiyārāt 'alā l-buyūt al-itnai 'asar*, by Sahl ibn Bišr al-Isra'ili, with its Latin Translation *De Electionibus*" (Ph.D. diss., Glasgow University, 1985)

Denningmann, Susanne, *Die Astrologische Lehre der Doryphorie* (Munich: K.G. Saur, 2005)

Dykes, Benjamin trans. and ed., *Works of Sahl & Māshā'allāh* (Golden Valley, MN: The Cazimi Press, 2008)

Dykes, Benjamin trans. and ed., *Persian Nativities* vols. I-III (Minneapolis, MN: The Cazimi Press, 2009-10).

Gansten, Martin, *Primary Directions: Astrology's Old Master Technique* (England: The Wessex Astrologer, 2009)

Ibn Ezra, Abraham, *The Beginning of Wisdom*, trans. Meira Epstein, ed. Robert Hand (Arhat Publications, 1998)

Ibn Ezra, Abraham, *The Beginning of Wisdom*, trans. Peter of Abano, (Venice: Peter Leichtenstein, 1507)

Lilly, William, *Christian Astrology*, vols. I-II, ed. David R. Roell (Abingdon, MD: Astrology Center of America, 2004)

Māshā'allāh, *On the Knowledge of the Motion of the Orb*, in Dykes 2008.

Maternus, Julius Firmicus, *Matheseos Libri VIII* [*Mathesis*] (Stuttgard: B.G. Teubner, 1968)

Morin, Jean-Baptiste, *The Morinus System of Horoscope Interpretation* (*Astrologia Gallica* Book 21), trans. Richard S. Baldwin (Washington, DC: The American Federation of Astrologers, Inc., 1974)

Paulus Alexandrinus, *Late Classical Astrology: Paulus Alexandrinus and Olympiodorus*, trans. Dorian Gieseler Greenbaum, ed. Robert Hand (Reston, VA: ARHAT Publications, 2001)

Ptolemy, Claudius, *Quadripartitum* [Tetrabiblos], trans. Plato of Tivoli (1138) (Basel: Johannes Hervagius, 1533)

Ptolemy, Claudius, *Tetrabiblos* vols. 1, 2, 4, trans. Robert Schmidt, ed. Robert Hand (Berkeley Springs, WV: The Golden Hind Press, 1994-98)

Rhetorius of Egypt, *Astrological Compendium*, trans. and ed. James H. Holden (Tempe, AZ: American Federation of Astrologers, Inc., 2009)

Robson, Vivian, *The Fixed Stars & Constellations in Astrology* (Abingdon, MD: Astrology Classics, 2003)

Schmidt, Robert E., *Kepler College Sourcebook of Hellenistic Astrological Texts* (Cumberland, MA: The Phaser Foundation, 2005)

Schmidt, Robert H., trans. and ed. *Definitions and Foundations* (Cumberland, MD: The Golden Hind Press, 2009)

INDEX

For topics which entire sections, references are typically to the section heading. Not every instance of every concept is listed, especially for Book III (where many sections are interrelated and ought to be read together anyway).

Also available at www.bendykes.com:

The three volumes of *Persian Nativities* represents works on natal interpretation and numerous predictive techniques by Masha'allah, Abu 'Ali al-Khayyat, 'Umar al-Tabari, Abu Bakr, and Abu Ma'shar. These works represent the natal portion of the *Essential Medieval Astrology* series.

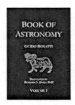

This classic medieval text by Guido Bonatti, the *Book of Astronomy* is now available in paperback reprints. This famous work is a complete guide to basic principles, horary, elections, mundane, and natal astrology.

This compilation of sixteen works by Sahl bin Bishr and Masha'allah covers all areas of traditional astrology, from basic concepts to horary, elections, natal interpretation, and mundane astrology. It is also available as two separate paperbacks.

Expand your knowledge of astrology and esoteric thought with the *Logos & Light* audio series: downloadable, college-level lectures and courses on CD at a fraction of the university cost! It is ideal for people with some knowledge of traditional thought but who want to enrich their understanding.